Sustainable E-learning and Education with Intelligence

Sustainable E-learning and Education with Intelligence

Editor

Hao-Chiang Koong Lin

Basel • Beijing • Wuhan • Barcelona • Belgrade • Novi Sad • Cluj • Manchester

Editor
Hao-Chiang Koong Lin
Information & Learning Technology
National University of Tainan
Tainan
Taiwan

Editorial Office
MDPI
St. Alban-Anlage 66
4052 Basel, Switzerland

This is a reprint of articles from the Special Issue published online in the open access journal *Sustainability* (ISSN 2071-1050) (available at: www.mdpi.com/journal/sustainability/special_issues/e-lerning_education_ai).

For citation purposes, cite each article independently as indicated on the article page online and as indicated below:

Lastname, A.A.; Lastname, B.B. Article Title. *Journal Name* **Year**, *Volume Number*, Page Range.

ISBN 978-3-0365-8723-3 (Hbk)
ISBN 978-3-0365-8722-6 (PDF)
doi.org/10.3390/books978-3-0365-8722-6

© 2023 by the authors. Articles in this book are Open Access and distributed under the Creative Commons Attribution (CC BY) license. The book as a whole is distributed by MDPI under the terms and conditions of the Creative Commons Attribution-NonCommercial-NoDerivs (CC BY-NC-ND) license.

Contents

About the Editor vii

Preface ix

Yu-Hsuan Lin, Hao-Chiang Koong Lin, Tao-Hua Wang and Cheng-Hsun Wu
Integrating the STEAM-6E Model with Virtual Reality Instruction: The Contribution to Motivation, Effectiveness, Satisfaction, and Creativity of Learners with Diverse Cognitive Styles
Reprinted from: *Sustainability* 2023, 15, 6269, doi:10.3390/su15076269 1

Yu-Chen Kuo, Hao-Chiang Koong Lin, Yu-Hsuan Lin, Tao-Hua Wang and Bo-Yue Chuang
The Influence of Distance Education and Peer Self-Regulated Learning Mechanism on Learning Effectiveness, Motivation, Self-Efficacy, Reflective Ability, and Cognitive Load
Reprinted from: *Sustainability* 2023, 15, 4501, doi:10.3390/su15054501 18

Ting-Ting Wu, Chia-Ju Lin, Shih-Cheng Wang and Yueh-Min Huang
Tracking Visual Programming Language-Based Learning Progress for Computational Thinking Education
Reprinted from: *Sustainability* 2023, 15, 1983, doi:10.3390/su15031983 40

Ye Zhang and Xinrong Chen
Students' Perceptions of Online Learning in the Post-COVID Era: A Focused Case from the Universities of Applied Sciences in China
Reprinted from: *Sustainability* 2023, 15, 946, doi:10.3390/su15020946 52

Yujian Ma, Yantao Wei, Yafei Shi, Xiuhan Li, Yi Tian and Zhongjin Zhao
Online Learning Engagement Recognition Using Bidirectional Long-Term Recurrent Convolutional Networks
Reprinted from: *Sustainability* 2022, 15, 198, doi:10.3390/su15010198 66

Chih-Hung Wu and Chien-Yu Liu
Educational Applications of Non-Fungible Token (NFT)
Reprinted from: *Sustainability* 2022, 15, 7, doi:10.3390/su15010007 80

Hao-Chiang Koong Lin, Yi-Cheng Liao and Hung-Ta Wang
Eye Movement Analysis and Usability Assessment on Affective Computing Combined with Intelligent Tutoring System
Reprinted from: *Sustainability* 2022, 14, 16680, doi:10.3390/su142416680 102

Xiulan Chen, Xiaofei Xu, Yenchun Jim Wu and Wei Fong Pok
Learners' Continuous Use Intention of Blended Learning: TAM-SET Model
Reprinted from: *Sustainability* 2022, 14, 16428, doi:10.3390/su142416428 119

Khurram Jawad, Muhammad Arif Shah and Muhammad Tahir
Students' Academic Performance and Engagement Prediction in a Virtual Learning Environment Using Random Forest with Data Balancing
Reprinted from: *Sustainability* 2022, 14, 14795, doi:10.3390/su142214795 133

Tidarat Luangrungruang and Urachart Kokaew
E-Learning Model to Identify the Learning Styles of Hearing-Impaired Students
Reprinted from: *Sustainability* 2022, 14, 13280, doi:10.3390/su142013280 148

Mengfan Li, Ting Wang, Wei Lu and Mengke Wang
Optimizing the Systematic Characteristics of Online Learning Systems to Enhance the Continuance Intention of Chinese College Students
Reprinted from: *Sustainability* **2022**, *14*, 11774, doi:10.3390/su141811774 . . . . **167**

Chao-Ming Wang, Cheng-Hao Shao and Cheng-En Han
Construction of a Tangible VR-Based Interactive System for Intergenerational Learning
Reprinted from: *Sustainability* **2022**, *14*, 6067, doi:10.3390/su14106067 . . . . **184**

Vacius Jusas, Rita Butkiene, Algimantas Venčkauskas, Šarūnas Grigaliūnas, Daina Gudoniene and Renata Burbaite et al.
Sustainable and Security Focused Multimodal Models for Distance Learning
Reprinted from: *Sustainability* **2022**, *14*, 3414, doi:10.3390/su14063414 . . . . **225**

Shang-Chin Tsai and Hao-Chiang Koong Lin
Effect of Adding Emotion Recognition to Film Teaching—Impact of Emotion Feedback on Learning through Puzzle Films
Reprinted from: *Sustainability* **2021**, *13*, 11107, doi:10.3390/su131911107 . . . . **251**

About the Editor

Hao-Chiang Koong Lin

Prof. Hao-Chiang Koong Lin works as the Chair and Professor of the Department of Information and Learning Technology at the National University of Tainan. He is now the President of the Association of Technology Arts Education and the Director of the Research Group on Innovative Design of Learning Software, Ministry of Science and Technology, Taiwan. He also worked as a CIO at Tainan National University of Arts. He received his Ph.D. degree in Computer Science from National Tsing-Hua University in 1997. He has published more than 400 internationally refereed research papers focused on affective computing, learning and education technology, digital arts, interaction design, e-commerce, and artificial intelligence. He serves as a guest editor and member of the editorial review board for several international journals (SSCI, SCI, and Scopus) and many international conferences.

Preface

In this era of rapid technological evolution, the landscape of education continually transforms. This compilation is a timely endeavor, capturing the intersection of technology and learning, a synergy pivotal for the future. Starting with Lin et al., we venture into the fusion of the STEAM-6E model with virtual reality, demonstrating how technology can enhance various learning parameters. Kuo's team underscores the merits of distance education, highlighting the essence of peer self-regulation.

Wu and her team delve into computational thinking, emphasizing the power of visual programming. Zhang and Chen's chapter brings to light students' perceptions in the wake of the pandemic, focusing on Chinese institutions. Ma and collaborators employ advanced neural networks to analyze online engagement patterns. The educational potential of NFTs, a buzzword of our times, is elaborated upon by Wu and Liu. A dive into the nuances of eye movements and their potential for learning is championed by Lin, Liao, and Wang. This seamlessly leads to Chen et al.'s insights on blended learning's continuity and the TAM-SET model.

Jawad and colleagues harness machine learning to forecast student success on virtual platforms, while Luangrungruang and Kokaew pioneer an e-learning model catering to the hearing-impaired. Li's ensemble examines online learning optimization for Chinese students, and Wang's team introduces us to VR's power in bridging generational divides.

Jusas and co-authors address the paramount importance of sustainability and security in e-learning, culminating with Tsai and Lin's exploration of emotion recognition's role in film-based pedagogy. This anthology, a mosaic of innovation and insight, beckons readers to witness the dawn of a transformative epoch in education.

Hao-Chiang Koong Lin
Editor

Article

Integrating the STEAM-6E Model with Virtual Reality Instruction: The Contribution to Motivation, Effectiveness, Satisfaction, and Creativity of Learners with Diverse Cognitive Styles

Yu-Hsuan Lin [1], Hao-Chiang Koong Lin [2], Tao-Hua Wang [3],* and Cheng-Hsun Wu [2]

1. General Research Service Center, National Pingtung University Science and Technology, Pingtung 912, Taiwan
2. Department of Information and Learning Technology, National University of Tainan, Tainan 700, Taiwan
3. Science Education Department, National Museum of Natural Science, Taichung City 404, Taiwan
* Correspondence: wangsab@gmail.com; Tel.: +886-04-2322-6940 (ext. 249)

Abstract: In today's digital age, where smartphones are ubiquitous among the younger generation, they can add to the cognitive load on the brain, even when not in use. This can affect students' learning outcomes and creativity, leading to negative emotions or creativity blocks during the learning process. Thus, this study investigates the relationship between differences in students' cognitive styles and their learning motivation, learning outcomes, creativity, and learning satisfaction. The primary objective is to use the STEAM-6E instructional model in virtual reality (VR) courses to understand how students with different cognitive styles can be stimulated to unleash their diverse and vibrant creativity based on their learning preferences during hands-on experiences. The study also aims to explore whether there are disparities in their learning motivation and learning outcomes, and whether there are differences in their overall learning satisfaction. The findings of the study indicate that for the two cognitive styles of holistic and sequential, the subjects showed significant differences in their learning motivation regarding intrinsic goals, extrinsic goals, task value, control beliefs, self-efficacy, and test anxiety. Significant differences were also observed in their learning preferences, learning outcomes, and creative performance. However, the two groups had no significant differences in the effectiveness, efficiency, and overall satisfaction of the learning activities.

Keywords: cognitive style; STEAM-6E model; virtual reality; motivation for learning; creativity

1. Introduction

The responsibility of education is to effectively guide learners in improving their knowledge, being willing to imagine and develop creativity, and preparing for the future. Therefore, it is important to discuss how to motivate students with different cognitive styles and learning preferences to learn and stimulate their creativity. This study enriches digital learning technology literacy through STEAM-6E instructional scaffolding to improve learning effectiveness through hands-on experience and group dynamics of cooperate promotion because the recent integration of the STEAM-6E model and VR (virtual reality) into digital courses rarely includes the "differences in cognitive styles of learners". Moreover, students in Taiwan are digital natives, and cannot live without their mobile phones. Studies have shown that even if we do not use our phones and there is no notification sound, the normal functioning of our brains may still be disturbed. The reason is that individuals need extra effort to self-control to avoid reaching or using mobile phones [1,2], which can affect the proper working memory, cognitive capacity, and hinder the generation of flow. It will produce creative blocks in the process of inspiration or imagination, which eventually makes it hard for the individual to applicate his inner internal creativity. Winterstein and Jungwirth [3] studied the drawings of 1859 children through the Menschenzeichentest to

analyze the impact on children's "visual perception" and "hand-eye coordination" based on the amount of time spent watching TV, and then they found differences in internal cognitive abilities and emotional development ensued. Przybylski and Weinstein [4] pointed out that mobile devices, such as smartphones, will interfere with the ideal relationship between team members, and may impair group creativity. Based on the above, such issues hinder the normal development of children's creative ability, which gives the researcher the motivation to explore these issues in depth.

This research takes junior high school students as a primary group using the hands-on experience of a VR campus-guiding course combined with immediate issues in daily life based on their two cognitive styles, holist and serialist, in response to the new era led by digital technology. This study plans STEAM curriculum content with participation, exploration, explanation, construction, deepening, and evaluation in 6E multi-axis teaching strategies. We conducted VR problem-based learning based on tasks at each stage, from finding the problem, collecting, analyzing, designing coordination, executive management, and posting comments to reflective corrections and other cross-domain integrated dynamic learning knowledge.

Combining the STEAM-6E model with virtual reality instruction can help students better understand and apply knowledge in science, technology, engineering, arts, and mathematics. This teaching method can stimulate students' learning motivation and creativity, helping them better respond to future challenges and opportunities. At the same time, this teaching method can also help students cultivate environmental awareness and concepts of sustainable development, as it can educate them on how to solve real-life problems in the fields of science and technology to achieve economic, social, and environmental sustainability. In addition, we conducted VR courses through the STEAM-6E teaching model and implemented a VR campus tour. Using virtual reality technology on campus tours can provide a more realistic, interactive, and vivid experience while also reducing the consumption of natural resources, thereby better adhering to the principles of sustainable development.

The study will investigate the effects of implementing the STEAM-6E model for VR courses on learning motivation and creativity, and whether there are significant differences in learning preferences, outcomes, and satisfaction of junior high school students with different cognitive styles. The study hypothesizes that implementing STEAM-6E for VR courses positively affects learning motivation and creativity, and significant differences in learning preferences, outcomes, and satisfaction exist among students with different cognitive styles. The rationale for each hypothesis will be based on the literature review.

Based on the purpose of this study, the following research questions are proposed:

1. Does implementing the STEAM-6E model for VR courses affect the learning motivation of junior high school students with different cognitive styles?
2. Does implementing the STEAM-6E model for VR courses impact the creativity of junior high school students with different cognitive styles?
3. After conducting VR courses in the STEAM-6E model, are there any significant differences in the learning preferences, learning outcomes, and learning satisfaction of junior high school students with different cognitive styles?

2. Literature Review

2.1. The Influence of Cognitive Style on Learning Strategies

Pask's team [5] proposed the concept of "Holist-Serialist." The learning strategies of the holistic cognitive style tend to adopt an overall considerate orientation, and their behavioral traits prefer a hypothesis-based method. On the other hand, the serialist cognitive style preference adopts hierarchical focusing and has a step-by-step behavior. Messick [6] pointed out that cognitive style is the behavioral trait of individuals' organizing or processing information, different from intelligence. Riding and Sadler-Smith [7] defined cognitive style as an individual's inertial strategy for information construction during the learning process. It has a general structure, it is stable, and it is deeply rooted, reflecting qualitative differences in the thought processes of different individuals. In addition, cognitive style is a preferred information-processing mode of individuals, and it is also the most habitual or preferred strategy in the learning process [8]. The serialist cognitive style is more active, focusing on deep and partial sequential learning strategies; the holistic cognitive style is more passive, learning with breadth and overview [9]. Therefore, teachers' in-depth understanding of students' learning preferences would be able to contribute to teaching effectiveness, while learners' cognitive style can affect their preference for Web-based instruction [10]. Chen and Tseng [11] found that holist and serialist cognitive style learners showed similar learning perceptions through E-based scaffolding assessment on English grammar learning. However, they exhibited differences in learned behavior that corresponded to their cognitive style characteristics. Naseer et al. [12] describe an ideal creative cognitive style that helps individuals focus their attention and engage their imagination, thereby fostering creativity and innovation. Therefore, the ideal of an educator lies in realizing the careful planning of lesson preparation, timely adjusting strategies during the teaching process according to individual differences in adaptive practice activities. It aims to provide the most effective and multi-functional learning scaffold customized for different cognitive styles and learning preference behaviors, and eventually achieve ideal learning effects and realize personal dreams through multiple growth paths.

2.2. Creativity in Education

Creativity is a phenomenon that creates new ideas and value, and it is also the ability to make or use new thoughts. In the field of education, Csikszentmihalyi [13] pointed out that creativity is a mental activity, mastering the original insights of people's unique minds through dedicated learning and by imitating others. Therefore, the ways in which education can implement teaching strategies effectively, assisting students in launching creative thinking skills, originality, flexibility, refinement, and productivity through teachers' metacognition has become the focus of today's creativity education.

The importance of creativity can be further explored in the classroom through the interweaving of students, teachers, and teaching materials. Students' curiosity and interests are primary sources of potential creativity [14]. Hu [15] indicates that creative thinking teaching is more sensitive and fluent than traditional teaching since students can demonstrate their highest levels of sensitivity and fluency in creative thinking while using immersive VR. Saorin [16] pointed out that innovative ideas can be stimulated through the STEAM maker offices and creative thinking ability can be improved by turning ideas into actual products. Nikkola [17] indicates that children's creativity and thinking ability are closely related to whether they are willing to participate in activities. They will change their will by paying attention to their surroundings. Jumadi et al. [18] proposed an instructional design that allows students to develop problem-solving and creativity. This can help students enhance their system's thinking, and intensify their creative performance by engaging in meaningful reflection and taking action through questioning and discussing critical thinking situations

In summary, creativity means a process that produces original and unique ideas or creations to integrate knowledge for problem-solving, and eventually achieves the real purpose of solving problems. Individuals, based on prior knowledge or experience, can have the ability to break through the framework with an unprecedented perspective, urging them to bring out new theories and dare to unlock the unknown through continuous practice, perceiving, understanding, and exploring the essence of questions.

2.3. STEAM and 6E Instructional Scaffolding Model in Education

Radziwill et al. [19] proposed that the STEAM learning development plan is divided into four stages, the cumulative sum of knowledge, creating knowledge exchange between individuals and organizations, self-awareness and update, and the recognition and value obtained by the previous knowledge and ability. STEAM education aims to ensure that lifelong learning takes place at all times accessible to learners, allowing them to unleash their potential and creativity, continuing to utilize the integration of multi-stakeholder dialogue and cross-domain literacy to activate actual learning experiences and eventually bring maximum benefit to society through teamwork and problem-solving.

The 6E (engage, explore, explain, engineer, enrich, and evaluate) instructional scaffolding model emphasizes that students are the main body of learning. It is a sequential teaching model that combines science education and engineering design processes combining students in heterogeneous groups to stimulate design, practice, inquiry, and reflection. Sanjayanti et al. [20] found that the 6E design learning program can improve students' logical thinking and awareness. Hashim et al. [21] illustrated that science educators should emphasize meaningful learning environments to stimulate students' creativity. Cultivating sophisticated thinking skills from learning by design according to their diverse background knowledge, cognitive style, and learning tendency is believed to be the basis for stimulating students' creativity. In executing the 6E model, students repeatedly deepen their thinking, which is especially suitable for STEAM courses, learning STEAM knowledge sequentially and competently through hands-on subject content and teacher step-by-step guidance. As a result, it can improve the learning effect of various disciplines and interdisciplinary subjects, and improve collaborative learning, professional knowledge, and self-confidence [22].

To sum up, based on the core concept of STEAM education, this study deeply explores and carefully plans the activation curriculum that can break through the subject framework. It strengthens the basis of student engagement as the primary body of learning, combined with the 6E teaching model interwoven into the STEAM-6E pedagogy to guide students to actively participate, explore, explain, build, enrich and evaluate. It guides students step by step to use their imagination, self-control their learning strategies, develop their learned and practical concepts, and develop their skills in innovative and creative thinking, action response, and problem-solving.

2.4. The Application of VR in Education

For educational applications, the initial stage of VR is often used as a high-risk training tasks. It can be seen in the standard operation procedure (SOP) training that is widely used in the daily duties of the police, firefighters, medical staff, actual combat simulation or logistics special training courses for military officers and soldiers, precision microscopic medical practice training for brain surgery, etc. The purpose is to provide a safe and secure educational environment where mastery can be practiced. Walcutt et al. [23] pointed out that with the maturity of waterproof hardware and educational software technology, VR is more and more widely used in marine science as educational materials for scientific exploration. VR is an extraordinarily engaging educational tool compared to data analysis or flat images. Shim [24] mentioned that the fusion of VR and educational applications are based on three basic principles: immersion, interaction, and user participation in the environment and story. These elements make the learning process more engaging and improve student motivation, offering exciting educational potential. Chen et al. [25] pointed out that students using VR technology while learning has significantly improved academic performance and hands-on ability. Demonstrating virtual reality can help students understand abstract scientific concepts and build mental conceptual models to help them internalize and organize into knowledge structures. Looking forward, the combination of VR and education in the future, may be able to carry out an international virtual course that allows teachers and students around the world to discuss language, culture, or science all together without distance and time problems to conduct self-directed flipped learning and mastery training. It can also be used in a digital guided tour of museums before the outdoor education starts as a knowledge preview, or as pre-fire fire extinguishing and escape simulation training. In conclusion, as VR and related technologies mature, the only thing that can slow their evolution is human imagination.

Therefore, this study plans a set of "STEAM-6E Teaching Methods" for VR teaching and aims to enrich the diversified content of STEAM education. We adopt the 6E model to expand the spectrum of interdisciplinary thinking and deepen the learning experience while combining school-based characteristic courses and actual conditions. Engaging in meaningful observation and reflection to stimulate learning motivation and team dynamics further initiates unlimited imagination for original and unique innovation output. Knowledgeable and systematic self-examination, internal management growth, and dynamic learning from the design process eventually produces original and interesting VR guide works, guiding students with different cognitive styles to deeply perceive and feel the beauty of the campus, and also make good use of creative thinking skills to solve practical problems in life. We hope students can improve their learning effect and learning satisfaction, enhance self-efficacy, and affirm their self-worth after taking this course.

2.5. Learning Motivation

Motivation refers to the activities that can arouse the learners and prompt the learners to lead the activities to a certain goal that is to be achieved, and towards an internal motivation of learning with active participation. This has a considerable impact on the positive correlation of learning outcomes. Additionally, Some studies also pointed out that there is a highly positive relationship between learning motivation and achievement [26–28].

According to MSLQ, the motivation scale section consists of six components: intrinsic motivation, extrinsic motivation, task value, control of learning beliefs, self-efficacy, and test anxiety [29]. Learning motivation is an important factor affecting students' learning behavior [30], which represents students' motivation to pursue their learning goals. Therefore, educators should understand students' learning motivation and adopt appropriate teaching strategies and methods to improve students' learning motivation and promote their learning achievement and growth.

2.6. Learning Satisfaction

Learning activity satisfaction refers to learners' satisfaction with the activities they participate in during the learning process. The level of satisfaction with learning activities will have an impact on learning motivation and learning outcomes [31]. According to Tough [32] students exhibit positive and enthusiastic attitudes toward learning activities can be seen as a measure of satisfaction in learning. Conversely, showing negative and pessimistic emotions can be viewed as a measure of dissatisfaction.

ASQ (after-scenario questionnaire) is a measurement tool that was first proposed and used by Lewis [33] for post-task ratings. The ASQ scale includes three questions that represent effectiveness, efficiency, and overall satisfaction [34]. This questionnaire has been widely used in evaluating user experience in various scenarios, including learning activities. Cabral's [35] results of the ASQ questionnaire indicated high levels of user satisfaction with the virtual experience.

3. Methods
3.1. Research Design

In this study, we use the experimental method of one-group pretest–posttest design from pre-experimental design, focusing on learners with the two cognitive styles of "Holist" and "Serialist", and integrating STEAM-6E to the VR campus tour practice course. We designed the course based on the essential techniques of VR to plan the teaching material required in curriculum planning, prepare for teaching materials, and then, assessment. We have taken the STEAM-6E teaching model as our main axis and choosing the VR campus guiding as the research category to explore the quality of the impacts on creative thinking, learning effectiveness, learning motivation, and learning satisfaction related to learners with different cognitive styles. According to the VR courses planned in the life and technology courses in senior, junior, and elementary schools, most of the teaching materials only have basic introductions, lacking application reflection and practical activities. Therefore, in terms of practical application value, participants can acquire a VR design project through the course, and plan the ideal guiding route on the campus where they live every day. This plan can not only allow the trainees to express their ideas and creativity through their cognitive style and develop independent creative thinking skills and practical problem-solving knowledge that resonates with their learning and life to carry forward into meaningful learning, but also help the school to build its resources. This course is planned for 40 min per week, and 8 weeks in total, including 320 min altogether. Figure 1 shows the plan of this course, Figure 2 shows the implementation records in this course, Table 1 is the correspondence table between STEAM fields and students' learning performance.

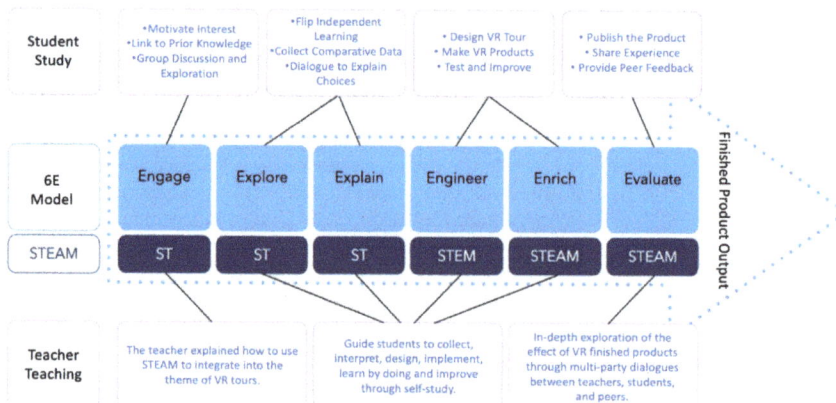

Figure 1. The planning process of STEAM-6E integrated into the VR campus tour practice course.

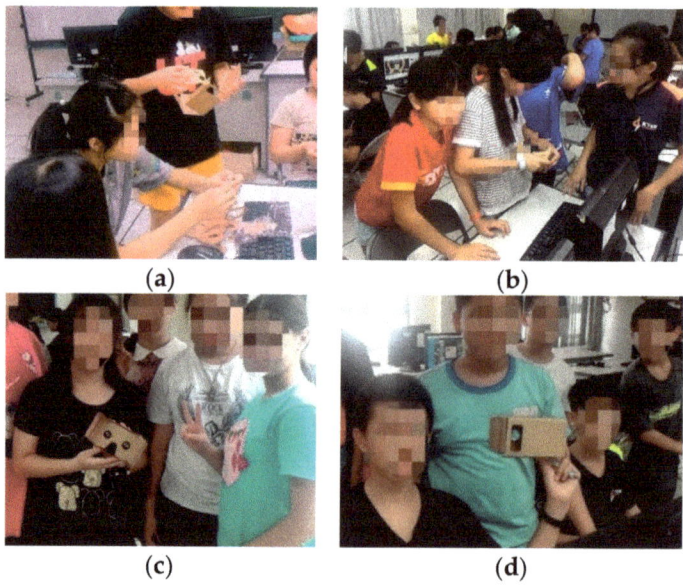

Figure 2. Implementation records of the integration with STEAM-6E and Google Cardboard VR school guiding campus. (**a**) After the explanation, they conducted research in groups. (**b**) Making the Google Cardboard with members. (**c**) Students finishing and publishing their work of VR guiding. (**d**) Group discussion for peer feedback and work improvement.

Table 1. Corresponding to the learning performance of students in the STEAM field.

STEAM Field	Students' Performance
Science	• Understand the principle of 3D Stereo Vision/Tour Creator.
Technology	• Learn the basics of virtual reality. • Learn about the applications of virtual reality in real life.
Engineering	• VR guiding map. • Identify the problems at work then improve and optimize them.
Art	• Beautify the VR map. • Discover the beauty of the school through the guiding map.
Math	• Three-dimensional coordinates with latitude and longitude.

3.2. Research Tool

In the beginning, we identified the two cognitive styles of holistic and serialist by using the study preference questionnaire (SPQ); then, we sorted out the comparison table proposed by Mampadi et al. [36]. Consulting the version used by Tsai and Lin [37], we described the content of each question in two sentences or pairs. After the respondents answered based on first intuition, we distinguished them as holists or serialists by calculating which type of choice was selected in more than half of their answers.

Next, we used MSLQ to explore their intrinsic goal orientation, extrinsic goal orientation, control of learning beliefs, task value, test anxiety, and self-efficacy, etc. We also added three dimensions of value, expectation, and emotion to explore the shift in their learning motivation. In addition, we applied the learning activity satisfaction scale learning activity satisfaction scale (ASQ) in the assessment questionnaire after the post-task ratings and gave a score based on the 7-point scale to investigate effectiveness, efficiency, and satisfaction [34]. We used the pre- and post-test prepared by IT teachers based on the STEAM-6E VR learning effect, including 6 true or false questions with 30 points and 10 multiple choice questions with 70 points, 100 points in total. Pre-test papers were used to see if there are any differences between students' prior knowledge. The post-test paper was used to understand the impact on students' learning after adding the STEAM-6E teaching method to the VR practice. Finally, we explored whether their creative thinking ability changes during the teaching activities by five normative reference scores, including fluency, elaboration, originality, titles, and closure, from the TTCT graphic and streamlined scoring.

3.3. Experimental Procedure

Figure 3 shows the flow chart of the STEAM-6E teaching method in the VR course teaching experiment: (1) Before the course, take a pre-test for 40 min. The questionnaires include: learning performance scale, TTCT(A), MSLQ, SPQ; (2) Subsequent teaching courses will last for 240 min, with a total of 6 lessons. Integrate the VR course with the STEAM-6E scaffolding teaching mode and use Google Cardboard to watch the finished VR campus tour produced by the course; (3) After the course is over, there will be a 40 min post-test. The questionnaires include: learning performance scale, TTCT(B), MSLQ, ASQ. Evaluate the students' learning effects according to the learning effect test paper, use the TTCT graphic version to evaluate the impact of the students' creative thinking ability after passing the course, and analyze the students' learning motivation and satisfaction with the learning activities.

3.4. Participants

The participants of this study were in a junior high school in Tainan city. A total of 44 students participated in this study, with an average age of 13 to 14 years. However, three students asked to leave during the pre- and post-test for two sessions. Therefore, a total of 41 participants were in this study.

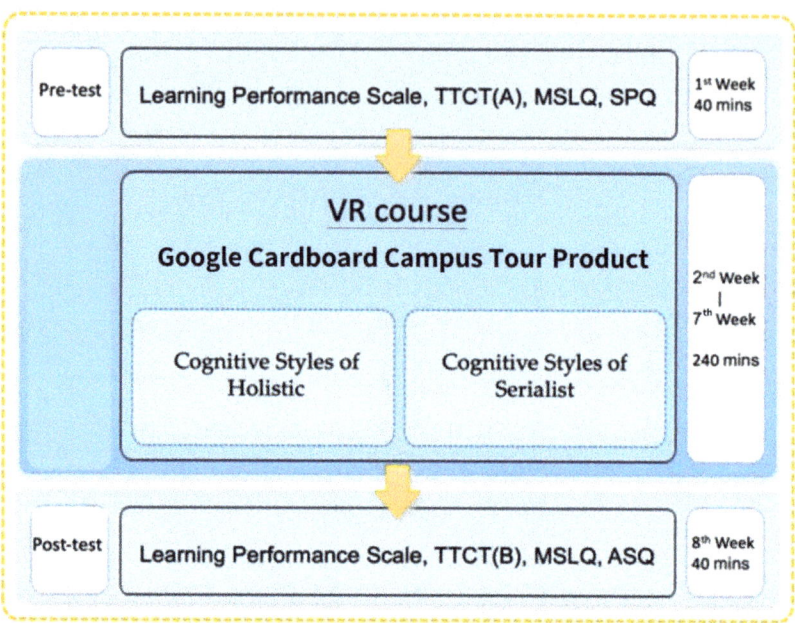

Figure 3. Experimental flow chart.

4. Results

The study aims to investigate the differences in learning motivation, learning effectiveness, and creativity among junior high school students with different cognitive styles who participated in a VR campus tour course integrated with the STEAM-6E model. A total of 41 students participated in the study. Before the course, the students completed questionnaires on the learning performance scale, TTCT(A), MSLQ, and SPQ. Then, all participants took the course, which involved using Google Cardboard to watch the finished VR campus tour produced by the course with the STEAM-6E scaffolding teaching mode. After completing the course, the students completed the post-test, which included the learning performance scale, TTCT(B), MSLQ, and ASQ questionnaires. We analyzed the data collected from the experiment based on the SPQ, and explored the differences in learning motivation, learning effectiveness, and creativity among students with different cognitive styles. Due to a pre-existing difference between holistic and serialist learners, ANCOVA was conducted to ensure the accuracy of the results.

4.1. Analysis of the Current Situation of Participants

This study used SPQ to differentiate the types of cognitive styles: holist and serialist. There were 44 participants involved in the experiment, but 3 were excluded due to being unable to fully complete the experiment. Therefore, a total of 41 participants comprised the valid sample; 21 participants with the serialist cognitive style and 20 participants with the holist cognitive style, as seen in Table 2.

Table 2. Distribution of the number of respondents' cognitive styles.

Cognitive Style	Numbers of Participants
Serialist	21
Holist	20

4.2. The Difference in the Learning Motivations for Different Cognitive Styles in the Combined STEAM-6E VR Course

This section is to discuss the differences in learning motivations between the different cognitive styles of students in the combined STEAM-6E VR-guided course. Learning motivation involved several dimensions, including intrinsic goal orientation, extrinsic goal orientation, task value, control of learning beliefs, self-efficacy, and test anxiety.

Analysis of Learning Motivations in the Different Cognitive Styles

This study was conducted to clarify the difference in learning motivation between the holist (N = 20) style and the serialist (N = 21) style in the combined STEAM-6E VR-guided course. The homogeneity of regression was examined according to the motivated strategies for learning questionnaire, MSLQ.

Table 3 shows the result of the assumption of homogeneity of regression. From the result, no significant levels were found in the pre-test of intrinsic goal orientation ($F = 2.536$, $p = 0.120 > 0.05$), the pre-test of extrinsic goal orientation ($F = 2.825$, $p = 0.101 > 0.05$), the pre-test of control of learning beliefs ($F = 0.219$, $p = 0.642 > 0.05$), the pre-test of task value ($F = 2.255$, $p = 0.142 > 0.05$), the pre-test of self-efficacy ($F = 1.191$, $p = 0.282 > 0.05$), and the pre-test of test anxiety ($F = 0.509$, $p = 0.480 > 0.05$). It showed the variables of the group, pre-test, and group*pre-test accorded with the hypothesis of homogeneity (homogeneity of variance was not violated when using the pre-test as a covariate and the post-test as the dependent variable), and suggested that a common slope of regression was appropriate for the three groups. Therefore, the analysis of covariance (ANCOVA) was adopted, where the assumption of homogeneity of regression was met, and the pre-test acted as a covariate to reduce the effect of any existing differences on the results.

Table 3. Results of the homogeneity for the within-group regression coefficients regarding the pre-test of each dimension of learning motivation.

Dimension	SS	df	MS	F	p
Intrinsic goal orientation	0.866	1	0.866	2.536	0.120
Extrinsic goal orientation	0.877	1	0.877	2.825	0.101
Control of learning beliefs	0.038	1	0.038	0.219	0.642
Task value	0.623	1	0.623	2.255	0.142
Self-efficacy	0.209	1	0.209	1.191	0.282
Test anxiety	0.164	1	0.164	0.509	0.480

Descriptive statistics for the means regarding the pre-test of intrinsic goal orientation were the means of the original post-test: 4.345 for the serialist style and 3.788 for the holist style. The descriptive statistics for the means regarding the pre-test of extrinsic goal orientation were the means of the original post-test: 3.964 for the serialist style and 3.325 for the holist style. The descriptive statistics for the means regarding the pre-test of control of learning beliefs were the means of the original post-test: 4.262 for the serialist style and 3.838 for the holist style. The descriptive statistics for the means regarding the pre-test of task value were the means of the original post-test: 4.175 for the serialist style and 3.792 for the holist style. The descriptive statistics for the means regarding the pre-test of self-efficacy were the means of the original post-test: 4.202 for the serialist style and 3.750 for the holist style. The descriptive statistics for the means regarding the pre-test of test anxiety were the means of the original post-test: 2.295 for the serialist style and 2.850 for the holist style. The above data did not exclude the influence of covariates (the pre-test), nor did it present the adjusted means.

The result of Levene's test of error variances for the pre-test of intrinsic goal orientation was not found to be significant ($F = 3.036$, $p = 0.089 > 0.05$). The result of Levene's test of error variances for the pre-test of extrinsic goal orientation was not found to be significant ($F = 0.050$, $p = 0.824 > 0.05$). The result of Levene's test of error variances for the pre-test of control of learning beliefs was not found to be significant ($F = 2.673$, $p = 0.110 > 0.05$).

The result of Levene's test of error variances for the pre-test of task value was not found to be significant ($F = 3.457, p = 0.071 > 0.05$). Levene's test of error variances for the pre-test of self-efficacy was not found to be significant ($F = 2.047, p = 0.160 > 0.05$). The result of Levene's test of error variances for the pre-test of test anxiety was not found to be significant ($F = 1.583, p = 0.216 > 0.05$). The above results suggested that homogeneity of variances was met, as error variances were equal across groups regarding the dependent variables of the post-test.

Table 4 reports the analysis of ANCOVA regarding each dimension of learning motivation, indicating the results of dependent variables (post-test scores) on the independent variables after eliminating the effects of the pre-test scores (covariates). According to the results, a significant difference was found between the two different cognitive styles ($F = 5.082, p = 0.03 < 0.05$) in terms of intrinsic goal orientation, indicating that there was a significant level of intrinsic goal orientation between the two different cognitive styles regarding involvement in the combined STEAM-6E VR-guided course. The adjusted mean value of post-test scores was 4.284 for the serialist style and 3.852 for the holist style. Students with the serialist style appear to have learnt significantly more than those with the holist style via the combined STEAM-6 combined course (Table 4).

Table 4. ANCOVA results of each dimension of learning motivation.

Dimension	Dependent Variable: Post-Test Scores						
	SS	df	MS	F	p	Effect Sizes	Partial Eta Square
Intrinsic goal orientation	1.805	1	1.805	5.082	0.030	0.394	0.118
Extrinsic goal orientation	4.231	1	4.231	13.004	0.001	0.493	0.255
Control of learning beliefs	2.606	1	2.606	15.244	0.000	0.424	0.286
Task value	1.245	1	1.245	4.360	0.044	0.533	0.103
Self-efficacy	2.103	1	2.103	11.947	0.001	0.477	0.239
Test anxiety	3.254	1	3.254	10.212	0.003	0.430	0.212

As for the extrinsic goal orientation, there was a significant difference in intrinsic goal orientation across the two different cognitive styles ($F = 13.004, p = 0.001 < 0.05$). This indicates that there was a significant level of extrinsic goal orientation between the two different cognitive styles regarding involvement in the combined STEAM-6E VR-guided course. The adjusted mean value of post-test scores was 3.967 for the serialist style and 3.323 for the holist style. Students with the serialist style appear to have learnt significantly more than those with the holist style via the combined STEAM-6E VR-guided course (Table 4).

In terms of control of learning beliefs, there was a significant difference in intrinsic goal orientation across the two different cognitive styles ($F = 15.244, p = 0.000 < 0.05$). This indicates that there was a significant level of control of learning beliefs between the two different cognitive styles regarding involvement in the combined STEAM-6E VR-guided course. The adjusted mean value of post-test scores was 4.309 for the serialist style and 3.788 for the holist style. Students with the serialist style appear to have learnt significantly more than those with the holist style via the combined STEAM-6E VR-guided course (Table 4).

Regarding task value, there was a significant difference in task value across the two different cognitive styles ($F = 4.36, p = 0.044 < 0.05$), indicating that there was a significant level of task value between the two different cognitive styles regarding involvement in the combined STEAM-6E VR-guided course. The adjusted mean value of post-test scores was 4.159 for the serialist style and 3.808 for the holist style. Students with the serialist style appear to have learnt significantly more than those with the holist style via the combined STEAM-6E VR-guided course (Table 4).

As for self-efficacy, there was a significant difference in self-efficacy across the two different cognitive styles ($F = 11.947, p = 0.001 < 0.05$), indicating that a significant level of self-efficacy was in self-efficacy between the two different cognitive styles when involved in the combined STEAM-6E VR-guided course. The adjusted mean value of post-test scores was 4.205 for the serialist style and 3.748 for the holist style. Students with the serialist style appear to have learnt significantly more than those with the holist style via the combined STEAM-6E VR-guided course (Table 4).

In terms of test anxiety, there was a significant difference in task anxiety across the two different cognitive styles ($F = 10.212$, $p = 0.003 < 0.05$), indicating that a significant level of task anxiety was found between the two different cognitive styles when involved in the combined STEAM-6E VR-guided course. The adjusted mean value of post-test scores was 2.291 for the serialist style and 2.855 for the holist style. Students with the serialist style appear to have learnt significantly more than those with the holist style via the combined STEAM-6E VR-guided course (Table 4).

4.3. The Difference in the Learning Preference for Different Cognitive Styles in the Combined STEAM-6E VR-Guided Course

The study aimed to explore the difference in learning preference between the holist (N = 20) style and the serialist (N = 21) style in the combined STEAM-6E VR-guided course. The homogeneity of regression was examined and not violated, as shown in Table 5. The variables of the group, pre-test, and group*pre-test, accorded with the hypothesis of homogeneity, were presented (homogeneity of variance was not violated when using the pre-test as a covariate and the post-test as the dependent variable, $F = 3.420$, $p = 0.072 > 0.05$), and suggested that a common slope of regression was appropriate for the three groups.

Table 5. Results of the homogeneity for the within-group regression coefficients regarding the pre-test of each dimension of learning preference.

Variable	SS	df	MS	F	p
Group	0.323	1	0.323	3.862	0.057
Pre-test	0.074	1	0.074	0.882	0.354
Group*pre-test	0.286	1	0.286	3.420	0.072

The descriptive statistics for the means regarding the pre-test of learning preference were the means of the original post-test: 3.874 for the serialist style and 3.557 for the holist style. The above data did not exclude the influence of covariates (the pre-test), nor did they present the adjusted means. The result of Levene's test of error variances for the pre-test of learning preference was not found to be significant ($F = 3.036$, $p = 0.089 > 0.05$), indicating that the null hypothesis is accepted and homogeneity of variances was met, as error variances were equal across groups regarding the dependent variables of the post-test.

Table 6 reports the ANCOVA results of learning preference, indicating the results of dependent variables (post-test scores) on the independent variables after eliminating the effects of the pre-test scores (covariates). According to the result, there was a significant difference in learning preference across the two different cognitive styles ($F = 11.791$, $p = 0.001 < 0.05$), indicating that a significant level of learning preference was found between the two different cognitive styles when involved in the combined STEAM-6E VR-guided course. The adjusted mean values of post-test scores in learning preference were 3.878 for the serialist style and 3.553 for the holist style. Students with the serialist style appear to have better learning preference than those with the holist style in the combined STEAM-6E VR-guided course (Table 6).

Table 6. ANCOVA results of learning motivation.

Variables	SS	df	MS	F	p	Effect Sizes	Partial Eta Square
Group	1.048	1	1.048	11.791	0.001	0.474	0.237

4.4. The Difference in the Learning Satisfaction for Different Cognitive Styles in the Combined STEAM-6E VR-Guided Course

The study aimed to discuss the difference in learning satisfaction with the three dimensions of effectiveness, efficiency, and overall satisfaction between the holist (N = 20) style and the serialist (N = 21) style in the combined STEAM-6E VR-guided course. In terms of the first dimension of learning satisfaction, the independent sample *t*-test was employed to analyze the effectiveness of learning satisfaction for the two styles. As seen in Table 7, the mean and standard deviation of the effectiveness scores were 6.19 and 0.873, respectively, for the serialist style, while the effectiveness scored 6.15 and 1.348, respectively for the holist style. The *t*-test results showed that there was no significant difference in the effectiveness of learning satisfaction between two different cognitive styles regarding involvement in the combined STEAM-6E VR-guided course ($t(39) = 0.115, p = 0.070 > 0.05$).

Table 7. The independent sample *t*-test result of the learning satisfaction.

	Mean (SD)		df	t	p
	Serialist (N = 21)	Holist (N = 20)			
Effectiveness	6.19 (0.873)	6.15 (1.348)	39	0.115	0.070
Efficiency	6.10 (0.995)	5.85 (1.461)	39	0.631	0.532
Overall satisfaction	6.14 (0.964)	5.70 (1.525)	39	1.117	0.271

As for the second dimension of learning satisfaction, the independent sample *t*-test was employed to analyze the efficiency of learning satisfaction for the two styles. As seen in Table 7, the mean and standard deviation of the effectiveness scores were 6.10 and 0.995, respectively, for the serialist style, while the effectiveness scored 5.85 and 1.461, respectively, for the holist style. The *t*-test results showed that there was no significant difference in the efficiency of learning satisfaction between the two different cognitive styles when involved in the combined STEAM-6E VR-guided course ($t(39) = 0.631, p = 0.0531 > 0.05$).

Regarding overall learning satisfaction, the independent sample *t*-test was employed to analyze the overall learning satisfaction for the two styles. As seen in Table 7, the mean and standard deviation of the effectiveness scores were 6.14 and 0.954, respectively, for the serialist style, while the effectiveness scored 5.70 and 1.525, respectively, for the holist style. The *t*-test results showed that there was no significant difference in the efficiency of learning satisfaction between the two different cognitive styles regarding their involvement in the combined STEAM-6E VR-guided course ($t(39) = 1.117, p = 0.271 > 0.05$).

4.5. The Difference in the Learning Achievement for Different Cognitive Styles in the Combined STEAM-6E VR-Guided Course

The study explored the difference in learning achievement between the holist (N = 20) style and the serialist (N = 21) style in the combined STEAM-6E VR-guided course. The homogeneity of regression was examined and not violated, as shown in Table 8. The variables of the group, pre-test, and group*pre-test, accorded with the hypothesis of homogeneity, were presented (homogeneity of variance was not violated when using the pre-test as a covariate and the post-test as the dependent variable, $F = 3.350, p = 0.075 > 0.05$), and suggested that a common slope of regression was appropriate for the three groups.

Table 8. Results of the homogeneity for the within-group regression coefficients regarding the pre-test of learning achievement.

Variable	SS	df	MS	F	p
Group	851.082	1	851.082	10.924	0.002
Pre-test	260.979	1	260.979	3.350	0.075
Group*pre-test	260.979	1	260.979	3.350	0.075

The descriptive statistics for the means regarding the pre-test of learning achievement were the means of the original post-test: 78.571 for the serialist style and 59.688 for the holist style. The above data did not exclude the influence of covariates (the pre-test), nor did they show the adjusted means. The result of Levene's test of error variances for the pre-test of learning achievement was not found to be significant ($F = 1.314, p = 0.259 > 0.05$), indicating that the null hypothesis is accepted and homogeneity of variances was met, as error variances were equal across groups regarding dependent variables of the post-test.

Table 9 shows ANCOVA results of learning achievement, indicating the results of dependent variables (post-test scores) on the independent variables after eliminating the effects of the pre-test scores (covariates). According to the result, there was a significant difference in the learning achievement across the two different cognitive styles ($F = 43.128$, $p = 0.000 < 0.05$), indicating that a significant level of learning achievement was found between the two different cognitive styles when involved in the combined STEAM-6E VR-guided course. The adjusted mean values of post-test scores in the learning achievement were 78.476 for the serialist style and 59.788 for the holist style. Students with the serialist style appear to have a significantly higher learning achievement than those with the holist style in the combined STEAM-6E VR-guided course (Table 9).

Table 9. ANCOVA results of learning achievement.

Variables	SS	df	MS	F	p	Effect Sizes	Partial Eta Square
Group	3567.920	1	3567.920	43.128	0.000	0.718	0.532

4.6. The Difference in the Creativity for Different Cognitive Styles in the Combined STEAM-6E VR-Guided Course

This study aimed to understand the difference in creativity between the holist (N = 20) style and the serialist (N = 21) style in the combined STEAM-6E VR-guided course. The homogeneity of regression was examined according to the Torrance tests of creative thinking (TTCT), and the result was not violated, as shown in Table 10. The variables of the group, pre-test, and group*pre-test, accorded with the hypothesis of homogeneity, were presented (homogeneity of variance was not violated when using the pre-test as a covariate and the post-test as the dependent variable, $F = 2.909$, $p = 0.096 > 0.05$), and suggested that a common slope of regression was appropriate for the three groups.

Table 10. Results of the homogeneity for the within-group regression coefficients regarding the pre-test of the creativity.

Variables	SS	df	MS	F	p
Group	146.523	1	146.523	1.789	0.189
Pre-test	1409.147	1	1409.147	17.202	0.000
Group*pre-test	238.296	1	238.296	2.909	0.096

Descriptive statistics for the means regarding the pre-test of the creativity were the means of the original post-test: 83.990 for the serialist and 78.070 for the holist style. The above data did not exclude the influence of covariates (the pre-test), nor did they present the adjusted means. The result of Levene's test of error variances for the pre-test of creativity was not found to be significant ($F = 2.945$, $p = 0.094 > 0.05$), indicating that the null hypothesis is accepted and homogeneity of variances was met, as error variances were equal across groups regarding dependent variables of the post-test.

Table 11 presents ANCOVA results of learning preferences, indicating the results of dependent variables (post-test scores) on the independent variables after eliminating the effects of the pre-test scores (covariates). According to the result, there was a significant difference in creativity across the two different cognitive styles ($F = 6.840$, $p = 0.013 < 0.05$), indicating that a significant level of creativity was found between the two different cognitive styles when involved in the combined STEAM-6E VR-guided course. The adjusted mean values of post-test scores in creativity were 84.841 for the serialist style and 77.177 for the holist style. Students with the serialist style appear to have better learning creativity than those who with the holist style in the combined STEAM-6E VR-guided course (Table 11).

Table 11. ANCOVA results of the creativity.

Variables	SS	df	MS	F	p	Effect Sizes	Partial Eta Square
Group	588.440	1	588.440	6.840	0.013	0.262	0.153

5. Discussion

When talking about the learning motivation of respondents with different cognitive styles, a serialist is yields better results compared to a holist and has remarkable differentiation. Therefore, teachers can arrange more efficient learning strategies for individual differences between students by planning and implementing adaptive teaching. Learners finish tasks based on self-motivation or outer encouragement to pursue self-affirmation and others' approval to further identify with the core value of the work. This theory also works in concert with the research [38–40]. Furthermore, learning preference is not associated with good or bad. It is just the skill they are used to applying based on their personality, background, and culture. In an environment that meets their learning preferences, the serialists' results have a notable discrepancy compared to the results of the holist cognitive style. Therefore, learners can achieve better absorption efficiency through real experiences or generalization techniques to transform learning content into knowledge. This self-efficacy helps them reach learning goals, in accordance with the research [41,42]. The only domain where there are no significant differences is satisfaction with learning activities. Adaptive teaching is carried out through teachers' close observation of learners, in line with Confucius' philosophy of teaching students according to their aptitude, as well as the Socratic method, providing students the opportunities for self-exploration and growth, conforming to research [43]. Furthermore, to improve learning results, such as cognitive strategies and intrinsic motivation, the analysis showed that serialists with higher learning motivation performed better than holists. It shows that the suitability of the cognitive method is positively correlated with learning outcomes, reflecting [44–46], that point out that adaptive learning can effectively promote learning results.

This study allows respondents with different cognitive styles to engage in a creative process with their exploration and development through hands-on experiential learning. There are significant disparities in creativity performance between different cognitive styles that also conform to studies [47,48]. These confirm that the serialist cognitive style is suitable for this research's creative practice activities. In short, previous studies [49,50] have pointed out that the satisfaction of learning activities often varies significantly due to individual differences. Nonetheless, the method used in this study improves the problems in this aspect thanks to the adoption of the STEAM-6E model and teaching strategies that accommodate cognitive style preferences. Taking students as the most important element of learning, we provide them with the necessary support at different levels according to their learning abilities.

This research aims to enhance children's learning motivation and creativity by using digital technology, leading them to find a better future and serving as role models for educators. The students in this study were from a small junior high school in Tainan city. Because the total number of students is not large, only 44 students could participate in this experiment. Therefore, the results of this experiment cannot be extrapolated to all situations. The recommendation of this study is to expand the sample size to obtain complete and diverse statistics. This research only focuses on the VR course due to time considerations, so other digital learning technologies are not addressed in this discussion. It is suggested that the STEAM-6E scaffolding instructional method is used in further experiments and that the scope of VR teaching resources is expanded, such as mixed reality, augmented reality, and tangible interaction. They can strengthen digital learning literacy gradually to improve the effectiveness of hands-on and experiential learning activities through the process they designed based on the 6E model. They can improve their concentration in learning and promote knowledge integration to make the process more impressive and attractive through the sense of touch and movement from touchable materials. In addition, fully immersive experiential learning products can achieve educational value in museums, exhibitions, sightseeing, and even space travel by applying them in multiple industries. Especially during the pandemic, they can help us obtain a balance between distance prevention and sustainable learning. In short, follow-up research can focus on an in-depth analysis of learners' flow and self-efficacy to further discuss understanding their learning status. Adding in a learners' interview supplement would be a feasible method. Qualitative texts can help us comprehend their psychological state and feelings during the process more accurately, and carry out instant and precise fit correction according to the slight changes in learners' cognitive experience to achieve effective teaching and intrinsic motivation in active learning processes.

6. Conclusions

This research focuses on learners with holistic and sequential cognitive styles and learning preferences, using the STEAM-6E model to set up an instructional scaffolding, adding VR digital technology to integrate into the school guiding program. Through the previous analyses, we found out that goal orientation, extrinsic goal orientation, task value, control of learning beliefs, self-efficacy, and test anxiety differed between the two cognitive styles. There is also significant discrepancy in learning orientation, effectiveness, and creative performances. However, in terms of satisfaction with learning activities, there was no significant difference between the two groups in effectiveness, efficiency, and overall satisfaction. The learning goal of this research is to combine VR with real-life situations and integrate the STEAM-6E mode to create a clear and potent instructional scaffold to help learners complete their tasks.

The scope and limitations of this study are described in detail as follows:

1. Scope and Limitations of the Study:

This study focuses on students from a junior high school in southern Taiwan. Students of different educational levels and living in other areas were not included in the this study. Therefore, the inferences drawn from this study should be limited to students with similar backgrounds and should not be overgeneralized to other populations;

2. Scope and Limitations of Cognitive Styles:

This study focuses mainly on the cognitive styles of "holistic" and "serialist", and other types of cognitive styles were not included in this study. The classification of cognitive styles is based on the "Study Process Questionnaire (SPQ)", which is filled out freely by learners and is subject to individual subjective thinking. Therefore, individual biases may exist and affect the research results;

3. Scope and Limitations of the Study:

This study aims to investigate the performance differences in learning effectiveness and creativity between "holistic" and "serialist" learners. The curriculum content is based on the emerging technologies mentioned in the Ministry of Education's news release, such as "VR virtual reality/AR augmented reality, AI artificial intelligence, IoT Internet of Things, big data, smart machinery, and green energy". The study selected the "VR virtual reality" course content to produce digital multimedia hands-on teaching materials for experimentation. The digital learning materials should be primarily composed of graphic, video, and textual content, while materials consisting of only pictures or text were not included in this study.

Author Contributions: Conceptualization, Y.-H.L. and T.-H.W.; methodology, H.-C.K.L.; software, C.-H.W.; validation, T.-H.W.; formal analysis, C.-H.W.; investigation, C.-H.W.; resources, T.-H.W.; data curation, H.-C.K.L. and T.-H.W.; writing—original draft preparation, Y.-H.L.; writing review and editing, Y.-H.L.; visualization, T.-H.W.; supervision, H.-C.K.L. and Y.-H.L.; project administration, Y.-H.L. All authors have read and agreed to the published version of the manuscript.

Funding: This research received no external funding.

Institutional Review Board Statement: Not applicable.

Informed Consent Statement: Informed consent was obtained from all subjects involved in the study.

Data Availability Statement: Not applicable.

Conflicts of Interest: The authors declare no conflict of interest.

References

1. Thornton, B.; Faires, A.; Robbins, M.; Rollins, E. The mere presence of a cell phone may be distracting. *Soc. Psychol.* **2014**, *45*, 479–488. [CrossRef]
2. Ward, A.F.; Duke, K.; Gneezy, A.; Bos, M.W. Brain drain: The mere presence of one's own smartphone reduces available cognitive capacity. *J. Assoc. Consum. Res.* **2017**, *2*, 140–154. [CrossRef]
3. Winterstein, P.; Jungwirth, R.J. Medienkonsum und Passivrauchen bei Vorschulkindern: Risikofaktoren für die kognitive Entwicklung. *Kinder-Und Jugendarzt* **2006**, *37*, 205–211.
4. Przybylski, A.K.; Weinstein, N. Can you connect with me now? How the presence of mobile communication technology influences face-to-face conversation quality. *J. Soc. Pers. Relatsh.* **2013**, *30*, 237–246. [CrossRef]
5. Pask, G. Styles and strategies of learning. *Br. J. Educ. Psychol.* **1976**, *46*, 128–148. [CrossRef]
6. Messick, S. The nature of cognitive styles: Problems and promise in educational practice. *Educ. Psychol.* **1984**, *19*, 59–74. [CrossRef]
7. Riding, R.J.; Sadler-Smith, E. Cognitive style and learning strategies: Some implications for training design. *Int. J. Train. Dev.* **1997**, *1*, 199–208. [CrossRef]
8. Sadler-Smith, E.; Badger, B. Cognitive style, learning and innovation. *Technol. Anal. Strateg. Manag.* **1998**, *10*, 247–266. [CrossRef]
9. Ford, N.; Chen, S.Y. Matching/mismatching revisited: An empirical study of learning and teaching styles. *Br. J. Educ. Technol.* **2001**, *32*, 5–22. [CrossRef]
10. Graf, S.; Kinshuk; Liu, T.-C. Supporting teachers in identifying students' learning styles in learning management systems: An automatic student modelling approach. *J. Educ. Technol. Soc.* **2009**, *12*, 3–14.
11. Chen, S.Y.; Tseng, Y.-F. The impacts of scaffolding e-assessment English learning: A cognitive style perspective. *Comput. Assist. Lang. Learn.* **2021**, *34*, 1105–1127. [CrossRef]
12. Naseer, S.; Khawaja, K.F.; Qazi, S.; Syed, F.; Shamim, F. How and when information proactiveness leads to operational firm performance in the banking sector of Pakistan? The roles of open innovation, creative cognitive style, and climate for innovation. *Int. J. Inf. Manag.* **2021**, *56*, 102260. [CrossRef]
13. Csikszentmihalyi, M. *Society, Culture, and Person: A Systems View of Creativity*; Springer: Berlin/Heidelberg, Germany, 2014.
14. Csikszentmihalyi, M. *Flow and the Psychology of Discovery and Invention*; HarperPerennial: New York, NY, USA, 1997; Volume 39, pp. 1–16.
15. Hu, R.; Wu, Y.-Y.; Shieh, C.-J. Effects of virtual reality integrated creative thinking instruction on students' creative thinking abilities. *Eurasia J. Math. Sci. Technol. Educ.* **2016**, *12*, 477–486.
16. Saorín, J.L.; Melian-Díaz, D.; Bonnet, A.; Carrera, C.C.; Meier, C.; De La Torre-Cantero, J. Makerspace teaching-learning environment to enhance creative competence in engineering students. *Think. Ski. Creat.* **2017**, *23*, 188–198. [CrossRef]
17. Nikkola, T.; Reunamo, J.; Ruokonen, I. Children's creative thinking abilities and social orientations in Finnish early childhood education and care. *Early Child Dev. Care* **2022**, *192*, 872–886. [CrossRef]
18. Jumadi, J.; Perdana, R.; Hariad, M.H.; Warsono, W.; Wahyudi, A. The Impact of Collaborative Model Assisted by Google Classroom to Improve Students' Creative Thinking Skills. *Int. J. Eval. Res. Educ.* **2021**, *10*, 396–403. [CrossRef]
19. Radziwill, N.M.; Benton, M.C.; Moellers, C. From STEM to STEAM: Reframing what it means to learn. *STEAM J.* **2015**, *2*, 3. [CrossRef]
20. Sanjayanti, A.; Rustaman, N.; Hidayat, T. 6E learning by design in facilitating logical thinking and identifying algae. *AIP Conf. Proc.* **2019**, *2194*, 020109.
21. Hashim, H.; Ali, M.N.; Samsudin, M.A. *Adapting Thinking Based Learning Approach and 6E Instructional Model in Implementing Green STEM Project*; The Scholarship of Teaching and Learning: Chicago, IL, USA, 2017.
22. Chung, C.-C.; Lin, C.-L.; Lou, S.-J. Analysis of the learning effectiveness of the STEAM-6E special course—A case study about the creative design of IoT assistant devices for the elderly. *Sustainability* **2018**, *10*, 3040. [CrossRef]
23. Walcutt, N.L.; Knörlein, B.; Sgouros, T.; Cetinić, I.; Omand, M.M. Virtual Reality and Oceanography: Overview, Applications, and Perspective. *Front. Mar. Sci.* **2019**, *6*, 644. [CrossRef]
24. Shim, J. Investigating the effectiveness of introducing virtual reality to elementary school students' moral education. *Comput. Educ. X Real.* **2023**, *2*, 100010. [CrossRef]
25. Chen, J.C.; Huang, Y.; Lin, K.Y.; Chang, Y.S.; Lin, H.C.; Lin, C.Y.; Hsiao, H.S. Developing a hands-on activity using virtual reality to help students learn by doing. *J. Comput. Assist. Learn.* **2020**, *36*, 46–60. [CrossRef]
26. Garate, J.V.; Iragui, J.C. Bilingualism and Third Language Acquisition. 1993.
27. Pambudi, D.S. The Effect of Outdoor Learning Method on Elementary Students' Motivation and Achievement in Geometry. *Int. J. Instr.* **2022**, *15*, 747–764. [CrossRef]

28. Tokan, M.K.; Imakulata, M.M. The effect of motivation and learning behaviour on student achievement. *S. Afr. J. Educ.* **2019**, *39*, 1510. [CrossRef]
29. Lim, S.L.; Yeo, K.J. A systematic review of the relationship between motivational constructs and self-regulated learning. *Int. J. Eval. Res. Educ. ISSN* **2021**, *2252*, 8822. [CrossRef]
30. Bovermann, K.; Bastiaens, T.J. Towards a motivational design? Connecting gamification user types and online learning activities. *Res. Pract. Technol. Enhanc. Learn.* **2020**, *15*, 1. [CrossRef]
31. Chen, K.-C.; Jang, S.-J. Motivation in online learning: Testing a model of self-determination theory. *Comput. Hum. Behav.* **2010**, *26*, 741–752. [CrossRef]
32. Chang, S.-C.; Hsu, T.-C.; Jong, M.S.-Y. Integration of the peer assessment approach with a virtual reality design system for learning earth science. *Comput. Educ.* **2020**, *146*, 103758. [CrossRef]
33. Lewis, J.R. Psychometric evaluation of an after-scenario questionnaire for computer usability studies: The ASQ. *ACM Sigchi Bull.* **1991**, *23*, 78–81. [CrossRef]
34. Albert, B.; Tullis, T. *Measuring the User Experience: Collecting, Analyzing, and Presenting Usability Metrics*; Morgan Kaufmann: Burlington, MA, USA, 2013.
35. Cabral, L.; Bessa, M. Using Virtual Reality Tools for Teaching Foreign Languages. In *New Knowledge in Information Systems and Technologies*; Springer: Cham, Switzerland, 2019.
36. Mampadi, F.; Chen, S.Y.; Ghinea, G.; Chen, M.-P. Design of adaptive hypermedia learning systems: A cognitive style approach. *Comput. Educ.* **2011**, *56*, 1003–1011. [CrossRef]
37. Tsai, M.-C.; Lin, H.-C.-K. A Study on the Behavioral Patterns Formed by Subjects with Different Cognitive Styles in Playing Augmented Reality Interaction Games. In *Emerging Technologies for Education: Second International Symposium, Proceedings of the SETE 2017, Held in Conjunction with ICWL 2017, Cape Town, South Africa, 20–22 September 2017, Revised Selected Papers*; Springer: Cham, Switzerland, 2017; pp. 372–381.
38. Rotter, J.B. Generalized expectancies for internal versus external control of reinforcement. *Psychol. Monogr. Gen. Appl.* **1966**, *80*, 1. [CrossRef]
39. Raffini, J.P. *Winners without Losers: Structures and Strategies for Increasing Student Motivation to Learn*; ERIC: Washington, DC, USA, 1993.
40. Prabhu, V.; Sutton, C.; Sauser, W. Creativity and certain personality traits: Understanding the mediating effect of intrinsic motivation. *Creat. Res. J.* **2008**, *20*, 53–66. [CrossRef]
41. Liang, J.-C.; Tsai, C.-C. Internet self-efficacy and preferences toward constructivist Internet-based learning environments: A study of pre-school teachers in Taiwan. *J. Educ. Technol. Soc.* **2008**, *11*, 226–237.
42. Frisby, B.N.; Sellnow, D.D.; Lane, D.R.; Veil, S.R.; Sellnow, T.L. Instruction in crisis situations: Targeting learning preferences and self-efficacy. *Risk Manag.* **2013**, *15*, 250–271. [CrossRef]
43. Gajos, K.Z.; Everitt, K.; Tan, D.S.; Czerwinski, M.; Weld, D.S. Predictability and accuracy in adaptive user interfaces. In Proceedings of the SIGCHI Conference on Human Factors in Computing Systems, Florence, Italy, 5–10 April 2008; pp. 1271–1274.
44. Hubalovsky, S.; Hubalovska, M.; Musilek, M. Assessment of the influence of adaptive E-learning on learning effectiveness of primary school pupils. *Comput. Hum. Behav.* **2019**, *92*, 691–705. [CrossRef]
45. Sun, Q.; Norman, T.J.; Abdourazakou, Y. Perceived value of interactive digital textbook and adaptive learning: Implications on student learning effectiveness. *J. Educ. Bus.* **2018**, *93*, 323–331. [CrossRef]
46. Zaccone, M.C.; Pedrini, M. The effects of intrinsic and extrinsic motivation on students learning effectiveness. Exploring the moderating role of gender. *Int. J. Educ. Manag.* **2019**, *33*, 1381–1394.
47. Aggarwal, I.; Woolley, A.W. Team creativity, cognition, and cognitive style diversity. *Manag. Sci.* **2019**, *65*, 1586–1599. [CrossRef]
48. Saha, S.; Sharma, R. The impact of leaders' cognitive style and creativity on organizational problem-solving. *Benchmarking Int. J.* **2020**, *27*, 2261–2281. [CrossRef]
49. Lu, H.-P.; Chiou, M.-J. The impact of individual differences on e-learning system satisfaction: A contingency approach. *Br. J. Educ. Technol.* **2010**, *41*, 307–323. [CrossRef]
50. Collins, S. Statutory Social Workers: Stress, Job Satisfaction, Coping, Social Support and Individual Differences. *Br. J. Soc. Work* **2007**, *38*, 1173–1193. [CrossRef]

Disclaimer/Publisher's Note: The statements, opinions and data contained in all publications are solely those of the individual author(s) and contributor(s) and not of MDPI and/or the editor(s). MDPI and/or the editor(s) disclaim responsibility for any injury to people or property resulting from any ideas, methods, instructions or products referred to in the content.

Article

The Influence of Distance Education and Peer Self-Regulated Learning Mechanism on Learning Effectiveness, Motivation, Self-Efficacy, Reflective Ability, and Cognitive Load

Yu-Chen Kuo [1], Hao-Chiang Koong Lin [2], Yu-Hsuan Lin [3,*], Tao-Hua Wang [4] and Bo-Yue Chuang [1]

1. Department of Computer Science and Information Management, Soochow University, Taipei City 100, Taiwan
2. Department of Information and Learning Technology, National University of Tainan, Tainan 700, Taiwan
3. General Research Service Center, National Pingtung University Science and Technology, Pingtung City 912, Taiwan
4. Science Education Department, National Museum of Natural Science, Taichung City 404, Taiwan
* Correspondence: yu.hsuan@mail.npust.edu.tw; Tel.: +886-985054200

Abstract: COVID-19 has resulted in the increased use of distance learning around the world. With the advancement of information technology, traditional classroom teaching has gradually integrated the Internet and distance learning methods. Students need to be able to learn on their own in a distance learning environment, so their ability to self-regulate their learning in a distance learning environment cannot be ignored. However, in previous studies on self-regulated learning, most learners learn alone. When they have academic doubts, they cannot obtain help and support from their studies, resulting in reduced learning outcomes. This study uses the peer self-disciplined learning mechanism to establish a distance teaching system that assists students and to improve their own learning status by meeting with peers at a distance. It can also help learners orient themselves by observing their peers' learning status and goal considerations. The participants in this study were 112 college students in the department of information management. The control group used a general self-regulated teaching system for learning, and the experimental group used a distance learning system, incorporating peer self-regulated learning. The results of the study found that learners who used the distance peer learning mechanism were more effective than those who used the general distance self-regulated learning system; learners who used the distance peer-regulated learning mechanism had better motivation, self-efficacy, and reflection after the learning activity than those who used the general distance self-regulated learning system. In addition, with the aid of such mechanisms, learners' cognitive load can be reduced, and learning effectiveness can be improved.

Keywords: distance education; self-regulated learning; self-explanation

Citation: Kuo, Y.-C.; Lin, H.-C.K.; Lin, Y.-H.; Wang, T.-H.; Chuang, B.-Y. The Influence of Distance Education and Peer Self-Regulated Learning Mechanism on Learning Effectiveness, Motivation, Self-Efficacy, Reflective Ability, and Cognitive Load. Sustainability 2023, 15, 4501. https://doi.org/10.3390/su15054501

Academic Editor: Antonio P. Gutierrez de Blume

Received: 3 February 2023
Revised: 27 February 2023
Accepted: 1 March 2023
Published: 2 March 2023

Copyright: © 2023 by the authors. Licensee MDPI, Basel, Switzerland. This article is an open access article distributed under the terms and conditions of the Creative Commons Attribution (CC BY) license (https://creativecommons.org/licenses/by/4.0/).

1. Introduction

The outbreak of COVID-19 has caused significant disruptions to traditional classroom teaching around the world, leading to increased use of distance-learning methods [1–3]. This change has been made possible by the rapid development of information technology, which has made it possible for students to complete their education at a distance. Traditional classroom teaching has gradually integrated the Internet and distance learning methods [4]. While this transition has been challenging for some educators and students, it has also opened up new opportunities for flexible and accessible learning [5,6]. With the ongoing global pandemic, distance learning will likely continue to play an important role in the future of education. Due to the rapid development of technology, distance learning has become a new learning trend that allows learners to create a learning environment that is not limited by space and time. Learners have the flexibility to learn at anytime and anywhere, allowing them to customise their learning plans according to their progress and paces [7]. However, because learning can take place without the constraints of space and time, it is difficult for students to feel engaged in the actual classroom [8]. Teachers are also unable to provide more personalised instruction.

Cognitive load refers to the mental effort required to process information during learning. The complexity of the textbook content and the way the content is presented can impact cognitive load. When students experience a high cognitive load, it can impede their ability to process information and negatively impact their learning outcomes. Therefore, it is important to consider the impact of cognitive load on students in a distance learning environment and to develop effective learning strategies to minimise its effects. Research indicates that students who are low achievers are more passive in the learning process. They struggle with achieving a thorough understanding of the subject area, developing effective learning skills, and identifying opportunities for success in their studies. Thus, they gradually lose motivation for learning and achieving the necessary goals. It has also been shown that students who do not employ efficient learning strategies during the self-adjustment phase of learning in a distance environment cannot efficiently gain knowledge [9]. Therefore, in order to learn in a distance environment and achieve good learning outcomes, students' self-regulated learning skills must not be neglected.

The development of students' self-regulated learning is an important goal of education today. Prior studies on self-regulated learning have mostly focused on how learners monitor their own learning outcomes, self-adjustments, and improvements. Reflective ability plays a crucial role in this process, as learners who are able to reflect on their learning experiences can identify their strengths and weaknesses and make necessary adjustments to their learning strategies. Yet, in certain situations where learners experience psychological or theoretical doubts, they may not be able to receive emotional, academic, instrumental, and informational assistance from a self-regulated learning environment.

If students can receive feedback and interact with others, it might make them feel less isolated. Such interactions with others can also help the learners work through various psychological and emotional issues, thus ultimately increasing learning effectiveness [10]. Effective self-discipline practices are essential for enhancing students' learning outcomes since they have a positive influence on their self-motivation and self-efficacy [11]. While teaching students knowledge, it is crucial to cultivate good self-discipline habits and enhance peer support in the learning environment.

This can significantly enhance students' learning results while enhancing their motivation for studying, self-efficacy, sense of accomplishment, and ability to cope with stress [12–14]. Hence, this study will use the remote peer self-regulated learning mechanism to (1) construct a self-regulated learning system to aid learners in observing their peers' learning status and goals during the learning process, and (2) enable learners to set their own learning goals and provide mutual support through remote peer learning. It aims to investigate the impact of incorporating a distance peer learning mechanism on learners' motivation and learning effectiveness in the self-regulated learning process, and further analyze the effect of students' varying levels of learning achievements.

The research questions are as follows:

(1) Can learners improve learning outcomes when involved in distance peer self-regulated learning mechanisms?
(2) Do high achievers enhance learning outcomes when involved in a distance peer self-regulated learning mechanism?
(3) Do low achievers enhance learning outcomes when involved in a distance peer self-regulated learning mechanism?
(4) Do both homogeneous groups and heterogeneous groups improve their learning outcomes when involved in a distance peer self-regulated learning mechanism?
(5) What are the differences in learning motivation, reflective ability, self-efficacy, cognitive load, and technology acceptance between learners who are involved in a distance peer self-regulated learning and those who are involved in a general self-regulated learning?

2. Related Work

2.1. Distance Learning

With the progress of technology, people's use of the Internet has also changed with the development of the times. Thus, traditional face-to-face teaching methods are gradually being replaced by distance learning in teaching and learning. This allows learners to create a learning environment that is not limited by space and time. Learners can adjust their own learning plans to fit with their paces. As distance learning offers diverse resources for learning, it has become an increasingly popular mode of education [15].

When learning in a digital environment, learners gain greater control than in traditional learning. They have more flexibility in their management of time and space, and choose methods and tools that match their preferences, abilities, and learning pace. Therefore, in the digital learning environment, the ability of learners to control themselves and use learning strategies will have a profound impact on learning outcomes.

Among the types of distance learning, several types of teaching materials for students are listed. These include "lecture capture, talking-head lecture", which records students' reactions and the teachers teaching in the classroom. Another type is "voice-after entering the screen", which briefs the teacher's voice and picture-in-picture. A third type is "picture-in-picture", which includes images, sounds, and digital teaching materials in the teacher's classroom through post-production and their integration with digital teaching materials, etc. [16].

The effectiveness of instruction in distance education was assessed in light of students' self-learning abilities, teaching skills, teachers' instruction, and textbook content. The results revealed that most students have a positive view toward the implementation of distance education and appreciate its effectiveness. On the contrary, the are several disadvantages associated with distance education, including the following [17–20]:

1. One-way or asynchronous course model: little interaction between instructor and students. While students watch pre-recorded videos, they do not take part in real-time class discussions, which makes learning less motivating;
2. Lack of immersion in the course: in distance learning, students may have trouble concentrating on the course content due to distractions in their learning environment or personal events;
3. Uniformity of course materials: the uniformity of materials in distance learning can prevent instructors from giving personalised feedback and guidance to students. It may result in students with weaker self-regulated learning skills falling behind.

Therefore, this study developed a distance peer learning system for an algorithms course to explore how students can receive peer support and assistance in a self-regulated learning process, focussing on course materials to enhance learning effectiveness and motivation.

2.2. Self-Regulated Learning

Self-regulated learning is a set of behaviour adopted by individuals to achieve learning goals, including control of thoughts, emotions, and environmental behaviour. Learning can be adjusted through strategies such as goal setting, strategy selection, and monitoring [21]. Therefore, it has been crucial to build students' self-regulation skills during the learning process in aid of strengthening areas of deficiency based on their past learning experiences.

According to past research, high achievers are more likely to plan their learning according to their learning status, set clear goals, use more learning strategies in the learning process, and constantly review themselves and adjust their learning status. The four steps of the self-regulated learning cycle model proposed by Zimmerman [21] include self-assessment and monitoring, goal setting and planning of strategies, implementation and monitoring of strategies, and monitoring of strategy outcomes, as described below:

1. Self-Assessment and Self-Monitoring: first, students will assess their level of performance on a learning task and determine how effective their learning is based on their past performance and effectiveness;

2. Goal Setting and Strategy Planning: first, students will analyse the learning task then set a clear goal for learning and plan strategies to achieve the goal;
3. Strategy Implementation and Strategy Monitoring: in a structuration learning environment, students try to implement a learning strategy and monitor the impact of its implementation;
4. Strategy Outcome Monitoring: students focus their attention on the "process of the strategy" and "learning outcomes" to determine the effectiveness of the strategy.

Self-regulated learning systems allow distance learners to have plans and goals, and learners can adjust their learning status during the self-regulated learning based on past learning experiences to address deficiencies. Zimmerman illustrates that learners go through a three-stage cycle of self-regulated learning, consisting of forethought, performance or volitional control, and self-reflection [12]. Forethought is a process in which learners analyze a task, set goals, and plan how to achieve them before performing the task. Performance or Volitional Control is the process by which learners monitor their progress while performing tasks and using self-control strategies to maintain their motivation to participate. Self-Reflection is an assessment of how well a student completes tasks that are attributed to their success or failure. These attributions produce self-reactions that can have a negative or positive effect on students' performance in the later stages of learning.

According to previous research on self-regulated learning systems, most students can only see their own learning performance and cannot see the learning status and performance of other learners, nor can they interact with each other. When learners encounter difficulties or face setbacks in the learning process, peer support is a buffer that helps learners express their emotions and restore their learning goals. Therefore, this study developed a model based on the three-stage cycle of self-regulated learning described by Zimmerman above. In the forethought stage, past learning records and peer set goals are provided for learners, allowing them to evaluate and formulate learning strategies in a structured manner according to their own learning conditions, rather than setting them haphazardly, which may result in poor learning outcomes. Test questions are employed to monitor learners' learning to ensure that learners are focusing on the curriculum and to compare their learning with that of their peers, thereby identifying appropriate learning strategies.

With the prevalence of distance teaching, research on self-disciplined learning has received increasing attention in recent years. Joo et al. [22] used the MSLQ scale to explore the "self-efficacy of traditional teaching", "self-efficacy of self-disciplined learning", and "self-efficacy of online learning". The results of the study found that "self-efficacy of online learning" is better than "self-efficacy of traditional teaching". Kao [23] proposed scaffold-assisted research on self-disciplined learning in asynchronous network teaching. The experimental background is a general course of asynchronous network teaching at a university. The setting of learning goals is used to explore college students' self-disciplined learning abilities. The results showed that this teaching environment and the mechanism of self-disciplined learning can effectively improve the situation, quality, and regularity of learning.

Hwang et al. [24] proposed that using a computer-assisted self-disciplined learning system helps assist students in classroom learning. With the availability of current school equipment resources, teachers can have a considerable impact on students' self-disciplined learning by formulating learning strategies. Therefore, it is feasible and essential to develop a self-disciplined learning system. Chen [25] established a personalised learning systems, "PELS", assisted by a self-disciplined learning mechanism. This system can help students increase their learning performance in a self-disciplined learning setting. The empirical results have proved that the self-disciplined learning mechanism, built by scholars, can facilitate students' learning effectiveness and self-discipline abilities.

The above research on self-disciplined learning found that most learning systems are aimed only at individuals and offer limited chances for peer learning via distance learning systems. Real-time detection and monitoring of student performance in self-disciplined learning are also missing. Therefore, this study aims to (1) enhance students' learning status by monitoring and detecting their performance during self-disciplined learning and providing peer support, while (2) also promoting students' learning effectiveness and motivation.

2.3. Self-Explanation

Self-explanation is a related discourse on solving problems or things [26]. It is a learning activity that can enhance the depth of learning. Many studies have also demonstrated the effectiveness of self-explaining learning and teaching strategies, and they have been widely used in different learning areas [27], such as programming, math, refs. [28–32], science [33–36], and biology [37–39]. These studies have confirmed that self-explanation has a positive effect; it helps to improve students' learning achievement and problem-solving skills.

Chi [40] believes that self-explanation integrates prior knowledge and external knowledge via reflection, which allows students to identify gaps in their understanding and fill them in the learning process [41]. In order to produce better quality descriptive knowledge [42], many scholars also mentioned that reflection is crucial to the construction of knowledge and can significantly boost students' learning performance [24,43–45].

Therefore, when learning reaches a certain level, the system provides test questions. When accessing incorrect answers in the test, they are engaged in self-explanation to reflect on their problem or seek help from peers if they are unable to solve the problem. By reflecting first and then gaining feedback from peers, learners can enhance their understanding and solve problems more easily. In this study, a distance peer self-regulated learning system was developed to investigate the effect of the peer self-regulated learning mechanism on the learning outcomes. During the learning process, learners can see the progress of their peers to stimulate their motivation to learn. When a student encounters a problem, they can seek help from peers by reflecting on the options for the question they answered incorrectly. Peers will explain the options based on the reflection. After the study, students can review their learning results and reflect on and adjust their learning to the areas where they fall short of their peers. Therefore, this study explores the effect of a distance peer learning mechanism on students' learning effectiveness and motivation and analyses the effects of different learning achievements on students' learning effectiveness.

3. Research Method
3.1. Conceptual Framework

In this study, students enrolled in an algorithm course at the Department of Information Management of a university in Taipei were divided into the control group and the experimental group. The variables of self-efficacy, motivation, learning effectiveness, reflective ability, and cognitive load of learners with different learning outcomes are all explored separately in relation to the effects of self-regulated learning with and without distant peer learning mechanisms The independent variables include learning strategies and learning achievement. The section on learning strategies includes general self-regulated learning mechanisms and peer self-regulated learning mechanisms and discusses the impact of different teaching strategies on learners. Additionally, the section on earning achievement will discuss whether two different types of learning achievement learners have different effects on the effectiveness of distance peer self-regulated learning mechanisms. The dependent variables are the effects and differences in learning effectiveness, motivation, self-efficacy, reflective ability, and cognitive load after the learners have completed learning. The control variable was examined before learning to ensure that students in both groups had the same prior knowledge of the algorithm and that both the control and experimental groups used the same materials and learning system.

The research structure of this study is shown in Figure 1, which includes the following three research variables:

1. Arguments

    It contains two independent variables: teaching strategy and learning achievement. The section on teaching strategies discusses two methods: the general self-regulated learning system and the self-regulated learning system using the distance peer learning mechanism. The results of different learning strategies and learning effectiveness on learners are also examined. In addition, the section on learning achievement explores whether successful learners demonstrate different effects and differences as a result of the distance peer self-disciplined learning mechanism.

2. Dependent variables

    It comprises six dependent variables: learning effectiveness, learning motivation, self-efficacy, reflective ability, cognitive load, and technology acceptance. When the students have completed the learning, the system will display the learning results in the post-learning test. The study uses an independent sample t-test analysis to explore the differences between the control group and the experimental group before and after the test. Then, the covariate analysis was used to compare learning effectiveness, self-efficacy, and reflective ability before and after the changes from the questionnaire results. Finally, the study uses an independent sample t-test analysis to examine the results of learners' acceptance of technology and cognitive load after learning.

3. Control variables

    The variables work to strengthen the study's internal validity of this study and prevent against unrelated variables. Thus, the teaching materials and learning systems used in the control group and the experimental group must be the same, and the "Divide-and-Conquer" in the algorithm, "Dynamic Programming", "The Greedy Approach", and "Backtracking" are the four units of this study. A pre-test was used to make sure that both sets of students had the same prior algorithmic knowledge before the learning activities began.

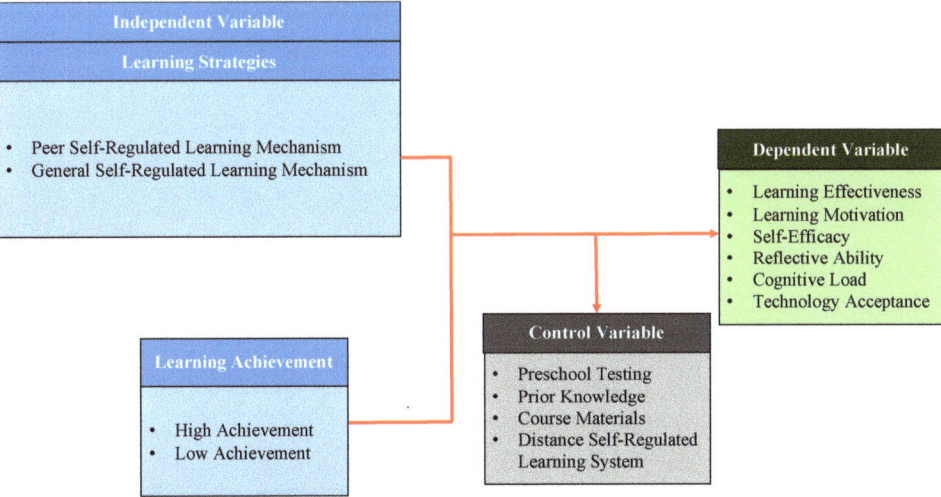

Figure 1. Conceptual Framework.

3.2. System Interface

This study uses distance education and the peer self-regulated system, and the following is a description of the system function and system screen.

The system's peer grouping rooms: in each study session, the system will set seven periods for peers to choose freely. The system will limit the number of students in each session to four, with two of them being high achievers and the other two being low achievers. If the number of high achievers or low achievers reaches two, they will no longer be able to join the session, and the system will hide the session option (Figure 2).

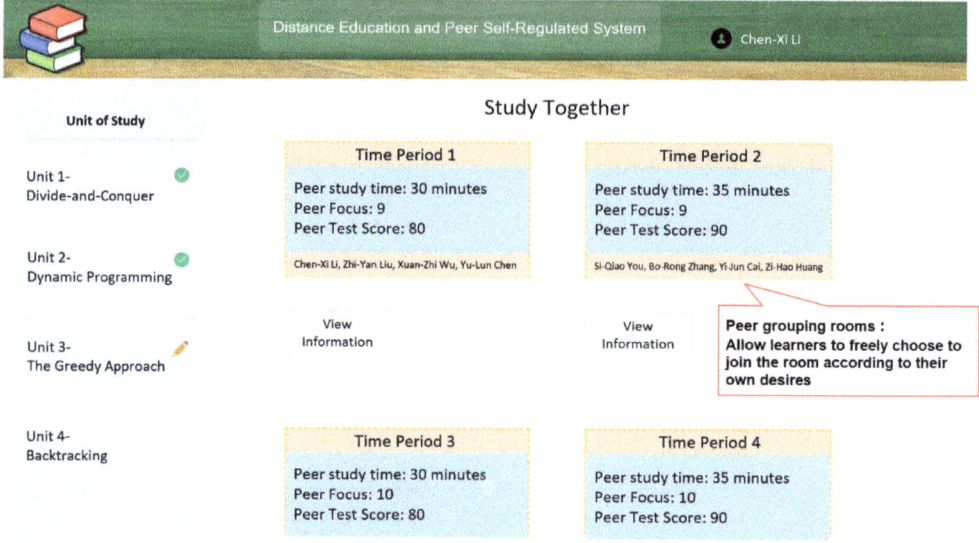

Figure 2. Self-regulated learning goal setting form.

Self-regulated learning goal setting: learners can set individual goals for this learning unit based on their past learning experiences and the goals of the team learning in this group room (Figure 3). The system will measure the learning effectiveness based on the learning goals set by the students themselves, as the study [12] suggests, when students can achieve their self-set goals, they can increase their motivation to learn.

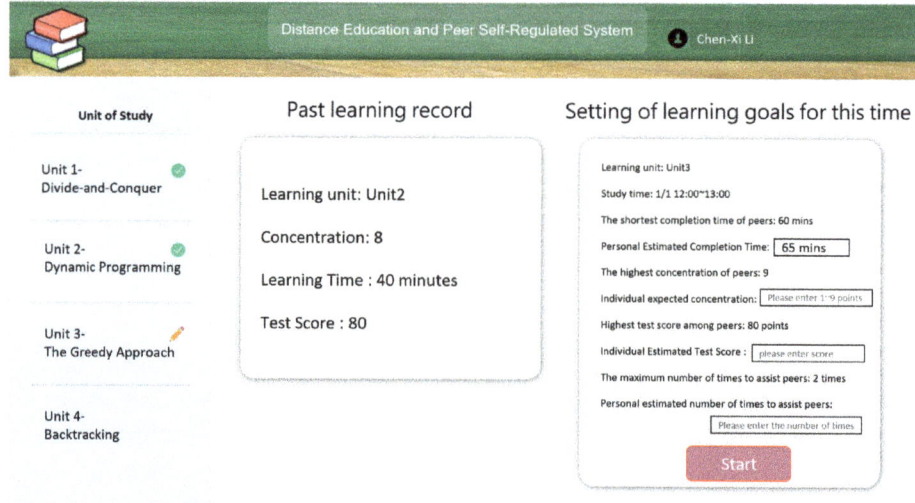

Figure 3. Self-regulated learning goal setting.

Peer progress: during the learning process, the progress bar at the bottom allows you to see the progress of the peers, and you can use it to help you improve your own learning status (Figure 4).

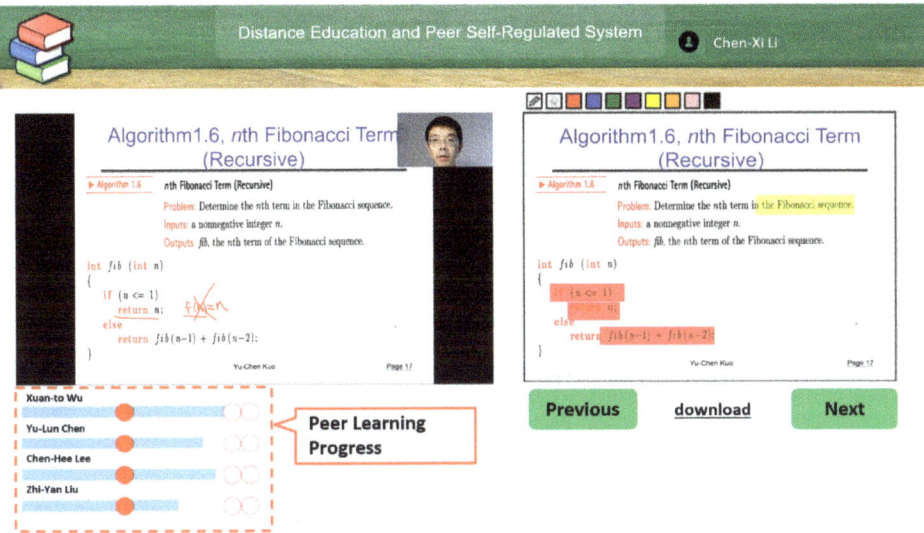

Figure 4. Peer progress.

Peer assistance: if a student responds to a question incorrectly, she or he may seek peer assistance. However, they must first reflect on the question and identify the specific part of it that they do not understand (Figure 5).

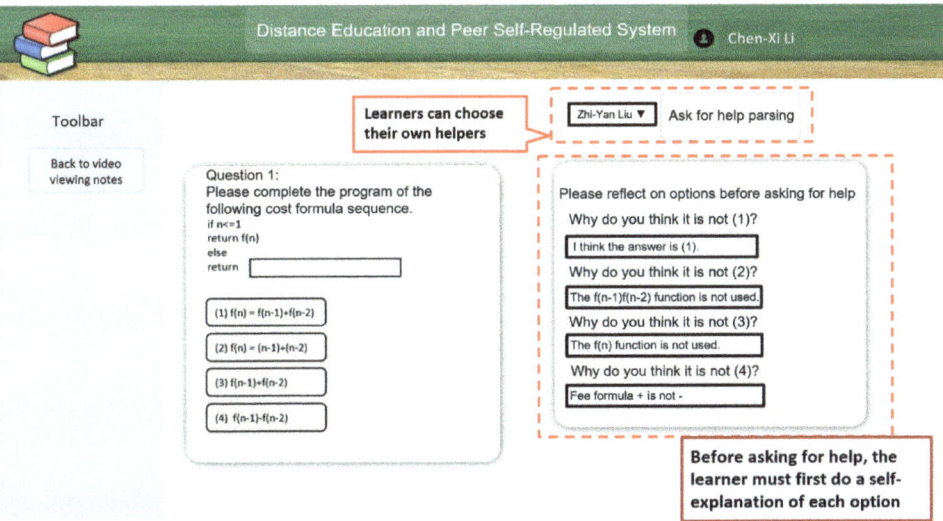

Figure 5. Seeking peer assistance.

When a learner is chosen to be a helper, the current video will be paused and the question from the requester will pop up. The helper will reply to the learner after giving the explanation (Figure 6).

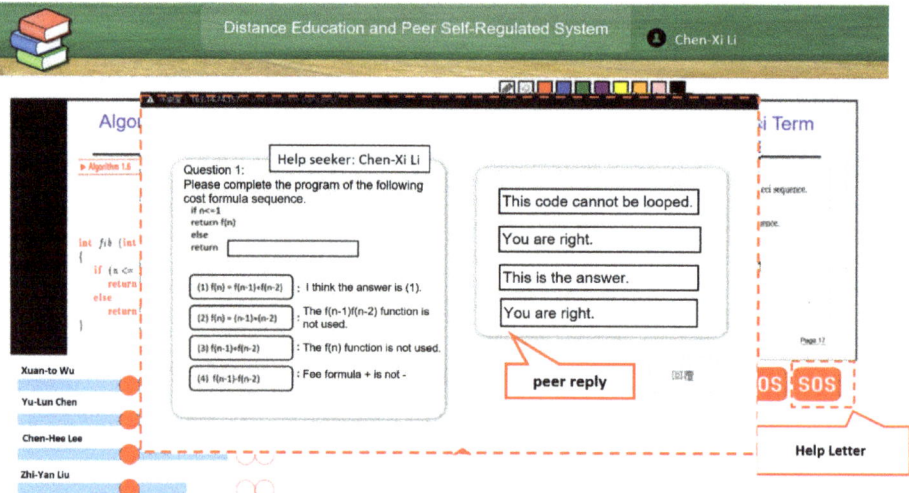

Figure 6. Peer assistance.

Peer feedback function: after the peers finished the learning activity, the tutor and tutee can enter the peer feedback room to complete a feedback form and evaluate the performance of both parties during the real-time instruction (Figure 6).

Self-regulated learning effectiveness view: once a student completes a learning task, the system will display his or her learning effectiveness on the page. The report includes learning units, learning time, test scores, peer averages, grade curves, and the number of times the students assisted their peers and received help. This is intended to help promote self-regulated skills (Figure 7).

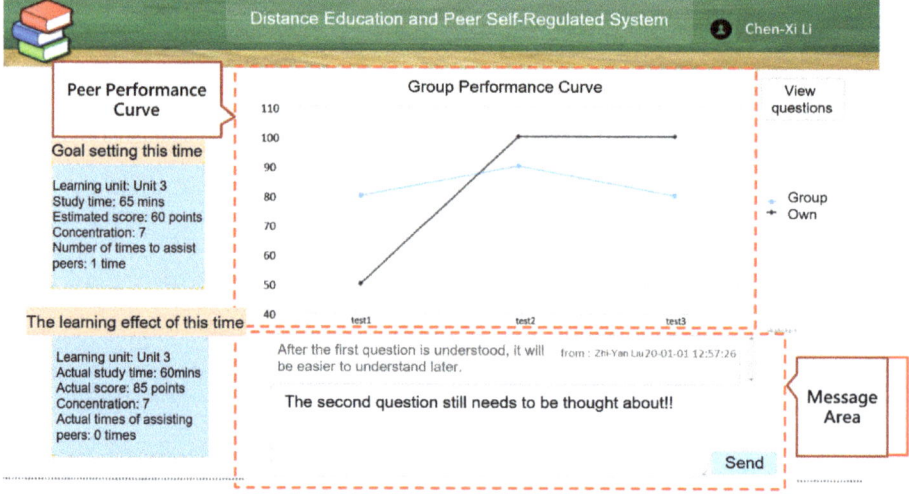

Figure 7. Self-regulated learning effectiveness view.

3.3. Experimental Design

3.3.1. Participants

The participants in this experiment were 112 college students in the department of information management. They were divided into the experimental and control groups, with 56 in the experimental group and 56 in the control group.

3.3.2. Grouping Method

The experimental group used the best grouping method proposed by Chen [46] to conduct paired groupings of students. After sorting the students' pre-test scores from large to small, the median was used as the standard value. The number of people closest to the standard value was taken as a homogeneous group, and the rest of the students were grouped into a heterogeneous group. In order to divide both groups evenly, 28 people are divided into the homogeneous group (a group of 4 people), with 7 groups, and 28 people are divided into the heterogeneous group (a group of 4 people), with 7 groups.

3.3.3. Learning Process

This study discusses the effect of using a distance peer learning mechanism on students' learning effectiveness and analyses the effect of students' learning outcomes with different learning achievements during the self-regulated learning process (Figure 8).

Students in the control group used a general, distance learning self-regulated system in which learners set their learning goals before learning. During the learning process, there are unit tests. If the learner answers the questions incorrectly, the system will give an analysis directly. At the end of the learning process, students can examine their learning results. They are expected to enhance their learning by adjusting their learning strategies. The system also collected learners' scores to compare with those of the experimental group. On the other hand, students in the experimental group were taught using a distance learning system with a peer self-regulated learning mechanism. Students in the experimental group will be classified into three categories of academic achievement based on their pre-test scores: high achievement, moderate achievement, and low achievement. Meanwhile, the high-achievement and low-achievement groups will be combined into a heterogeneous group, while the moderate-achievement group will be combined into a homogeneous group.

Before learning, the experimental group can set their team's learning goals with their peers and forecast their scores, learning time, and the number of times they offered help and received help from their peers. During the learning process, they can study together with their peers and watch their learning progress to improve their own learning status. There will be unit tests during the study. When learners answer a question incorrectly, they can ask for help from their peers. At the end of the study, they can watch the average score of their peers and the set and adjust their learning goals themselves.

The experiment was conducted for 4 weeks, with each week lasting 50 min. At the end of the experiment, tests and questionnaires will be administered to analyse the effects of a peer self-regulated learning mechanism on students' learning effectiveness, self-efficacy, reflective ability, motivation, cognitive load, and technology acceptance. The procedure is as follows:

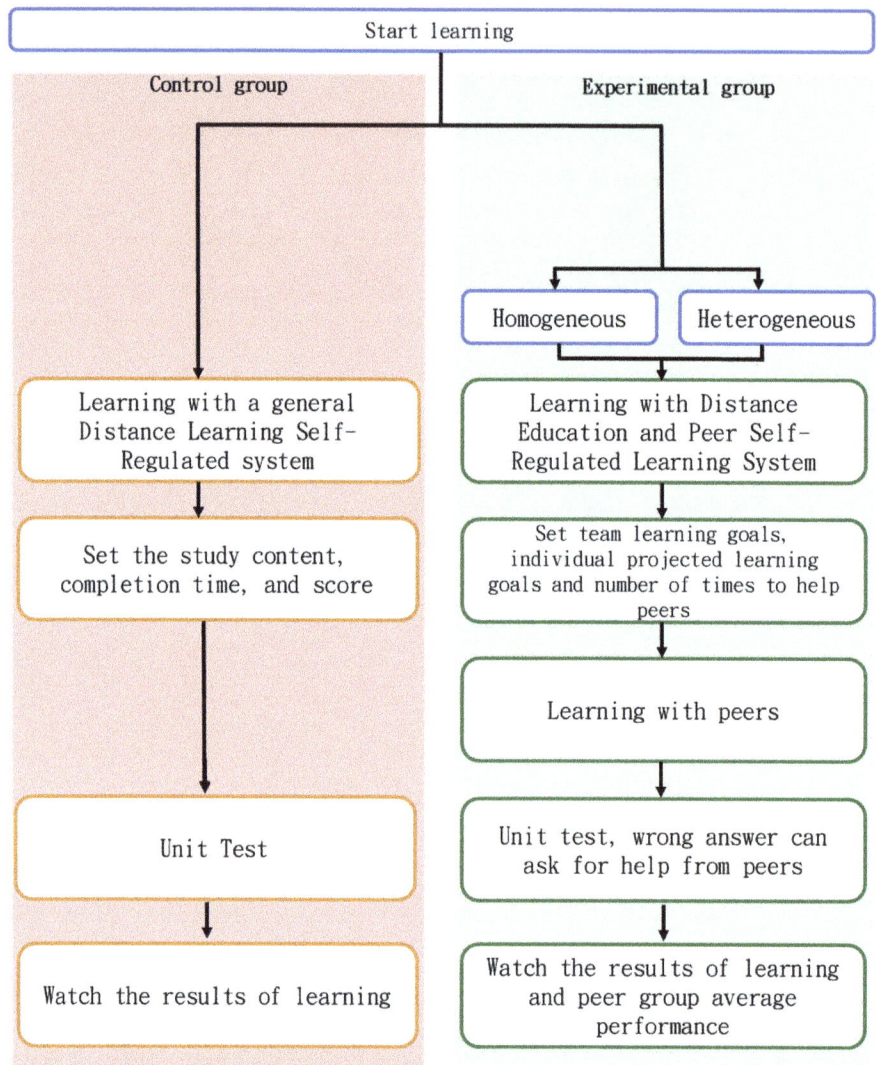

Figure 8. Experimental flowchart.

3.3.4. Research Tool

- Learning Materials and Learning Effectiveness Quiz:

The content of the textbook used in this study is an algorithm course, and 4 units are selected as the learning topics, namely "Divide-and-Conquer", "Dynamic Programming", "The Greedy Approach", and "Backtracking".

The learning achievement test is divided into "effectiveness of the pre-test" and "effectiveness of the post-learning test". Before the experimental activity, a pre-learning test will be carried out on the learner. The test content is algorithm-related questions, with a total of 5 questions and a total score of 100 points. The pre-test is to determine whether learners have the same prior knowledge before participating in the activity, and to use this as a standard to classify learners' learning achievements into three categories, namely, high, medium, and low achievement. High- and low-achievement students are classified as a heterogeneous group, while middle-achievement students are classified as a homogeneous group. Further, using S-shaped grouping in the homogeneous group, middle-achieving learners will also be divided into the two groups of high and low achievement based on their level of achievement.

After the experimental activity, a post-learning test is conducted for the learners. The post-learning test is based on the teaching material in the learning activity. The teacher will select the test questions related to the content of the teaching material. The test content is the unit content of the learning video. There are 5 questions in total. The score is 100 points. It mainly analyses the impact of using a distance peer learning mechanism on learners' learning effectiveness, and deeply analyses the impact of students' effectiveness with different learning achievements.

- Learning Motivation Questionnaire: The study's questionnaire is based on Pintrich's [47] learning motivation, which primarily investigates changes in students' learning motivation for algorithms before and after learning. Using a 5-point Likert scale, the Cronbach's alpha of the pre- and post-questionnaires was 0.85 and 0.87, respectively;
- Self-Efficacy Questionnaire: The questionnaire for this study is quoted from the self-efficacy questionnaire proposed by Pintrich [47], which mainly explores the changes in students' self-efficacy of algorithms before and after learning. Using a 5-point Likert scale, the Cronbach's alphas of the before and after questionnaires was 0.83 and 0.83, respectively;
- Reflective Ability Questionnaire: The questionnaire employed in this study is based on the reflective ability questionnaire proposed by Kember et al. [48], which mainly examines how students' reflective abilities to algorithms alter both before and after learning. Using a 5-point Likert scale, the Cronbach's alphas of the before and after questionnaires was 0.77 and 0.78, respectively;
- Technology Acceptance Questionnaire: The questionnaire of this study was quoted from the questionnaire proposed by Wang, Yang, and Hwang [49], which mainly examines whether students' use of the functions of the system is helpful for learning and whether the operation is simple and easy to use. Using a 5-point Likert scale, the Cronbach's alpha is 0.83;
- Cognitive Load Questionnaire: The questionnaire for this study was adapted from the cognitive load questionnaire proposed by Paas [50] and Hwang et al. [49]. The content of the questionnaire is divided into two categories: mental load and mental effort. Both aspects use a 7-point Likert scale, and the respective Cronbach's alphas are 0.92 and 0.89;
- Interview Questions: The interview questionnaire for this study was adapted from Kuo et al. [51] and Hwang, Yang, Tsai, and Yang [52], with a total of 7 questions. The experimental group's students were asked to participate in one-on-one interviews after the experiment to acquire a better understanding of their opinions and suggestions for improving the learning activities.

3.3.5. Analytical Method

The analysis of the experimental results of this study is carried out using two analysis methods, "independent sample t-test" and "covariate analysis". Firstly, a pre-class test was implemented in both groups using the independent sample t-test to determine whether they all had the same prior knowledge before participating in the activity. After the experimental activities, a post-learning test will be given to the learners. The post-learning test will be based on the teaching materials in the learning activities. The teacher will select the test questions related to the content covered in the teaching materials.

The test contains the entirety of the instructional video material and consists of 100 points. Its main focus is on analyzing the effect of the distance peer learning mechanism on the learning effectiveness of both groups during the self-regulated learning process.

Meanwhile, the study further analyses the homogeneous and heterogeneous groups of the experimental group, which aims to explore whether there is a significant difference in the learning outcomes of high-achieving students. In addition, a post-learning questionnaire is implemented to examine how learners' learning motivation, self-efficacy, cognitive load, and technology acceptance changed during the entire learning activity.

The survey results are utilised to help explain the findings of the statistical test.

4. Results
4.1. Learning Performance

In order to find out whether the students in the experimental and control groups had the same basic algorithmic skills, a pre-test was conducted before the experimental activity and the differences in the prior knowledge of the students in the experimental and control groups in terms of algorithms were analysed using an independent samples t-test. The results of the analysis are shown in Table 1. It was found that there was no significant difference between the pre-test scores of the experimental and control groups ($t = 0.25$, $p = 0.803 > 0.05$); therefore, it can be considered that the experimental and control groups have the comparable basic algorithmic ability.

Table 1. Pre-test of learners between the experimental group and the control group.

Group	N	Mean	SD	t
Experimental	56	75.53	11.09	0.25
Control	56	76.07	11.60	
Experimental High Achievement	28	82.52	8.96	0.98
Control High Achievement	28	82.92	9.82	
Experimental Low Achievement	28	68.54	10.23	0.84
Control Low Achievement	28	69.22	9.18	
Homogeneous	28	72.82	10.28	0.15
Heterogeneous	28	78.24	8.46	

The experimental group and the control group were further divided into high and low achievement samples for the independent sample t-test. The analysis revealed that there was no significant difference between the pre-test scores of high and low achievement learners in the experimental and control groups ($t = 0.98$, $p = 0.749 > 0.05$) and ($t = 0.84$, $p = 0.403 > 0.05$).

The experimental group was further divided into homogeneous and heterogeneous groups to conduct an independent sample t-test. It was found that there was no significant difference between the homogeneous group and the heterogeneous group ($t = 0.15$, $p = 0.748 > 0.05$).

After the learning activities, to analyse whether there were significant differences in the student's learning outcomes in the experimental and control groups, a post-learning test will be implemented at the end of the learning activity. An independent sample t-test will be administered with the post-learning test results to discuss the difference in algorithmic ability between the experimental and control groups. The results of the analysis are shown in Table 2. The post-learning test scores of the experimental group were significantly higher than those of the control group ($t = -2.05$, $p = 0.008 < 0.01$, $d = -0.501$). Therefore, the experimental group using the distance peer self-regulated learning mechanism helped to improve the students' learning effectiveness.

Further, post-learning tests were administered to high achievement and low achievement learners, and independent sample t-tests were administered using the results of the post-learning tests. The results of the analysis are shown in Table 3. The post-learning test scores of experimental high achievements were significantly higher than those of control high achievement ($t = -2.18$, $p = 0.000 < 0.001$, $d = -1.043$). The post-learning test scores of experimental low achievements were also significantly higher than those of control low achievement ($t = -1.29$, $p = 0.025 < 0.05$, $d = -0.603$). Thus, both experimental high achievement and experimental low achievement using distance peer self-regulated learning mechanisms help to improve learners' learning effectiveness.

Table 2. Post-learning test of learners between the experimental group and the control group.

Group	N	Mean	SD	t	d
Experimental	56	80.78	19.68	−2.05 **	−0.501
Control	56	70.96	19.55		

** $p < 0.01$.

Table 3. Post-learning test of learners with different learning achievements in the experimental and control groups.

Group	N	Mean	SD	t	d
Experimental High Achievement	28	96.90	8.96	−2.18 ***	−1.043
Control High Achievement	28	85.96	11.82		
Experimental Low Achievement	28	64.44	13.23	−1.29 *	−0.603
Control Low Achievement	28	56.48	13.18		

*** $p < 0.001$; * $p < 0.05$.

Pre-tests were administered to both homogeneous and heterogeneous groups of learners, and independent sample t-tests were conducted with the pre-test scores to investigate the differences in the algorithmic abilities of different groups of learners. The results of the analysis are shown in Table 4, where the learning effectiveness of the heterogeneous group was significantly higher than that of the homogeneous group ($t = 2.05$, $p = 0.04 < 0.05$, $d = 0.531$). The results showed that the heterogeneous group of learners who adopted the distance peer self-regulated learning mechanism demonstrated enhanced learning effectiveness.

Table 4. Post-learning test of learners in homogeneous and heterogeneous groups.

Group	N	Mean	SD	t	d
Homogeneous	28	75.03	18.63	2.05 *	0.531
Heterogeneous	28	84.96	18.74		

* $p < 0.05$.

4.2. Learning Motivation of Learners between the Two Group

The analysis of the pre-questionnaire on learning motivation was conducted using an independent sample t-test. As shown in Table 5, there was no significant difference in the learning motivation between the experimental and control groups ($t = 0.84$, $p = 0.40 > 0.05$).

Table 5. Pre-questionnaire of motivation of learners between the experimental group and the control group.

Group	N	Mean	SD	t
Experimental	56	3.90	0.51	0.84
Control	56	4.03	0.47	

After the learning activities, the two groups were given a post-questionnaire of learning motivation and the results were analysed by ANCOVA with the pre-questionnaire of learning motivation as a covariate. The results of the analysis are shown in Table 6, the learning motivation of the experimental group was significantly higher than that of the control group ($F = 5.49$, $p = 0.023 < 0.05$). Therefore, the experimental group that adopted the distance peer self-regulated learning mechanism demonstrated enhanced learning motivation.

Table 6. Post-questionnaire of motivation of learners between the experimental group and the control group.

Group	N	Mean	SD	Adjusted Mean	F	η^2
Experimental	56	4.18	0.42	4.20	5.49 *	0.08
Control	56	3.94	0.49	3.95		

* $p < 0.05$.

4.3. Self-Efficacy of Learners between the Two Group

The pre-questionnaire of self-efficacy was analysed using independent samples *t*-test. As shown in Table 7, there was no significant difference in motivation between the experimental and control groups ($t = -0.97$, $p = 0.336 > 0.05$).

Table 7. Pre-questionnaire of self-efficacy of learners between the experimental group and the control group.

Group	N	Mean	SD	t
Experimental	56	3.48	0.65	-0.97
Control	56	3.31	0.64	

After the learning activities, the two groups were given a post-questionnaire of self-efficacy and the results were analysed by ANCOVA with the pre-questionnaire of self-efficacy as a covariate. The results of the analysis are shown in Table 8, the self-efficacy of the experimental group was significantly higher than that of the control group ($F = 4.03$, $p = 0.043 < 0.05$). Therefore, the experimental group that adopted the distance peer self-regulated learning mechanism demonstrated enhanced self-efficacy.

Table 8. Post-questionnaire of self-efficacy of learners between the experimental group and the control group.

Group	N	Mean	SD	Adjusted Mean	F	η^2
Experimental	56	3.78	0.57	3.78	4.03 *	0.06
Control	56	3.49	0.41	3.49		

* $p < 0.05$.

4.4. Reflective Ability of Learners between the Two Group

The pre-questionnaire of reflective ability was analysed using independent samples *t*-test. As shown in Table 9, there was no significant difference in reflective ability between the experimental and control groups ($t = -0.41$, $p = 0.87 > 0.05$).

Table 9. Pre-questionnaire of reflective ability of learners between the experimental group and the control group.

Group	N	Mean	SD	t
Experimental	56	3.19	0.83	-0.41
Control	56	3.12	0.81	

After the learning activities, the two groups were given a post-questionnaire of reflective ability and the results were analysed by ANCOVA with the pre-questionnaire of reflective ability as a covariate. The results of the analysis are shown in Table 10, the reflective ability of the experimental group was significantly higher than that of the control group ($F = 0.786$, $p = 0.03 < 0.05$). Therefore, the experimental group that adopted the distance peer self-regulated learning mechanism demonstrated enhanced reflective ability.

Table 10. Post-questionnaire of reflective ability of learners between the experimental group and the control group.

Group	N	Mean	SD	Adjusted Mean	F	η²
Experimental	56	4.18	0.72	4.15	0.786 *	0.33
Control	56	3.76	0.49	3.46		

* $p < 0.05$.

4.5. Cognitive Load of Learners between the Two Group

After the learning activities, the cognitive load questionnaire was administered to the experimental and control group students, and the questionnaire was divided into two aspects: mental workload and mental effort. The results of the analysis are shown in Table 11. The students in the experimental group achieved significant results in both mental workload ($t = 3.12$, $p = 0.04 < 0.05$, $d = 0.710$) and mental effort ($t = 2.63$, $p = 0.03 < 0.05$, $d = 1.034$). Therefore, although the content of the materials in the experimental and control groups were the same, the peer self-regulated learning mechanism helped the learners not only to improve their own learning status, but also to seek peer assistance for problems that could not be solved so that the learners could solve subsequent problems, thus reducing mental workload and mental effort.

Table 11. Questionnaire of cognitive load of learners between the experimental group and the control group.

	Group	N	Mean	SD	t	d
Mental Workload	Experimental	56	3.13	0.95	3.12 *	0.710
	Control	56	3.83	1.02		
Mental Effort	Experimental	56	2.19	1.27	2.63 *	1.034
	Control	56	3.54	1.34		

* $p < 0.05$.

4.6. Technology Acceptance of Learners between the Two Group

A technology acceptance questionnaire was administered to students in the experimental and control groups after the learning activities, and an independent sample t-test was used. As shown in Table 12, the acceptance of distance peer self-regulated learning system by the experimental group was significantly better than that of the control group ($t = -3.33$, $p = 0.009 < 0.01$, $d = -0.784$). The students who adopted the distance peer self-regulated learning system found the interface of the system clear and easy to understand and operate.

Table 12. Questionnaire of technology acceptance of learners between the experimental group and the control group.

Group	N	Mean	SD	t	d
Experimental	56	4.11	0.49	−3.33 **	−0.784
Control	56	3.80	0.27		

** $p < 0.01$.

4.7. Interview Method

To understand more about the experimental group learners' ideas of adopting the distance peer self-regulated learning system, four experimental group learners were invited to conduct individual interviews after the experimental activity: Homogeneous group A, Homogeneous group B, Heterogeneous group C, and Heterogeneous group D. The interviews focused on the interviewees' thoughts on the learning system, the areas for improvement and the learning mechanism.

Based on the results of the interviews, the core categories of the interviews were divided into two main categories: "Peer intervention" and "Reflecting on the theme and the function of helping peers". "Peer intervention" is intended to analyse the impact of peer intervention on students. "Peer intervention" makes students more engaged, and watching peers' learning progress during the learning process can make students more motivated to continue learning and can increase students' effectiveness and motivation.

"Reflecting on the theme and the function of helping peers" is intended to analyse the impact of reflecting on the theme and helping peers' learning. Reflecting on the theme and the function of helping peers can effectively help students develop a deeper understanding in their learning. The study further found that the homogeneous group was less active in helping their peers and did not receive immediate feedback when they were asked. In contrast, the heterogeneous group was more active in helping their peers, and the low achievers in the heterogeneous group asked their peers more often than the high achievers. Therefore, from the interview analysis, it can roughly be inferred that the heterogeneous group of learners is more suitable to use this mechanism for learning.

5. Conclusions and Discussion

(1) Learners who used a distance peer self-regulated learning mechanism can help improve their learning effectiveness compared with those who used a general distance self-disciplined learning system.

Under the condition that both groups of students have the equivalent basic ability of calculation, the analysis of this experiment shows that the students in the experimental group have significantly better scores on the learning effectiveness scale than the control group after the learning activities. During the interview, it can be found that although it is stressful to see the learning progress of peers while studying, it can also improve one's own learning status and make one more focused on the teaching materials. This echoes Zimmerman's [53] self-regulated learning concept, which suggests that the peers with whom you are learning can significantly affect your learning outcomes.

Apart from learning together and choosing learning objects, learners can also gain support and assistance from their peers, thereby improving learning motivation and learning effectiveness. This also echoes the earlier discussion about how peer intervention can effectively improve students' learning performance. It follows that using the distance peer self-regulated learning system developed by this study in the algorithm learning course has the benefit of enhancing the learning effect.

(2) High-achievers using the distance peer self-regulated learning mechanism can help improve learners' learning effectiveness compared with those high-achievers in the general distance self-regulated learning system.

As the students in both groups had similar prior knowledge of the subject of the algorithms, the analysis results further revealed that the learners in the experimental group with high achievement had significantly better scores on the learning effectiveness test than those in the control group. In light of findings from the interview, students with high academic achievement in the experimental group will improve their sense of accomplishment by helping their peers. Apart from more goals setting in the learning process, students with high academic achievement demonstrate their behaviours during examination and evaluation of their learning progress [47]. While offering responses to peers, they also review the learning content, which helps them focus more on the learning activities. Based on the above findings, the results are consistent with the concept of self-explanation associated with the development of students' reflection. While offering the response to peers, students would think of how to give explanations (self-explanations) and then integrate prior knowledge and external knowledge through reflection. While conducting self-explanation and reflection, they are able to identify possible gaps in knowledge and find out the solutions in order to produce better quality descriptive knowledge, which aligns with VanLehn, Johns, and Chi's [42] statement on the development of descriptive knowledge. The findings are also echoed in the interview that reflected on the topic; along with assisting peers, the process can effectively help students in their learning. Since a deeper understanding can be gained, it thus enhances learning effectiveness. Students with high academic achievement in the experimental group are more aware of arranging learning plans according to their own learning conditions. Therefore, in the algorithm learning course, it can be concluded that the distance peer self-regulated learning system developed by this research will have the advantage of enhancing the learning effect for the experimental group's high achievers.

(3) Low-achievers using the distance peer self-regulated learning mechanism can improve their learning effectiveness compared with low-achievers in the general distance self-regulated learning system.

As the students in both groups had similar prior knowledge of the subject of the algorithms, the analysis results further found that the learners in the experimental group with low achievement had significantly better scores on the learning effectiveness test than those in the control group. During the interview, it can be found that when learners in the control group with low achievement answer questions incorrectly, they can seek help from their peers. However, they must first respond to the questions and explain the parts that they do not understand. This method not only reduces learners' feelings of loss and frustration during their learning, but it also helps them internalise the knowledge given to them by their peers, thereby achieving the goal of teaching and learning. This echoes the extremely important role of reflection in the construction of knowledge, which can effectively improve the learning performance of the learner [54].

Reflection is a crucial learning activity that can increase the depth of learning and enhance learning [40]. Reflection is an important learning activity that can increase the depth of learning and improve learning, which echoes the previous analysis results. Students reflect on achieving the goal of teaching and learning. This echoes the extremely important role of reflection in the construction of knowledge, which can effectively improve the learning performance of the learner [54], which, in turn, echoes the previous analysis results. Reflecting on topics and assisting peers can effectively help students gain a deeper understanding of learning, thereby enhancing learning effectiveness. Therefore, in the process of learning algorithms, it can be inferred that the use of the distance peer self-regulated learning system developed by this research has the benefit of improving the learning effect for the low achievers in the experimental group.

(4) In comparison to homogeneous group learners, the heterogeneous group learners who used the distance peer self-regulated learning mechanism can improve learners' learning effect.

In this study, the experimental group is divided into two groups: the homogeneous group and the heterogeneous group. The results of the analysis further found that after the activities, the heterogeneous group had significantly better scores on the learning effectiveness test than the homogeneous group. Therefore, it can roughly be concluded that the learners in the heterogeneous group would benefit more from using the distance peer self-disciplined learning mechanism. Based on the interview, it was found that the students in the heterogeneous group were more active than those in the homogeneous group in terms of the number of times they assisted their peers. Immediate feedback can be provided to low achievers in heterogeneous groups. Students can increase their sense of accomplishment and reduce their frustration by helping their peers and being assisted, which helps them learn again. Students become more focused and motivated to work harder on the teaching materials, aligning with the learning content of the self-regulated learning concept proposed by Zimmerman [53]. The learning system will provide students with their learning history so that they can assess their progress and the effectiveness and status of their peers' learning. The learning situation aligns with the analysis results from the previous discussion. The learners in the heterogeneous group of the experimental group are more suitable to use this mechanism for learning. Therefore, in the algorithm learning course, it can be concluded that the use of the distance peer self-regulated learning system developed by this research has the benefit of improving the learning effect of the experimental group's heterogeneous group learners.

(5) Learners who used the distance peer self-regulated learning mechanism have a significant impact on their learning motivation, self-efficacy, reflective ability, and cognitive load after learning.

The results of the questionnaire analysis found that the learning motivation, self-efficacy, and reflection abilities of the students in the experimental group after learning were significantly better than those before the experiment in the distance peer self-disciplined learning system. The learning motivation, self-efficacy, performance, and reflective ability in the experimental group were also better than those of the control group. With the assistance of the peer self-regulated learning mechanism, the cognitive load of the learners can be reduced at the same time. This leads back to the previous discussion about how peer intervention can motivate students to work harder, continue learning, and improve their learning motivation. As a result, it can be concluded in the algorithm learning course that the distance peer self-regulated learning system developed in this study can effectively improve learners' learning motivation, self-efficacy, and reflection ability. Although the learners in the experimental group put more pressure on their peers to intervene at the beginning, they became more motivated to continue learning after receiving assistance from their peers and feedback from the learners. Therefore, the assistance of the peer self-regulated learning mechanism can not only sharpen the learners' own learning status, but also seek peer assistance for unsolvable problems. Learners can solve subsequent problems, thereby reducing mental load and mental effort. This study's distance peer-self-regulated learning system demonstrated that peer assistance can effectively improve learners' learning effects in a distance learning setting.

However, some limitations must be taken into account, which are described in detail as follows:

(1) Sample limit

The samples for this study are from 112 students who are studying algorithmic courses in the Department of Information Management of a university in Taipei City, including 56 students in the experimental group and 56 in the control group. The sample size for this study is too small since it only includes university department students. Thus, the inference cannot be generalised to learners in other levels and grades; it can only be applied to learners who share the same characteristics as those in this study.

(2) Study subjects

The chosen learning activities of this study are associated with an algorithm with four thematic units: "Divide-and-Conquer", "Dynamic Programming", "The Greedy Approach", and "Backtracking". The material is restricted to the article in this study. Thus, it remains to be determined if the findings of this study may be applied to other subjects or groups. The distance peer self-regulated learning system developed by this research shows that the experimental group students' outcomes in the algorithm course are significantly superior to those of the control group students. Still, due to the intervention and support of peers, learners can compare their learning status with that of their peers, and then find the learning strategies that suit them. According to the interview, the learning mode of four-person groups can be altered to two-person groups, which can better cater to low-achieving learners. In the future, the system will be able to support "Sharing Note". When studying, students are able to highlight key ideas and make notes in their textbooks. Shared notes can organise peers' notes, making it simple for learners to learn from others, observe how their peers make notes, and understand what the other party learns.

Author Contributions: Conceptualization, Y.-C.K. and B.-Y.C.; methodology, Y.-C.K.; software, B.-Y.C.; validation, Y.-C.K., H.-C.K.L. and Y.-H.L.; formal analysis, B.-Y.C.; investigation, B.-Y.C.; resources, Y.-C.K.; data curation, H.-C.K.L. and T.-H.W.; writing—original draft preparation, Y.-C.K.; writing review and editing, Y.-H.L.; visualization, Y.-C.K.; supervision, H.-C.K.L. and T.-H.W.; project administration, Y.-H.L. All authors have read and agreed to the published version of the manuscript.

Funding: This research received no external funding.

Institutional Review Board Statement: Not applicable.

Informed Consent Statement: Informed consent was obtained from all subjects involved in the study.

Data Availability Statement: Not applicable.

Conflicts of Interest: The authors declare no conflict of interest.

References

1. Krishnakumari, S.; Subathra, C.; Arul, K. A descriptive study on the behavior of students in online classes during COVID-19 pandemic. In Proceedings of the Eighth International Conference on New Trends in the Applications of Differential Equations in Sciences (NTADES2021), St. Constantin and Helena, Bulgaria, 7–10 September 2021; p. 030028.
2. Singh, J.; Singh, L.; Matthees, B. Establishing social, cognitive, and teaching presence in online learning—A panacea in COVID-19 pandemic, post vaccine and post pandemic times. *J. Educ. Technol. Syst.* **2022**, *51*, 28–45. [CrossRef]
3. Salta, K.; Paschalidou, K.; Tsetseri, M.; Koulougliotis, D. Shift from a traditional to a distance learning environment during the COVID-19 pandemic: University students' engagement and interactions. *Sci. Educ.* **2022**, *31*, 93–122. [CrossRef] [PubMed]
4. Cui, Y.; Ma, Z.; Wang, L.; Yang, A.; Liu, Q.; Kong, S.; Wang, H. A survey on big data-enabled innovative online education systems during the COVID-19 pandemic. *J. Innov. Knowl.* **2023**, *8*, 100295. [CrossRef]
5. O'Keefe, R.; Auffermann, K. Exploring the effect of COVID-19 on graduate nursing education. *Acad. Med.* **2022**, *97*, S61. [CrossRef]
6. Kelly, S. Instructional Communication during Pandemics. In *Pandemic Communication*; Routledge: Oxfordshire, UK, 2023; pp. 197–214.
7. Lassoued, Z.; Alhendawi, M.; Bashitialshaaer, R. An exploratory study of the obstacles for achieving quality in distance learning during the COVID-19 pandemic. *Educ. Sci.* **2020**, *10*, 232. [CrossRef]
8. Raes, A.; Vanneste, P.; Pieters, M.; Windey, I.; Van Den Noortgate, W.; Depaepe, F. Learning and instruction in the hybrid virtual classroom: An investigation of students' engagement and the effect of quizzes. *Comput. Educ.* **2020**, *143*, 103682. [CrossRef]
9. Azevedo, R.; Cromley, J.G. Does training on self-regulated learning facilitate students' learning with hypermedia? *J. Educ. Psychol.* **2004**, *96*, 523. [CrossRef]
10. Caplan, G. *Support Systems and Community Mental Health: Lectures on Concept Development*; Behavioral Scientist: New York, NY, USA, 1974.
11. Cheng, C.K.E. The role of self-regulated learning in enhancing learning performance. *Int. J. Res. Rev.* **2011**, *6*, 1–16.
12. Zimmerman, B.J. Attaining self-regulation: A social cognitive perspective. In *Handbook of Self-Regulation*; Elsevier: Amsterdam, The Netherlands, 2000; pp. 13–39.
13. Wentzel, K.R. Social relationships and motivation in middle school: The role of parents, teachers, and peers. *J. Educ. Psychol.* **1998**, *90*, 202. [CrossRef]
14. Lim, C.; Ab Jalil, H.; Ma'rof, A.; Saad, W. Peer learning, self-regulated learning and academic achievement in blended learning courses: A structural equation modeling approach. *Int. J. Emerg. Technol. Learn.* **2020**, *15*, 110–125. [CrossRef]
15. Schneider, S.L.; Council, M.L. Distance learning in the era of COVID-19. *Arch. Dermatol. Res.* **2021**, *313*, 389–390. [CrossRef]
16. Chen, C.-M.; Wu, C.-H. Effects of different video lecture types on sustained attention, emotion, cognitive load, and learning performance. *Comput. Educ.* **2015**, *80*, 108–121. [CrossRef]
17. Drokina, K. Distance education in universities: Advantages and disadvantages. *Int. J. Humanit. Nat. Sci.* **2020**, *9-2*, 46–48.
18. Mirkholikovna, D.K. Advantages and disadvantages of distance learning. *Sci. Educ. Today* **2020**, *7*, 70–72.
19. Yueh, H.P. A study of classroom management in real-time multicast distance education. *Curric. Instr. Q.* **2000**, *3*, 63–74.
20. Vlasenko, L.; Bozhok, N. *Advantages and Disadvantages of Distance Learning*; National University of Food Technologies: Kyiv, Ukraine, 2014.
21. Zimmerman, B.J. Investigating self-regulation and motivation: Historical background, methodological developments, and future prospects. *Am. Educ. Res. J.* **2008**, *45*, 166–183. [CrossRef]
22. Joo, Y.-J.; Bong, M.; Choi, H.-J. Self-efficacy for self-regulated learning, academic self-efficacy, and internet self-efficacy in web-based instruction. *Educ. Technol. Res. Dev.* **2000**, *48*, 5–17. [CrossRef]
23. Kao, T.C. Scaffolding-Assisted Research on Self-Disciplined Learning in Asynchronous Online Teaching. 2002. Available online: https://scholar.google.com.tw/scholar?hl=zh-TW&as_sdt=0%2C5&q=%E9%9D%9E%E5%90%8C%E6%AD%A5%E7%B6%B2%E8%B7%AF%E6%95%99%E5%AD%B8%E4%B8%AD%E8%87%AA%E5%BE%8B%E5%AD%B8%E7%BF%92%E7%9A%84%E9%B7%B9%E6%9E%B6%E8%BC%94%E5%8A%A9%E7%A0%94%E7%A9%B6&btnG= (accessed on 2 February 2023).
24. Chen, M.R.A.; Hwang, G.J.; Chang, Y.Y. A reflective thinking-promoting approach to enhancing graduate students' flipped learning engagement, participation behaviors, reflective thinking and project learning outcomes. *Br. J. Educ. Technol.* **2019**, *50*, 2288–2307. [CrossRef]
25. Chen, C.-M. Personalized E-learning system with self-regulated learning assisted mechanisms for promoting learning performance. *Expert Syst. Appl.* **2009**, *36*, 8816–8829. [CrossRef]
26. Miller-Cotto, D.; Booth, J.L.; Newcombe, N.S. Sketching and verbal self-explanation: Do they help middle school children solve science problems? *Appl. Cogn. Psychol.* **2022**, *36*, 919–935. [CrossRef]

27. Chang, Y.-C. *The Self-Explanations on the Effectiveness of Learning*; National Taichung University of Education: Taichung, Taiwan, 2016.
28. Siegler, R.S. Microgenetic studies of self-explanation. In *Microdevelopment: Transition Processes in Development and Learning*; Granott, N., Parziale, J., Eds.; Cambridge University Press: Cambridge, UK, 2002; pp. 31–58.
29. Wong, R.M.; Lawson, M.J.; Keeves, J. The effects of self-explanation training on students' problem solving in high-school mathematics. *Learn. Instr.* 2002, *12*, 233–262. [CrossRef]
30. Maarif, S.; Alyani, F.; Pradipta, T.R. The implementation of self-explanation strategy to develop understanding proof in geometry. *J. Res. Adv. Math. Educ.* 2020, *5*, 262–275. [CrossRef]
31. Nakamoto, R.; Flanagan, B.; Dai, Y.; Takami, K.; Ogata, H. An Automatic Self-explanation Sample Answer Generation with Knowledge Components in a Math Quiz. In Proceedings of the 23rd International Conference on Artificial Intelligence in Education, Durham, UK, 27–31 July 2022; pp. 254–258.
32. Vest, N.A.; Silla, E.M.; Bartel, A.N.; Nagashima, T.; Aleven, V.; Alibali, M.W. Self-Explanation of Worked Examples Integrated in an Intelligent Tutoring System Enhances Problem Solving and Efficiency in Algebra. In Proceedings of the Annual Meeting of the Cognitive Science Society, Toronto, ON, Canada, 27–30 July 2022.
33. Andersen, T.; Watkins, K. The value of peer mentorship as an educational strategy in nursing. *J. Nurs. Educ.* 2018, *57*, 217–224. [CrossRef]
34. Huang, Q.-Z.; Hsu, C.-C.; Wang, T.I. An Open-Ended Question Self-Explanation Classification Methodology for a Virtual Laboratory Learning System. In Proceedings of the 2018 7th International Congress on Advanced Applied Informatics (IIAI-AAI), Yonago, Japan, 8–13 July 2018; pp. 232–237.
35. Bisra, K.; Liu, Q.; Nesbit, J.C.; Salimi, F.; Winne, P.H. Inducing self-explanation: A meta-analysis. *Educ. Psychol. Rev.* 2018, *30*, 703–725. [CrossRef]
36. Hsu, C.-C.; Wang, T.-I. Applying game mechanics and student-generated questions to an online puzzle-based game learning system to promote algorithmic thinking skills. *Comput. Educ.* 2018, *121*, 73–88. [CrossRef]
37. Oliver, M.; Renken, M.; Williams, J.J. *Revising Biology Misconceptions Using Retrieval Practice and Explanation Prompts*; International Society of the Learning Sciences, Inc. [ISLS]: Montréal, QC, Canada, 2018.
38. Ainsworth, S.; Th Loizou, A. The effects of self-explaining when learning with text or diagrams. *Cogn. Sci.* 2003, *27*, 669–681. [CrossRef]
39. O'Reilly, T.; Symons, S.; MacLatchy-Gaudet, H. A comparison of self-explanation and elaborative interrogation. *Contemp. Educ. Psychol.* 1998, *23*, 434–445. [CrossRef]
40. Chi, M.T.; Bassok, M.; Lewis, M.W.; Reimann, P.; Glaser, R. Self-explanations: How students study and use examples in learning to solve problems. *Cogn. Sci.* 1989, *13*, 145–182. [CrossRef]
41. Chi, M.T.; De Leeuw, N.; Chiu, M.-H.; LaVancher, C. Eliciting self-explanations improves understanding. *Cogn. Sci.* 1994, *18*, 439–477.
42. VanLehn, K.; Jones, R.M.; Chi, M.T. A model of the self-explanation effect. *J. Learn. Sci.* 1992, *2*, 1–59. [CrossRef]
43. Yang, Y.; van Aalst, J.; Chan, C.K. Dynamics of reflective assessment and knowledge building for academically low-achieving students. *Am. Educ. Res. J.* 2020, *57*, 1241–1289. [CrossRef]
44. Leijen, Ä.; Lam, I.; Wildschut, L.; Simons, P.R.-J.; Admiraal, W. Streaming video to enhance students' reflection in dance education. *Comput. Educ.* 2009, *52*, 169–176. [CrossRef]
45. Lin, F.; Chan, C.K. Promoting elementary students' epistemology of science through computer-supported knowledge-building discourse and epistemic reflection. *Int. J. Sci. Educ.* 2018, *40*, 668–687. [CrossRef]
46. Chen, C.H. *A Study of Optimal Grouping in Collaborative Learning*; National Tainan University: Tainan, Taiwan, 2006.
47. Pintrich, P.R.; Smith, D.A.F.; Duncan, T.; Mckeachie, W.J. *A Manual for the Use of the Motivated Strategies for Learning Questionnaire (MSLQ)*; 1991. Available online: https://eric.ed.gov/?id=ED338122 (accessed on 2 February 2023).
48. Kember, D.; Leung, D.Y.; Jones, A.; Loke, A.Y.; McKay, J.; Sinclair, K.; Tse, H.; Webb, C.; Yuet Wong, F.K.; Wong, M. Development of a questionnaire to measure the level of reflective thinking. *Assess. Eval. High. Educ.* 2000, *25*, 381–395. [CrossRef]
49. Hwang, G.-J.; Yang, L.-H.; Wang, S.-Y. A concept map-embedded educational computer game for improving students' learning performance in natural science courses. *Comput. Educ.* 2013, *69*, 121–130. [CrossRef]
50. Paas, F.G. Training strategies for attaining transfer of problem-solving skill in statistics: A cognitive-load approach. *J. Educ. Psychol.* 1992, *84*, 429. [CrossRef]
51. Kuo, Y.-C.; Chu, H.-C.; Tsai, M.-C. Effects of an integrated physiological signal-based attention-promoting and English listening system on students' learning performance and behavioral patterns. *Comput. Hum. Behav.* 2017, *75*, 218–227. [CrossRef]
52. Hwang, G.-J.; Yang, T.-C.; Tsai, C.-C.; Yang, S.J. A context-aware ubiquitous learning environment for conducting complex science experiments. *Comput. Educ.* 2009, *53*, 402–413. [CrossRef]

53. Zimmerman, B.J. Dimensions of academic self-regulation: A conceptual framework for education. In *Self-Regulation of Learning and Performance: Issues and Educational Applications*; Routledge: Oxfordshire, UK, 1994; Volume 1, pp. 3–21.
54. Quinton, S.; Smallbone, T. Feeding forward: Using feedback to promote student reflection and learning–A teaching model. *Innov. Educ. Teach. Int.* **2010**, *47*, 125–135. [CrossRef]

Disclaimer/Publisher's Note: The statements, opinions and data contained in all publications are solely those of the individual author(s) and contributor(s) and not of MDPI and/or the editor(s). MDPI and/or the editor(s) disclaim responsibility for any injury to people or property resulting from any ideas, methods, instructions or products referred to in the content.

Article

Tracking Visual Programming Language-Based Learning Progress for Computational Thinking Education

Ting-Ting Wu [1], Chia-Ju Lin [2], Shih-Cheng Wang [2] and Yueh-Min Huang [2,*]

1. Graduate School of Technological and Vocational Education, National Yunlin University of Science and Technology, Yunlin 64002, Taiwan
2. Department of Engineering Science, National Cheng Kung University, Tainan City 70101, Taiwan
* Correspondence: huang@mail.ncku.edu.tw

Abstract: Maker education that incorporates computational thinking streamlines learning and helps familiarize learners with recent advances in science and technology. Computational thinking (CT) is a vital core capability that anyone can learn. CT can be learned through programming, in particular, via visual programming languages. The conclusions of most studies were based on quantitative or system-based results, whereas we automatically assessed CT learning progress using the Scratch visual programming language as a CT teaching tool and an integrated learning tracking system. The study shows that Scratch helped teachers to diagnose students' individual weaknesses and provide timely intervention. Our results demonstrate that learners could complete tasks and solve problems using the core CT steps. After accomplishing numerous tasks, learners became familiar with the core CT concepts. The study also shows that despite increased learning anxiety when solving problems, all learners were confident and interested in learning, and completed each task step by step.

Keywords: computational thinking; visual programming language; Scratch; learning tracking system

1. Introduction

With the global rise of the maker movement, governments across the world have begun to focus on the impact of maker activities on learners. The philosophy of maker education is learning by making; this indicates a transformation from the conventional dissemination of knowledge to learning relevant concepts by doing. That is, maker education allows students to implicitly acquire knowledge while completing maker projects. This method of learning has a positive and effective impact on learners. Compared with conventional teaching methods, students think about and apply their knowledge, during which they proactively identify and address problems instead of acquiring knowledge passively.

Scientific, manufacturing, and other technological advances have reduced the costs of maker equipment. Also, as the maker movement has developed, embedded development systems have matured, and sensors have become more affordable and diverse, helping learners develop their creativity. Information technology (IT) has resulted in new development and applications for maker education, and it is now cheaper and easier to integrate maker education into on-site education than it once was. These developments all significantly benefit learners. Countries all over the world have developed maker education, and the U.S. Department of Education is cooperating with Exploratorium in offering maker courses to high-poverty and low-performing regions [1]. In Europe, the Fabrication Laboratory (FabLabs), the EU-initiated MakerSpace, and organizations such as Maker Faire Rome and Startup Europe provide maker spaces for learners to tap into their creativity. In Taiwan, the movement has been nurtured by the Workforce Development Agency, which has established maker bases and factories. In addition to hardware developments, the maker concept has been brought into the classroom. Maker education requires not only hardware investments but also integrated software, as well as teachers and teaching materials, helping learners to gain a better understanding of the potential value of the maker movement. Furthermore, students can be trained to acquire existing knowledge from tasks.

The literature shows that maker education integrates well with emerging science and technology, such as STEAM education [2,3], virtual reality (VR) [4], and computational thinking (CT) [5]. This gives learners access to emerging science and technology in a better and faster manner, reflecting today's rapidly changing culture. Additionally, the literature indicates that maker education assists students in developing their creativity, collaborative skills, and problem-solving abilities [6] and improves their engagement in classes [7], all of which have long-term, vertical impacts on learners rather than short-term impacts [8].

CT has been a popular research topic in recent years [9]. In 2006, Professor Wing of CMU indicated that CT is a basic skill needed in daily life and that CT is a key element for elementary education. She re-defined CT and showed that it is just as important as the "3 Rs" (reading, writing, and arithmetic) and that every child should be encouraged to hone their analytical skills using CT [10]. CT is a thinking process in which people use basic concepts and logical methods from computer science to identify and seek solutions step by step [10,11]. Accordingly, learning CT helps us tackle problems more effectively, understand root causes, and address more sophisticated problems [12,13]. In addition, the increasing importance of CT has motivated countries throughout the world to implement CT training policies [14,15].

CT is generally learned through programming [16,17]. Though current programming languages closely resemble natural languages, abstract concepts that are implicit in text-based programming languages are difficult for beginners to learn [18]. In contrast to such text-based programming languages, visual programming languages (VPLs) present language structures via visual blocks of different colors and shapes. This enables beginners to design programs by manipulating blocks, thus significantly lowering the threshold of programming [19]. Relevant studies demonstrate that VPL is an effective learning method for CT, which explains the increasing use of VPL in CT education using systems such as Scratch [20] and Blocky [21]. Scratch facilitates user-defined block-based design to design programs using VPLs and also connects with IoT devices. Therefore, Scratch is the most popular learning instrument for CT [22]. Despite the fact that many studies have attested to the effectiveness of VPL for learning CT [22,23], most determined it by quantitative methods [24,25] involving CT tests or scales [25–27]. Some assessed student programming projects through operating systems [25,28]. However, such methods failed to comprehensively analyze the programming and learning processes and thus did not investigate students' operations during visual programming (VP). It is also important to effectively and automatically assess the learning effectiveness of CT [29] and determine whether students understand CT, particularly in problem-solving.

We thus tapped the Scratch VPL as a programming language tool to teach CT and developed a learning and tracking system for CT education. This system facilitated real-time tracking of programming projects and tasks, allowing teachers to grasp the learning pace of every student as well as the various project results. The system logged the writing procedures and paths of students during programming assignments to help teachers diagnose students' learning weaknesses. Timely intervention and assistance then alleviated students' anxiety and boosted learning motivation and confidence. We posed the following research questions:

(1) After participating in the course of Scratch programming, is there any difference in the frequency of using computational thinking skills?
(2) Does participation in the Scratch programming course affect learning motivation, learning anxiety, and learning confidence?

2. Research Method

2.1. Participants

To equip subjects with basic computer and programming skills, we recruited fifth- and sixth-grade students from elementary schools as participants. Twenty-eight participants (16 boys and 12 girls) voluntarily participated in this course. With the help of CT concepts, the participants completed tasks and challenges by using the Scratch-based learning platform while the system recorded and visualized their progress in real time. The teacher had teaching experience in using Scratch and participated in the overall course design and planning.

2.2. Experimental Design

Figure 1 shows the experimental procedures of this study. The Scratch programming course was taught in two 40-min sections each week for six weeks. In the first week, the teacher explained the learning procedures and programs to give students a preliminary understanding of the Scratch tasks. The teacher explained the core CT concepts and steps so that learners would grasp course structure, after which the teacher demonstrated and explained the learning system's functions and procedures to familiarize students with the operating environment and prepare them for follow-up courses. In addition, students completed questionnaires and scales about learning motivation, learning confidence, and learning anxiety to record their own feelings before the activities. The experimental activities commenced in the second week. The teacher explained the course content and samples and showed how to complete the problem-solving tasks step by step via the four core CT steps (decomposition, pattern recognition, abstraction, and algorithms). An example description is shown in Table 1. After the teacher explained the tasks, the learners logged into the system to complete the tasks: five basic tasks and five advanced tasks, including maze and math problems, as shown in Table 2. The question types all reflected questions designed by Chien [30] and were modified to suit the activities so that students could use Scratch to complete the tasks and solve the problems according to the core CT steps. The tasks and events lasted for four weeks, and post-tests and interviews were administered in the last week, during which students completed questionnaires and scales again. The learners' viewpoints and thoughts concerning the teaching activities, procedures, and content were then solicited via interviews.

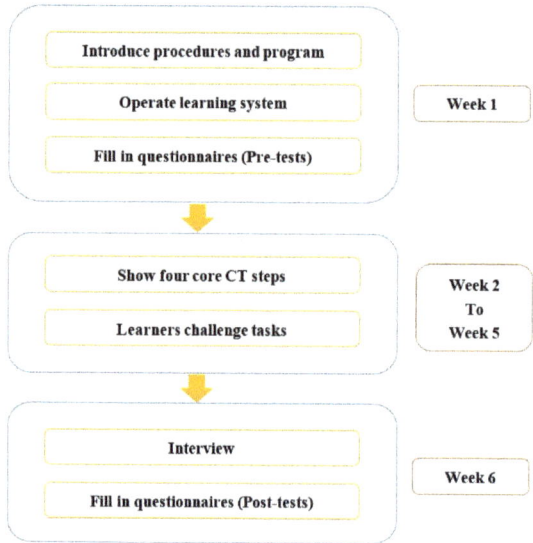

Figure 1. Experimental procedure of this study.

Table 1. Complete the problem-solving tasks via the four core CT steps.

Core CT Step	Step Statement	System Interface
Decomposition	1. Polar bears cannot hit icebergs 2. A polar bear must touch a fish to successfully eat it 3. Polar bears can only go where the blue water is	
Pattern recognition	1. Two steps to the right 2. Two steps down	
Abstraction	1. Two steps to the right: building blocks to the right 2. Two steps down: building down blocks	
Algorithms	Use program blocks to control the polar bear, have the polar bear move in the order of the blocks	

Table 2. Five basic tasks and five advanced tasks of this study.

Level	Task	Statement	System Interface
Basic task 1	Maze problem: polar bear eating fish	Complete tasks using blocks with defined topics	

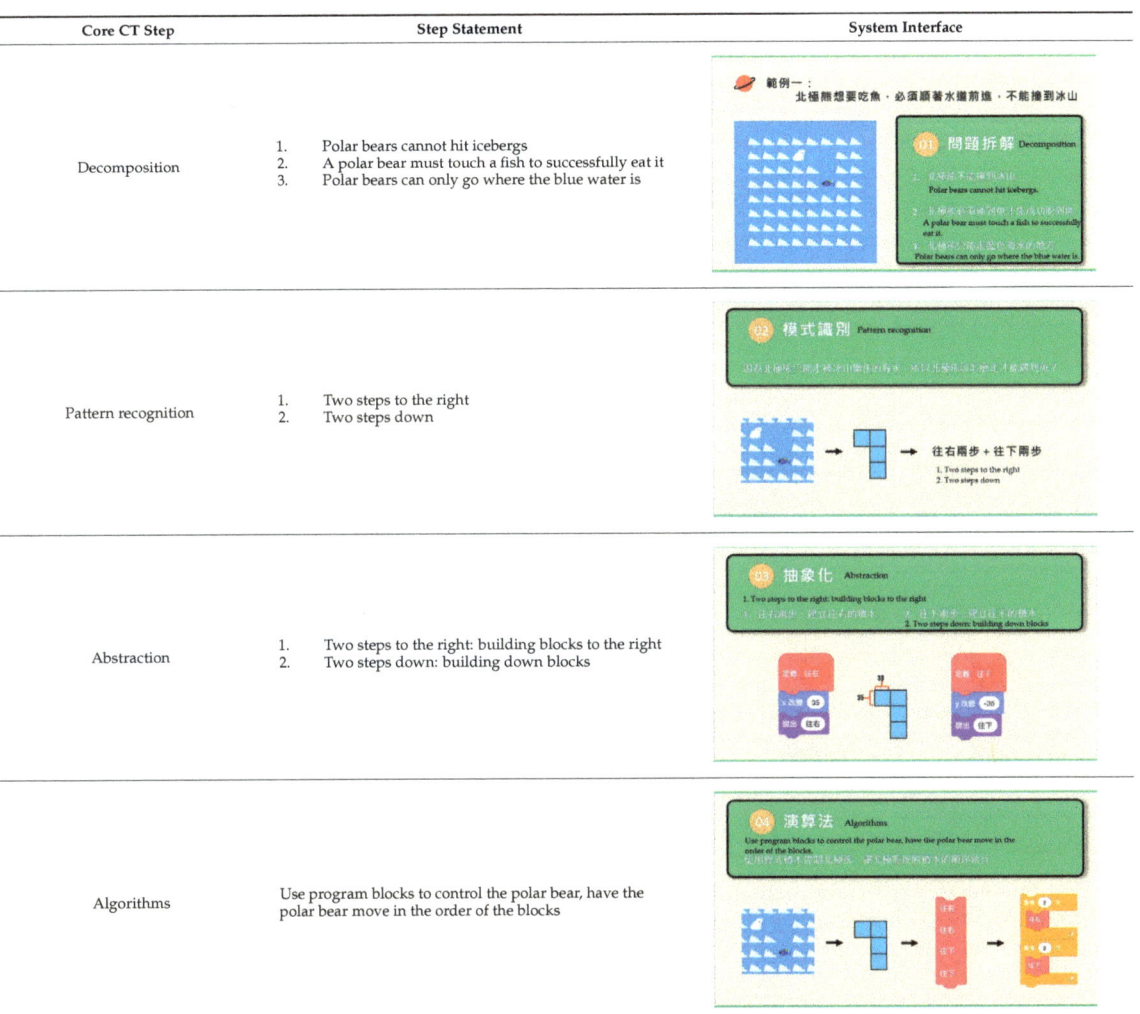

Table 2. Cont.

Level	Task	Statement	System Interface
Basic task 2	Maze problem: polar bear eating fish	Use topic blocks and repeat blocks to complete tasks	
Basic task 3	Maze problem: polar bear eating fish	Define blocks and repeat blocks to complete tasks	
Basic task 4	Draw a rectangle	Repeat blocks to draw rectangles	
Basic task 5	Draw three squares	Define blocks and repeat blocks to draw three squares	
Advanced task 1	Maze problem: polar bear eating fish	Complete tasks with a limited number of blocks	
Advanced task 2	Maze problem: polar bear eating fish	Use conditional judgment blocks to complete tasks	
Advanced task 3	Maze problem: polar bear eating fish	Use specified blocks and conditional judgment blocks to complete tasks	

Table 2. *Cont.*

Level	Task	Statement	System Interface
Advanced task 4	Draw five triangles	Define blocks and repeat blocks to draw five triangles	
Advanced task 5	Automated obstacle-avoiding vehicle	Define building blocks and use conditions to judge building blocks to complete tasks	

2.3. Learning Platform

We customized the interfaces and functions of the VP platform in this study in line with the research design and created cross-platform learning environments for VP using website features, as shown in Figure 2. The Scratch interface was divided into six major parts: (1) block programming categories; (2) blocks; (3) canvas; (4) staging area; (5) roles; and (6) tools. From those parts, students reflected on and selected the desired block programming category and then dragged the programs to the canvas to combine the blocks. After constructing the program, they clicked the green flag to run it or the red button to suspend it in the staging area to preview the logical results of the program.

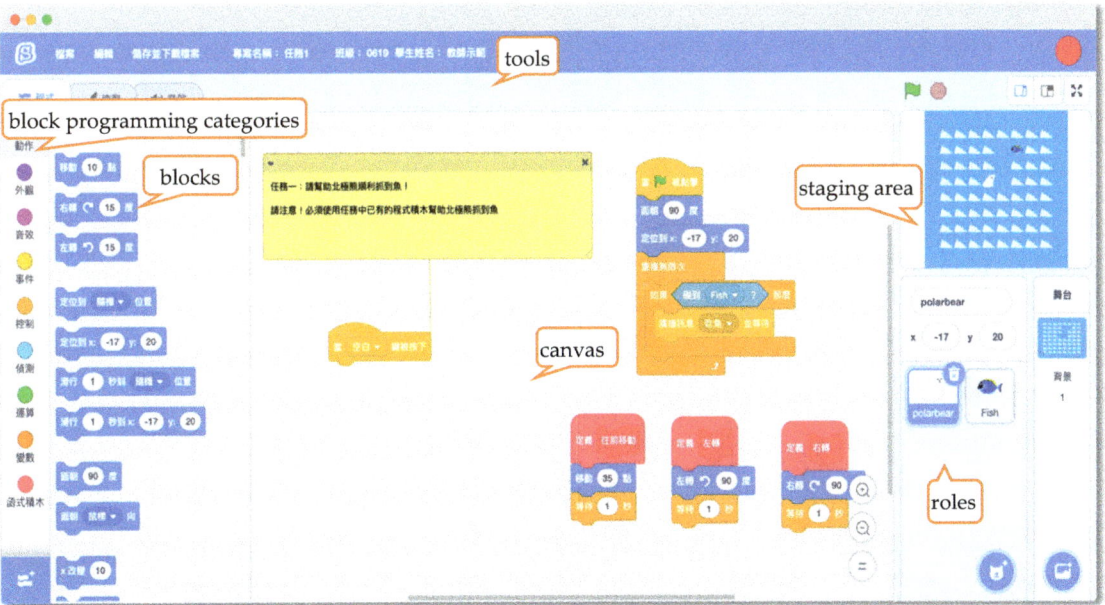

Figure 2. Interfaces and functions of the VP platform in this study.

We assembled the integrated learning and tracking system on the Scratch VP platform. The system recorded the time-stamped operations of students. Once these records were transformed in the backend system, students' behaviors were extracted from the logs, and the files were stored in the cloud servers. We used coding and analysis tools to better understand students' behavior when completing the programming tasks and to determine the role that the platform played in the learning process. The behavior logs not only recorded the students' actions during programming tasks but also grasped the creation of them via the coding and analysis instrument. This helped teachers to provide timely assistance to students or adjustments to the course content.

2.4. Assessment Tools

1. Frequency of CT Skill Use (FCT)

In this study, we modified the Frequency of Using CT Skills Questionnaire (FCTQ) by Yin, Hadad [31] to evaluate the results of our experiment. We analyzed the reliability of the questionnaire, yielding a Cronbach's α of 0.939. The scale had nine items in total to understand how frequently the learners use CT to think and solve problems in the implementation of task-challenge activities after the teacher explained the four core steps of CT.

2. Learning anxiety

To understand student anxiety during the tasks and Scratch challenges, we used a modified Computer Anxiety Scale Venkatesh [32] ($\alpha = 0.887$). Of the nine items on the scale, five were inverse items to measure learner anxiety about the courses and tasks.

3. Learning motivations

We used the Motivated Strategies for Learning Questionnaire (MSLQ) Pintrich [33] ($\alpha = 0.981$) which was divided into an intrinsic motivation part and an extrinsic motivation part, each with four questions. This allowed us to better understand the impact of proper intervention and assistance on learners' motivation.

4. Learning confidence

We used the Computer Attitudes and Confidence Questionnaire [34] ($\alpha = 0.975$) which included 8 questions to understand the learning self-confidence of the participants before and after the experiments.

5. Interviews

During the experiment of the previous week, we randomly interviewed four learners to solicit their impressions and thoughts on the activity design, course content, and system interface, as face-to-face interviews yielded better understanding of the students' standpoints. The interviews were recorded and videotaped, and the interview results were utilized to assist when quantitative materials were insufficient.

3. Research Results

3.1. FCTQ

The t-test (as shown in Table 3), showed that the FCTQ questions were all significant ($p < 0.05$) at a confidence level of 95%. FCTQ used a five-point Likert scale. The larger the value means the more frequent the use.

This questionnaire revealed that learners gained an in-depth understanding of the CT steps and concepts and completed the tasks and solved the problems using the four core steps. Teachers took advantage of the system's behavior tracking to offer real-time instruction and assistance to familiarize students with CT concepts and help learners apply them to solve the problems. As the learners completed various tasks, they became more familiar with CT steps and concepts, increasing their CT usage frequency and even transferring what they had learned to solve problems in daily life.

Table 3. t-test results of FCTQ questions.

Items	N	Mean	SD	df	t	p
CT_F1	28	4.50	0.51	27	46.77 *	0.00
CT_F2	28	4.36	0.49	27	47.25 *	0.00
CT_F3	28	4.43	0.50	27	46.50 *	0.00
CT_F4	28	4.46	0.51	27	46.51 *	0.00
CT_F5	28	4.39	0.50	27	46.74 *	0.00
CT_F6	28	4.46	0.51	27	46.51 *	0.00
CT_F7	28	4.46	0.51	27	46.51 *	0.00
CT_F8	28	4.39	0.50	27	46.74 *	0.00
CT_F9	28	4.43	0.50	27	46.50 *	0.00

* $p < 0.05$.

3.2. Learning Anxiety

As shown in Table 4, a paired samples *t*-test for the learning anxiety questionnaire revealed significant differences in the pre- and post-tests of items ($p < 0.05$) at a confidence level of 95%. The anxiety questionnaire used a five-point Likert scale. Larger values mean more anxiety. The average value indicates that the post-test results were greater than the pre-test results, which shows that the learning anxiety of the learners during the task challenges was greater than that before starting the tasks. This suggests that the task content and problem-solving methods increased the students' anxiety. Nevertheless, the post-test average ranged from 2.5 to 2.9, which is acceptable. A suitable amount of learning anxiety enhanced learning effectiveness [35]. This suggests that the teaching content, tasks, teaching procedures, and system presentation were suitable for students at this age.

Table 4. Paired samples' t-test results for learning anxiety analysis.

	Mean		SD			
Items	Pre	Post	Pre	Post	t	p
A1	1.54	2.96	0.51	0.84	−10.95 *	0.00
A2	1.46	2.82	0.51	0.61	−12.85 *	0.00
A3	1.57	2.82	0.50	0.67	−11.30 *	0.00
A4	1.54	2.82	0.51	0.55	−14.79 *	0.00
A5	1.54	2.93	0.51	0.72	−11.72 *	0.00
A6	1.57	2.89	0.50	0.69	−12.76 *	0.00
A7	1.54	2.89	0.51	0.61	−10.23 *	0.00
A8	1.46	2.64	0.51	0.62	−11.38 *	0.00
A9	1.46	2.53	0.51	0.64	−7.91 *	0.00

* $p < 0.05$.

3.3. Learning Motivation

Motivation is a complicated mental process composed of intrinsic interest, attitudes and desires, the selection of people for experience and targets, and a driving force that influences behavioral attitudes and results in changes in those attitudes [36]. As shown in Table 5, a paired samples *t*-test of the results revealed significant differences between the eight items of learning motivations ($p < 0.05$) at a confidence level of 95%. The learning motivation questionnaire used a five-point Likert scale. Larger values mean more motivation. The post-test results were greater than those of the pre-test (Mean). Thus, the lively and friendly interfaces of systems and task challenges increased the students' learning motivation during the activities. Moreover, the interfaces not only improved extrinsic motivation but also familiarized the students with the system and helped them complete their tasks. The tasks proceeded from easy to difficult. Meanwhile, being able to solve each problem along with the peer pressure stimulated learners' intrinsic motivation, promoting learners to use CT for problem-solving. Repeated practice and thinking helped learners gain proficiency in the CT steps.

Table 5. Paired samples' t-test results of learning motivation analysis.

Items	Mean		SD		t	p
	Pre	Post	Pre	Post		
A1	3.21	4.39	0.83	0.69	−11.38 *	0.00
A2	3.29	4.36	0.85	0.62	−9.38 *	0.00
A3	3.25	4.50	0.89	0.51	−12.76 *	0.00
A4	3.29	4.50	0.85	0.51	−12.89 *	0.00
A5	3.32	4.46	0.82	0.58	−13.49 *	0.00
A6	3.36	4.57	0.78	0.50	−15.38 *	0.00
A7	3.21	4.43	0.83	0.50	−12.89 *	0.00
A8	3.32	4.50	0.82	0.51	−13.11 *	0.00

* $p < 0.05$.

3.4. Learning Confidence

Confidence, a measure of self-assessment adjusted to the environment [37,38], is closely related to self-efficacy, the belief in the mastery of our own capabilities and competence. We conducted analyses using paired samples' t-tests, yielding the results in Table 6. The learning confidence questionnaire used a five-point Likert scale. Larger values mean more confidence. There were significant differences in all items ($p < 0.05$) at a confidence level of 95%, and the results of post-tests were better than those of pre-tests (Mean). We thus observed that detailed CT steps and programs helped learners solve problems efficiently while bolstering their confidence. When students got stuck, teachers were able to directly address their weaknesses with real-time assistance, which helped lower the students' frustration level and boost their confidence. This helped students to focus on solving the problem at hand.

Table 6. Paired samples' t-test results of learning confidence analysis.

Items	Mean		SD		t	p
	Pre	Post	Pre	Post		
A1	3.18	4.32	0.82	0.67	−10.23 *	0.00
A2	3.29	4.36	0.81	0.62	−10.51 *	0.00
A3	3.21	4.43	0.83	0.50	−11.31 *	0.00
A4	3.25	4.46	0.84	0.51	−12.89 *	0.00
A5	3.29	4.46	0.81	0.58	−15.99 *	0.00
A6	3.36	4.57	0.78	0.50	−15.38 *	0.00
A7	3.21	4.39	0.79	0.57	−13.11 *	0.00
A8	3.32	4.50	0.82	0.51	−13.11 *	0.00

* $p < 0.05$.

3.5. Findings from Interviews

We coded and summarized the interviews with the four students, finding that the learners were satisfied with the system design: the system was easy to use, and the content was at an appropriate level for the students. However, for the tasks, although participants possessed basic computer and programming skills, it took time to become familiar with the four core CT steps for problem-solving. In particular, when students observed their peers completing the tasks, they felt stressed, which manifested as learning anxiety.

Some students mentioned that when they got stuck, the teacher provided timely instruction and assistance and was aware of the steps and procedures that the students had used earlier. This assistance relieved the students and alleviated their anxiety. Furthermore, the tasks helped them to be more familiar with CT: solving the various problems increased their confidence and their intrinsic and extrinsic motivation and helped them to further devote themselves to problem-solving.

4. Discussion

We developed a CT learning platform and established a learning and tracking system for Scratch. We used the behavior records to better understand the learners' VPL programming approaches for various tasks. The analysis results helped teachers understand the students' programming progress and offer timely support when necessary. CT problem-solving not only improved the logical skills and systemic thinking of learners but also enhanced their problem-solving skills, which were equally valuable for problems encountered in daily life.

The FCT analysis showed that most learners understood the four core CT steps and solved the problems based on CT concepts. Nonetheless, when they attempted to solve the problems for the first time, they were not able to master the CT steps. Different attempts to solve the problems and tasks only increased their learning anxiety. Since the learners' progress was tracked and recorded in the backend database, the teacher was able to know what difficulties each student faced by consulting their logs, and was thus able to render timely assistance and offer helpful instructions. Such assistance relieved anxiety generated during tasks, improving the students' motivation and confidence.

In addition, learners mastered the four core CT steps and concepts as they completed the tasks. Learning anxiety did occur during the process, but a certain amount of anxiety is necessary to enhance learning efficiency [35]. Moreover, using the concept of computational thinking could improve the logic and systematisms of learners; learners could also apply computational thinking in the process of solving problems in the future and even effectively achieve the effect of learning transfer. Solving the various problems familiarized students with the CT steps, boosted their confidence, and taught them to keep trying in the face of difficulty. Timely assistance and explanations from the teacher also helped students maintain their motivation and gave them the confidence to complete the tasks.

The results of this study are consistent with the drive theory [39], in which the intrinsic drive motivates intrinsic physiological needs, resulting in behavior. Motivation is indispensable for learning. When the needs of individuals are not met, the internal drive is stimulated, leading to reactions. Needs must be satisfied to achieve the desired result. Accordingly, teachers consulted the system's learning logs and analyses to understand the programming progress of each student and offered instruction and assistance to meet their needs. Repeated success in solving problems enhanced learners' confidence and motivation, and the desire to complete more tasks stimulated internal drive, motivating students to accomplish the tasks. The inverted U-shape theory [40] also supports these results: there is a U-shape curvilinear relationship between learning performance and anxiety. As anxiety rises, performance will gradually improve, and when anxiety rises to a certain level, the best performance will be produced. In the tasks in this experiment, learner anxiety was maintained at an acceptable range, promoting learners' confidence and interest in the system activities and helping them to complete the tasks.

5. Conclusions and Recommendations for Future Work

In this study, we developed a CT learning platform and established a learning and tracking system for Scratch. The system tracked and recorded programming activities during the course so that teachers could better understand each student's progress and difficulties. Using this learning and analysis system, teachers could offer timely assistance and relevant explanations to students at different levels. The analysis results show that all participants were able to complete the tasks and solve the problems according to the four core CT steps. When the students faced difficulties, the teacher offered instructions and assistance to reduce their anxiety. Additionally, various tasks served to familiarize the students with CT, and problem-solving boosted their confidence and motivation.

From interviews, we learned that the course was too fast-paced. As a result, though participants had basic computer and programming skills, they still needed time to familiarize themselves with the four core CT steps for problem-solving. In addition, we learned that the proposed CT learning platform has many potential applications. Specifically, the learning and tracking system is well-suited for higher education. The CT-based problem-solving, pattern recognition, abstraction, and algorithm design can be incorporated into course designs to train students' logical thinking and problem-solving capabilities.

Author Contributions: Conceptualization, T.-T.W. and S.-C.W.; methodology, T.-T.W. and S.-C.W.; validation, C.-J.L.; formal analysis, T.-T.W. and S.-C.W.; investigation, T.-T.W. and S.-C.W.; writing—original draft preparation, T.-T.W. and C.-J.L.; Writing—review and editing, T.-T.W. and Y.-M.H.; supervision, Y.-M.H. All authors have read and agreed to the published version of the manuscript.

Funding: This research was partially supported by the Ministry of Science and Technology, Taiwan under Grant No. MOST 110-2511-H-224-003-MY3 and MOST 111-2628-H-224-001-MY3.

Institutional Review Board Statement: Not applicable.

Informed Consent Statement: Not applicable.

Data Availability Statement: The data presented in this study are available upon reasonable request from the corresponding author, except Experimental Research Participation Consent Form and Declaration of Parental Consent.

Conflicts of Interest: The authors declare no conflict of interest.

References

1. House, W. *FACT SHEET: President Obama Announces New Actions to Promote Rehabilitation and Reintegration for the Formerly-Incarcerated*; The White House, Office of the Press Secretary: Washington, DC, USA, 2015.
2. Wang, T.-H.; Lim, K.-Y.T.; Lavonen, J.; Clark-Wilson, A. Maker-Centred Science and Mathematics Education: Lenses, Scales and Contexts. *Int. J. Sci. Math. Educ.* **2019**, *17*, 1–11. [CrossRef]
3. Clapp, E.P.; Jimenez, R.L. Implementing STEAM in maker-centered learning. *Psychol. Aesthet. Creat. Arts* **2016**, *10*, 481–491. [CrossRef]
4. Chen, J.; Huang, Y.; Lin, K.; Chang, Y.; Lin, H.; Lin, C.; Hsiao, H. Developing a hands-on activity using virtual reality to help students learn by doing. *J. Comput. Assist. Learn.* **2019**, *36*, 46–60. [CrossRef]
5. Hadad, R.; Thomas, K.; Kachovska, M.; Yin, Y. Practicing Formative Assessment for Computational Thinking in Making Environments. *J. Sci. Educ. Technol.* **2019**, *29*, 162–173. [CrossRef]
6. Taylor, B. Evaluating the benefit of the maker movement in K-12 STEM education. *Electron. Int. J. Educ. Arts Sci. EIJEAS* **2016**, *2*, 1–22.
7. Lee, V.R.; Fischback, L.; Cain, R. A wearables-based approach to detect and identify momentary engagement in afterschool Makerspace programs. *Contemp. Educ. Psychol.* **2019**, *59*, 101789. [CrossRef]
8. Schlegel, R.J.; Chu, S.L.; Chen, K.; Deuermeyer, E.; Christy, A.G.; Quek, F. Making in the classroom: Longitudinal evidence of increases in self-efficacy and STEM possible selves over time. *Comput. Educ.* **2019**, *142*, 103637. [CrossRef]
9. Tang, X.; Yin, Y.; Lin, Q.; Hadad, R.; Zhai, X. Assessing computational thinking: A systematic review of empirical studies. *Comput. Educ.* **2020**, *148*, 103798. [CrossRef]
10. Wing, J.M. Computational thinking. *Commun. ACM* **2006**, *49*, 33–35. [CrossRef]
11. Hu, C. Computational thinking: What it might mean and what we might do about it. In Proceedings of the 16th Annual Joint Conference on Innovation and Technology in Computer Science Education, Darmstadt, Germany, 27–29 June 2011.
12. Grover, S.; Pea, R. Computational thinking: A competency whose time has come. *Comput. Sci. Educ. Perspect. Teach. Learn. Sch.* **2018**, *19*, 1257–1258.
13. Slisko, J. Self-Regulated Learning in A General University Course: Design of Learning Tasks, Their Implementation and Measured Cognitive Effects. *J. Eur. Educ.* **2017**, *7*, 12–24.
14. Hsu, T.-C.; Chang, S.-C.; Hung, Y.-T. How to learn and how to teach computational thinking: Suggestions based on a review of the literature. *Comput. Educ.* **2018**, *126*, 296–310. [CrossRef]
15. Selby, C.; Woollard, J. Computational Thinking: The Developing Definition. In Proceedings of the 45th ACM Technical Symposium on Computer Science Education, SIGCSE 2014, Atlanta, GA, USA, 5–8 March 2014; ACM: Atlanta, GA, USA, 2013.
16. Futschek, G.; Moschitz, J. Learning algorithmic thinking with tangible objects eases transition to computer programming. In Proceedings of the International Conference on Informatics in Schools: Situation, Evolution, and Perspectives, Bratislava, Slovakia, 26–29 October 2011; Springer: Berlin/Heidelberg, Germany, 2011.
17. Sung, W.; Ahn, J.; Black, J.B. Introducing Computational Thinking to Young Learners: Practicing Computational Perspectives Through Embodiment in Mathematics Education. *Technol. Knowl. Learn.* **2017**, *22*, 443–463. [CrossRef]
18. Papadakis, S. Evaluating a game-development approach to teach introductory programming concepts in secondary education. *Int. J. Technol. Enhanc. Learn.* **2020**, *12*, 127. [CrossRef]
19. Bau, D.; Gray, J.; Kelleher, C.; Sheldon, J.; Turbak, F. Learnable programming: Blocks and beyond. *Commun. ACM* **2017**, *60*, 72–80. [CrossRef]

20. Resnick, M.; Maloney, J.; Monroy-Hernández, A.; Rusk, N.; Eastmond, E.; Brennan, K.; Millner, A.; Rosenbaum, E.; Silver, J.; Silverman, B.; et al. Scratch: Programming for all. *Commun. ACM* **2009**, *52*, 60–67. [CrossRef]
21. Pasternak, E.; Fenichel, R.; Marshall, A.N. *Tips for Creating a Block Language with Blockly*; IEEE blocks and beyond workshop (B&B); IEEE: Piscataway, NJ, USA, 2017.
22. Zhang, L.; Nouri, J. A systematic review of learning computational thinking through Scratch in K-9. *Comput. Educ.* **2019**, *141*, 103607. [CrossRef]
23. Kalelioğlu, F. A new way of teaching programming skills to K-12 students: Code.org. *Comput. Hum. Behav.* **2015**, *52*, 200–210. [CrossRef]
24. Cutumisu, M.; Adams, C.; Lu, C. A Scoping Review of Empirical Research on Recent Computational Thinking Assessments. *J. Sci. Educ. Technol.* **2019**, *28*, 651–676. [CrossRef]
25. Moreno-León, J.; Robles, G.; Román-González, M. Dr. Scratch: Automatic analysis of scratch projects to assess and foster computational thinking. *RED Rev. Educ. Distancia* **2015**, *46*, 1–23.
26. Korkmaz, Ö.; Çakir, R.; Özden, M.Y. A validity and reliability study of the computational thinking scales (CTS). *Comput. Hum. Behav.* **2017**, *72*, 558–569. [CrossRef]
27. Tsai, M.-J.; Liang, J.-C.; Hsu, C.-Y. The Computational Thinking Scale for Computer Literacy Education. *J. Educ. Comput. Res.* **2020**, *59*, 579–602. [CrossRef]
28. Jiang, B.; Zhao, W.; Zhang, N.; Qiu, F. Programming trajectories analytics in block-based programming language learning. *Interact. Learn. Environ.* **2019**, *30*, 113–126. [CrossRef]
29. Zhong, B.; Wang, Q.; Chen, J.; Li, Y. An Exploration of Three-Dimensional Integrated Assessment for Computational Thinking. *J. Educ. Comput. Res.* **2015**, *53*, 562–590. [CrossRef]
30. Chien, Y.-C. *Evaluating the Learning Experience and Performance of Computational Thinking with Visual and Tangible Programming Tools for Elementary School Students*; Department of Engineering Science, National Cheng Kung University: Taiwan, China, 2018.
31. Yin, Y.; Hadad, R.; Tang, X.; Lin, Q. Improving and Assessing Computational Thinking in Maker Activities: The Integration with Physics and Engineering Learning. *J. Sci. Educ. Technol.* **2019**, *29*, 189–214. [CrossRef]
32. Venkatesh, V. Determinants of Perceived Ease of Use: Integrating Control, Intrinsic Motivation, and Emotion into the Technology Acceptance Model. *Inf. Syst. Res.* **2000**, *11*, 342–365. [CrossRef]
33. Pintrich, P.R.; Smith, D.A.F.; Garcia, T.; McKeachie, W.J. *A Manual for the Use of the Motivated Strategies for Learning Questionnaire (MSLQ)*; Michigan State University: East Lansing, MI, USA, 1991.
34. Levine, T.; Donitsa-Schmidt, S. Computer use, confidence, attitudes, and knowledge: A causal analysis. *Comput. Hum. Behav.* **1998**, *14*, 125–146. [CrossRef]
35. Young, D.J. An Investigation of Students' Perspectives on Anxiety and Speaking. *Foreign Lang. Ann.* **1990**, *23*, 539–553. [CrossRef]
36. Munn, N.L.; Fernald, L.D., Jr.; Fernald, P.S. *Introduction to Psychology*, 2nd ed.; Houghton Mifflin: Oxford, UK, 1969; p. 752-xvi.
37. Bandura, A. Self-efficacy: Toward a unifying theory of behavioral change. *Psychol. Rev.* **1977**, *84*, 191. [CrossRef]
38. Jackson, P.R.; Warr, P.B. Unemployment and psychological ill-health: The moderating role of duration and age. *Psychol. Med.* **1984**, *14*, 605–614. [CrossRef]
39. Hull, C.L. *Principles of Behavior: An Introduction to Behavior Theory*; Appleton-Century: New York, NY, USA, 1943.
40. Yerkes, R.M.; Dodson, J.D. The relation of strength of stimulus to rapidity of habit-formation. *J. Comp. Neurol. Psychol.* **1908**, *18*, 459–482. [CrossRef]

Disclaimer/Publisher's Note: The statements, opinions and data contained in all publications are solely those of the individual author(s) and contributor(s) and not of MDPI and/or the editor(s). MDPI and/or the editor(s) disclaim responsibility for any injury to people or property resulting from any ideas, methods, instructions or products referred to in the content.

Article

Students' Perceptions of Online Learning in the Post-COVID Era: A Focused Case from the Universities of Applied Sciences in China

Ye Zhang [1] and Xinrong Chen [2,*]

1. School of International Exchange, Shanghai Polytechnic University, Shanghai 201209, China
2. Academy for Engineering and Technology, Fudan University, Shanghai 200433, China
* Correspondence: chenxinrong@fudan.edu.cn

Abstract: Currently, while most universities around the world have returned to offline teaching, most universities in China are still using online teaching. In the current educational context, Chinese universities switch between online and offline teaching modes at any time depending on the epidemic situation in their city. This paper discusses students' perceptions of online learning in the post-COVID era in China. Based on the data collected from student questionnaires, the teaching and learning situation in the post-COVID era and student preferences for online learning are discussed. In addition to this, the statistics program JMP was used to perform the data analysis. The correlations among study characteristics, socio-economic factors, organisational and didactic design, and the acceptance and use of online learning are analysed. The results show that students spend more time in university courses in the post-COVID era than in previous academic years. Students prefer to study alone and at individual times that are set by themselves. Study characteristics and the socio-economic situation of the students are not related to the acceptance and usage behaviour of online learning. The organisational and didactic design of online learning is correlated with its acceptance. In the end, the reflection on opportunities for online learning in the post-COVID era is concluded.

Keywords: online learning; emergency remote teaching; post-COVID era; universities of applied sciences; student preference; China

Citation: Zhang, Y.; Chen, X. Students' Perceptions of Online Learning in the Post-COVID Era: A Focused Case from the Universities of Applied Sciences in China. *Sustainability* **2023**, *15*, 946. https://doi.org/10.3390/su15020946

Academic Editor: Hao-Chiang Koong Lin

Received: 15 November 2022
Revised: 27 December 2022
Accepted: 1 January 2023
Published: 4 January 2023

Copyright: © 2023 by the authors. Licensee MDPI, Basel, Switzerland. This article is an open access article distributed under the terms and conditions of the Creative Commons Attribution (CC BY) license (https://creativecommons.org/licenses/by/4.0/).

1. Introduction

For several decades, online learning has not received enough attention, especially at universities [1,2]. Although numerous virtual universities, such as open universities and distance teaching universities, already offer online learning, most ordinary universities prefer to offer face-to-face courses [3]. Since the 1990s, the widespread use of the internet has greatly promoted the development of online education and has had a potential impact on university teaching methods, resource allocation, and development strategies [4,5]. Since 2013, there has been an explosive growth of large-scale online courses [6].

In early 2020, various industries and sectors were affected by the massive global spread of COVID-19 [7]. For example, total urban traffic has seen a significant drop due to the impact of travel controls. The home quarantine policy has led to high growth in the size of transactions in the new retail industry. The rapid changes in the epidemic have led to large fluctuations in the psychological situation of the population [6]. Similarly, universities around the world have struggled to return to normal teaching and learning in the wake of the epidemic due to the excessive range of movement of people. This situation forced all universities to operate remotely and to put emergency remote teaching into practice [8]. University students and teachers have to use online learning as a supplement to traditional face-to-face teaching and learning [9]. To ensure the safety of students, the education authorities in each country have taken measures to ensure the normal teaching and learning process at universities, requiring them to rely on various online course platforms and online learning spaces during the COVID-19 pandemic [10]. Universities have also asked students to postpone their return to university and engage with online teaching. In this case, students are studying online off-campus through platforms such as Zoom, Tencent Meeting, etc. [11]. As learning styles and learning environments change, so do students' choices of courses and attitudes towards learning. Students and faculty often found themselves logging onto Zoom or other platforms for the first time, with little knowledge of how to use virtual learning. As the COVID-19 pandemic eases, many universities are realising that well-planned online platforms will allow them to better serve students [12,13].

Online learning became the default in 2020. Nevertheless, remote learning via Zoom and Tencent Meeting is now used by the majority of universities [14]. However, a variety of new platforms and technologies have emerged in recent years, grounded in machine learning, artificial intelligence, etc. MOOC platforms such as Coursera and EdX use machine learning to automatically grade assignments and deliver adaptive content and exams by combining data from billions of course datapoints and tens of millions of students [15].

The need for online education is enormous and expanding quickly during the epidemic [16]. From 2016 to 2023, the online education industry is anticipated to expand at a 16.4% CAGR. In ten to fifteen years, it is possible that the teaching style in schools may alter due to the internet's rapid development. More and more students are favouring online learning [17]. However, few studies have involved the influencing factors of students' perceptions of the online learning situation during COVID-19, especially the students of universities of applied sciences. Higher education that emphasises applications is essential for a nation's development since it fosters employment and raises competitiveness [16]. Its potential to enhance learners' capacity to gain knowledge, develop skills, and express creativity is what gives it its distinctive worth [18–20].

In order to improve the understanding of the overall evaluation of online learning in the post-COVID era from the perspective of students of universities of applied sciences in China, it is necessary to identify which implicit and explicit factors are present in the research on online learning. This is a necessary first step towards having a robust debate about the influencing factors in online learning.

2. Theoretical Frameworks

Just as COVID-19 spread to many countries in 2020, the COVID-19 pandemic affected universities in these countries around the world. During lockdowns, university teachers have almost exclusively used digital tools to ensure the continuation of teaching and learning [7]. However, not all countries, universities, and students were equally affected. At this point, central aspects from the educational, sociological, and economical perspectives that influence online learning are presented. This includes various forms of the digital divide and other factors. The digital divide is a fundamental problem for online learning [21]. This approach is, in turn, influenced by other aspects such as socio-economic factors. At the beginning of the research on the digital divide, the focus was on access to the internet and digital media. Internet skills are addressed as a second digital divide [22,23].

2.1. The Expectation Confirmation Theory (ECT)

In 1980, Oliver proposed the expectancy disconfirmation theory (EDT). Before purchasing a product or service, users have certain expectations of it. After the product or service is actually used, the difference between the user's perceived performance and their expectations is known as expectation disconfirmation [24]. Expectancy confirmation theory (ECT) was developed based on EDT and provides an important basis for the study of sustained use by users [25]. Patterson et al. [26] were the first to apply ECT to information systems. Bhattacherjee [27] proposed the expectation confirmation model (ECM), which includes four main variables: expectation confirmation, perceived usefulness, satisfaction, and repurchase intention. After ECM was proposed, many academics confirmed the validity of the ECM. For example, Larsen et al. [28] examined mobile commerce using the ECM, Tang and Chiang [29] verifies the effectiveness of the ECM by examining blogs, Doong and Lai [30] examined knowledge sharing using the ECM, and Kim [31] explored the effectiveness of the ECM by examining mobile data services. Moreover, many academics have combined online learning with the ECM. Wang et al. [32] determined if online learning helps students accomplish learning activities during the pandemic and increases their motivation to continue utilising online learning in the future. In order to investigate the potential drivers of continuous learning willingness in a Massive Open Online Course (MOOC) environment, Hai et al. [33] developed and extended the ECM by including cognitive and emotional variables (including intrinsic motivation, attitude, and curiosity). Based on the foregoing literature, the ECM can be utilised to describe the impact of online learning on students' learning experiences.

2.2. The First and Second Digital Divides

The digital divide is also called Digital Gap or Digital Division; that is, the gap between the information-rich and the information-poor [34]. It was first proposed by the National Telecommunications and Information Administration (NTIA) in 1999 in a report titled "Falling Through the Net: Defining the Digital Divide Lost in the Network: Defining the Digital Divide". Subsequently, the digital divide was first formally proposed in a report entitled "Filling the Digital Divide", published by the United States in July 1999. In July 2000, the World Economic Forum (WEF) submitted a special report, "From the Global Digital Divide to the Global Digital Opportunity", to the G8 summit. As time goes by, the digital divide has received more and more attention [35–38].

In all countries, there are always some people who have better information technology provided by society. They have computers, good telephone services, and fast internet services. There are also some people who, for various reasons, cannot access the latest computers, reliable telephone services, or fast and convenient internet services. The difference between these two groups of people is the digital divide [39]. Being on the negative side of this divide means that they have few opportunities to participate in the new information-based economy and there are few opportunities to participate in online education, training, shopping, entertainment, and communication. The differences caused by the digital divide are mainly reflected in different classes, races, industries, ages, genders, generations, and educational backgrounds [40].

The first digital divide is related to computer ownership and internet access [41]. In the 1990s, many poor people could not afford computers and had no access to the internet at home. As time goes by, computer prices decreased gradually and most families bought computers. Therefore, the first digital divide became smaller than before.

The second digital divide is about computer use. Many studies show that not all students have equal computer use at university and at home [42]. There are differences between urban and rural students. Different income levels and educational backgrounds are causes of the second digital divide, too. The second digital divide was first proposed by Hargittai [20]. He emphasised that online skills play an important role in the digital divide. It is not only important to gain access to digital media, but also the ability to find and process useful information. Recent studies expand the approach of Hargittai and argue that not only is access to digital media unevenly distributed but that there are differences in the quality and intensity of use [43]. They conclude that the use of digital media is strongly related to the initial conditions of the users and their social context in real life [23].

By now many studies have illuminated the consequences of digital inequalities for many different offline activities [44]. To date, the recent developments in online learning have been seen as potentially positive disruptions to higher education, but have failed to move higher education away from business as usual [21]. Online learning was thought to be a game-changer for higher education, especially regarding access to knowledge. At universities, taking a course online is now normal. The digital divide between rich and poor is an expression of class inequality. Online learning has failed to nudge elite universities in a direction that will ultimately narrow global wealth gaps. Thus, the matter of the digital divide is very crucial.

2.3. Online Learning at Universities of Applied Sciences

Online learning is defined as the provision and use of learning material by using electronic media and is a collective term for all forms of media-based learning that integrate multimedia and communicative technologies [45,46]. The phrase "online learning" was originally used in 1995 when Web CT, the first Learning Management System (LMS), subsequently known as Blackboard, was created. Online learning then meant using LMS or posting text and PDF files online. Since then, there have been numerous names associated with online learning, including e-learning, blended learning, online education, online courses, etc. Students learn in a traditional classroom by listening to the teacher and conversing with their classmates. These classes are normally scheduled at a specified time and place. However, with online learning, students may be anywhere in the world and still receive the same high-quality instruction as if they were in the classroom [5]. Online learning is usually done via the internet as a series of courses that students can access at any time and from any location [47]. Students who desire to gain new skills or educate themselves can benefit from online learning. Although many people still believe that traditional institutions are the better method for learning, online learning has been shown to be an excellent substitute or supplement [48].

The following are some advantages of online learning: (i) The total costs are lower. Online programs might be less expensive than traditional learning institutions. (ii) Students learning online already have access to a wide range of courses and instructors from which to choose. Students can discover online learning courses or programs in a variety of subjects. (iii) Commuting or relocating can be avoided. By learning online, students can save money on travel and living expenditures, as well as commute time. (iv) Convenience and flexibility. Students have access to all resources at any time, allowing them to learn wherever they are and at their own pace. (v) Instant feedback and outcomes. (vi) Access to good teachers. In any field of study, there are only a few professionals. If the constraints of geography are removed, expertise can travel to any location. This shift makes highly specialised material more accessible to a wider audience [49].

However, the majority of students continue to take traditional classes. As opposed to traditional classroom education, there are still a few disadvantages to online learning. The students need to be self-disciplined. Because online courses are inexpensive, students are less motivated to complete them, and only a small percentage of students complete them. Aside from the cost, few of these online courses are accredited, which further reduces the incentive to complete them. Online courses require good time-management skills to complete the course and lack the social aspect of regular classes [47,50].

Online learning is considered a central component and essential key for innovative university teaching [51,52]. For this reason, universities are increasingly relying on digital formats for learning as part of their training and further education. Many studies showed that online learning is available at a large number of universities, but these can vary considerably depending on the type, sponsorship, and size of the universities [53,54]. In recent years, online learning has been developed, tested, and used many times at universities of applied sciences [55]. In the last few decades, attempts have been made to promote the growth of online learning through a series of funding programs [56,57]. The advantages of using new educational technologies in university teaching are seen primarily in the development of new student groups through increased student flexibility in terms of time and space, financial savings, increased international competitiveness, and improved quality of university teaching [57]. Nevertheless, it must be pointed out that until today, the widespread use of media-based teaching in universities has not come true [52,58]. The dissemination of online learning in university teaching continues to face challenges, including in the areas of technological equipment, acceptance and willingness to innovate, legal management, and curricular integration [55,59].

Due to the COVID-19 pandemic, all educational institutions, including universities, were forced to switch to online teaching [11]. Previous teaching and learning formats had to be implemented exclusively online at short notice, which posed hurdles for many universities, teachers, and students [60]. Instead of a well-planned digital transformation, both students and teachers were confronted with many innovations and requirements within a very short period [61].

In recent years, universities of applied sciences have become a significant part of higher education. Unlike academic universities, universities of applied sciences generally have subjects in engineering, technology, agriculture and forestry, economics, finance, business administration, design, and nursing. The subjects are derived from the practice and there are usually no humanities subjects. The curriculum and its contents, apart from the necessary basic theories, are mostly application-oriented, with a fine classification of professions and a compact teaching schedule, focusing on training and improving students' independent learning and practical hands-on skills [61]. Therefore, online learning at universities of applied sciences faces even greater challenges [60].

The teaching aim of universities of applied sciences is to meet the special needs of the industry, and set up subjects and courses mainly for the industry. It needs cooperation between universities of applied sciences and industry. One aim of this study is to sketch a picture of teaching and learning during the 2021–2022 academic year, from the perspective of the students of universities of applied sciences, and to identify factors that influence studying. Above all, currently relevant needs and recommendations for action for the design of university teaching are to be derived. It is therefore important to uncover relevant criteria for a successful and sustainable anchoring of online teaching and learning in universities of applied sciences. It is of interest to what extent the students of universities of applied sciences accepted and used online teaching and learning formats during the 2021–2022 academic year and which factors influenced them.

3. Methodology

3.1. Research Questions and Hypotheses

From the perspective of the students of universities of applied sciences, central conditions are to be identified that are necessary for the success of online learning [41,42]. Knowledge of such conditions for success is currently of enormous importance to enable all students to study in classes that can only take place online and to design them to be of high quality. It is important to research the background of a lack of student acceptance and low usage rates of online learning in universities of applied sciences [62,63]. In summary, it can be said that the use of online learning as an innovation in the field of education is confronted with various hurdles.

The aim of this paper is, therefore, firstly to provide a description of the teaching and learning situation in the post-COVID era in China. The investigated question is whether the COVID-19 pandemic has already caused changes in university teaching at this point. Second, the paper tries to understand the willingness, acceptance, and use of online learning from the perspective of the students of universities of applied sciences in China. As a result, the following research questions were examined in more detail in this study. How did the students evaluate the post-COVID era, which was still influenced by the COVID-19 pandemic? What are the conditions for the success of online learning from the students' perspectives? What suggestions can be made for universities of applied sciences in China?

A hypothesis is a statement of fact, or a concept that is made for the sake of debate and then evaluated to see if it is correct [64]. Apart from a basic background assessment, the hypothesis is established using the scientific method before any relevant research is conducted [65]. The following hypotheses result from the literature review [48,66,67] and research questions: During the post-COVID era, more time was spent on university courses than in previous academic years (H1). Students prefer asynchronous online learning formats over synchronous ones (H2). Students prefer to study at specific times set by the teacher than at individual times set by themselves (H3). Students prefer to study alone than in groups (H4). Study characteristics are related to the acceptance and usage behaviour of online learning formats (H5). The socio-economic situation of students is related to the acceptance and usage behaviour of online learning formats (H6). The better the organisational design of online learning, the higher the acceptance and use by students (H7). The better the didactic design of online learning, the higher the acceptance and use by students (H8).

3.2. Quantitative Analysis

Quantitative methods were used to test the hypotheses of the study [68–72]. Students of a university of applied sciences in China were asked to fill out an online questionnaire and the questionnaire is anonymous. The reason to choose this university is that this is one of the top universities of applied sciences in China and during and after COVID-19, student engagement in online learning and student performance at this university are typical in comparison with other universities. The survey was delivered at a university of applied sciences in China from January to March 2022. In this study, a sample of students from three major fields (Natural Sciences, Social Sciences, and Humanities) was selected for the survey using a random-type sampling method. The questionnaires consisted of closed and open questions with different response formats. In addition to descriptive features, the teaching and learning situation in the post-COVID era and student preference for online learning were examined. In addition, the extent to which there are connections between the aspects of the socio-economic situation of the students, didactic design, organisational design as well as study characteristics, and student acceptance and usage behaviour of online learning were examined. The response format for this questionnaire was a five-point Likert scale from strongly disagree to strongly agree. In this study, a self-administered questionnaire was developed to investigate the students' evaluation (see Appendix A). It consists of 11 items. All items were measured by using a five-point Likert scale ranging from 1—very dissatisfied to 5—very satisfied. We developed the five-point Likert-type scale based on Jashapara and Liaw's scales [73,74]. The name of the five-point Likert-type scale applied is "Students' perceptions of online learning in the post-COVID era". The reliability of variables is evaluated using Cronbach's alpha test. This study used the statistics program JMP (SAS JMP Statistical Discovery Pro 16) for data processing and obtained Cronbach's alpha of the questionnaire as 0.864, indicating that the questionnaire had good reliability. Validity is the degree to which a measurement instrument or tool accurately reflects the characteristics or function of a thing, and reflects the validity of the measurement instrument. It is divided into three types, content validity, structural validity, and validity associated with validity criteria. This study used a structural validity test, and the method used for structural validity analysis was factor analysis. The examination of the exploratory factor analysis revealed that the self-efficacy subscales contained questions that loaded between 0.625 and 0.832 on each factor for each dimension, with an explanatory variance of 71.3%. Therefore, the scales in this study all have good structural validity.

4. Results

In this part, the descriptive parameters of the sample are first described. The teaching and learning situation and the student preference for online learning in the post-COVID era are then presented. At the end, the assumed relationships between the acceptance and use of online learning and various influential factors are discussed.

4.1. Characteristics of the Sample

A survey conducted by UNESCO on the impact of the COVID-19 epidemic on higher education shows that the main impact of the COVID-19 pandemic on teaching and learning has been the increase in online education, with blended learning models having become the most popular format. The case study university is one of the top universities of applied sciences in China. It is located in East China. With around 13,000 students enrolled at this university, a total of 480 questionnaires were distributed, 476 of which were returned. Before the pandemic, this university adopted face-to-face teaching and learning and sometimes used blended learning. With the massive global spread of COVID-19, the case study university had to fully adopt online learning by using platforms such as Zoom, Tencent Meeting, etc.

In this study, 476 students completed the questionnaires. A total of 72.7% of the students are male and 27.3% female, which is the usual gender distribution in universities of applied sciences; 33.2% of the respondents were sophomores, 28.6% juniors, 21.0% seniors, and 17.2% freshmen. Most of the respondents major in Natural Sciences (68.1%), while only 14.3% of the respondents major in Social Sciences and 17.6% in Humanities (see Table 1).

Table 1. Characteristics of the sample.

Characteristic	Group	F	%
Gender	1—Male	346	72.7
	2—Female	130	27.3
Grade	1—Freshman	82	17.2
	2—Sophomore	158	33.2
	3—Junior	136	28.6
	4—Senior	100	21.0
Major field	1—Natural Sciences	324	68.1
	2—Social Sciences	68	14.3
	3—Humanities	84	17.6

4.2. The Teaching and Learning Situation in the Post-COVID Era

Student evaluations of the teaching and learning situation in the post-COVID era were analysed. It was hardly possible to calculate inferential statistical methods to adequately test the hypotheses. Therefore, the following part of the results is limited to descriptive frequencies.

Many students found that their learning processes were more self-directed and flexible than in previous academic years. The teaching often took place asynchronously. H1 postulated that more time was spent on university courses than in the previous academic years. A total of 61% of the respondents stated that they had spent more time than usual, 28% said no, and another 11% could not assess this. The results show that more time was spent on university courses than in the previous academic years ($r = 0.42$, $p = 0.02$). Therefore, H1 is true (see Table 2).

Table 2. Summary of the hypothesis tests.

Hypothesis	Correlation Coefficient	p	Results
H1	0.42	0.02	Accepted
H2	0.05	0.19	Rejected
H3	0.04	0.22	Rejected
H4	0.49	0.03	Accepted
H5	0.03	0.21	Rejected
H6	0.59	0.02	Accepted
H7	0.63	0.01	Accepted
H8	0.51	0.04	Accepted

It was also criticised that students have fewer interactive behaviours than usual because of online learning. Online learning can be understood as the process of using the internet to obtain learning materials, interact with learning content, teachers, and other learners, gain knowledge, obtain support, and grow from the learning experience [69]. The study of learning behaviours helps to distinguish the commonalities and differences between learner groups and individuals. Interactive behaviour is a very important part of the teaching process. Arbaugh [72] found that the higher the degree of student–student interaction and teacher–student interaction in online teaching, the better the student's academic performance. According to the students' opinions, virtual communication only worked perfectly for 4%, predominantly for 15%, partially for 29%, hardly at all for 41%, and not at all as well for 11% as it usually did when present. In addition, new digital tools have been used by students. This particularly includes video conference tools, whereby Zoom seems to have convinced the most. Overall, 59% of the respondents are completely or predominantly of the opinion that digital tools support them in learning, 38% partially, and 3% hardly or not at all.

4.3. Student Preference for Online Learning

It was assumed that students prefer asynchronous online learning formats over synchronous ones (H2). While 21% consider synchronous online learning to be more effective, a further 17% prefer asynchronous online learning and 62% consider both to be equally effective. It was assumed that students prefer to study at specific times than at individual times (H3). In this regard, 32% report preferring to learn at specific times set by the teachers, while 68% prefer to study at individual times that are set by themselves. A total of 79% of students prefer to study alone, while 21% said they prefer to study in groups. Students prefer to study alone rather than in groups ($r = 0.49$, $p = 0.03$).

The relationship between the acceptance and use of online learning was also calculated. There is a significantly positive correlation between the acceptance and the frequency of the use of online learning ($r = 0.51$, $p = 0.03$). Students who have a positive view of online learning use such formats more frequently.

4.4. Study Characteristics and Socio-Economic Factors

In this study, the assumed relationship between study characteristics and the acceptance and use of online learning could not be confirmed ($r = 0.03$, $p = 0.21$). Neither of the variables shows a significant correlation with the acceptance of online learning.

Also, hardly any significant correlations could be found between parameters of the socio-economic situation of the surveyed students and the acceptance and usage behaviour of online learning. On the other hand, access to stable internet seems to play a decisive role. Those who have a stable internet connection are more likely to accept online learning ($r = 0.59$, $p = 0.02$).

4.5. Organisational and Didactic Design

The organisation and implementation of online learning is a fundamental tool to guarantee maximum learning outcomes in the limited time available to students in these special times. Based on the teacher's perspective, improving teachers' teaching methods, adjusting teaching status, stimulating students' independent learning, organising and implementing online teaching, and achieving efficient teaching could help students to learn effectively online with clear objectives, reduce students' learning pressure, improve the effectiveness of online learning, and enhance the quality of learning.

The better the organisational design of online learning, the higher its acceptance ($r = 0.63$, $p = 0.01$). Problem-oriented support and the absence of technical difficulties are consequently related to increased acceptance. If there was a need for support, 13% of the respondents felt the support was complete, 39% predominantly, 26% partially, and 21% thought it was hardly as competent. A total of 59% of the respondents hardly have technical difficulties, 30% partially, and 11% have more technical difficulties.

The didactic design of online learning is also correlated with its acceptance ($r = 0.51$, $p = 0.04$). The better the didactic design of online learning, the higher its acceptance. A total of 29% of the respondents rated the teaching and learning content as completely didactically well-prepared and understandable, 26% as predominantly, 43% as partially, and 2% as hardly. Exercises were completely available for 37%, predominantly for 23%, partially for 31%, and barely sufficient for 9%. Constructive feedback from teachers was complete for 18%, predominant for 23%, partial for 35%, hardly at all for 18%, and not at all for 6%.

In addition, there is a positive relationship between the organisational and didactic design itself with high significance ($r = 0.69$, $p = 0.01$). If the organisational design is successful, the didactic design is just as well thought out and rated positively.

5. Discussion

The massive disruption to education triggered by the COVID-19 epidemic has exposed the vulnerability of education systems and the lack of preparedness for the future on a global scale. As universities close and reopen, millions of students are being excluded from education systems due to the significant digital divide. With approximately half of the world's population (around 3.6 billion) still without access to the internet, due to reasons such as the lack of online learning policies or the equipment needed to connect to the internet at home, connectivity has become a key factor in guaranteeing students' right to education. From the findings of this study, it is clear that online learning can not only help universities of applied sciences in China to complement the courses they cannot offer, but also meet the needs of students to study at home or to take or retake certain courses. However, it is worth noting that online learning in the context of the epidemic has also revealed some issues of concern, such as the fact that online learning is less likely to guarantee student motivation than offline classes, and that the effectiveness of teaching and learning needs to be improved.

This study aimed to outline the current teaching and learning situation at universities of applied sciences in China, which was influenced by the COVID-19 pandemic. Some students were asked to fill out the online questionnaire. It can be seen from the findings that most students have mobile devices, especially smartphones. Two-thirds of students have a stable internet connection in their place of residence. Technically, they almost have no problems studying online.

In addition, the post-COVID era seems to have presented a challenge from students' perspectives. This assumption is confirmed by the finding that 61% stated that they had spent more time on university courses than usual. Furthermore, the students seem to lack exchanges with other students and teachers. Communication and cooperation were therefore presumably not entirely successful in the post-COVID era. In subsequent academic years, teachers should create more impetus for discussion and cooperation. In this regard, teachers should be familiar with suitable digital methods and tools, and be willing to participate and innovate in online teaching and learning. Students seem to be able to get used to digital tools well.

This study also analysed student preference for online learning. Most students consider both synchronous online learning and asynchronous online learning to be equally effective. Students prefer to study alone and at individual times that are set by themselves. There are many known inter-individual differences in learning behaviour between students. However, the COVID-19 pandemic forced teachers to digitise their teaching [11]. The aim of imparting the same learning content to students and achieving the same teaching and learning goals as in the previous academic years was mostly the focus of teachers. The difficulties faced by students were ignored. In the future, different requirements and needs for online learning should be identified on an individual basis and appropriate measures should be established.

Another aim of this study was the analysis of factors that influence the acceptance and use of online learning by students. This study showed hardly any connections between socio-economic factors and study characteristics with the acceptance and use of online learning. Only access to stable internet correlated positively with student acceptance. Significant positive relationships could be demonstrated between acceptance and organisational and didactic design. Based on this finding, teachers should take organisational and didactic design into account and improve online teaching skills.

In addition, we can see from the findings that the education system, in general, is unprepared for online learning. As a response to the global education crisis, emergency remote teaching (ERT) has been put into practice [75]. Courses delivered online in reaction to a catastrophe or tragedy are significantly different from well-planned online learning experiences. When analysing this emergency remote teaching, universities attempting to preserve education during and after the COVID-19 pandemic should be aware of the differences. For decades, researchers have researched online education, including online teaching and learning. Quality online learning, online teaching, and online course design are the subject of numerous research papers, theories, models, standards, and evaluation criteria. According to studies, efficient online learning is the result of meticulous instructional design and planning, as well as the use of a systematic design and development process. The quality of the teaching is influenced by the design process and the thorough evaluation of various design options. In most circumstances, during these emergency shifts, this meticulous design process will be missing.

6. Conclusions

This study discusses online learning in the post-COVID era in China. According to the data analysis results, students spent more time in university courses in the post-COVID era than in the previous academic years. Students prefer to study alone and at individual times that are set by themselves. Study characteristics and the socio-economic situation of the students are not related to the acceptance and usage behaviour of online learning. The organisational and didactic design of online learning is correlated with its acceptance.

Emergency remote teaching is a temporary change in instructional delivery to an alternate delivery channel owing to crisis conditions, as opposed to experiences that are planned from the start and designed to be online. It entails the use of entirely remote teaching solutions for instruction or education that would ordinarily be offered face-to-face or as blended or hybrid courses, with the intention of returning to that format after the crisis or emergency has passed. The major goal in these situations is to give temporary access to instruction and instructional aids in a way that is easy to put up and reliable during an emergency or crisis, rather than to re-create a comprehensive educational ecosystem. Online emergency remote teaching involves more than uploading educational content; rather, it is a learning process that provides learners flexibility and choice [8]. In post-COVID higher education, online learning under the circumstance of emergency remote teaching will play a significant role in universities of applied sciences.

The process of change that has picked up speed due to the COVID-19 pandemic can only succeed in the long term through the cooperation of students, teachers, and universities. If universities of applied sciences in China hope to have sustainable teaching and learning, it requires active cooperation and willingness to innovate. Online learning would not only be a supplement to face-to-face teaching and learning but also be equally important.

7. Limitations and Future Research Directions

COVID-19 has posed some particular issues for higher education institutions in China. Everyone involved in the university's sudden shift to online learning must recognise that these crises also cause disturbances in the lives of students, staff, and teachers. Online teaching and learning are complex educational activities. To effectively integrate information technology into the teaching process requires the creation of universities, teachers, and students. The main purpose of this study is not to prove that online and offline learning are homogenous and equivalent, but to provide suggestions for continuous improvement from good to better learning. It needs to be pointed out that the questionnaire determines that its data comes from student evaluation. In terms of judging the learning effect, more evidence, such as process management, needs to be considered. In follow-up research, it is necessary to further integrate subjective and objective data and conduct more comprehensive investigations.

Author Contributions: Conceptualisation and writing original draft, Y.Z.; data curation, Y.Z. and X.C.; review and editing, X.C. All authors have read and agreed to the published version of the manuscript.

Funding: This work was sponsored by the Humanity and Social Science Youth Foundation of the Ministry of Education of China (Grant No. 20YJC880125) and the Shanghai Pujiang Program (Grant No. 21PJC063).

Institutional Review Board Statement: Not applicable.

Informed Consent Statement: Informed consent was obtained from all subjects involved in the study.

Data Availability Statement: Data can be available from the corresponding author upon request.

Acknowledgments: The authors wish to thank the reviewers for their invaluable comments and suggestions that enhanced the quality of the paper.

Conflicts of Interest: The authors declare no conflict of interest.

Appendix A. Evaluation Questionnaire (Likert-Type Survey)

Item	Definition
Q1	Gender
Q2	Grade
Q3	Major field
Q4	I spent more time on university courses than in the previous academic years.
Q5	I prefer asynchronous online learning formats over synchronous ones.
Q6	I prefer to study at specific times set by the teacher than at individual times that are set by myself.
Q7	I prefer to study alone than in groups.
Q8	Study characteristics are related to the acceptance and usage behaviour of online learning formats.
Q9	The socio-economic situation of students is related to the acceptance and usage behaviour of online learning formats.
Q10	The better the organisational design of online learning, the higher the acceptance and use by students.
Q11	The better the didactic design of online learning, the higher the acceptance and use by students.

References

1. Barker, P. Electronic course delivery, virtual universities and lifelong learning. *AACE Rev. Former. AACE J.* **2020**, *1*, 14–18.
2. Barnard, J. The World Wide Web and higher education: The promise of virtual universities and online libraries. *Educ. Technol.* **1997**, *37*, 30–35.
3. Gros, B.; Garcia, I.; Escofet, A. Beyond the net generation debate: A comparison of digital learners in face-to-face and virtual universities. *Int. Rev. Res. Open Distrib. Learn.* **2012**, *13*, 190–210. [CrossRef]
4. Sun, A.; Chen, X. Online education and its effective practice: A research review. *J. Inf. Technol. Educ.* **2016**, *15*, 157–190. [CrossRef] [PubMed]
5. Li, Y.Q.; Hu, F.F.; He, X. How to make students happy during periods of online learning: The effect of playfulness on university students' study outcomes. *Front. Psychol.* **2021**, *12*, 753568. [CrossRef] [PubMed]
6. Favale, T.; Soro, F.; Trevisan, M.; Drago, I.; Mellia, M. Campus traffic and e-Learning during COVID-19 pandemic. *Comput. Netw.* **2020**, *176*, 107290. [CrossRef]
7. Daniel, J. Education and the COVID-19 pandemic. *Prospects* **2020**, *49*, 91–96. [CrossRef]
8. Bozkurt, A.; Sharma, R.C. Emergency remote teaching in a time of global crisis due to Corona Virus pandemic. *Asian J. Distance Educ.* **2020**, *15*, i–vi.
9. Dhawan, S. Online learning: A panacea in the time of COVID-19 crisis. *J. Educ. Technol. Syst.* **2020**, *49*, 5–22. [CrossRef]
10. Adnan, M.; Anwar, K. Online Learning amid the COVID-19 Pandemic: Students' Perspectives. *Online Submiss.* **2020**, *2*, 45–51. [CrossRef]
11. Mishra, L.; Gupta, T.; Shree, A. Online teaching-learning in higher education during lockdown period of COVID-19 pandemic. *Int. J. Educ. Res. Open* **2020**, *1*, 100012. [CrossRef]

12. Abuhassna, H.; Al-Rahmi, W.M.; Yahya, N.; Zakaria, M.A.Z.M.; Kosnin, A.B.; Darwish, M. Development of a new model on utilizing online learning platforms to improve students' academic achievements and satisfaction. *Int. J. Educ. Technol. High. Educ.* **2020**, *17*, 1–23. [CrossRef]
13. Liu, Z.Y.; Lomovtseva, N.; Korobeynikova, E. Online learning platforms: Reconstructing modern higher education. *Int. J. Emerg. Technol. Learn.* **2020**, *15*, 4–21. [CrossRef]
14. Niu, X.; Wu, X. Factors influencing vocational college students' creativity in online learning during the COVID-19 pandemic: The group comparison between male and female. *Front. Psychol.* **2022**, *13*, 967890. [CrossRef]
15. Lu, Y.; Wang, B.; Lu, Y. Understanding key drivers of MOOC satisfaction and continuance intention to use. *J. Electron. Commer. Res.* **2019**, *20*, 105–117.
16. Moser, K.M.; Wei, T.E.; Brenner, D. Remote teaching During COVID-19: Implications from a National Survey of language educators. *System* **2020**, *97*, 102431. [CrossRef]
17. Shahzad, A.; Hassan, R.; Aremu, A.Y.; Hussain, A.; Lodhi, R.N. Effects of COVID-19 in E-learning on higher education institution students: The group comparison between male and female. *Qual. Quant.* **2020**, *55*, 805–826. [CrossRef]
18. Teclehaimanot, B.; Hamady, C.; Arter, M. Infusing creativity into the K-12 classroom: A model for 21st century education. In *Proceedings of the Society for Information Technology and Teacher Education International Conference, 5 March 2012, Austin, TX, USA*; AACE: Morgantown, WV, USA, 2012; ISBN 9781880094921.
19. Sari, F.M.; Oktaviani, L. Undergraduate Students' Views on the Use of Online Learning Platform during COVID-19 Pandemic. *Teknosastik* **2021**, *19*, 41–47. [CrossRef]
20. Almusharraf, N.; Khahro, S. Students satisfaction with online learning experiences during the COVID-19 pandemic. *Int. J. Emerg. Technol. Learn.* **2020**, *15*, 246–267. [CrossRef]
21. Hill, C.; Lawton, W. Universities, the digital divide and global inequality. *J. High. Educ. Policy Manag.* **2018**, *40*, 598–610. [CrossRef]
22. Hargittai, E. Second-Level Digital Divide: Differences in People's Online Skills. *arXiv* **2002**, arXiv:cs/0109068. [CrossRef]
23. Büchi, M.; Just, N.; Latzer, M. Modeling the second-level digital divide: A five-country study of social differences in Internet use. *New Media Soc.* **2016**, *18*, 2703–2722. [CrossRef]
24. Oliver, R.L. A cognitive model of the antecedents and consequences of satisfaction decisions. *J. Mark. Res.* **1980**, *17*, 460–469. [CrossRef]
25. Hossain, M.A.; Quaddus, M. Expectation–confirmation theory in information system research: A review and analysis. *Inf. Syst. Theory* **2012**, *17*, 441–469.
26. Patterson, P.G.; Johnson, L.W.; Spreng, R.A. Modeling the determinants of customer satisfaction for business-to-business professional services. *J. Acad. Mark. Sci.* **1996**, *25*, 4–17. [CrossRef]
27. Bhattacherjee, A. Understanding information systems continuance: An expectation-confirmation model. *MIS Q.* **2001**, *25*, 351–370. [CrossRef]
28. Larsen, T.J.; Sørebø, A.M.; Sørebø, Ø. The role of task-technology fit as users' motivation to continue information system use. *Comput. Hum. Behav.* **2009**, *25*, 778–784. [CrossRef]
29. Tang, J.T.E.; Chiang, C.H. Integrating experiential value of blog use into the expectation-confirmation theory model. *Soc. Behav. Personal. Int. J.* **2010**, *38*, 1377–1389. [CrossRef]
30. Doong, H.S.; Lai, H. Exploring usage continuance of e-negotiation systems: Expectation and disconfirmation approach. *Group Decis. Negot.* **2008**, *17*, 111–126. [CrossRef]
31. Kim, B. An empirical investigation of mobile data service continuance: Incorporating the theory of planned behavior into the expectation–confirmation model. *Expert Syst. Appl.* **2010**, *37*, 7033–7039. [CrossRef]
32. Wang, T.; Lin, C.-L.; Su, Y.-S. Continuance intention of university students and online learning during the COVID-19 pandemic: A modified expectation confirmation model perspective. *Sustain. For.* **2021**, *13*, 4586. [CrossRef]
33. Hai, M.; Tt, A.; Nar, A.; Fang, H.C. Explaining Chinese university students' continuance learning intention in the MOOC setting: A modified expectation confirmation model perspective. *Comp. Educ.* **2020**, *150*, 103850. [CrossRef]
34. Journell, W. The Inequities of the Digital Divide: Is e-learning a solution? *E-Learn. Digit. Media* **2007**, *4*, 138–149. [CrossRef]
35. Muir, A.; Oppenheim, C. National Information Policy developments worldwide II: Universal access-addressing the digital divide. *J. Inf. Sci.* **2002**, *28*, 263–273.
36. DiBello, L.C. Issues in education: Are we addressing the digital divide? Issues, access, and real commitment. *Child. Educ.* **2005**, *81*, 239–241. [CrossRef]
37. Epstein, D.; Nisbet, E.C.; Gillespie, T. Who's responsible for the digital divide? Public perceptions and policy implications. *Inf. Soc.* **2011**, *27*, 92–104. [CrossRef]
38. Buzzetto-Hollywood, N.A.; Elobeid, M.; Elobaid, M.E. Addressing information literacy and the digital divide in higher education. *Interdiscip. J. e-Ski. Lifelong Learn.* **2018**, *14*, 077–093. [CrossRef] [PubMed]
39. Van Dijk, J. *The Digital Divide*; John Wiley & Sons: Hoboken, NJ, USA, 2020.
40. Warschauer, M. *Technology and Social Inclusion: Rethinking the Digital Divide*; MIT Press: Cambridge, MA, USA, 2004.
41. Attewell, P. Comment: The First and Second Digital Divides. *Sociol. Educ.* **2001**, *74*, 252–259. [CrossRef]

42. Scheerder, A.; Van Deursen, A.; Van Dijk, J. Determinants of Internet skills, uses and outcomes. A systematic review of the second-and third-level digital divide. *Telemat. Inform.* **2017**, *34*, 1607–1624. [CrossRef]
43. Ignatow, G.; Robinson, L. Pierre Bourdieu: Theorizing the digital. *Inf. Commun. Soc.* **2017**, *20*, 950–966. [CrossRef]
44. Van Deursen, A.J.; Helsper, E.J. The third-level digital divide: Who benefits most from being online? In *Communication and Information Technologies Annual*; Emerald Group Publishing Limited: Bingley, UK, 2015.
45. Singh, V.; Thurman, A. How many ways can we define online learning? A systematic literature review of definitions of online learning (1988–2018). *Am. J. Distance Educ.* **2019**, *33*, 289–306. [CrossRef]
46. Anderson, T. (Ed.) *The Theory and Practice of Online Learning*; Athabasca University Press: Athabasca, AB, Canada, 2008.
47. Kumpikaite-Valiuniene, V.; Aslan, I.; Duobiene, J.; Glinska, E.; Anandkumar, V. Influence of digital competence on perceived stress, burnout and well-being among students studying online during the COVID-19 lockdown: A 4-country perspective. *Front. Psychol.* **2021**, *14*, 1483–1498. [CrossRef]
48. Binali, T.; Tsai, C.C.; Chang, H.Y. University students' profiles of online learning and their relation to online metacognitive regulation and internet-specific epistemic justification. *Comput. Educ.* **2021**, *175*, 104315. [CrossRef]
49. Turk, M.; Heddy, B.C.; Danielson, R.W. Teaching and social presences supporting basic needs satisfaction in online learning environments: How can presences and basic needs happily meet online? *Comput. Educ.* **2022**, *180*, 104432. [CrossRef]
50. Perozzi, B.; Al-Rfou, R.; Skiena, S. Deepwalk: Online learning of social representations. In *20th ACM SIGKDD International Conference on Knowledge Discovery and Data Mining, New York, NY, USA, 24–27 August 2014*; ACM: New York, NY, USA, 2014; pp. 701–710.
51. Shao, M.; Hong, J.C.; Zhao, L. Impact of the self-directed learning approach and attitude on online learning ineffectiveness: The mediating roles of internet cognitive fatigue and flow state. *Front. Public Health* **2022**, *10*, 927454. [CrossRef] [PubMed]
52. Salmon, G. *E-Tivities: The Key to Active Online Learning*; Routledge: Oxfordshire, UK, 2013.
53. Yang, G.; Sun, W.; Jiang, R. Interrelationship Amongst University Student Perceived Learning Burnout, Academic Self-Efficacy, and Teacher Emotional Support in China's English Online Learning Context. *Front. Psychol.* **2022**, *13*, 829193. [CrossRef]
54. McClelland, B. Digital learning and teaching: Evaluation of developments for students in higher education. *Eur. J. Eng. Educ.* **2001**, *26*, 107–115. [CrossRef]
55. Wang, X.H.; Zhang, R.X.; Wang, Z.; Li, T.T. How does digital competence preserve university students' psychological well-being during the pandemic? An investigation from self-determined theory. *Front. Psychol.* **2021**, *12*, 652594. [CrossRef]
56. Appana, S. A review of benefits and limitations of online learning in the context of the student, the instructor and the tenured faculty. *Int. J. E-Learn.* **2008**, *7*, 5–22.
57. Kjeldstad, B.; Alvestrand, H.; Elvestad, O.E.; Ingebretsen, T.; Melve, I.; Bongo, M.; Landstad, B. MOOCs for Norway: New digital learning methods in higher education. *Retrieved May* **2014**, *1*, 2015.
58. Sahito, Z.; Shah, S.S.; Pelser, A.M. Online Teaching During COVID-19: Exploration of Challenges and Their Coping Strategies Faced by University Teachers in Pakistan. *Front. Educ.* **2022**, *7*, 1–12. [CrossRef]
59. Kearns, L.R. Student assessment in online learning: Challenges and effective practices. *J. Online Learn. Teach.* **2012**, *8*, 198.
60. Correia, A.P. Healing the Digital Divide During the COVID-19 Pandemic. *Q. Rev. Distance Educ.* **2020**, *21*, 13–21.
61. Rapanta, C.; Botturi, L.; Goodyear, P.; Guàrdia, L.; Koole, M. Online university teaching during and after the Covid-19 crisis: Refocusing teacher presence and learning activity. *Postdigital Sci. Educ.* **2020**, *2*, 923–945. [CrossRef]
62. Al-Salman, S.; Haider, A.S. Jordanian University Students' Views on Emergency Online Learning during COVID-19. *Online Learn.* **2021**, *25*, 286–302. [CrossRef]
63. Herguner, G.; Son, S.B.; Herguner Son, S.; Donmez, A. The Effect of Online Learning Attitudes of University Students on Their Online Learning Readiness. *Turk. Online J. Educ. Technol.-TOJET* **2020**, *19*, 102–110.
64. Means, B.; Toyama, Y.; Murphy, R.; Bakia, M.; Jones, K. *Evaluation of Evidence-Based Practices in Online Learning: A Meta-Analysis and Review of Online Learning Studies*; ALT: Washington, DC, USA, 2009.
65. Lehmann, E.L.; Romano, J.P.; Casella, G. *Testing Statistical Hypotheses*; Springer: New York, NY, USA, 2005; Volume 3.
66. Wang, C.H.; Shannon, D.M.; Ross, M.E. Students' characteristics, self-regulated learning, technology self-efficacy, and course outcomes in online learning. *Distance Educ.* **2013**, *34*, 302–323. [CrossRef]
67. Sher, A. Assessing the relationship of student-instructor and student-student interaction to student learning and satisfaction in web-based online learning environment. *J. Interact. Online Learn.* **2009**, *8*, 102–120.
68. Stockemer, D.; Stockemer, G.; Glaeser. *Quantitative Methods for the Social Sciences*; Quantitative Methods for the Social Sciences; Springer International Publishing: Berlin/Heidelberg, Germany, 2019; Volume 50, p. 185.
69. Osborne, J.W. (Ed.) *Best Practices in Quantitative Methods*; Sage: Newcastle upon Tyne, UK, 2008.
70. Steckler, A.; McLeroy, K.R.; Goodman, R.M.; Bird, S.T.; McCormick, L. Toward integrating qualitative and quantitative methods: An introduction. *Health Educ. Q.* **1992**, *19*, 1–8. [CrossRef]
71. Ally, M. Foundations of educational theory for online learning. *Theory Pract. Online Learn.* **2004**, *2*, 15–44.
72. Arbaugh, J.B. Does the community of inquiry framework predict outcomes in online MBA courses? *Int. Rev. Res. Open Distrib. Learn.* **2008**, *9*, 1–21. [CrossRef]
73. Jashapara, A.; Tai, W.C. Knowledge mobilization through e-learning systems: Understanding the mediating roles of self-efficacy and anxiety on perceptions of ease of use. *Inf. Syst. Manag.* **2011**, *28*, 71–83. [CrossRef]

74. Liaw, S.S.; Huang, H.M. Perceived satisfaction, perceived usefulness and interactive learning environments as predictors to self-regulation in e-learning environments. *Comput. Educ.* **2013**, *60*, 14–24. [CrossRef]
75. Hodges, C.B.; Moore, S.L.; Lockee, B.B.; Trust, T.; Bond, M.A. The Difference Between Emergency Remote Teaching and Online Learning. *Educ. Rev.* **2020**, *3*, 1–12.

Disclaimer/Publisher's Note: The statements, opinions and data contained in all publications are solely those of the individual author(s) and contributor(s) and not of MDPI and/or the editor(s). MDPI and/or the editor(s) disclaim responsibility for any injury to people or property resulting from any ideas, methods, instructions or products referred to in the content.

Article

Online Learning Engagement Recognition Using Bidirectional Long-Term Recurrent Convolutional Networks

Yujian Ma [1,2], Yantao Wei [1,2,*], Yafei Shi [3], Xiuhan Li [1,2], Yi Tian [1,2] and Zhongjin Zhao [1,2]

[1] Hubei Research Center for Educational Informationization, Central China Normal University, Wuhan 430079, China
[2] Faculty of Artificial Intelligence in Education, Central China Normal University, Wuhan 430079, China
[3] School of Educational Technology, Northwest Normal University, Lanzhou 730070, China
* Correspondence: yantaowei@mail.ccnu.edu.cn

Abstract: **Background:** Online learning is currently adopted by educational institutions worldwide to provide students with ongoing education during the COVID-19 pandemic. However, online learning has seen students lose interest and become anxious, which affects learning performance and leads to dropout. Thus, measuring students' engagement in online learning has become imperative. It is challenging to recognize online learning engagement due to the lack of effective recognition methods and publicly accessible datasets. **Methods:** This study gathered a large number of online learning videos of students at a normal university. Engagement cues were used to annotate the dataset, which was constructed with three levels of engagement: low engagement, engagement, and high engagement. Then, we introduced a bi-directional long-term recurrent convolutional network (BiLRCN) for online learning engagement recognition in video. **Result:** An online learning engagement dataset has been constructed. We evaluated six methods using precision and recall, where BiLRCN obtained the best performance. **Conclusions:** Both category balance and category similarity of the data affect the performance of the results; it is more appropriate to consider learning engagement as a process-based evaluation; learning engagement can provide intervention strategies for teachers from a variety of perspectives and is associated with learning performance. Dataset construction and deep learning methods need to be improved, and learning data management also deserves attention.

Keywords: online learning; learning engagement; deep learning; learning evaluation

1. Introduction

1.1. Research Background

Since the breakout of COVID-19, online learning has garnered considerable attention from schools [1]. Online learning moves face-to-face classes online, which allows real-time interaction between instructors and students, even if they are not in the same classroom. In addition to helping students learn from home, online technology also increases the flexibility of learning, and the use of subsidies [2]. Yet, its widespread utilization has been accompanied by several problems. Online learning does not encourage meaningful relationships between teachers and students or between students themselves [2–4], which could lead to online education has a higher dropout rate than offline education [5]. Online learning in certain subjects can increase the anxiety of some students with a negative view of their abilities, which does not help them achieve better academic results [6,7]. These problems are very detrimental to the education and growth of students.

Teaching strategies can benefit students in online learning, and teachers can help students regain interest in studying in various ways, such as by offering instructional materials [8]. Due to the limitations of devices and networks, it is difficult for teachers to accurately assess each student's performance in the online learning environment, thus making it hard for them to effectively intervene in the classroom to ensure the quality of student learning [9,10]. A large number of students in Chinese classrooms also makes it difficult for teachers to pay attention to each student. Therefore, it is important to be able to help teachers obtain the status of their students' online learning so that they can target their teaching strategies.

Monitoring the quality of students' online learning to save those who are about to dropout will become the future entry point of online education. Students learning can be evaluated by learning engagement, which is directly related to learning performance [11]. The effective recognition of students' online learning engagement has become an essential consideration of teachers' intervention in student learning and improving teaching quality. Initially, manual methods were used to assess student engagement, but this method is time-consuming and labor-intensive, and the results can be significantly subjectively influenced. There are also methods for assessing student engagement through external observations that have high demands for the observer. Since the development of information technology, automatic recognition methods based on learning data have received much attention from researchers. Automatic recognition methods are non-intrusive and do not interrupt the student learning process compared to other methods.

Currently, most of the automated methods used to learn engagement recognition are based on deep learning models [7,12]. Data drive deep learning, but data on learning engagement now face problems, including complicated data modalities, a shortage of open-access datasets, and uneven data annotation standards, which directly limit the results of learning engagement for automatic recognition. In addition, differences in learning performance across ethnic groups make it more difficult to systematically advance the automatic recognition of learning engagement appropriate for China.

There are two main methods of learning engagement in recognition: using physiological signals (e.g., heart rate, brainwave, skin electricity, etc.) and using behaviors (e.g., posture, gestures, facial expressions, etc.) [12]. However, collecting physiological signals in an online learning context requires wearable equipment, which is more difficult to achieve. Instead, it is more feasible to use student behavior in learning videos recorded via webcam because this method allows data to be collected without invading the student learning process.

1.2. Learning Engagement and Its Measurement Methods

Learning engagement often appears as an antithesis to learning burnout, which was introduced in 1985 by Meier et al. [13]. They believe that learning burnout is a state of physical and mental exhaustion that originates from a vicious cycle between the learning environment and the learner, including three aspects of emotional exhaustion, behavioral misconduct, and low personal achievement. In 2004, Fredricks et al. [14] provided a widely accepted definition of learning engagement, asserting that learning engagement consists of a multidimensional structure of emotional, behavioral, and cognitive engagement.

The level of student engagement in learning is directly correlated with the learning's quality [15]. Learning engagement refers to the learner's positive and engaged mind in the learning situation and activity. Learning engagement measurement dates back as far as 1980. The main methods of learning engagement measurement include self-feedback reports, external observations, and automated recognition. Self-feedback reporting methods mark student engagement through student self-report or questionnaires, such as Greene et al. [16], who used the Likert scale to investigate student engagement. Self-feedback reports often depend on the learner's apparent understanding of the learning engagement, their level of compliance, and their memory of the learning process, even if they are frequently convenient and useful. External observation is another important method for assessing learning engagement [17]. Still, it requires a certain level of expertise from the observer, which makes it difficult to deal with large amounts of data. The automatic recognition method aims to evaluate student engagement by utilizing trimming technologies such as machine learning and computer vision, which can successfully address the aforementioned shortcomings [18]. Although the automatic recognition method of learning engagement currently has problems such as difficult data collection and annotation, low recognition performance, and low interpretability, we still believe that automatic recognition is promising for the future.

1.3. Video-Based Recognition of Learning Engagement

Compared to the constraints of self-feedback reporting methods and external observation methods (e.g., time-consuming and labor-intensive, unable to handle huge amounts of data, etc.), automated recognition systems perform better. The automated recognition method collects many performance indicators from the student's learning process and evaluates the learning engagement based on the gathered data without interfering with the student's learning process. Video data have evolved into the primary modality used in learning engagement recognition studies due to their convenience of collection and heavy information content [19,20]. There are additional examples of engagement recognition studies that utilize other modal data types such as images [21], audio [22], and physiological data [23].

In this study, we concentrated on learning engagement recognition work based on video data (see Table 1). Gupta et al. [24] proposed the DaiSEE dataset and used traditional Long-term Recurrent Convolutional Networks, C3D, and other networks for four classification learning engagement predictions. Zaletelj et al. [19] proposed a large-scale analysis mechanism of student classroom behavior data obtained by the Kinect One sensor, which can estimate the level of student attention and engagement in the classroom and give teachers feedback on instructional evaluation based upon which teachers can adjust instruction in a way that is tailored to students to support learning performance. Huang et al. [25] proposed an engagement recognition network (DERN) based on temporal convolution, Bi-directional Long Short Term Memory, and an attention mechanism for the DAiSEE dataset. Abedi et al. [26] used the hybrid end-to-end network of ResNet (Residual Network) and TCN (Temporal Convolution Network) to analyze the original video sequences, and the results outperformed other approaches for the same dataset. Sümer et al. [20] collected facial video data from 128 students in grades 5–12 in a classroom and utilized three methods—SVM, MLP, and LSTM—to predict student learning engagement using a scale of −2 to 2 to represent off-task to on-task and to compare the engagement levels of students in different grades. Liao et al. [27] extracted facial features from the DAiSEE dataset using a pre-trained SENet and then utilized an LSTM network with a global attention mechanism to predict learning engagement. Mehta et al. [28] proposed a three-dimensional DenseNet self-attentive network, compared the results to current methods for two- and four-classification metrics, and verified the network's robustness using the EmotiW dataset.

Although learning engagement measurement had garnered attention before the pandemic, its widespread growth was nonetheless a result of the epidemic. Deep learning, a branch of machine learning that uses data for feature learning with artificial neural networks, has emerged as a major feasible approach to learning engagement automated recognition. The models chosen by current deep learning methods for learning engagement mostly focus on the temporal features of students' behavioral performance, but it is also a simple use. It has become a consensus among researchers that videos of students' facial expressions are the most representative data of student learning engagement. Still, there is no standard paradigm for handling the data. In addition, the evaluation of existing methods is mostly based on the accuracy and mean square error, which is intuitive but lacks a certain degree of comprehensiveness.

Table 1. Automatic recognition of learning engagement.

Research	Year	Data	Method	Setting	Accuracy
Gupta et al. [24]	2016	DAiSEE	LRCN	Online learning	57.9%
Zaletelj et al. [19]	2017	posture, expression	DT, KNN	watch Lectures	-
Kaur et al. [29]	2018	in-the-wild	LSTM	watch videos	-
Huang et al. [25]	2019	DAiSEE	DERN	Online learning	60.0%
Abedi et al. [26]	2021	DaiSEE	ResTCN	Online learning	63.9%
Sümer et al. [20]	2021	posture, expression	SVM, DNN	Traditional classroom	-
Liao et al. [27]	2021	DAiSEE	DFSTN	Online learning	58.84%
Mehta et al. [28]	2022	DAiSEE, EmotiW	DenseNet	Online learning	63.59%

1.4. Dataset for Engagement Recognition

Most studies based on open-access database learning engagement measures are based on HBUC [30], DAiSEE (Dataset for Affective States in E-Environments) [24] and in-the-wild datasets [29]. The HBUC data were collected from thirty-four people from two distinct pools; nine men and thirty-five women. Individuals in both pools participated in Cognitive Skills Training research coordinated by a Historically Black College/University (HBCU) and the University of California (UC). The DAiSEE dataset is a multi-label video classification dataset made up of 9068 video clips from 112 subjects with labels for boredom, confusion, engagement, and frustration. Each label is represented by level 0 (very low), level 1 (low), level 2 (high), and level 3 (very high). Of these, the number of engagements is 61, 459, 4477, and 4071, respectively. The in-the-wild dataset included 78 people and 195 movies (each lasting around 5 min), collected in unrestricted settings such as computer laboratories, dorm rooms, open spaces, and so on. Labels of in-the-wild are disengaged, barely engaged, normally engaged, and highly engaged. The labels in the DAiSEE and "in-the-wild" were determined by crowdsourcing, while human experts were used for labeling in the HBCU. Considering differing labeling standards might result in unclear engagement labels; some research excludes data with ambiguous labels, which improves the results' accuracy but reduces the data's amount and variety. In addition, there is no dataset of learning engagement for Chinese students.

Additionally, it is more difficult to collect data because various learning environments, learning tasks, and student objects have different data-gathering and processing methods. So, the learning engagement data gathered via the collection are typically small samples. In conclusion, the data utilized in current learning engagement research range in terms of data unit duration, annotators differences, labeling criteria, and data collection processes, making it difficult to develop learning engagement recognition systematically. Data may be aligned by researchers using a variety of data processing techniques, but before undertaking a study, the researcher must discuss and set up the data annotation process.

1.5. Problem Statement

After the above description, the main problems of learning engagement recognition are currently as follows:

I   How to construct a more realistic dataset of online learning engagement due to the lack of publicly available datasets?
II How to improve the automatic recognition results of deep learning-based learning participation for practical applications?
III How should learning engagement results help teachers develop teaching intervention strategies?

1.6. Contributions

This study built an online learning engagement dataset of videos of students recruited from a university in Wuhan, Hubei Province. Learning engagement cues were used to establish the tri-categorized label for this dataset. Based on this dataset, we investigated the automatic recognition method of students' learning engagement in online learning scenarios through the BiLRCN network. Finally, we analyze and discuss the results, explore the feasible methods for the automatic recognition of learning engagement, and propose future research directions. The contributions of our work can be summarized as follows:

- We created a dataset for the learning engagement of Chinese students that is more quantifiable, interpretable, and annotated by multiple engagement cues. The dataset consists of online learning videos of Chinese students, with a video duration of 10 s.
- We introduced the Bi-directional Long-Term Recurrent Convolutional Neural Networks (BiLRCN) framework for recognizing engagement from videos. This method focuses on the sequential features of learning engagement using the TimeDistributed layer, and its effectiveness has been verified on the self-build dataset.

The rest of this article is structured as follows: Section 2 describes the processing of the collected dataset, which includes the collection process, annotation criteria, etc. Section 3 describes the bidirectional long-time convolutional network introduced in this study. Section 4 shows this experiment's experimental metrics and results and the comparison with the results of the other five state-of-the-art methods. Section 5 is a discussion of these results. Finally, conclusions and possible future research directions are given in Section 6.

2. Dataset Construction

2.1. Data Collection

An HD webcam (Logitech C930c, 1920*1080, 30 Fps) was mounted on a laptop computer and utilized to collect video data from students engaging in online learning. For this study, 58 undergraduate or graduate students between the ages of 21 and 25 were recruited; 42 females and 16 males. They spanned six majors, including educational technology, computer science, psychology, and more. We used OBS software (Open Broadcaster Software) to perform screen recordings of students' computers during the experiment to guarantee that they executed the learning tasks assigned. Additionally, we used a unique custom software program to record videos of the students' faces and their body parts, and the recorded films served as the raw data. Apart from being required to be in front of the computer, students were not constrained in any other manner.

Three online learning tasks were given to the participants in this experiment:

- Watch a one-minute, thirty-second medical video, then answer one easy multiple-choice question about the content within the allotted four minutes;
- Read documents related to machine learning material (accuracy and recall) and finish 9 challenging calculation questions with an 8-min time constraint based on the material;
- Answer two multiple-choice questions based on the content after watching a 6-min English video on the development of facial recognition. The participants in this exercise have a 7-min time constraint.

Besides completing the learning tasks, participants were also required to rate the difficulty of the learning tasks and indicate whether they had been exposed to the tasks' material. Before the experiment, student subjects were informed of the experimental procedure and the requirements of the experiment. It can reduce the Hawthorne effect by allowing students breaks before the experiment begins and between each task. Five staff members directed the experiment, but they did not interfere with the participants' experiment operation. After the experiment, students were asked to use the recorded video to recall each full minute of engagement. All student subjects featured in the video signed an informed consent form before the experiment, and each student subject provided only age, gender, and major as their identifying information. The experiment is shown in Figure 1.

Excluding the lost or missed videos during the experiment, we gathered 1073 min of raw video data (saved in avi format and encoded in H264 format). To align the data for subsequent data annotation, we used the FFmpeg tool to crop the videos after the initial data screening to obtain 6308 raw 10-s videos.

Figure 1. Data Collection. (**a**) Experimental procedure; (**b**) Experimental example.

2.2. Data Annotation

Three annotators with experience in learning engagement annotation performed the annotation work in this study. Before starting the data annotation work, the annotators systematically learned the annotation classification and criteria and completed the reliability assessment before the annotation. Based on the common trichotomous classification used in contemporary learning engagement recognition research, the data labels in this study were separated into three groups, namely low engagement, engagement, and high engagement (marked by 0, 1, and 2 from low to high, respectively). Low engagement indicates that the student is not engaged in the learning content or there is a clear indication of engagement in other non-learning content; engagement shows that learners are involved in the learning process, but this involvement is limited and susceptible to interruption; high engagement entails complete engagement in the learning process and a high level of stability under disturbance. Annotators were asked to use the intensity and proportion of brief learning engagement cues (see Table 2) observed in students' videos to determine the level of learning engagement.

Table 2. Distribution of online learning engagement dataset.

Cue	Student's Performance
Low Engagement	The vision drifts or leaves the computer. The gaze is dull, the expression is sleepy, blinks more often, or appears to raise and lower the head and turn the head.
Engagement	The line of sight is basically on the screen, the eye movement is small, the line of sight jumps out of the screen and flashes back quickly, the number of blinks is high, the expression is normal, the head and body posture is more upright, and the line of sight returns to the screen quickly after the presence of a clear head-down keyboarding action.
High Engagement	The head posture remains stable, the eyes are focused on the screen, the eyes are wide open, the eyes stare at the screen for a long time, or the eyes swing regularly. The expression is more serious, there is a tight frown or pursed mouth movement, and the body leans forward significantly.

Eye movement-related cues were used as the primary cue in labeling, followed by facial expressions, body movements, and pre-and post-temporal states to determine the degree of engagement. Given the annotation's subjective nature, the annotators considered the student subjects' self-feedback results on the annotation. Annotation quality control was performed through an MV (Most Voting) strategy and repeated annotation through collective discussion.

To facilitate the subsequent training, validation, and testing of the model, we disorganized the order of the labeled video data and divided the training, validation, and testing sets in the ratio of 6:2:2. The final distribution of the data is shown in Table 3. Unique subject numbers index the data, and subject 042 is used as an example; Figure 2 shows the partial performance of different engagements of this subject (chosen 10 frames).

Table 3. Distribution of online learning engagement dataset.

Label	Train	Valid	Test	Sum
0	766	242	208	1216
1	1162	403	30	1869
2	1982	650	510	3142
sum	3910	1295	1022	6227

Figure 2. Example of online learning engagement dataset. (a) disengagement; (b) engagement; (c) high engagement.

3. Online Learning Engagement Recognition Method

The Long-term Recurrent Convolutional Network (LRCN) [31] is a deep learning network that combines Convolutional Neural Networks (CNN) with Long Short-Term Memory (LSTM) networks. It can process temporal video or single-frame image inputs as well as single-value prediction and temporal prediction, making it an agglomeration network for processing sequential inputs or outputs. LRCN has been widely used in activity recognition, image description, video description, etc. Due to the excellent performance of LRCN, some improvements have been made. For example, Yan et al. [32] proposed bidirectional LRCN for stress recognition, and their results also show that bidirectional LSTM is helpful for video classification.

Given that learning engagement is a process performance, this paper utilized a Bidirectional Long-Term Recurrent Convolutional Network (BiLRCN) that combines a two-dimensional convolutional neural network (2DCNN) packed by a TimeDistributed layer with BiLSTM for learning engagement recognition. Taking video 0191012 in the dataset as an example, the BiLRCN network structure used in this study is shown in Figure 3. The network consists of four main parts, from left to right, video frame input layer, spatio-temporal feature extraction layer, time series learning layer, and determination layer. The model takes the video frame sequence as input and uses a 2D convolutional neural network (2DCNN) wrapped by a TimeDistributed layer to extract the spatio-temporal features. The extracted features are passed through a BiLSTM network for temporal feature learning to obtain the temporal output of the network. Then the final output of the network is obtained through a fully connected layer with softmax as the activation function.

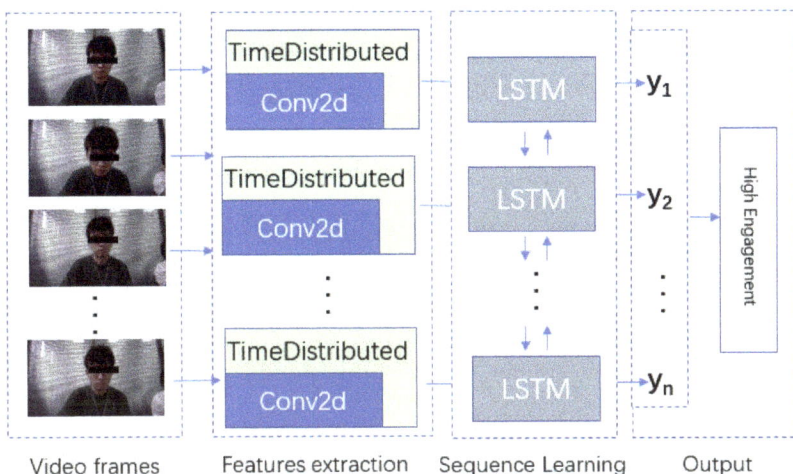

Figure 3. Architecture for BiLRCN.

3.1. Features Extraction

2DCNN means that the convolution kernel performs a sliding window operation in the two-dimensional space of the input image, which preserves the spatial features of individual video frames. The fact is that a 2DCNN can only receive one frame for convolution. While this can help us identify students in an image, we are now seeking to identify students at varying degrees of engagement, which requires numerous frames in a sequence to decide. If we train a convolutional network stream for each image, this requires a lot of computation time, so for sequential video frame sequences, TimeDistributed wrappers can focus on temporal features. The TimeDistributed wrapper enables the wrapped CNN layers to be applied to each time slice of the input, which allows the spatial features extracted by the convolutional network to preserve the temporal feature well. VGG16 inspired us to extract features with convolution-pooling-convolution-pooling, which allows for more nonlinear variations in the data. We employed tiny convolutional kernels (3 × 3) for feature extraction in the CNN section of the model, which inevitably deepens the network depth but also reduces parameters and improves model generalization ability.

3.2. Sequence Learning

Although BiLSTM is mostly used in NLP domains, such as sentence classification, the learning engagement is considered continuous, based upon which we also used BiLSTM for engagement classification. The BiLSTM network may consider the contextual information of learning engagement because it adds the inverse operation to the traditional LSTM, which enables the network to assess depending on students' pre- and post-learning states. BiLSTM will prevent us from classifying the video in real time. Still, it more follows our annotation work on the data than LSTM, i.e., utilizing one label to represent a whole 10 s video.

4. Experiment

4.1. Experimental Setting

The experimental environment for this study was configured with NVIDIA GeForce RTX 3070 8 G (GPU), intel i7-11700 (CPU), and Windows 10 (OS), with Keras (deep learning framework). The input dimension was 40 × 80 × 80 × 3 (NHWC), where 40 represents the length of the input video frame sequence, 80 × 80 represents the image resolution, and 3 represents the three channels of RGB color image; the output dimension was three-dimensional, representing its possibility for three engagement levels, respectively, and the dimension in which the maximum value was taken as the final prediction result.

4.2. Evaluation Metrics

The precision (P) and recall (R) metrics were used to measure model performance in this experiment, and they were computed as given in Equations (1) and (2), respectively.

$$P = \frac{TP}{TP+FP},\qquad(1)$$

$$R = \frac{TP}{TP+FN},\qquad(2)$$

where TP (True Positives) indicates the number of properly predicted target engagements, FP (False Positives) represents the number of mistakenly predicted target engagements, and FN (False Negatives) represents the number of target engagements that were not successfully identified.

4.3. Experimental Results

In the same experimental setting, this study compared the performance of different methods on our dataset, and the results are shown in Table 4 and Figure 4. In Figure 4, the horizontal rows show the real category of the video, the vertical columns show the model's predicted category, and the brackets represent the recall R of the current category.

Table 4. Classification results obtained by BiLRCN, LRCN, ResTcn, C3D, Xception, and SlowFast. The best results are expressed in bold. 0: Low engagement; 1: Engagement; 2: High engagement.

Method	$P_{overall}$	P_0	P_1	P_2	R_0	R_1	R_2
BiLRCN (ours)	**66.24%**	46.63%	55.32%	**73.12%**	**61.39%**	**52.96%**	82.16
LRCN [31]	63.01%	57.85%	53.56%	68.65%	33.65%	51.97%	81.57%
ResTCN [26]	61.65%	54.55%	51.46%	67.09%	37.50%	41.45%	**83.53%**
C3D [33]	56.46%	**62.50%**	55.85%	56.40%	7.21%	25.33%	95.10%
Xception [34]	62.04%	46.93%	52.65%	71.83%	51.44%	39.14%	80.00%
SlowFast [35]	61.94%	47.56%	**61.09%**	67.05%	37.50%	50.00%	79.02%

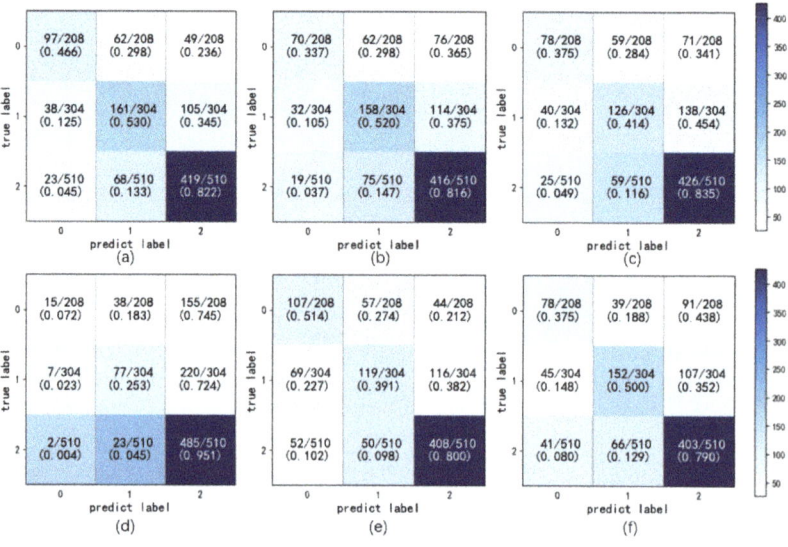

Figure 4. Confusion matrix for experimental results, (**a**) BiLRCN, (**b**) LRCN, (**c**) ResTCN, (**d**) C3D, (**e**) Xception, (**f**) SlowFast.

Compared to other methods, the accuracy of BiLRCN and LRCN is higher, and the accuracy and recall of BiLRCN in different categories are higher than those of LRCN, demonstrating that learning engagement as a process performance and considering its temporal features for assessment can effectively improve the accuracy. However, there is still space for improvement in deep learning, which could be due to the following factors: the first is that manual features were not extracted before the experiment, which will increase the noise in the training data; and the second is that the videos in the dataset are all adult learning videos, and the performance of adults when they learn may be more implicit, which will also raise the difficulty of judgment.

When comparing the results of different engagements, the results are more likely to be high engagement because the model's learning effects for different learning engagements are also imbalanced due to the uneven distribution of the dataset. The precision and recall of high engagement are generally and significantly higher than those of low engagement and engagement. The high precision means that the model is more accurately judged for high engagement because the continuous performance of students in the high engagement state is less variable than that of low engagement and engagement. Although high recall might lead to false detection, it also implies that the model will detect every conceivable high engagement, making the distinction between high learning engagement (high engagement) and low learning engagement (low engagement, engagement) more obvious. Teachers' instructional interventions are primarily addressed to students with low learning engagement [36] in practice, making the use of recall to evaluate the results of learning engagement measures more appropriate. Furthermore, most engagement false detection is high rather than low because of judging the students' internal cognitive processes solely through external observation of video data.

5. Discussion

Some of the arguments for the experimental results will be explained and discussed in this section. We found that the accuracy results of the automatic recognition of video-based learning engagement do not perform as well as the classification in other domains. Although the experimental results have been analyzed, a few points still need to be discussed after comparison with other studies.

5.1. Discussion of Experimental Results

Sample imbalance promotes unbalanced results. Regardless of the method used, the results show that the category with more training samples performs better in the testing stage. While we believe that the sample imbalance in the self-built dataset is realistic, the phenomenon would also show that misclassifying uncommon samples does not significantly impact the overall precision. So a general phenomenon in the experimental results is that the categories with a higher number in the training set perform better in the recognition results. Therefore, improving the precision performance from the algorithmic perspective requires focusing on categories with large data. It is not always proper to enhance numerical performance from an educational standpoint. For example, in [26], Abedi et al. conducted a study on learning engagement recognition methods based on DAiSEE. Although their method showed a good improvement in accuracy, it did not work well for the recognition of the few labels. Recall metrics indicate that high engagement is more efficiently and accurately detected in this experiment and that the meaning of recall is more consistent with actual instructional needs, which illustrates the validity of using recall to evaluate our results.

Samples of similar categories are prone to be misclassified. Our dataset identifies different learning engagements based on the proportion and timing of learning engagement cues, which annotators understand, but machines do not. Therefore, the data classification in the dataset is not a complete discrete value, especially between engagement and high engagement, making it difficult for deep learning models to distinguish between them. Therefore, misdetections of 0 (low engagement) and 2 (high engagement) are more likely than 1 (engagement). Although the study by Bergdahl et al. [37] concluded that engagement lacks intrinsic boundaries, it is uncertain for us to judge whether learning engagement is classified as a discrete or continuous value. The advantage of labeling learning videos with engagement cues is that learning engagements are treated as discrete values while maintaining continuity, which facilitates the development of subsequent extension studies. There is no convincing study of learning engagement as continuous values with labeled annotations and open-access datasets.

Learning engagement is appropriate as a process-based, comprehensive assessment. The method considering temporal features outperforms other approaches. Additionally, our method focuses more on temporal contextual features and produces the best results. In our annotation work, annotators make judgments based on continuous behavior. In this study, learning engagement was reported in ten-second intervals, and there is no accepted standard for exactly how long is most accurate. Video-based learning engagement recognition models are mostly end-to-end, reducing labor costs but exposing the model to more noise while learning. Although the difference in the three learning engagements' sequential performance has already been mentioned in earlier sections, they are still negligible compared to other study domains. Since learning engagement can be represented in three dimensions: behavioral, affective, and cognitive, it is more acceptable to consider more fine-grained features for engagement recognition in cases where observable cues are not evident from students during online learning. For example, we can achieve this by extracting more manual features from the video or integrating other modal data.

5.2. Discussion of Learning Engagement Application

Effective and diversified application of learning engagement is required. Teachers' attention cannot match the recognition of learning engagement when teaching online, which requires the integration or adjustment of individual students' online learning engagement. Applying learning engagement efficiently in diverse ways is also a future research direction for us. At the individual level, the evolution of student engagement can be a good indicator of how engaged students are throughout the classroom. We can alert teachers to chronically low-engagement students. At the class level, we can aggregate the overall engagement of all students in the class and promptly notify the teacher when class engagement is generally low. The teacher can increase class interest by selecting simple, attractive learning media or preparing short, clear, and easy-to-understand learning materials. In addition, teachers should regularly assess students' status and intervene with students who have lost interest in learning for a long time.

The relationship between learning engagement and learning performance is worth exploring. Before the study, we thought his performance would probably be higher if a student's engagement status were consistently high and stable. Taking 0082 (student 008 for the second task) and 0032 as examples, 0082's learning engagement was more erratic than 0032's, with 0082 mostly low engagement (0) and engagement (1). At the same time, 0032 was mostly high engagement (2), and, as a result, 0082 did not complete the questions, while 0032 answered eight out of nine questions correctly. In addition, among low-performing students, most of them have low or fluctuating engagement statuses. Some data show the opposite result, and we believe there is an incompleteness in judging students' internal mental activity solely through external performance due to the cognitive dimension of learning engagement.

5.3. Discussion of Future Development

We envision a way to recognize learning engagement without recording raw data, and its application, in reality, requires more in-depth research on the automatic recognition of learning engagement.

More comprehensive datasets rely on more accurate automatic identification methods. The comprehensiveness here refers not only to the comprehensiveness of data types but also to the comprehensiveness of research subjects. There was no significant overall change in adult student performance during this study, making accurate annotation of labels more difficult. The research topic of learning engagement recognition should be expanded to explore the learning engagement characteristics of students at different levels and to create a comprehensive dataset with more explanatory labeling criteria. We believe that improving the performance of the results can be optimized in two parts: data feature extraction and deep learning network construction. In this study, we have shown that considering the temporal features of the learning engagement can improve recognition accuracy, but again we found that some data were wasted. The granularity of feature extraction and the complexity of deep learning networks are the future directions of automatic learning engagement recognition methods based on the video.

We must acknowledge that there are some risks in recognizing learning engagement. The security and ethical issues of educational data are of great importance, which not only requires researchers to maintain the confidentiality of data throughout the process but also requires stronger legislative efforts at the policy level. The data security risk mainly occurs during the data upload and storage process. Therefore, we envisage that in the data upload phase, students download the program with recognition on their computers, perform the recognition locally and upload only the recognition results; in the storage phase, the data should be encrypted and then stored in a private cloud which reduces the data risk since it can be built inside a firewall. Ethical issues of video data are mainly related to collection, representation, storage, and analysis [38]. The authenticity and objectivity of the data collection and representation process need to be paid attention to. We constructed a more realistic experimental environment for the characteristics of the Chinese online learning environment. We referred to the students' self-report for labeling, which, to a certain extent, does not have ethical problems. Storage and analytics are mainly concerned with security-oriented issues, which were also discussed previously.

6. Conclusions

This paper aims to deal with teachers' difficulty in perceiving students' online learning engagement in a timely and accurate way. In this paper, many online learning videos have been collected, and an online learning engagement dataset has been constructed. Furthermore, a deep learning-based engagement recognition method was also introduced in this paper, and we compared the performance of different methods on the dataset based on this method. Finally, we discussed experimental results, learning engagement applications, and future developments. This study could provide teachers with reliable assistance with evaluating student engagement and conducting learning interventions.

However, the present study also has some limitations. We will continue to improve the learning engagement automatic recognition research in the future. First, we will gather data from various stages, situations, and engagement categories, implement data annotation work using more interpretable standards and build a comprehensive learning engagement dataset. Second, we will constantly modify the model to enhance precision by dealing with data imbalance, extracting finer-grained features for learning, and so on. Finally, we will use multimodal data (such as physiological signals) for engagement recognition in the future.

Author Contributions: Conceptualization, Y.M., Y.S. and Y.W.; methodology, Y.W. and Y.M.; software, Y.M.; validation, Y.M., X.L. and Y.W.; formal analysis, Y.M., Y.T., Z.Z. and Y.W.; resources, Y.M., Y.S. and Y.W.; data curation, Y.M., Y.T. and Z.Z.; writing—original draft preparation, Y.M.; writing—review and editing, Y.W., Y.S. and X.L.; visualization, Y.M. and Y.S.; supervision, X.L. and Y.W.; project administration, Y.W.; funding acquisition, Y.W. All authors have read and agreed to the published version of the manuscript.

Funding: This work was supported in part by the National Natural Science Foundation of China under Grant 62277029, the National Collaborative Innovation Experimental Base Construction Project for Teacher Development of Central China Normal University under Grant CCNUTEIII-2021-19, the Humanities and Social Sciences of China MOE under Grants 20YJC880100 and 22YJC880061, the Fundamental Research Funds for the Central Universities under Grant CCNU22JC011, and Knowledge Innovation Project of Wuhan under Grant 2022010801010274.

Institutional Review Board Statement: This research study was conducted in accordance with the ethical standards of the Helsinki Declaration. The Central China Normal University Institutional Review Board (CCNU IRB) usually exempts educational research from the requirement of ethical approval.

Informed Consent Statement: Informed consent was obtained from all subjects involved in the study.

Data Availability Statement: Not applicable.

Conflicts of Interest: The authors declare no conflict of interest.

References

1. Ladino Nocua, A.C.; Cruz Gonzalez, J.P.; Castiblanco Jimenez, I.A.; Gomez Acevedo, J.S.; Marcolin, F.; Vezzetti, E. Assessment of Cognitive Student Engagement Using Heart Rate Data in Distance Learning during COVID-19. *Educ. Sci.* **2021**, *11*, 540. [CrossRef]
2. Pirrone, C.; Varrasi, S.; Platania, G.; Castellano, S. Face-to-Face and Online Learning: The Role of Technology in Students' Metacognition. *CEUR Workshop Proc.* **2021**, *2817*, 1–10.
3. Mubarak, A.A.; Cao, H.; Zhang, W. Prediction of students' early dropout based on their interaction logs in online learning environment. *Interact. Learn. Environ.* **2020**, *30*, 1414–1433. [CrossRef]
4. Wang, K.; Zhang, L.; Ye, L. A nationwide survey of online teaching strategies in dental education in China. *J. Dent. Educ.* **2021**, *85*, 128–134. [CrossRef] [PubMed]
5. Fei, M.; Yeung, D.Y. Temporal Models for Predicting Student Dropout in Massive Open Online Courses. In Proceedings of the 2015 IEEE International Conference on Data Mining Workshop (ICDMW), Atlantic City, NJ, USA, 14–17 November 2015; pp. 256–263. [CrossRef]
6. Pirrone, C.; Di Corrado, D.; Privitera, A.; Castellano, S.; Varrasi, S. Students' Mathematics Anxiety at Distance and In-Person Learning Conditions during COVID-19 Pandemic: Are There Any Differences? An Exploratory Study. *Educ. Sci.* **2022**, *12*, 379. [CrossRef]
7. Liu, S.; Liu, S.; Liu, Z.; Peng, X.; Yang, Z. Automated detection of emotional and cognitive engagement in MOOC discussions to predict learning achievement. *Comput. Educ.* **2022**, *181*, 104461. . [CrossRef]
8. Sutarto, S.; Sari, D.; Fathurrochman, I. Teacher strategies in online learning to increase students' interest in learning during COVID-19 pandemic. *J. Konseling Dan Pendidik.* **2020**, *8*, 129. [CrossRef]
9. Hoofman, J.; Secord, E. The Effect of COVID-19 on Education. *Pediatr. Clin. N. Am.* **2021**, *68*, 1071–1079. . [CrossRef]
10. El-Sayad, G.; Md Saad, N.H.; Thurasamy, R. How higher education students in Egypt perceived online learning engagement and satisfaction during the COVID-19 pandemic. *J. Comput. Educ.* **2021**, *8*, 527–550. [CrossRef]
11. You, W. Research on the Relationship between Learning Engagement and Learning Completion of Online Learning Students. *Int. J. Emerg. Technol. Learn. (iJET)* **2022**, *17*, 102–117. [CrossRef]
12. Shen, J.; Yang, H.; Li, J.; Cheng, Z. Assessing learning engagement based on facial expression recognition in MOOC's scenario. *Multimed. Syst.* **2022**, *28*, 469–478. [CrossRef] [PubMed]
13. Meier, S.T.; Schmeck, R.R. The Burned-Out College Student: A Descriptive Profile. *J. Coll. Stud. Pers.* **1985**, *26*, 63–69.
14. Fredricks, J.A.; Blumenfeld, P.C.; Paris, A.H. School Engagement: Potential of the Concept, State of the Evidence. *Rev. Educ. Res.* **2004**, *74*, 59–109. [CrossRef]
15. Lei, H.; Cui, Y.; Zhou, W. Relationships between student engagement and academic achievement: A meta-analysis. *Soc. Behav. Personal. Int. J.* **2018**, *46*, 517–528. [CrossRef]
16. Greene, B.A. Measuring Cognitive Engagement With Self-Report Scales: Reflections From Over 20 Years of Research. *Educ. Psychol.* **2015**, *50*, 14–30. [CrossRef]
17. Dewan, M.; Murshed, M.; Lin, F. Engagement detection in online learning: A review. *Smart Learn. Environ.* **2019**, *6*, 1. [CrossRef]
18. Hu, M.; Li, H. Student Engagement in Online Learning: A Review. In Proceedings of the 2017 International Symposium on Educational Technology (ISET), Hong Kong, China, 27–29 June 2017; pp. 39–43. [CrossRef]
19. Zaletelj, J.; Košir, A. Predicting students' attention in the classroom from Kinect facial and body features. *EURASIP J. Image Video Process.* **2017**, *2017*, 80. [CrossRef]
20. Sümer, Ö.; Goldberg, P.; D'Mello, S.; Gerjets, P.; Trautwein, U.; Kasneci, E. Multimodal Engagement Analysis from Facial Videos in the Classroom. *IEEE Trans. Affect. Comput.* **2021**. [CrossRef]
21. Zhang, Z.; Li, Z.; Liu, H.; Cao, T.; Liu, S. Data-driven Online Learning Engagement Detection via Facial Expression and Mouse Behavior Recognition Technology. *J. Educ. Comput. Res.* **2020**, *58*, 63–86. [CrossRef]
22. Standen, P.J.; Brown, D.J.; Taheri, M.; Galvez Trigo, M.J.; Boulton, H.; Burton, A.; Hallewell, M.J.; Lathe, J.G.; Shopland, N.; Blanco Gonzalez, M.A.; et al. An evaluation of an adaptive learning system based on multimodal affect recognition for learners with intellectual disabilities. *Br. J. Educ. Technol.* **2020**, *51*, 1748–1765. [CrossRef]
23. Apicella, A.; Arpaia, P.; Frosolone, M.; Improta, G.; Moccaldi, N.; Pollastro, A. EEG-based measurement system for monitoring student engagement in learning 4.0. *Sci. Rep.* **2022**, *12*, 5857. [CrossRef] [PubMed]

24. Gupta, A.; D'Cunha, A.; Awasthi, K.; Balasubramanian, V. DAiSEE: Towards User Engagement Recognition in the Wild. *arXiv* **2016**, arXiv:1609.01885.
25. Huang, T.; Mei, Y.; Zhang, H.; Liu, S.; Yang, H. Fine-grained Engagement Recognition in Online Learning Environment. In Proceedings of the 2019 IEEE 9th International Conference on Electronics Information and Emergency Communication (ICEIEC), Beijing, China, 12–14 July 2019; pp. 338–341. [CrossRef]
26. Abedi, A.; Khan, S.S. Improving state-of-the-art in Detecting Student Engagement with Resnet and TCN Hybrid Network. *arXiv* **2021**, arXiv:2104.10122.
27. Liao, J.; Liang, Y.; Pan, J. Deep facial spatiotemporal network for engagement prediction in online learning. *Appl. Intell.* **2021**, *51*, 6609–6621. [CrossRef]
28. Mehta, N.K.; Prasad, S.S.; Saurav, S.; Saini, R.; Singh, S. Three-Dimensional DenseNet Self-Attention Neural Network for Automatic Detection of Student's Engagement. *Appl. Intell.* **2022**, *52*, 13803–13823. [CrossRef] [PubMed]
29. Kaur, A.; Mustafa, A.; Mehta, L.; Dhall, A. Prediction and Localization of Student Engagement in the Wild. In Proceedings of the 2018 Digital Image Computing: Techniques and Applications (DICTA), Canberra, Australia, 10–13 December 2018; pp. 1–8. [CrossRef]
30. Whitehill, J.; Serpell, Z.; Lin, Y.C.; Foster, A.; Movellan, J.R. The Faces of Engagement: Automatic Recognition of Student Engagement from Facial Expressions. *IEEE Trans. Affect. Comput.* **2014**, *5*, 86–98. [CrossRef]
31. Donahue, J.; Hendricks, L.A.; Rohrbach, M.; Venugopalan, S.; Guadarrama, S.; Saenko, K.; Darrell, T. Long-term Recurrent Convolutional Networks for Visual Recognition and Description. *arXiv* **2014**, arXiv:1411.4389.
32. Yan, S.; Adhikary, A. Stress Recognition in Thermal Videos Using Bi-Directional Long-Term Recurrent Convolutional Neural Networks. In *Neural Information Processing: Proceedings of the 28th International Conference ICONIP 2021, Sanur, Bali, Indonesia, 8–12 December 2021*; Mantoro, T., Lee, M., Ayu, M.A., Wong, K.W., Hidayanto, A.N., Eds.; Springer International Publishing: Cham, Switzerland, 2021; pp. 491–501.
33. Tran, D.; Bourdev, L.; Fergus, R.; Torresani, L.; Paluri, M. Learning Spatiotemporal Features with 3D Convolutional Networks. *arXiv* **2014**, arXiv:1412.0767.
34. Chollet, F. Xception: Deep Learning with Depthwise Separable Convolutions. In Proceedings of the 2017 IEEE Conference on Computer Vision and Pattern Recognition (CVPR), Honolulu, HI, USA, 21–26 July 2017; IEEE Computer Society: Los Alamitos, CA, USA, 2017; pp. 1800–1807. [CrossRef]
35. Feichtenhofer, C.; Fan, H.; Malik, J.; He, K. SlowFast Networks for Video Recognition. *arXiv* **2018**, arXiv:1812.03982.
36. Parsons, J.; Taylor, L. Improving Student Engagement. *Curr. Issues Educ.* **2011**, *14*, 132.
37. Bergdahl, N. Engagement and disengagement in online learning. *Comput. Educ.* **2022**, *188*, 104561. [CrossRef]
38. Peters, M.; White, E.; Besley, T.; Locke, K.; Redder, B.; Novak, R.; Gibbons, A.; O'Neill, J.; Tesar, M.; Sturm, S. Video ethics in educational research involving children: Literature review and critical discussion. *Educ. Philos. Theory* **2020**, *53*, 1–9. [CrossRef]

Disclaimer/Publisher's Note: The statements, opinions and data contained in all publications are solely those of the individual author(s) and contributor(s) and not of MDPI and/or the editor(s). MDPI and/or the editor(s) disclaim responsibility for any injury to people or property resulting from any ideas, methods, instructions or products referred to in the content.

Case Report

Educational Applications of Non-Fungible Token (NFT)

Chih-Hung Wu * and Chien-Yu Liu

Department of Digital Content and Technology, National Taichung University of Education, Taichung 403, Taiwan
* Correspondence: chwu@mail.ntcu.edu.tw

Abstract: With the emergence of non-fungible tokens (NFTs) in blockchain technology, educational institutions have been able to use NFTs to reward students. This is done by automatically processing transaction information and the buying and selling process using smart contract technology. The technology enables the establishment of recognition levels and incentivizes students to receive NFT recognition rewards. According to the Taxonomy Learning Pyramid, learning through hands-on experiences plays a crucial role in attracting students' interest. In this study, we analyzed the potential for using NFTs in education and the current applications of NFTs in society. We conducted a case study and performed a preliminary investigation of the types of NFT applications in the education industry. We then analyzed different education industries using individual analysis combined with SWOT analysis to understand the impact, value, and challenges of NFT applications. The results revealed 10 educational applications of NFT: textbooks; micro-certificates; transcripts and records; scholarships and rights; master classes and content creation; learning experiences; registration and data collection; patents, innovation, and research; art; payment; and deposit. Finally, ways to reduce the negative impact of education NFTs on the sustainable environment are discussed.

Keywords: non-fungible token; NFT; educational applications; sustainable; education technology; blockchain; metaverse

1. Introduction

The global pandemic caused by the COVID-19 virus has been devastating to most industries and countries, and the education sector has also been affected, forcing a shift from face-to-face, on-site education to remote delivery of skills training and academic courses [1]. With the rise of information technology, some emerging intelligent technologies such as artificial intelligence with STEAM (Science, Technology, Engineering, Art, and Math) education [2], affective tutoring technologies [3], emotional intelligence [4], and affective computing [5] to assist education have become an important research topic.

Non-fungible tokens (NFTs) based on a blockchain are a record of ownership of digital assets. An NFT can be considered as a certificate of ownership. NFTs record the ownership of intangible objects and of tangible items [6]. NFTs help address dilemmas when it comes to trading digital contents [7]. Specifically, teachers distribute and sell the teaching materials or books they produce through NFTs. This innovative model helps transform teachers' knowledge into commercially viable products while avoiding piracy [8,9]. NFTs are an emerging application following cryptocurrencies and the rise of blockchain technology.

However, the types of applications and benefits of NFTs to education are still in need of research. NFTs can automatically process transaction information and buying and selling processes through smart contract technology, and it is irreplaceable, indivisible, and unique [10]. Educational institutions can reward NFT entities by establishing recognition levels through incentives so that students can receive NFT rewards when they are recognized, thus increasing the gamification process [1]. Taxonomy learning pyramid enhances the instructional trajectory by considering learning as a continuous process consisting of six structural blocks: classroom exercises, classroom tutorials, homework and assignments,

Citation: Wu, C.-H.; Liu, C.-Y. Educational Applications of Non-Fungible Token (NFT). *Sustainability* **2023**, *15*, 7. https://doi.org/10.3390/su15010007

Academic Editor: Alexander Mikroyannidis

Received: 14 November 2022
Revised: 14 December 2022
Accepted: 15 December 2022
Published: 20 December 2022

Copyright: © 2022 by the authors. Licensee MDPI, Basel, Switzerland. This article is an open access article distributed under the terms and conditions of the Creative Commons Attribution (CC BY) license (https://creativecommons.org/licenses/by/4.0/).

periodic tests, revision lectures, and final tests. In this study, we analyzed both the possibility of combining NFTs with education and the cases in which NFTs are applied in society, and we compared and analyzed the differences in the application of NFT in education and assessed the advantages and disadvantages.

2. Literature Review

2.1. Education and Teaching Methods

According to previous research [11], advanced pedagogy improves teaching and learning outcomes by increasing interactions between teachers and students through the use of multimedia and technology. Blended teaching and learning follow an integrated approach that combines students' interests and teachers' personalities, wherein teachers use their innovative teaching methods to allow students to enjoy freedom in the learning process. Therefore, the application of innovative teaching and learning methods is extremely important. Dale's theory suggests that learners retain more information by "doing" than they do by "listening" or "reading," as shown in Figure 1.

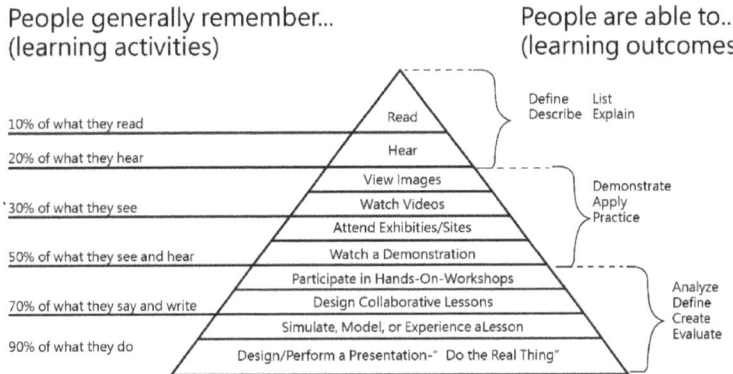

Figure 1. Edgar Dale's cone of learning experience. Source: [11].

NFTs are currently flourishing with art collections, although they can be involved in more than that. The current applications of NFTs in education are discussed in the following sections [8,12].

2.2. Textbook

Teachers distribute and sell the teaching materials or books they produce through NFTs. This innovative model helps transform teachers' knowledge into commercially viable products while avoiding piracy [8]. The sharing economy that relies on a blockchain platform is a new way to create value and distribution channel for various types of digital content such as e-books owned by individuals or organizations. In reality, numerous businesses are increasingly encrypting to protect their products from economic damage resulting from data forgery [13].

2.3. Micro-Credentials

Micro-certificates are a symbol of certification through skill verification. At present, certificates are usually provided in the form of printed or electronic badges. However, the biggest challenge is to verify and evaluate the value of the certificate [14,15]. Students' educational records can be encrypted, updated, and easily verified by any individual or organization with blockchain technology [9].

In addition, EchoLink is working on a blockchain platform to store verified skills and experiences. This platform stores users' professional profiles that can be used as a verified resume for the user [16]. Moreover, previous studies pointed out that graduates can find their diploma as a tamper-proof certificate that is strictly preserved and secured on blockchain-based systems of educational institutes [17,18].

2.4. Transcripts and Records

In addition to certificates, school transcripts can be obtained in the form of tokens, which include grades, reports, and annual achievements. If a student wants to view college transcripts, they must pay a fee to the school to get them printed [14]. Blockchain-based systems such as the Ethereum and DISCIPLINA platform were developed to store grades, track student achievements, and propose a system to create verified personal profiles based on academic and professional achievement [16,19]. These personal data can be linked to companies with recruitment needs.

2.5. Scholarships and Entitlements

If scholarships are provided to students in the form of tokens, students can exchange these tokens for online courses, event tickets, resource visits, counseling sessions, and other purposes [19]. Recent studies reported that students can receive rewards in the form of cryptocurrencies, which can be used to purchase goods and services because the universities accept tokens in their coffee shops, canteens, bookstores, and course enrollment [20,21].

2.6. Masterclass and Content Creation

Content creators who are interested in offering courses, curricula, video lectures, etc. can also benefit from NFTs. When content creators develop a course and sell it to a market or university, they can add the option of secondary sales royalties. If the NFT method is used, each transaction is recorded in the blockchain ledger [22]. Thus, publishers can set the commission and royalty for resale [23] and avoid pirated books, and students can easily find the required e-books through electronic data on the books, e.g., the BooksGoSocial website (https://booksgosocial.com/, accessed on 30 March 2022). They can not only buy books on the platform but also resell and publish their own books. Hence, creators and consumers can easily sell and buy digital contents that exist as an NFT. Each NFT is associated with a physical or digital asset that designates the asset's legal value, ownership, transaction rights, and other attributes [24]. Each NFT that is recorded on a blockchain system will not be tampered with or superseded in the digital encryption ecosystem [25].

In regard to classroom management, an online learning platform helps increase interaction between students and lecturers based on blockchain technology, which helps manage the quality of examinations or student assessments after each course, and it simultaneously improves the quality of system [19]. The blockchain system NOTA (a novel online teaching and assessment scheme using blockchain) can be used for course implementation and can maintain teaching quality and assessment fairness during courses and examination [26].

2.7. Learning Experiences

Learning is achieved not only through grades or accumulated knowledge but also through experience [27–29]. For example, the difficulties and solutions encountered by a surgeon during his first surgery, a fireman putting out a fire, and a salesman completing his first sale serve as key learning experiences in these different professions. If NFTs can be combined with these experiences, it may result in lifelong learning. Blockchain technology has opened up a great prospect for integrating academic teaching activities at schools with professional practices [18–21]. This contributes to a greater educational environment and an educational system that meets the actual needs of society [9].

With a technology platform managed by a blockchain system, students have the opportunity to choose from a variety of courses in the curriculum. By accumulating bitcoins on the system, students actively learn and interact with their lecturers. Blockchain-dependent technology enhances learning by allowing students to apply a range of career skills that help them think critically, work in groups, and solve problems [14].

2.8. Registration and Data Capturing

At present, most students use a student card to prove their identity, and if they want to prove that they are students in other areas, they need to apply to the school for a separate proof of attendance [16]. However, teachers do not have the relevant proof of teaching in a school. Thus, if NFTs are combined with one's identity, the identity of students and teachers can be marked in the form of NFTs and display detailed information through data of the smart contract, which can prevent identity theft and quickly prove identity [30].

The nature of the peer-to-peer topology in blockchains helps reduce security risks in the education sector. The blockchain's data are constantly updated during development, and the new cryptographic algorithm is simultaneously sent separately to the other users. These characteristics make personal data difficult to tamper with [18]. Blockchain technology can bring significant benefits to education, including high transparency and security at a low cost, improving student assessment, and improving control of stakeholders' identification [20].

2.9. Patenting, Innovations, and Research

Patent registration is not only a time-consuming process but is also high cost. Use of NFT has significant potential in the field of intellectual property [31]. It can promote transparency and open up new markets for innovators to effectively commercialize their inventions. With the help of the unique features of blockchain technology, the NFT can provide protection of intellectual properties [32] while the patent holders wait for the government to grant their products more formal protection. Therefore, NFTs in particular and blockchain in general will make it easier to buy and sell patents, providing new opportunities for educational institutions, businesses, and inventors to profit from these patents, which are encrypted, stored, and protected on the blockchain system [33].

Some inventors, creators, and experts have lost credit for their work simply because they could not patent it. NFTs can use the blockchain immutability principle to provide credit to the owner [34] and embed the metadata and parameters of this invention into irreplaceable tokens. For example, in 2021, UC Berkeley announced the public tokenization of patents for two Nobel Prize-winning inventions and auctioned off CRISPR-Cas9 gene editing and cancer immunotherapy, which were finally sold successfully for 22 ETH [35].

2.10. Arts

Currently, the creative development and production of art and architecture must consider the reality of life, such as the need to consider the structure in the production of architecture. If NFTs are combined with art, scholars of art, symbolism, and architecture can move their works or ideas into the world of NFT to build, develop, and create more products [22,36], which are irreplaceable assets [37].

The trend of NFT application in the creation of artworks has developed at an unprecedented scale. Based on the integration of art and technology, Wang (2022) [38] showed that NFT artworks have the following features: (1) Decentralized characteristics—on the basis of blockchain technology, artwork creators and purchasers can directly interact with each other instead of depending on an intermediary. This also improves transparency about the lifetime of the artwork. (2) Unique characteristics—the identification of NFT artworks is unique through blockchain's tamper-proof technology. This feature aims to make artworks more valuable because of scarcity in the market while also helping to protect NFT artworks from art forgery. (3) Reselling right—this is a solution to protect the rights of the creators. In detail, artists may be entitled to the benefits associated with the circulation of their artworks. (4) Separation of ownership—with NFTs, the proprietorship can divide the NFT artwork in the form of crypto and can be distributed to the collectors or other stakeholders.

2.11. Payments and Storage

The school needs to make payments, students need to use cash or credit cards to pay, and the school needs to deposit the money in the bank or other places for safekeeping [30]. Thus, the greater the number of monetary transactions, the higher the security risk. A new way of payment called smart contract on blockchain helps improve the efficiency of cash flow administration. Smart contract has been described as a secure and trustworthy platform for automated execution of contract terms and payments without requiring an intermediary (e.g., a bank). This leads to savings in transaction costs and other fees that would otherwise have to be paid to a third party [39].

Regarding the fees and credit transfers in an educational setting, educational institutions can adopt the EduCTX system to activate the transfer process using non-fungible tokens [20]. These tokens are based on blockchain technology, so they are highly secure and reliable. Non-fungible tokens can be used in any digital forms for units of learning such as diplomas, certificates, and courses. Each school should have its own EduCTX system to address the process in a secure way. Likewise, Williams (2019) [40] argued that by paying with a cryptocurrency called Woolf Tokens, which works on the basis of blockchain-based systems, the students would pay lower tuition and the lecturers may receive higher salaries.

2.12. Top 10 NFT Applications Mentioned in the Literature

Combining education through NFTs reduces the need for physical infrastructure and face-to-face interaction and enables students worldwide to transcend geographical barriers, which allows greater participation in education [1]. If education can take advantage of this feature, it will generate a new method of learning for students and teachers. The top 10 NFT applications in education and NFT education products are summarized in Table 1.

Scholars, such as LEDU [8] and DelSignore [12], have put forward their views on the application of NFTs to education. Based on the above discussion, we can infer that education combined with NFT is the most promising method to store transcripts and records. Most scholars have indicated that transcripts and records are easily lost and forgotten, making it impossible to retain data for a long period of time [41,42]. Therefore, if each piece of information is recorded in an NFT, it can be easily accessed and used as an educational file. When interviewing with companies or other schools, information can be quickly displayed without the need to apply for a complicated process. Another promising method is art. As NFTs provide art and collectibles for preservation, they can be combined with education, and students' creations can be sold as art on the Internet, which increases the visibility and scope of appreciation for students' works. In the field of education, copyright protection for students' works and projects is usually overlooked [43]. If these can be combined with NFTs, students' post-creation rights can be effectively protected.

Table 1. Top 10 NFT applications in education.

NFT Application Papers:	[A]	[B]	[C]	[D]	[E]	[F]	[G]	[H]	[I]	[J]	[K]	[L]	[M]	[N]	[O]	[P]	[Q]	[R]
Textbooks	✓				✓								✓				✓	
Micro-certificate	✓	✓				✓	✓	✓	✓				✓	✓	✓			
Transcripts and records		✓	✓	✓	✓	✓	✓			✓	✓	✓			✓			✓
Scholarships and rights (entitlements)	✓	✓				✓			✓	✓	✓		✓					
Master class and content creation		✓					✓		✓		✓			✓				
Learning experience		✓		✓			✓	✓	✓	✓	✓	✓						
Registration and data collection	✓	✓							✓					✓				
Patents, innovation, and research	✓															✓		
Art	✓		✓	✓	✓	✓										✓		
Payment and deposit	✓								✓				✓					✓

Note: The letter in [ ] denotes a code of the cited references. The symbol ✓ denotes that the NFT application is mentioned in the paper. [A]: [8]; [B]: [12]; [C]: [44]; [D]: [45]; [E]: [46]; [F]: [47]; [G]: [48]; [H]: [18]; [I]: [19]; [J]: [20]; [K]: [14]; [L]: [21]. [M]: [9]; [N]: [40]; [O]: [16]; [P]: [33]; [Q]: [6]; [R]: [30].

The above analysis shows that education combined with NFTs is primarily used for data preservation. In the past, transcripts were provided to students and parents in a paper form, but paper is easily lost or destroyed by external factors such as getting wet or burnt. Later, online transcripts were introduced to provide access to grades and records, which also allowed data to be preserved. However, data cannot be opened and reviewed at different stages due to different locations of accessing grades. The rise of NFT, which provides a platform for complete data retention, has made it easy to retain transcripts.

3. Research Design and Methodology

This study conducted a scoping review and a case study with a preliminary investigation of NFT education applications. In this study, we first conducted a scoping review to analyze the educational applications of NFT based on a review of the literature. Second, we conducted a case study to preliminarily investigate the possibility of combining NFTs with education and to introduce the cases in which NFTs are applied in the current society. Third, this study analyzed the differences before and after the application of NFTs in education as well as their advantages and disadvantages. Finally, this study discussed the idea of NFT application in education based on the aforementioned differences following NFT application and based on its advantages and disadvantages.

This study reviewed papers regarding NFT educational applications published in the ScienceDirect database (SDOS), Science Citation Index (SCI), and Social Science Citation Index (SSCI). The review procedure followed that of a previous study [5] that reviewed technology-assisted topics. Two researchers with NFT experience used the keyword 'NFT education application' or 'NFT educational application' to collect relevant research papers from the database. Because NFT in educational applications is an emerging topic, we also search all articles in google scholar and the google search engine to broaden our review database.

Based on the abovementioned data collection procedure, the selected NFT educational application papers included articles published in the following academic journals: *Applied Sciences*, *Business Horizons*, *Computer Applications in Engineering Education*, *Concurrency and Computation: Practice and Experience*, *European Journal of Education*, *Journal of Computing in Higher Education*, *Journal of Higher Education Policy and Management*, *Mobile Information Systems*, *Scientific Reports*, and *Sustainability*. The major contributing countries included England (2), Serbia/Romania/Portugal (2), China (2), United Arab Emirates (1), Mauritius (1), Malaysia (1), Austria (1), Saudi Arabia (1), Spain/USA/England (1), America (1), Hong Kong (1), and Iran/China (1). The number of papers regarding NFT educational applications are shown in Figure 2. Regarding the growing trend of research on NFT in education, only a few studies in the research topic of NFT educational applications were found from before 2020. The number of NFT studies has increased since 2021 due to flourishing of NFT research.

This study conducted an analysis of the frequency of keywords from the full text of NFT papers as shown in Table 2. The top five most critical keywords were blockchain (53), NFT (51), educator (44), technology (29), and digital (24). In addition, the terms asset (13), manage (11), and secure (10) were also important concepts in NFT education research. The word clouds based on keyword analyses in the abstract and full text are depicted in Figures 3 and 4, respectively.

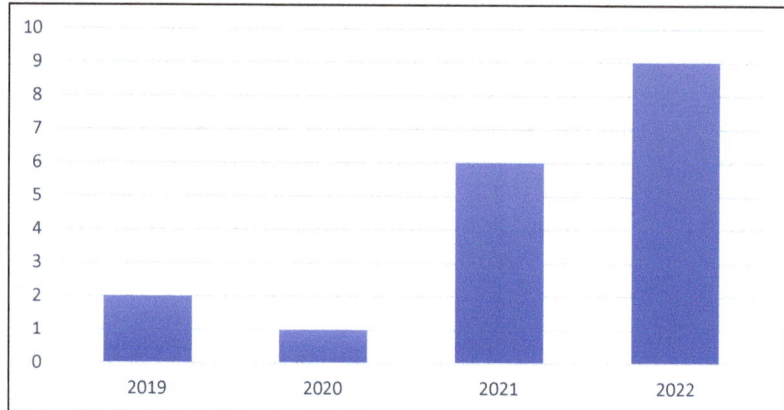

Figure 2. Number of papers regarding educational applications of NFTs.

Table 2. Frequency analysis of keywords in NFT education papers (full text).

Ranking	Keywords	Count	Ranking	Keyword	Count
1	Blockchain	53	11	World	14
2	NFT	51	12	Non	13
3	Educator	44	13	Fungible	13
4	Technology	29	14	Asset	13
5	Digital	24	15	Manage	11
6	Student	23	16	New	11
7	Use	22	17	Based	11
8	Token	18	18	Unique	10
9	Data	15	19	Secure	10
10	Learning	15	20	Application	10

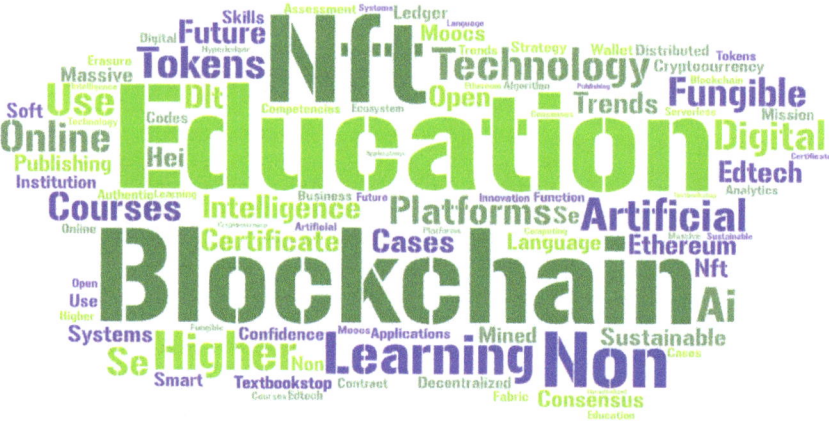

Figure 3. Abstract word cloud.

Figure 4. Full text word cloud.

4. Results

We first conducted a case study with a preliminary investigation of the types of NFT applications in the education industry. We then analyzed different education industries using individual analysis and combined it with SWOT analysis to understand the impact, value, and challenges of NFT applications.

4.1. Current Education versus Education Combined with NFT

Current educational applications of NFT include certificate, transcripts and records, scholarship, content creation, learning experiences, registration, patents, art, and payment and deposits [8,12,44–48]. Comparisons of current educational applications and NFT educational applications are summarized in Table 3. Educators can record certificates, transcripts, and learning records through NFTs and give NFTs to students in the form of scholarships, which students can exchange for courses by using a wide range of applications

Table 3. Comparison of current education and education combined with NFT.

	Current Education	**Education Combined with NFT**
Certificate	Printed on paper, the authenticity of which is difficult to discern	Unique electronic barcode for easy verification
Transcripts and records	Application process is cumbersome and difficult to retain for a long time	Easy application process for long-term storage
Scholarship and entitlements	Cash or coupon payment	Issued in the form of tokens, which can be exchanged for courses
Content creation	Publishers do not get a share of secondary sales of books	Publishers can set the commission and royalty for resale
Learning experience	Your learning experience is not recorded	Learning experiences can be recorded and made available for viewing by those who request them
Register	Use of paper or student ID card, making it difficult to distinguish the real from the fake	Registration using NFT method, data display details to avoid identity theft
Patents	The application requirements are complicated, and some people have lost credit for their work because they could not apply for a patent	Sell directly on the Internet through NFT, lowering the threshold for publication and providing credit to owners through NFT
Art	Need to consider the reality of the environment	You can enjoy your thoughts in the NFT world
Payment and deposits	Payment by credit card or cash and deposited in a bank or other institution	Payments can be made with NFT and stored in NFT books

4.2. NFT Application in Education: Study Abroad

The process of studying abroad is more complicated than studying locally and requires more information such as a university application and visa. Many people give up the opportunity to study abroad if they are not well prepared or do not know enough information about the content. NFT helps guide students through the entire process, informs them of the documents they need to provide, helps them evaluate suitable colleges and universities, and helps them apply for visas (Figure 5).

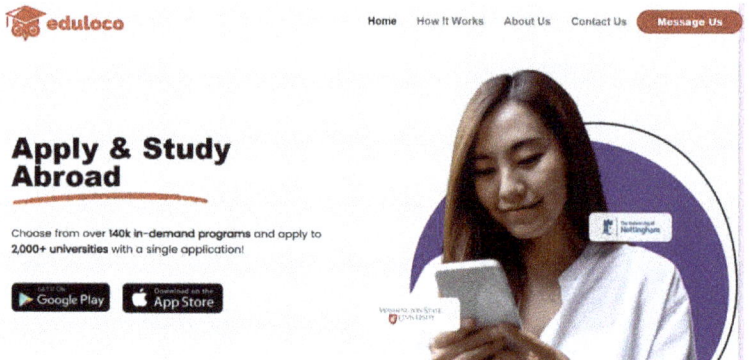

Figure 5. Eduloco interface. (Source: https://www.eduloco.com/, accessed on 23 April 2022).

4.2.1. Eduloco Value

Eduloco offers students a choice of different subjects and schools, and it provides detailed descriptions of the school of their choice, such as the campus environment, number of students, living expenses, and housing facilities. The website also provides scholarship descriptions of different schools for students in need of reference (Figure 6).

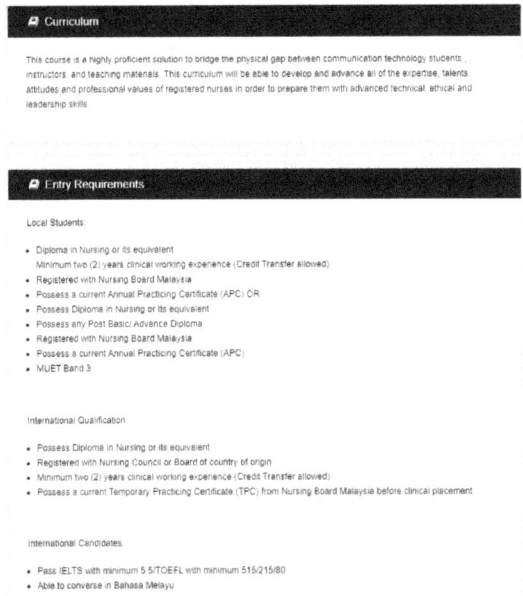

Figure 6. Interface description. (Source: https://www.eduloco.com/course/bachelor-of-nursing-sciences-hons-open-distance-learning-mode/, accessed on 23 April 2022).

4.2.2. Eduloco Applied in the Metaverse

The outbreak of COVID-19 led to a rapid rise in digital teaching methods. For example, the Korea Advanced Institute of Science and Technology (KAIST) offers its students a 60:40 ratio of live Zoom courses and pre-recorded courses. Students and parents do not need to drive far distances to attend the campus but can conveniently rely on the virtual space in the metaverse [48]. Although it may take some time for craft-based subjects to enter the world of the metaverse at this stage, virtual campuses are gradually being implemented, thus allowing students worldwide to attend classes from home regardless of distance.

4.2.3. Analysis of Strengths and Weaknesses

Before combining NFTs, studying abroad and attending school is necessary for face-to-face interactions and observation of each other's emotion through expressions or body movements. If students have questions, they can ask the teacher directly during or after class, and the teacher can use the time after class to ask students about their learning status. The disadvantage is that students have to wake up early to go to class and need to make some preparations before they go abroad, including obtaining a passport, daily necessities, and accommodation. Moreover, they may not be able to adapt to the environment in a completely unfamiliar place.

The disadvantage of online learning is that it is not as intimate as physical learning in terms of interaction with classmates. Moreover, because teachers do not know exactly how students are learning, if they are falling asleep in class, or not understanding the course, teachers cannot obtain a good solution. In addition, because students can study better in a familiar environment, they tend to lose the learning experience and foreign culture experience when studying abroad.

4.3. NFT Application in Education: Borrowing and Trading Books

In the past, students who needed to borrow books would go to the library, but it was not easy to find the books they wanted because of the limited number of books in the library. Moreover, not all locations had libraries. With the development of the Internet, books can be presented in an electronic form, which provides more books than libraries. The Internet has enabled students to borrow books at home, which is more convenient than borrowing from libraries.

BooksGoSocial is a website related to book trading, and it differs from traditional book trading in that BooksGoSocial uses the NFT method to sell books through the WAX blockchain, which is a certified carbon-neutral blockchain as seen on the BooksGoSocial website. The WAX blockchain uses 125,000 times less energy per transaction than its closest competitor, solving an environmental problem that exists with other blockchains.

In addition, traditional book sales consider a book sold for a certain price, which can have a high carbon footprint if the book is printed and sent to the purchaser's home. However, an online trading platform makes the transaction more convenient and faster, as anyone can trade at any time and place and can easily and quickly publish their works on the website (Figure 7).

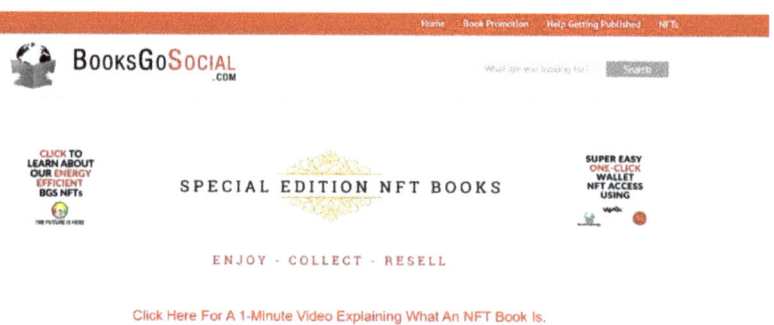

Figure 7. BooksGoSocial interface. (Source: https://booksgosocial.com/, accessed on 23 April 2022).

4.3.1. BooksGoSocial Value

On this website, users can enjoy additional stories, related video content and other valuable content, read e-books on any device, buy NFT books through their WAX wallet, or sell books through resale. Additionally, buyers with NFT books can visit the private members area, in which users can post comments and reviews, find other unique content, sell NFTs, view details of giveaways and sweepstakes, view collector points used to purchase NFTs, and visit and share the site. Finally, buyers who are not satisfied with their NFT books can get a refund within seven days.

4.3.2. Analysis of Strengths and Weaknesses

One of the reasons why many people would like to buy books is to touch or smell the books when flipping through them, but the disadvantage is that it takes more time to buy. If they are purchased on the Internet, you need to wait for the delivery; thus, if you need books urgently, you need to go to a physical store to look for them or choose a store with faster delivery time.

Using e-books with NFTs, all transactions are conducted on the blockchain, which saves a lot of transaction time, and the ownership of the e-book is protected. Therefore, everyone can post their articles and books on the NFT marketplace. However, the method of book publication may cause some problems, such as the quality of the books is not guaranteed due to the lack of a content and quality check conducted by book publishers and the protection of e-book recreation.

4.4. NFT Application in Education: Youth Technology Development

Recently, Taiwan began using the NFT approach to facilitate youth technical development through the website Bees2be. Around 20,000 different types of bees are available on Bees2be, which aims to celebrate the friendship between Lithuania and Taiwan and to encourage the technical development of youth in rural areas of Lithuania. Bees2be has also set several milestones and will start to achieve them once it reaches the target sales as shown in Table 4.

Table 4. Percentage target commitment.

Goal Commitment	%
Paying tribute to the mothers of the bees- Give back to the bee mothers and start preparing and building the infrastructure for the worker bees to work smoothly in the future	25%
The worker bees get to work- Start helping talented kids who may not have the opportunity to learn programming languages by providing them with a personal computer and programming language classes	50%
It's time to buzz together- Exclusive club open	75%
A new, unique collection of NFTs will be released- All beekeepers will have the exclusive opportunity to receive these NFTs made by children and supported and nurtured by beekeepers on the eco-friendly SOLANA blockchain.	100%

4.4.1. Bees2be Value

Bees2be.io is an NFT collection of 20,000 unique little bees that aims to celebrate the friendship between Lithuania and Taiwan and encourage the technological development of rural youth. According to the Bee2be website, some regions in Lithuania are technologically advanced, but many regions are still struggling to provide young people with specific education and opportunities. Bees2be hopes to change this situation through this NFT collection. Bees2be is an NFT-based education and training program aimed at helping children in the Lithuanian region by providing them with the necessary equipment and training to encourage and strengthen their digital literacy and assist in technological development. According to their development strategy, they will begin providing equipment and training to promising children once 50% of the NFTs are sold in order to help these young people better understand digital opportunities, programming, and NFT production. As part of this development strategy, the children will create their own new NFT works, which will be released for subscription after the Bees2be series is sold out.

The Beee2be NFT project is dedicated to providing regional children with the equipment and training they need to encourage and enhance their digital literacy and enable technological development. By purchasing a bee, buyers can ensure that their children have everything they need to learn to program a language and open up more opportunities and possibilities for their future (Figure 8).

Figure 8. Bee2be interface. (Source: http://bees2be.io/zh/, accessed on 23 April 2022).

4.4.2. Bees2be Sales Analysis

The price of each Bees2be is ETH 0.18, and the character consists of 13 different accessories: background, chain, earrings, exclusivity, eyes, eyewear, face, fur, hands, legs, mouth, stinger, and wings. The rarer the accessory, the lower the percentage, and the purchase method is provided in the Bees2be website. The work will be presented in Opensea. Currently, 113 people are enlisted to buy a bee character (Figure 9).

Figure 9. Bee2be character. (Source: http://bees2be.io/zh/, accessed on 23 April 2022).

4.4.3. Analysis of Strengths and Weaknesses

Before combining with NFT, in traditional education and training programs, buyers only purchased course content services. The advantage of this was being able to know the detailed information of the beneficiaries, such as their region and school. However, a possible disadvantage is that there are no other added values and services.

After combining with NFT, there are other added value to course content. The buyer acquires unique digital bee artwork and receives exclusive membership in a club whose benefits and gifts are set to increase over time. Those purchasing a bee will be supporting a great project to improve the digital literacy of youth in rural Lithuania. However, the disadvantage is that the buyer may not be able to obtain detailed information about the beneficiaries.

4.5. NFT Is Used in Education: Art

OMIA is an online learning platform that offers a variety of courses, such as handicraft and painting, and the creation of art and collectibles is the most common way to present NFTs [10]. According to OMIA's introduction, the platform has four features: online courses that can be watched at any time, diversified contents that are enjoyable and stress-relieving, masterclasses that are prepared from the beginning to the end, and handcrafted courses with purchased materials.

4.5.1. OMIA Learns the Value of the East and West

OMIA learning is divided into many categories: personal growth, education and learning, health and wellness, handicraft DIY, life hobbies, finance and investment, painting and illustration, photography and art, and workplace skills. Prices range from TWD 300 to TWD 15,000. Recently, due to the epidemic, online learning has become the primary way for children to learn on their own. OMIA's Learn Something video course platform has launched a special "parent-child online learning" activity to encourage parents to learn with their children. This creates a common topic between children and parents to make parent-child relationships more harmonious. Parents post their children's achievements on the Internet for everyone to enjoy. Simultaneously, the metaverse and blockchain have also attracted attention, and students can sell their works in the form of NFT. The sales of drawing courses on OMIA's Learning Stuff platform have doubled compared with that of the same period in the previous year (Figure 10).

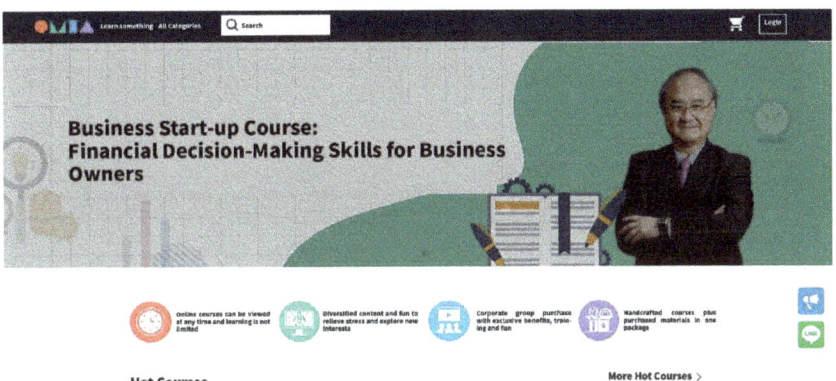

Figure 10. OMIA learning interface. (Source: https://www.omia.com.tw/, accessed on 23 April 2022).

4.5.2. Taiwan Arts University Advancement Universe and Casting NFT

In 2022, to encourage students' creativity, National Taiwan University of Arts combined NFT with ecology and selected 512 outstanding works under the theme of "Portrait of a Fish" to be sold as public service NFTs. Approximately 50% of the proceeds were donated to young art talents recommended by the National Museum of Art Education, and the other 50% was used for innovative work in technology and art [49], with the hope of motivating more art lovers to publish their works through this method.

4.5.3. Art Revolution Taipei

This exhibit was the first of its kind to present NFT-encrypted art in 2022, allowing everyone to enter and experience the new world of the metaverse. The New Art Revolution Taipei advocates that "Art is not only culture, but also education and promotion, it should never be limited to commercial interests, and the aim is to bring more artists into the world of NFT and to combine it with the metaverse so that artworks can be presented in a more diversified way" [50].

4.5.4. Gust and Her Friends

The abovementioned application of NFT has been combined with artworks, e.g., Gust and her friends, and it differs from other works on the market in that it adopts a lightweight commercial model with a limited edition of 10 rare releases and with unique collector's significance and value. This artwork was the creation of a six-year-old girl named MIUMIU who transformed her life story into the character "Gust", and each "Gust" has a special character, such as the love of candy and tooth decay, as well as a symbolic meaning behind the name. The purpose of this is to encourage each child to create their art universe character and to continue utilizing their creative energy [51] (Figure 11).

Figure 11. Gust and her friends. (Source: https://opensea.io/collection/nftboard-today-collection, accessed on 18 March 2022).

According to the introduction on the NFTBoard website, the ultimate goal of Gust is as follows: the first stage is to build children's meta-universe, the second stage is to create a model that presents generational love, the third stage is to encourage more children to join the project through Gust and Meta Kids Fun, the fourth stage is to hope that these Gust IP and new characters would help the real world through positive images, and finally, the fifth stage is to gather all the characters to build children's meta-universe (Figure 12).

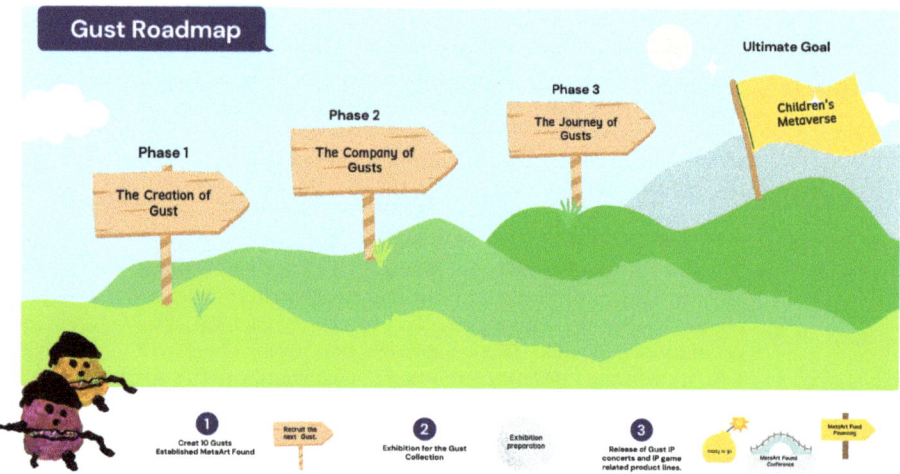

Figure 12. Gust roadmap. (Source: https://nftboard.today/gust-nft/, accessed on 18 March 2022).

4.5.5. Analysis of Strengths and Weaknesses

The biggest change that followed the combination of art with NFT is the restriction on the artworks' exhibition. Before the combination of art with NFT, the works were placed in real-world exhibitions, meaning the realistic aspect was considered and the works were touched by buyers for a more realistic experience. The possible disadvantage is pirated copies of the artwork because there is lack of public authentication. Moreover, it is difficult for the creators of the sold works to gain extra revenue.

After the combination of issuing artwork NFT, the works are sold on the NFT marketplace, eliminating the problem of searching the exhibition and reducing the exhibition fee. Thus, the creator is able to create more interesting works, and the works are located in cyberspace all the time. In the meta-universe, artworks are transformed into digital works with NFTs that are able to provide interaction functions with buyers. However, NFT artwork which may the possible problems the other creators to copy, steal, hack, and re-create the works.

4.6. NFT Applied to Educational: Historical Works

The National Palace Museum recently collaborated with Lootex, a Taiwan-based NFT trading platform, and released a series of co-branded NFT graphic art products with eight original illustrators to promote the museum's collection to the world.

The Palace emphasized that the purpose of issuing NFT merchandise was not the value of the transaction but the educational and promotional significance; they hope to use the secondary creation of cultural relics to attract more people to understand the works and regain an understanding of the content of the relics. They also aimed to play with traditional art in an innovative way through the digital technology network so that the Palace art is widely shared and so the Museum cultural and creative products the derived from national treasures open up a new page and lead the trend of NFT art goods in the country (Figure 13).

Figure 13. Lootex secondary creation works. (Source: https://lootex.io/zh-TW/stores/national-palace-museum-shop, accessed on 20 April 2022).

4.6.1. KANDER'S China Royal Art

According to the Opensea platform, KANDER'S is a strategic partnership with Steven Rockefeller's team. ENFT sis the heirloom art treasures that exist in the world (Figure 14).

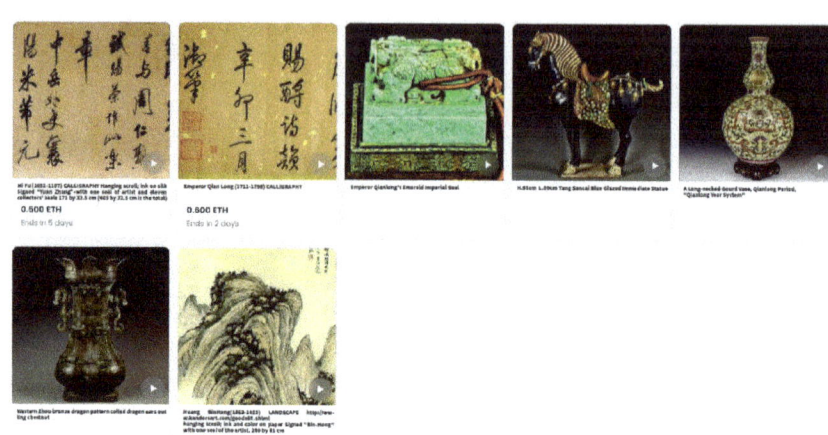

Figure 14. KANDER'S China royal art treasures. (Source: https://opensea.io/collection/kanders, accessed on 20 April 2022).

4.6.2. Analysis of Strengths and Weaknesses

Before the combination with NFT, the National Palace collection was placed in the same location so that visitors could directly view the complete content of the works on site. Because of the onsite introduction, they could understand the content of the works more comprehensively, but if they wanted to view the works, they had to go directly to the site, which took more time and money. In contrast, after the combination with NFT, visitors could directly view the works on the Internet. However, unlike onsite displays, no introduction of the work is provided by a specialist, which may result in a lack of deep understanding of the work. The greatest advantages of using secondary creation for the sale of the Palace collection are that it can increase the visibility of the work, make the work gathering more interesting, and attract people to buy the product, thereby increasing the revenue. However, because the secondary creation is different from the original style, the buyer may not be able to understand the original appearance of the artwork or the designer's original design concepts and philosophy.

5. Discussion and Conclusions

Finally, in this section, we present the discussion and conclusions of our study. The first section discusses and summarizes the educational applications of NFT across various industries. The conclusions are described in the next section.

5.1. Discussion

This section summarizes educational applications of NFT among various industries. The different activity styles between current educational applications and NFT educational applications are also discussed.

5.1.1. Education Industry

The comparison of current versus NFT educational activity in education industry are summarizes in Table 5. In study aboard programs, the most remarkable difference between the metaverse and education is whether students and teachers have to physically go to school. If the metaverse is not integrated, students and teachers have to go to the school campus to attend and teach classes, respectively. If combined with the metaverse, students and teachers can easily attend from home. In addition, another challenge for students studying abroad is accommodation. Metaverse integration allows students to continue to live in their original house.

Table 5. Current versus NFT educational activity (education industry).

Industry	Current	With NFT
Education industry		
Study abroad		
In class	Students must attend class in the classroom	Students take classes from home via the Internet
Accommodation	Students must spend additional money to find a home	Students can live in their homes
Teachers	Teachers must be present in the classroom	Teachers can take classes online
Buy Books	Money must be used to purchase	Available for purchase with NFT tokens
Textbook		
Book category	Physical books as the main, e-books as a supplement	E-Books
Book purchase	Purchase in physical stores or online	Purchase directly on the Internet
Book sales	Sold on the Internet or at second-hand bookstores	Sold directly on the Internet
Book publishing	Many things need to be prepared before publishing	Can be directly posted on the Internet for sale
Publishers	No revenue from books sold	Royalties can be set for sale to gain revenue
Energy consumption	Printed and delivered to the purchaser's home to produce a carbon footprint	Electricity consumption for casting
Course/Training		
Buy course	Purchase a course to study.	There are other added values besides learning after purchase
Member services	No member service	Exclusive club membership

Regarding textbooks, the difference between the book trade before and after the combination with NFT is both virtual and physical. Prior to combination with NFT, commercial processes mainly took place in stores, where sellers and buyers met directly to perform services. After combination with NFT, service encounters can be conducted both in stores and e-commerce systems. Before the combination, it was not easy to publish books. However, if combined with the NFT form of sales, everyone can easily publish their work. Because NFT books retain access to copyright, the copyright fee can be set when selling so that when the books are resold, authors can continue to receive royalties, and the publisher has protection and feedback.

Energy consumption is not similar. The energy required before the combination with NFT (from trees and the carbon footprint of transporting books) and after the combination with NFT (from casting costs and electricity consumption) would be very different. What needs to be assessed after the combination with NFT is how to inflict minimum damage to the environment and address the energy consumption problem.

Regarding online courses and training, the combination of educational methods with NFT is more optimal. Once training and education are integrated with NFT, learners not only own the course content but also receive additional values such as Bee2be, which enables learners to help people in Lithuania receive education and training, to obtain a unique bee, and to enjoy the exclusive membership services of the club.

5.1.2. Art Industry

The comparison of current versus NFT educational activity in architecture industry and art industry are summarizes in Table 6. In the architecture industry, architects need to consider the environment and structure when designing a house, but if combined with NFT, their works can be sold in cyberspace through NFTs. Because it is a completely virtual space, there is no need to consider any realistic aspects in the design, which can create more interesting works.

Table 6. Current versus NFT educational activity (art industry).

Industry	Current	With NFT
Architecture industry		
Architects		
Creation	Creating in the real world.	Creating in a new space or cyberspace.
Sale	No further revenue can be earned after the work is sold.	Royalties can be set to be earned upon resale.
Value	Collecting and reselling.	Collect, resell, and interact with buyers.
Art industry		
Art and historical works		
Watch	Visitors have to visit the exhibition (e.g., National Museum).	Directly viewing on the web.
Works sale	Artists usually sell their works through art exhibitions.	The works can be sold on cyberspace.

In the art industry, before the integration of NFT, a visit to the physical exhibition such as National Palace Museum was required to view the collection. After the integration of NFT, one can directly view it on the Internet. The works have been transformed from purely exhibition, but after using NFT, creators can sell their works on cyberspace, thus increasing the source of revenue.

5.2. Conclusions

NFTs provide several contributions to education, which includes (1) issuance and management of certificates, (2) protection of rights, (3) rewards for teachers, (4) impact beyond the classroom, and (5) privacy control [47]. NFTs are suitable for diplomas, recognition, or certificates and can securely verify academic credentials and achievements. The major benefits of NFTs in education are that NFTs use tokens of blockchain technology thus reducing the possibility of falsification while verifying student records and credits. The other benefit is that the NFT provides an effective tool for tracking students' learning progress and safely preserving educational data [47].

Educational Applications of the NFT's Impact on Sustainability

The NFT concept can develop and be involved in a sustainable education game. NFT game-based learning is able to cultivate a player's motivation to accept the concept of sustainability. Zeedz is one of the sustainable NFT games that provides players the opportunity to collect and grow little monsters and fight in the real world to combat climate change [52]. The player can learn about the reality of climate change and the relevance of three concepts of sustainability: awareness and knowledge of sustainability, financial resource allocation for sustainability, and motivation to become more sustainable.

NFTs themselves do not cause any environmental impact, but an impact on the climate can be caused by how NFTs are minted. NFTs may be harmful to the environment depending on how they are produced (minted), such as in highly energy-intensive minting processes for NFT production or NFT transactions. Minting an NFT usually utilizes the leading blockchain (Ethereum) with a proof-of-work blockchain. To reduce the environment impact, blockchain platforms can use the proof-of-stake operating method to generate NFTs with low energy intensity and without a negative impact on the climate. Other ways to improve sustainability are to use renewable energy, invest in renewable energy, invest in experimental technologies, and choose NFTs minted on proof-of-stake blockchains [53].

Educators can use green or renewable energy to mint educational NFTs. The education NFT issue can select energy-efficient blockchain technology to issue their NFT certification. Notable proof-of-stake blockchains include Ethereum, Solana, Algorand, Cradano, and Tezos. The minted education NFTs can be placed in the well-known NFT marketplace Opensea, which uses Ethereum.

A previous study [1] proposed a high-level educational establishment system of NFTs wherein able educators create their own certificates or reward system. This study proposed a new energy-efficient educational establishment system of NFTs based on [1] as shown in Figure 15. In the educational establishment step, educators have to create their own blockchain wallet called the establishment's wallet to save the NFT transaction information. The educators can use green or renewable energy to create the blockchain wallet. In the step of issuing NFTs, the educators can use proof-of-stake blockchains such as Ethereum to mint the NFT and can issue NFT awards for students to reduce energy-intensive consumption. Educators can place their NFTs in Opensea, which uses proof-of-stake blockchain technology for students to collect their NFT collections such as certifications or awards. Our proposed energy-efficient system for educational applications of NFTs is shown in Figure 15.

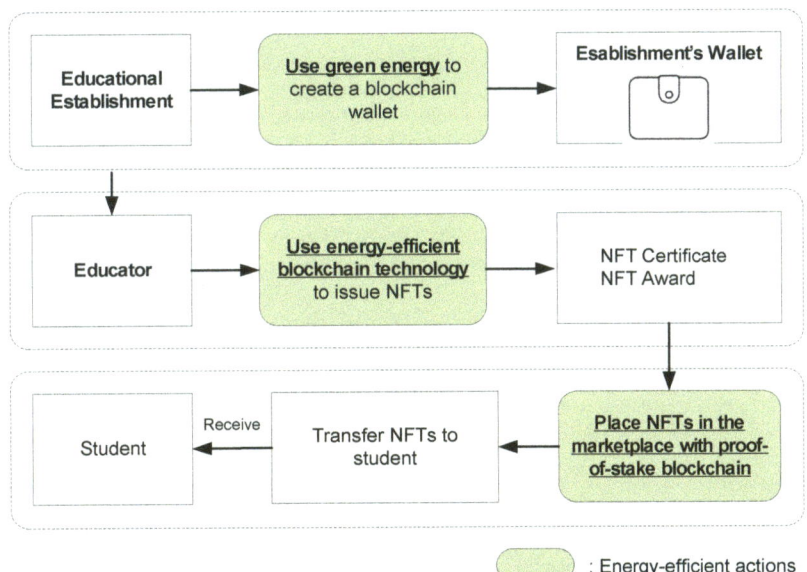

Figure 15. The proposed energy-efficient educational NFT establishment system.

From the above analysis, it can be concluded that the greatest value of combining with NFTs is to transform real-world objects into virtual ones. Progress and creativity in education have also been observed. NFT applications are not only limited to the purchase and sale of artwork but can also be expanded to the level of certificates, awards, and scholarships, making the process of education swifter and more convenient.

However, people still love real products that can be touched. More research is required to propose ways to balance the development of technology and energy and to enable most people to accept the combination of education with NFTs.

Funding: This research was funded by National Science and Technology Council with grant number [MOST 110-2511-H-142 -008 -MY2].

Institutional Review Board Statement: Not applicable.

Informed Consent Statement: Not applicable.

Data Availability Statement: Not applicable.

Conflicts of Interest: The authors declare no conflict of interest.

References

1. Elmessiry, A.; Elmessiry, M.; Bridgesmith, L. NFT student teacher incentive system (NFT-stis). *SSRN Electron. J.* **2021**, 4648–4656. [CrossRef]
2. Wu, C.-H.; Liu, C.-H.; Huang, Y.-M. The exploration of continuous learning intention in STEAM education through attitude, motivation, and cognitive load. *Int. J. STEM Educ.* **2022**, *9*, 1–22. [CrossRef]
3. Wu, C.H.; Lin, H.-C.K.; Wang, T.-H.; Huang, T.-H.; Huang, Y.-M. Affective Mobile Language Tutoring System for Supporting Language Learning. *Front. Psychol.* **2022**, *13*, 833327. [CrossRef]
4. Abdullah, A.H.; Julius, E.; Suhairom, N.; Ali, M.; Talib, C.A.; Ashari, Z.M.; Kohar, U.H.A.; Rahman, S.N.S.A. Relationship between Self-Concept, Emotional Intelligence and Problem-Solving Skills on Secondary School Students' Attitude towards Solving Algebraic Problems. *Sustainability* **2022**, *14*, 14402. [CrossRef]
5. Wu, C.-H.; Huang, Y.-M.; Hwang, J.-P. Review of affective computing in education/learning: Trends and challenges. *Br. J. Educ. Technol.* **2015**, *47*, 1304–1323. [CrossRef]
6. Wilson, K.B.; Karg, A.; Ghaderi, H. Prospecting non-fungible tokens in the digital economy: Stakeholders and ecosystem, risk and opportunity. *Bus. Horizons* **2021**, *65*, 657–670. [CrossRef]
7. Hofstetter, R.; de Bellis, E.; Brandes, L.; Clegg, M.; Lamberton, C.; Reibstein, D.; Rohlfsen, F.; Schmitt, B.; Zhang, J.Z. Crypto-marketing: How non-fungible tokens (NFTs) challenge traditional marketing. *Mark. Lett.* **2022**, *33*, 705–711. [CrossRef]
8. LEDU. 2021. Available online: https://ledu.educationecosystem.com/top-10-use-cases-of-nft-in-education/ (accessed on 20 March 2022).
9. Lizcano, D.; Lara, J.A.; White, B.; Aljawarneh, S. Blockchain-based approach to create a model of trust in open and ubiquitous higher education. *J. Comput. High. Educ.* **2020**, *32*, 109–134. [CrossRef]
10. Dowling, M. Fertile LAND: Pricing non-fungible tokens. *Financ. Res. Lett.* **2021**, *44*, 102096. [CrossRef]
11. Thusi, N.; Costa, K. A Practical Representation of NFT Pedagogy in a Learning Environment. 2020. Available online: https://osf.io/preprints/africarxiv/pjxvd/ (accessed on 30 November 2022).
12. DelSignore, P. 2021. Available online: https://medium.com/the-future-of-learning-and-education/nfts-in-education-957ce434047c (accessed on 18 March 2022).
13. Khan, U.; An, Z.Y.; Imran, A. A Blockchain Ethereum Technology-Enabled Digital Content: Development of Trading and Sharing Economy Data. *IEEE Access* **2020**, *8*, 217045–217056. [CrossRef]
14. Kuleto, V.; Bucea-Manea-Țoniș, R.; Bucea-Manea-Țoniș, R.; Ilić, M.P.; Martins, O.M.D.; Ranković, M.; Coelho, A.S. The Potential of Blockchain Technology in Higher Education as Perceived by Students in Serbia, Romania, and Portugal. *Sustainability* **2022**, *14*, 749. [CrossRef]
15. Palma, L.M.; Vigil, M.A.G.; Pereira, F.L.; Martina, J.E. Blockchain and smart contracts for higher education registry in Brazil. *Int. J. Netw. Manag.* **2019**, *29*, e2061. [CrossRef]
16. Deenmahomed, H.A.M.; Didier, M.M.; Sungkur, R.K. The future of university education: Examination, transcript, and certificate system using blockchain. *Comput. Appl. Eng. Educ.* **2021**, *29*, 1234–1256. [CrossRef]
17. Capece, G.; Ghiron, N.L.; Pasquale, F. Blockchain Technology: Redefining Trust for Digital Certificates. *Sustainability* **2020**, *12*, 8968. [CrossRef]
18. Chen, Y. The Impact of Artificial Intelligence and Blockchain Technology on the Development of Modern Educational Technology. *Mob. Inf. Syst.* **2022**, *2022*, 1–12. [CrossRef]
19. Panagiotidis, P. Blockchain in Education—The Case of Language Learning. *Eur. J. Educ.* **2022**, *5*, 66–82. [CrossRef]
20. Alammary, A.; Alhazmi, S.; Almasri, M.; Gillani, S. Blockchain-Based Applications in Education: A Systematic Review. *Appl. Sci.* **2019**, *9*, 2400. [CrossRef]
21. Bucea-Manea-Țoniș, R.; Martins, O.M.D.; Bucea-Manea-Țoniș, R.; Gheorghiță, C.; Kuleto, V.; Ilić, M.P.; Simion, V.-E. Blockchain Technology Enhances Sustainable Higher Education. *Sustainability* **2021**, *13*, 12347. [CrossRef]
22. Ante, L. Non-fungible token (NFT) markets on the Ethereum blockchain: Temporal development, cointegration and interrelations. *Econ. Innov. New Technol.* **2022**, 1–19. [CrossRef]
23. Kaczynski, S.; Kominers, S.D. How NFTs create value. *Harv. Bus. Rev.* **2021**, *10*.
24. Chohan, R.; Paschen, J. NFT marketing: How marketers can use nonfungible tokens in their campaigns. *Bus. Horizons* **2021**. [CrossRef]
25. Morkunas, V.J.; Paschen, J.; Boon, E. How blockchain technologies impact your business model. *Bus. Horiz.* **2019**, *62*, 295–306. [CrossRef]

26. Cheriguene, A.; Kabache, T.; Kerrache, C.A.; Calafate, C.T.; Cano, J.C. NOTA: A novel online teaching and assessment scheme using Blockchain for emergency cases. *Educ. Inf. Technol.* **2021**, *27*, 115–132. [CrossRef] [PubMed]
27. Griffin, J. Learning science through practical experiences in museums. *Int. J. Sci. Educ.* **1998**, *20*, 655–663. [CrossRef]
28. Mullen, J.; Byun, C.; Gadepally, V.; Samsi, S.; Reuther, A.; Kepner, J. Learning by doing, High Performance Computing education in the MOOC era. *J. Parallel Distrib. Comput.* **2017**, *105*, 105–115. [CrossRef]
29. Tran, T.A.; James, H.; Pittock, J. Social learning through rural communities of practice: Empirical evidence from farming households in the Vietnamese Mekong Delta. *Learn. Cult. Soc. Interact.* **2018**, *16*, 31–44. [CrossRef]
30. Liang, X.; Zhao, Q.; Zhang, Y.; Liu, H.; Zhang, Q. EduChain: A highly available education consortium blockchain platform based on Hyperledger Fabric. *Concurr. Comput. Pr. Exp.* **2021**, e6330. [CrossRef]
31. Zanella, G.; Liu, C.Z.; Choo, K.-K.R. Understanding the Trends in Blockchain Domain Through an Unsupervised Systematic Patent Analysis. *IEEE Trans. Eng. Manag.* **2021**, 1–15. [CrossRef]
32. Savelyev, A. Copyright in the blockchain era: Promises and challenges. *Comput. Law Secur. Rev.* **2018**, *34*, 550–561. [CrossRef]
33. Bamakan, S.M.H.; Nezhadsistani, N.; Bodaghi, O.; Qu, Q. Patents and intellectual property assets as non-fungible tokens; key technologies and challenges. *Sci. Rep.* **2022**, *12*, 1–13. [CrossRef]
34. Shin, D.D. Blockchain: The emerging technology of digital trust. *Telemat. Inform.* **2019**, *45*, 101278. [CrossRef]
35. Sanders, R. UC Berkeley Will Auction NFTs of Nobel Prize-Winning Inventions to Fund Research. Berkeley News. 2021. Available online: https://news.berkeley.edu/2021/05/27/uc-berkeley-will-auction-nfts-of-nobel-prize-winning-inventions-to-fund-research/ (accessed on 10 November 2022).
36. Tsang, Y.P.; Wu, C.H.; Lee, C.K.M. BlockTrainHK: An online learning game for experiencing blockchain concepts. *SoftwareX* **2022**, *19*, 101167. [CrossRef]
37. Dowling, M. Is non-fungible token pricing driven by cryptocurrencies? *Financ. Res. Lett.* **2022**, *44*, 102097. [CrossRef]
38. Wang, T. A Deep Learning-Based Programming and Creation Algorithm of NFT Artwork. *Mob. Inf. Syst.* **2022**, *2022*, 1–10. [CrossRef]
39. Ahmadisheykhsarmast, S.; Sonmez, R. A smart contract system for security of payment of construction contracts. *Autom. Constr.* **2020**, *120*, 103401. [CrossRef]
40. Williams, P. Does competency-based education with blockchain signal a new mission for universities? *J. High. Educ. Policy Manag.* **2018**, *41*, 104–117. [CrossRef]
41. Ngoasheng, C.; Ngoepe, M.; Marutha, N.S. Sounds like a broken record: Preservation and access of audio-visual records at the South African broadcasting corporation radio. *Glob. Knowledge Mem. Commun.* **2021**, *71*, 383–397. [CrossRef]
42. Rakemane, D.; Mosweu, O. Challenges of managing and preserving audio-visual archives in archival institutions in Sub Saharan Africa: A literature review. *Collect. Curation* **2020**, *40*, 42–50. [CrossRef]
43. Thomas, P. 2021. Available online: https://medium.com/@peterjthomas/nfts-in-education-fashion-fad-or-truly-non-fungible-252a662d4bce (accessed on 30 May 2022).
44. StartupBeat. Hong Kong Economic Journal Financial News. 2022. Available online: https://www1.hkej.com/features/article?q=%23%E8%99%9B%E5%B9%A3%E5%8B%95%E6%85%8B%23&suid=451160638 (accessed on 30 November 2022).
45. Johnson, S. How Will NFTs Disrupt the Education Sector? Cyptocurrency. 2022. Available online: https://biz.crast.net/how-will-nfts-disrupt-the-education-sector/ (accessed on 12 November 2022).
46. Bambury, S. 3 Ways NFTs Will Disrupt the Education Sector. 2022. Available online: https://www.gesseducation.com/gess-talks/articles/3-ways-nfts-will-disrupt-the-education-sector (accessed on 30 November 2022).
47. Vilchis, N. How Do NFTs Support Education? Institute for the Future of Education. 2022. Available online: https://observatory.tec.mx/edu-news/how-do-nfts-support-education (accessed on 30 November 2022).
48. Cheng, J. 2021. Available online: https://www.eduloco.com/blog/how-nft-metaverse-will-accelerate-virtual-education/ (accessed on 15 March 2022).
49. V, C. Yahoo News. 2022. Available online: https://tw.news.yahoo.com/%E8%87%BA%E8%97%9D%E54%A7%E9%BC%93%E5%8B%B5%E5%AD%B8%E7%94%9F%E8%87%AA%E7%94%B1%E5%89%B5%E4%BD%9C%E7%99%BC%E8%A1%8Cnft-114730350.html (accessed on 22 May 2022).
50. Hong, S.T. China Times News Network. 2022. Available online: https://www.chinatimes.com/realtimenews/20220407001850-260405?ctrack=pc_main_rtime_p05&chdtv&fbclid=IwAR1EGTz12fAmjIwHHR2Ic-HZlZFFg_95GKbhB8_PC3z_jlmQWTd9iNSo4ao (accessed on 10 April 2022).
51. NFTBoard. 2022. Available online: https://nftboard.today/nftboard-gust-and-her-friends/ (accessed on 31 March 2022).
52. Zeedz. 2022. Available online: https://www.zeedz.io/?gclid=CjwKCAjwtp2bBhAGEiwAOZZTuMlh8i_YdxJRJathsn16pvMsI3-c0reWhnVSQIRLuG9HpDeQoGjDHhoC9FgQAvD_BwE (accessed on 30 November 2022).
53. Investopedia. Do Non-Fungible Tokens (NFTs) Harm the Environment? 2022. Available online: https://www.investopedia.com/nfts-and-the-environment-5220221 (accessed on 10 November 2022).

Disclaimer/Publisher's Note: The statements, opinions and data contained in all publications are solely those of the individual author(s) and contributor(s) and not of MDPI and/or the editor(s). MDPI and/or the editor(s) disclaim responsibility for any injury to people or property resulting from any ideas, methods, instructions or products referred to in the content.

Article

Eye Movement Analysis and Usability Assessment on Affective Computing Combined with Intelligent Tutoring System

Hao-Chiang Koong Lin [1], Yi-Cheng Liao [1,*] and Hung-Ta Wang [2]

1 Department of Information and Learning Technology, National University of Tainan, Tainan 700, Taiwan
2 COPLUS Inc. Tainan Branch, Tainan 702, Taiwan
* Correspondence: edcr0328@gmail.com

Abstract: Education is the key to achieving sustainable development goals in the future, and quality education is the basis for improving the quality of human life and achieving sustainable development. In addition to quality education, emotions are an important factor to knowledge acquisition and skill training. Affective computing makes computers more humane and intelligent, and good emotional performance can create successful learning. In this study, affective computing is combined with an intelligent tutoring system to achieve relevant and effective learning results through affective intelligent learning. The system aims to change negative emotions into positive ones of learning to improve students' interest in learning. With a total of 30 participants, this study adopts quantitative research design to explore the learning situations. We adopt the System Usability Scale (SUS) to evaluate overall availability of the system and use the Scan Path to explore if the subject stays longer in learning the course. This study found that both availability and satisfaction of affective tutoring system are high. The emotional feedback mechanism of the system can help users in transforming negative emotions into positive ones. In addition, the system is able to increase the learning duration the user spends on learning the course as well.

Keywords: affective computing; affective tutoring system; eye movement analysis; sentiment analysis; usability assessment

1. Introduction

1.1. Research Background and Motivation

Due to vigorous development of information technology, digital learning development and applied education are very common. Emotions are an important part of everyone and can affect behavior, thinking skills, decision-making, resilience, well-being, and the way human beings communicate with each other [1]. Based on the discussions, emotion not only is the driving factor that promotes learning but also is the primary factor that hinders the learning process as well. Hence, it is crucial to have reliable methods of emotion recognition in academic contexts [2]. The term "affective computing" was proposed by Professor Rosalind Picard in 1997 [3], and it has been guiding computers to identify and express emotions and respond intelligently to human emotions [4]. Owing to this, a trend has developed that applies emotional lenses to emerging academic research and positions emotion at the core of learning [5,6]. Kort and other scholars have proposed an emotion conceptualization module (2001) to combine affective computing with intelligent tutoring system for the purpose of identifying learners' emotions, responding to affections of current learners and promoting learning effectiveness [7]. Moreover, it can also identify the user's emotions and corresponding system responses as well as guide how to keep positive emotions via "mood proxy" and promote the achievement of learning objectives [8,9]. As Chen Huang Cheng mentioned in this book (2006), the best way to relieve negative emotions is to shift your thinking direction and appropriately reduce the expansion of negative emotions. Impacted with positive emotions, determination to solve problems will be generated when encountering difficulties [10]. In many studies on the affective tutoring system, the experimental results mainly discuss the usability and interactivity of the system. In this study, we use Scan Path to understand the subject's eye movement trajectory and observe his/her eye movement fixation duration in each ROI block to understand if the subject is more willing to stay in the digital course after combining the tutoring system with the affective computing module.

1.2. Research Purpose

With the advancement of technology, diversified learning modes can create richer teaching materials and learning methods. Based on the aforementioned research background and motivation, this study aimed to combine affective computing with intelligent tutoring system to understand the user's learning emotions, convert the user's negative emotions into positive ones and improve his/her interest of learning. Moreover, we used an eye tracker to perform eye movement analysis and understand if the user is able to increase the course learning duration by using the affective tutoring system. Based on the research background and motivation as well as the above discussions, the purpose of this study was set as follows: 1. Exploring the usability assessment of the affective tutoring system. 2. Understanding the fixation duration when using the affective tutoring system through eye movement analysis. 3. Understanding if the user is able to increase the course learning duration by using the affective tutoring system through eye movement analysis. Eye movement analysis was conducted to explore if the affective tutoring system can improve learners' attention and increase the course learning duration. The study themes are as follows:

1. How satisfied are the users with the affective tutoring system?
2. Is the user able to effectively increase the course learning duration by using the affective tutoring system?

2. Literature Review

2.1. Affective Computing

Affective computing methods have been applied to many fields such as training and learning environments [11]. In learning environments, the most important emotions to be dealt with are those associated with the teaching process (such as boredom, frustration, confusion, and engagement). Picard (1997) proposed four levels of affective computing: Recognize Emotion, Understand Emotion, Express Emotion and Emotion Intelligence. Affective Computing aims to detect signals caused by emotions and affections, such as language, physiological changes and body movements through various sensors. The computers will analyze these signals and make appropriate responses to current emotions. Emotion recognition can be detected by heartbeat, skin potential difference and facial emotion expression [12].

2.2. Affective Tutoring System

Emotions play a significant role in human behaviors in individual and social communities. This can happen in any kind of human activity such as learning online [13]. Recently, researchers have acknowledged the role of emotions in online learning in improving learning outcomes and enhancing students' experience [14–16]. The significance of incorporating emotional states with the learning process has necessitated the development of ATSs, which is the extended research of ITSs and with the ability to adapt to the learner's adverse emotion effectively to spark the learner's motivation to learn [17]. The affective tutoring system is based on the intelligent tutoring system, combining with affective computing and featuring the ability to detect the learners' emotions when they are learning [18]. The affective computer-based digital learning system proposed by Duo and Song (2012) aims to simulate the traditional teaching mode to analyze and recognize learners' emotions and improve learners' moods with virtual agents [19]. Mao and Li (2010) proposed that success in teaching lay in the ability to quickly identify the learners' emotional state, timely adjust the learners' emotions and enhance the learners' learning motivation. Ammar et al. (2010) added a facial expression detection module to the affective tutoring system to boost the learners' moods and improve the emotional communication between the system and the learner. The final results indicate that affective computing can effectively monitor the learners' emotions, appropriately lead to positive emotions and thus improve the learning motivation [20]. As Gerald (2004) said, learners may greatly reduce their learning motivation due to negative emotions, but positive emotions can effectively improve the learners' learning willingness. Graesser et al. (2004) used natural language to set up an emotion module for about 1000 subjects who are students in computer or physics majors. As the test results showed, such an emotion module has significantly improved the learning effects on both basic knowledge learning and in-depth research and discussion [21]. The indicators for measuring the satisfaction of using the affective tutoring system include learners' attitude and affective computing, the performance ability of the tutoring system, the accuracy of emotion recognition, the quantity of emotion recognition, the teaching course activities and the availability of the system etc. [17]. This study will therefore take the above characteristics into account in the design of the system.

2.3. Intelligent Virtual Agents

Intelligent virtual agents (IVAs) powered by artificial intelligence (AI) are prevalent in our daily lives. Amazon's Alexa, Apple's Siri, and Microsoft's Cortana are all IVAs that search information in real-time and verbally communicate the results to human beings [22]. Intelligent Virtual Agents are programs that can be assigned to perform user-specified jobs in a way that is comparable to human beings, featuring reactivity, positivity [23], autonomy [24], social ability and veracity [25], etc. which is different from traditional software. It is personalized, autonomous, proactive, adaptive and continuously running.

2.4. Emotion and Learning

The research carried out in education and psychology shows that emotion and learning have a hidden correlation, which will ultimately enhance learning performance [26]. Russell (1980) has built a 2D emotion model diagram and the eight emotions are divided into four quadrants, namely, happiness, surprise, boredom, fear, calmness, sadness, disgust and anger [27]. Ekman and Friesen (1971) defined six facial expressions: happiness, anger, fear, disgust, surprise and sadness [28]. Because emotions may affect learning effectiveness and the learning process may also influence the emotions, the correlation has therefore led many studies to focus on emotions and teaching. As Guo Shuzhen pointed out (2010), tutors need to be able to guide students to think in a right direction, influence students in a practical way, cultivate positive thinking and problem-solving ability, trigger students' potential abilities and improve learning effects in a happy learning way [29]. As Wen-Tzu Chiang (2004) proposed, the best way to adjust your emotion is to shift your attention away from your current mood and change the way you think and the point of view with which you view things [30]. Ying-Chun Sun (2009) pointed out that the cognitive style can generate different learning effects for understanding different emotions during the learning process. Therefore, in order to improve learning motivation, students shall be guided to maintain positive thinking over time to achieve optimal effect of learning [31].

2.5. Eye Movement Analysis

In recent years, eye tracking has been widely used as a research tool in many fields [32,33]. By tracking the user's fixation and analyzing eye movements and pupil size, his/her cognitive state can be studied, such as attention pattern and learning preferences [34,35]. Eye movement analysis mainly seeks to detect the learner's distraction process and understand the learner's attention on news reading through fixation points and eye movement trajectories [36]. As for eye movements upon reading, as Rayner (2009) said, tracking eye movements is regarded as an intuitive and effective approach to explore people's cognitive process in reading, scene perception and visual search [37]. The average fixation duration is 260–330 ms when the reader views images and 225–250 ms when reading words. The movement of fixation is to follow the texts from left to right or up to down. About 10–15% of fixation is associated with looking back, moving in an opposite direction of the text order. The situation is due to the fact that the reader spends a longer time reading the text and has to look back. If more than ten words are looked back by the reader, it indicates that the reader does not understand the current texts. Attention is a very important step for learning education because you shall first attract the attentions of learners before starting to tutor knowledge [38]. Many researchers agree that the direction of the head in interpersonal interaction is the easiest way to know the direction of the individual's fixation. When the head is fixed, the eye direction is almost the same as that of the individual's attention, except when the subject suffers from severe strabismus [39]. When the head is fixed, the eye direction is the same as that of the individual's fixation [36].

3. Methods

The objects of this study included 30 college students or above aged 20 to 30 who are divided into an experiment group and a control group, each with 15 subjects. The former conducted the experiment with the affective tutoring system and the latter conducted the experiment with the traditional tutoring system. The eye tracker was applied to perform eye movement analysis and tracking on both groups, and the whole experiment took about 15 min. At the end of the experiment, the subjects were asked to fill in the System Usability Scale, which took 10 min.

3.1. Interface Design

The system interface is divided into Interfaces A, B and C. A is an intelligent virtual agent, B is a course module and C is a course menu, as shown in Figure 1. The specific functions of the three interfaces are as follows:

A. Intelligent Virtual Agent: The intelligent virtual agent gives feedback to the user by combining Chinese semantic emotion recognition. When the user types in text sentences in the text input box, the system will identify the emotional keywords contained in the sentences and timely respond to the user's emotional results. The agent will interact with the user with different emotions and the system will finally propose new emotional questions to achieve real-time interaction and communication between the user and the system.
B. Course Module: The experimental textbook contains information about interactive technology describing the main development of interactive technology and other related technologies in recent years (such as wearable device, interactive technology, somatosensory and five-sense experience etc.). It helps the user to know more about the current course by combining with relevant online videos.
C. Course Menu: The menu displays each chapter in the course, allowing the user to control the reading time for each chapter and then select the next chapter.

3.2. Course Model

The course refers to digital art. In addition to the textual description of the course, picture and video examples are used to help the users understand the course contents. It takes 15 min for the subject to watch the course. Interactive design-related technologies are added in the learning process to improve the user's interest of learning.

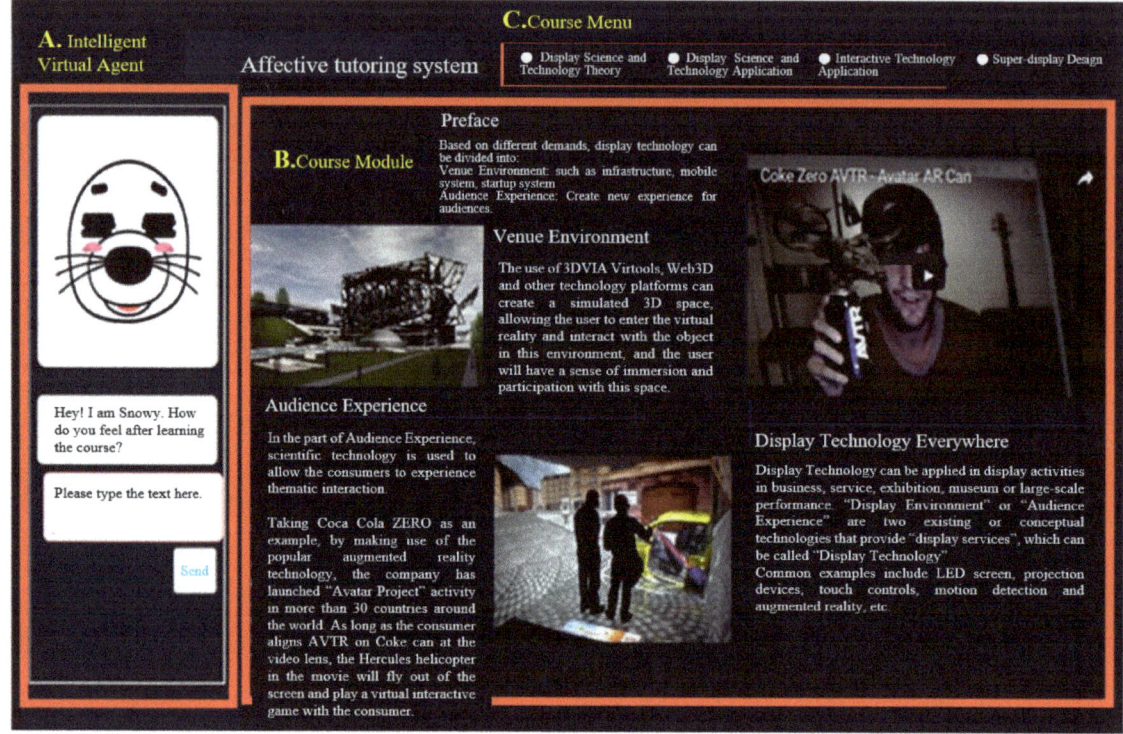

Figure 1. Affective Tutoring System Interface.

3.3. Agent Model

The agent model can affect the learner's learning emotion, perceive the learner's learning situation and give corresponding emotional guidance. In this study, the semantic analysis of affective computing was used to judge the semantics of dialogue between the user and the agent and provide appropriate emotional feedback to the agent to adjust the user's learning emotion and enhance his/her learning willingness. Therefore, the system set up an agent model as a bridge between the learner and the system. During the recognition, the system will respond to corresponding sentences and change the graphs of the agent model to enhance the learner's willingness to operate. For example, when any positive emotion is recognized in the learner's sentences by the system, the agent module will display a graph of positive emotion, and when any negative emotion is identified from the learner's sentences by the system, the emotion agent model will display a graph of negative emotion. If no emotional keywords are contained in the sentence or the system is unable to recognize the input sentence, a dynamic confusion graph without emotional feedback will be displayed. After the user's emotions are recognized by the system, the agent's emotional feedback will be given to the user in the set emotional performance state, and eight kinds of agent emotion feedback will be set up, including happiness, sadness, fear, frustration, anger, surprise, disgust, and doubt, as shown in Figure 2 below.

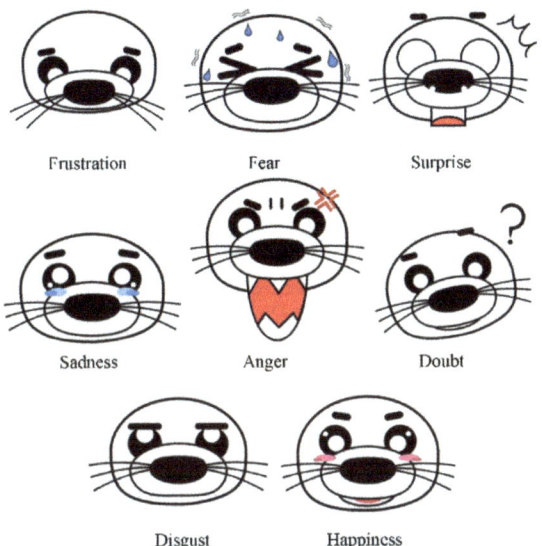

Figure 2. The icons of the emotional agent's positive and negative emotions.

3.4. Analysis of Eye Movement Statistics

The proportion and duration of time spent on the ROI blocks of the subject. In this study, an eye tracker gifted by Professor He Hongfa of National Taiwan Normal University was used. It is a research outcome from developing the eye tracker hardware and software in a five-year project for the Top University Project sponsored by the Ministry of Education of the Republic of China. The statistics analysis software developed by this study was analyzed according to the calculation formula in the eye tracker's manual, as shown below.

1. Total Time in Zone (ms) [Formula Definition: Total Time in ROI (fix.txt; duration totaling in ROI)] [Meaning: Total fixation time in zone]
2. Total Fixation Duration (ms) [Formula Definition: Total fixation duration of fix.txt] [Meaning: Total fixation duration of the subject during the experiment]
3. Average Fixation Duration (ms) [Formula Definition: Average fixation duration of fix.txt] [Meaning: Average fixation duration of the subject during the experiment]
4. Fixation Counts [Formula Definition: Total fixation counts of fix.txt] [Meaning: Total fixation counts of the subject during the experiment]
5. Percent Time Fixated Related to Total Fixation Duration (%) [Formula Definition: fix.txt; duration totaling/fixation duration in ROI (duration totaling of fix.txt)] [Meaning: Fixation duration in the zone to total fixation duration]

3.5. System Usability Scale

In this study, the System Usability Scale (SUS) was used. It was developed by Equipment Co., Ltd. in 1986 and mainly used to evaluate the usability of the system. The System Usability Scale is a low-cost, reliable and rapid method to effectively assess the user's subjective feelings toward the system [40]. The Likert scale was used to measure the scale from point 1 to 5 from strongly disagree to strongly agree. The formula was, however, divided into even numbers and odd numbers. For even-numbered questions, the numerical value 5 was subtracted from the original scores of the question to be the score available. For odd-numbered questions, the original scores were subtracted from the numerical value 1 to be the score available. Finally, the scores of the even and odd-numbered questions were added and multiplied by 2.5 to obtain the final satisfied scores [41]. The scale was analyzed by the formula, and the statistics selected by the subjects according to the statistics scale were scored with a total of 100 points for evaluation and analysis. The higher the score, the higher the degree of satisfaction on the system evaluated.

4. Data Analysis and Results

4.1. System Usability Analysis

In order to analyze the user's usability of the system, the statistical analysis was conducted with the System Usability Scale. A total of 15 participants took part in the experiment and all of them filled in the scale, which means that all the 15 scales are effective.

4.1.1. System Usability Scale—Reliability Analysis

Some of questions in the System Usability Scale are roundabout questions. Therefore, it is required to invert these roundabout questions first, and then to perform the statistical analysis according to the scale statistics filled in by the users to determine the user's usability of the system. From the overall usability scale, the average value is 4.01 with a standard deviation of 0.512. This means that the internal consistency reliability of the scale is high. Figure 3 shows the histogram of the overall usability scale.

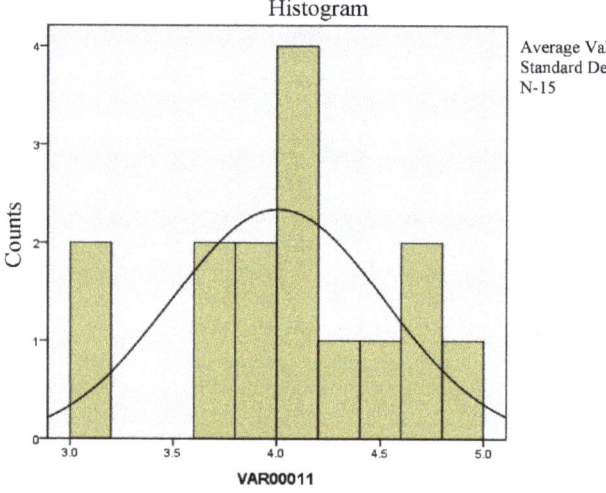

Figure 3. Overall Usability Scale.

4.1.2. System Usability Scale—Descriptive Statistics

This refers to the statistical result of each question of the System Usability Scale. Table 1 shows the analysis statistics of the System Usability Scale (percentage of five-point scale) and Table 2 shows the results of the analysis of each question of the Usability Scale.

Table 1. Analysis Statistics of System Usability Scale (Percentage of five-point scale).

	1	2	3	4	5
Q1	0%	0%	6.7%	53.3%	40.0%
Q2	0%	13.3%	40%	33.4%	13.3%
Q3	0%	0%	26.7%	40%	33%
Q4	0%	13.3%	46.7%	26.7%	13.3%
Q5	0%	0%	40%	40%	20%
Q6	0%	0%	26.7%	46.7%	26.6%
Q7	0%	0%	6.7%	46.7%	46.6%
Q8	0%	0%	6.7%	46.7%	46.6%
Q9	0%	0%	20%	26.7%	53.3%
Q10	0%	13.3%	26.7%	20%	40%

Table 2. Results of Analysis of Each Question of the Usability Scale.

	N	Minimum Value	Maximum Value	Summation	Average Number	Standard Deviation	Variance
Q1	15	3	5	65	4.33	0.617	0.381
Q2	15	2	5	52	3.47	0.915	0.838
Q3	15	3	5	61	4.07	0.799	0.638
Q4	15	2	5	51	3.40	0.910	0.829
Q5	15	3	5	57	3.80	0.775	0.600
Q6	15	3	5	60	4.00	0.756	0.571
Q7	15	3	5	66	4.40	0.632	0.400
Q8	15	3	5	66	4.40	0.632	0.400
Q9	15	3	5	65	4.33	0.816	0.667
Q10	15	2	5	58	3.87	1.125	1.267

The sum of the highest and second highest percentages for each question on a 5-point Likert scale represents agreement. The third highest percentages for each question on a 5-point Likert scale represent neutrality and the second lowest and lowest percentages for each question on 5-point Likert scale represent disagreement. Analysis results are as follows.

Q1: I think I would often use the system. This is a straightforward question with an average number of 4.33 and standard deviation of 0.617. In all, 40% of users are very willing to use the affective tutoring system often for learning, 53.3% of users would like to use the affective tutoring system for learning often and 6.7% of users are generally willing to use the system. As the system is a combination of emotion recognition and the course, emotion feedback is given to users in the aspect of emotion recognition, which has increased the enjoyment of the users. Therefore, it is inferred that most users are satisfied with this system.

Q2: I think the system is too complicated. This is a roundabout question with an average number of 3.47 and standard deviation of 0.915. In all, 13.3% of users strongly disagree that the system is too complicated, 33.4% of users disagree that the system is too complicated, 40% of users are neutral about the complexity of the system and 13.3% of users think that the system is too complicated.

Q3: I think the system is easy to use. This is a straightforward question with an average number of 4.07 and standard deviation of 0.799. In all, 33% of users think the system is very easy to use, 40% of users think the system is easy to use and 26.7% of users are neutral about the complexity of the system.

Q4: I think I need a technician's help to use the system. This is a roundabout question with an average number of 3.40 and a standard deviation of 0.910. In all, 13.30% of users think that it is absolutely necessary to have a technician to help use the system, 26.7% of users think that it is necessary to have a technician to help use the system, 46.70% of users are neutral about whether it is necessary to have a technician to help use the system and 13.3% of users think that it is unnecessary to have a technician to help use the system. Therefore, we are getting to a conclusion that the users do not have sufficient knowledge of affective computing and the functions of the agents need to be introduced. Human resources are required to be of assistance to guide the users.

Q5: I think all functions of the system are integrated well. This is a straightforward question with an average number of 3.80 and standard deviation of 0.775. In all, 20% of users strongly agree that all functions of the system are integrated well, 40% of users agree that all functions of the system are integrated well and 40% of users are neutral about whether all functions of the system are integrated well.

Q6: I think there is too much contradiction in the system. This is a roundabout question with an average number of 4.00 and standard deviation of 0.756. In all, 26.60% of users strongly disagree that there is too much contradiction in the system, 46.70% of users disagree that there is too much contradiction in the system and 26.70% of users are neutral about whether there is too much contradiction in the system.

Q7: I think most people could learn how to use the system fast. This is a straightforward question with an average number of 4.40 and standard deviation of 0.632. In all, 46.60% of users strongly agree that most people could learn how to use the system fast; 46.70% of users agree that most people could learn how to use the system fast and 6.70% of users are neutral about whether most people could learn how to use the system fast.

Q8: I think the system is very difficult to use. This is a roundabout question with an average number of 4.40 and standard deviation of 0.632. In all, 46.60% of users strongly disagree that the system is very difficult to use, 46.70% of users disagree that the system is very difficult to use and 6.70% of users are neutral about whether the system is very difficult to use.

Q9: I think I am very confident of using the system. This is a straightforward question with an average number of 4.33 and standard deviation of 0.816. In all, 53.30% of users strongly agree that they are very confident about using the system, 26.70% of users agree that they are very confident about using the system and 20% of users are neutral about whether they are very confident about using the system.

Q10: I think I have to learn something to use the system. This is a roundabout question with an average number of 3.87 and standard deviation of 1.125. In all, 40% of users strongly agree that they have to learn something to use the system, 20% of users agree that they have to learn something to use the system, 26.70% of users are neutral about whether they have to learn something to use the system and 40% of users disagree that they have to learn something to use the system. The researcher arrived at a conclusion that he/she does not know about affective computing and needs the help of technicians; he/she therefore thinks he/she needs to learn relevant knowledge before using the system.

4.1.3. Users' Satisfaction Analysis

For the score of each question, the odd-numbered questions are straightforward, with the score of each question being subtracted by the numerical value 1 to get final score; for example, if the score is 3, the calculated result will be 2. The even-numbered questions are roundabout, with the numerical value of 5 being subtracted by the score of each question to get final score; for example, if the score is 4, the calculated results will be 1. After the scores of each question are calculated, all the scores are added and multiplied by 2.5 to get the total score. The statistics obtained after the score conversion are shown in Table 3. According to the calculated results of the SUS formula, the average score of the subject for the system is 81.5. Figure 4 shows how the adjective ratings compare to both the school grading scale and the acceptability ranges [41]. The statistical results show that the users are satisfied with the usability of the system.

Table 3. Calculated Results of SUS Formula.

	Sample Size	Average Number	Median	Maximum Value	Minimum Value	Standard Deviation
Overall	15	81.5	82.5	95	67.5	7.245688

4.2. Eye Movement Analysis

The 30 objects of this study were divided into an experiment group and a control group with each 15 subjects. The former conducted the experiment by using the affective tutoring system, while the latter conducted the experiment by using the traditional tutoring system. The eye tracker was applied to both groups in order to perform the eye movement analysis and tracking. The whole experiment took about 15 min.

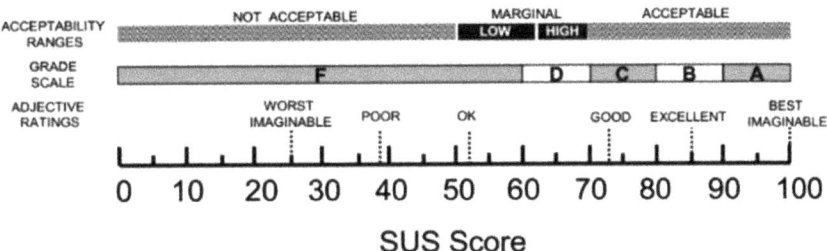

Figure 4. A comparison of the adjective ratings, acceptability scores and school grading scales with the average SUS score.

4.2.1. Eye Movement Fixation Analysis

The teaching contents of the system were divided into four sessions. The control group was compared with the experiment group in each session to understand the fixation duration of the subjects using the affective tutoring system. After finishing the experiment, the aggregate and average data of both the control group and the experiment group, as shown in Table 4, were calculated to obtain the total average fixation duration: 80,889.27 for the control group and 120,477.2 for the experiment group. The total average fixation duration at the course contents was 80,687.73 for the control group and 86,751.6 for the experiment group. The total average fixation count on the course contents was 796,133 for the control group and 803,533 for the experiment group. The single average fixation duration was 101,349 for the control group and 107,962 for the experiment group. In the analysis of eye movement statistics, the results of the experiment group were better than those of the control group, which indicates that using the affective tutoring system increased the course learning fixation duration.

Table 4. Sessions one to four—Overall Average Table.

	Control Group	Experiment Group
Total Average Fixation Duration	80,889.27	120,477.2
Course Contents Total Average Fixation Duration	80,687.73	86,751.6
Course Contents Total Average Fixation Counts	796,133	803,533
Course Contents Single Average Fixation Duration	101,349	107,962

4.2.2. Learning Duration Analysis of Eye Movement Course

The teaching contents of the system were divided into four sessions. The control group was compared with the experiment group in each session to understand if the affective tutoring system can effectively increase the learners' course learning duration. According to Table 5, the average number of the experiment group and the control group was 1,084,836.47 and 851,582.27 respectively. The former was higher than the latter, which indicates that the affective tutoring system lengthened the learning duration compared with the traditional tutoring system. According to the significance judgment and analysis results of the data in Table 6, the significance was 0.000 < 0.05. We can say that the total course learning duration of the experiment group using the affective tutoring system is significantly different from that of the control group using the traditional tutoring system.

According to Table 7 below, the average number of the experiment group and control group is 86,751.60 and 80,687.73 respectively. Based on the significance judgment and analysis results of the data in Table 8, the significance is 0.242 > 0.05. According to Tables 7 and 8, the Test (T) table shows that there is no significant difference in the total fixation duration of the control group, but the average duration is increased.

Table 5. T Verification—Group Statistical Analysis (Total Course Learning Duration).

	Average Number	Person(s)	Standard Deviation	Standard Error Mean Value
Control Group	851,582.27	15	109,821.034	28,355.669
Experiment Group	1,084,836.47	15	171,437.643	44,265.009

Table 6. T Verification—Independent Sample Verification (Total Course Learning Duration).

	Levene Variance Equality Test		Test (T) to Check if the Average Value Is Equal		
F	Significance	T	df	Significance (two-tailed)	
0.881	0.356	−4.437	23.834	0.000	

Table 7. Test (T)—Group Statistics (Fixation duration at the course contents).

	Average Number	Person(s)	Standard Deviation	Standard Error Mean Value
Control Group	80,687.73	15	12,762.089	3295.157
Experiment Group	86,751.60	15	17,452.989	4506.342

Table 8. Test (T)—Independent sample test (course content gaze time).

	Levene Variance Equality Test		Test (T) to Check if the Average Value Is Equal		
	F	Significance	T	df	Significance (Two-Tailed)
Fixation at the course contents	1.427	0.242	−1.086	25.643	0.287

According to Table 9 below, the average number of the experiment group and the control group is 1,084,836.47 and 851,582.27, respectively. Based on the significance judgment and analysis results of data in Table 10, the significance is 0.003 < 0.05. According to Tables 9 and 10, it can be found that there is a significant difference in the total fixation duration of the experiment group using the affective tutoring system compared with the control group using the general tutoring system. It shows that the fixation duration of the users with the affective tutoring system is longer than that of the users with the general tutoring system.

Table 9. Test (T)—Group Statistics (Total fixation duration).

	Average Number	Person(s)	Standard Deviation	Standard Error Mean Value
Control Group	80,889.27	15	12,842.757	3315.986
Experiment Group	120,477.20	15	24,068.766	3315.986

Table 10. Test (T)—Independent Sample Test (Total fixation duration).

	Levene Variance Equality Test		Test (T) to Check if the Average Value Is Equal		
	F	Significance	T	df	Significance (Two-Tailed)
Fixation at the course contents	10.209	0.003	−5.620	28	0.000

4.2.3. Eye Movement ROI Block Analysis

The teaching contents of the system were divided into four sessions. The control group was compared with the experiment group in respect of the time before the first visit of ROI block and the counts of fixation before the first visit.

Time before the first visit of the ROI block, the time before the first visit of the ROI block from sessions one to four of both the control group and the experiment group is zero. In this study, the course contents were in the middle position of the page layout, and after the nine-point correction, all subjects looked straight ahead and waited for the experiment to start, so they had already looked into the ROI block of the course contents at the very beginning of the first time, and thus the statistics show zero.

Fixation counts before the first visit, the fixation counts before the first visit from sessions one to four of both the control group and the experiment group are zero. In this study, the course contents were in the middle position of the page layout, and after the nine-point correction, all subjects looked straight ahead and waited for the experiment to start, and the standard fixation duration is 80 ms and the count statistics show zero.

4.2.4. Analysis of Eye Movement Hot Zone

The teaching contents of the system were divided into four sessions for analysis and comparison of hot zones to understand the hot zones of learners' attention to the contents of the textbook in the course of study. Figures 5 and 6 are the first session of the course contents of the control group and the experiment group. Figures 7 and 8 are the hot zones for the course contents of the control group and the experiment group in the second session. Figures 9 and 10 are the course contents of the control group and the experiment group in the third session of the fixation hot zone. Figures 11 and 12 show the course contents in the fourth session of the control group and the experiment group. The experiment shows that both the control group and the experiment group were completely fixated on the course contents in the course content fixation hot zone.

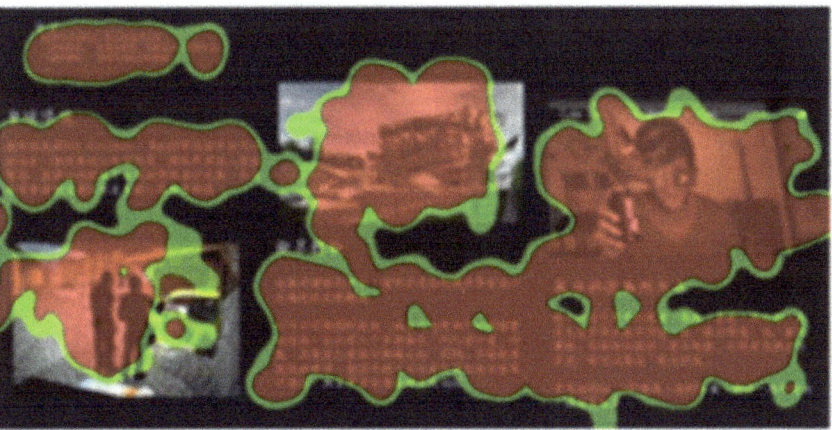

Figure 5. Control group (session 1).

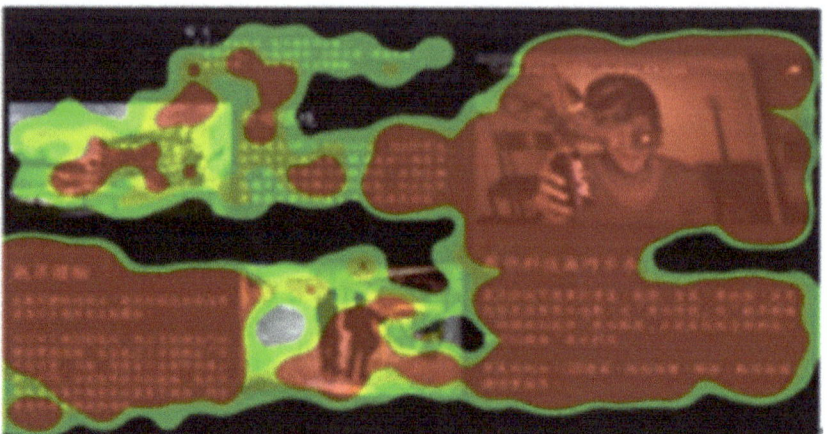

Figure 6. Experiment group (session 1).

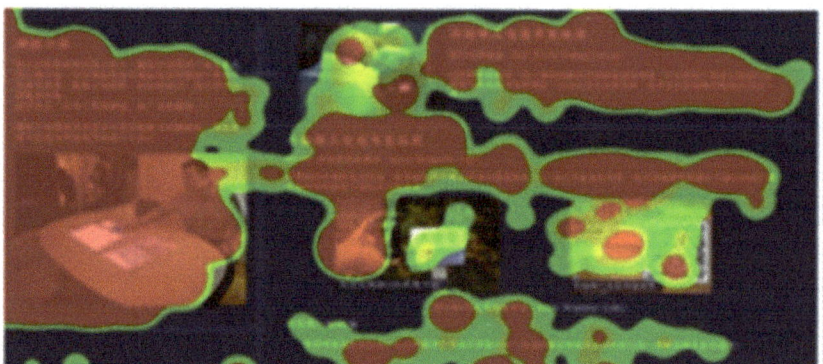

Figure 7. Control group (session 2).

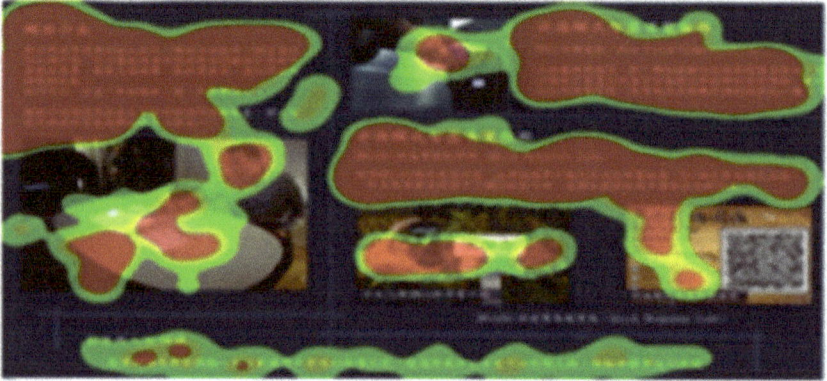

Figure 8. Experiment group (session 2).

Figure 9. Control group (session 3).

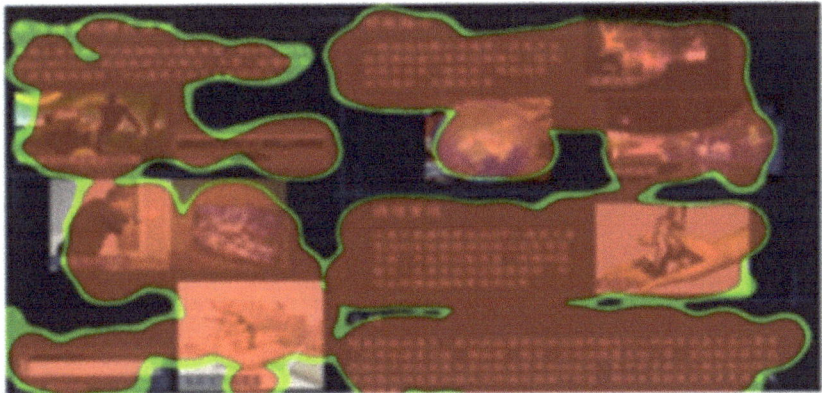

Figure 10. Experiment group (session 3).

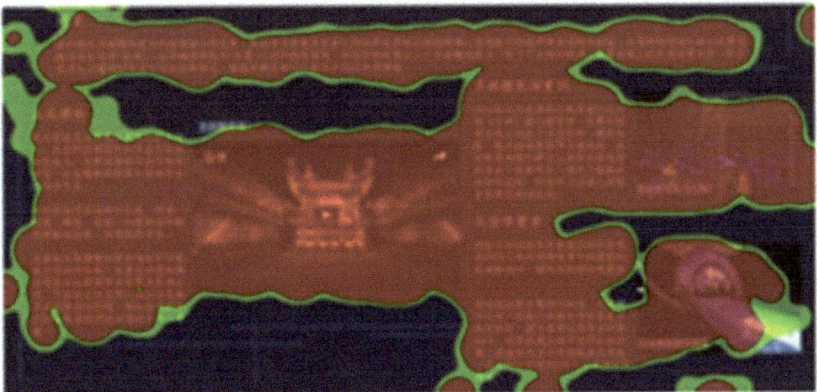

Figure 11. Control group (session 4).

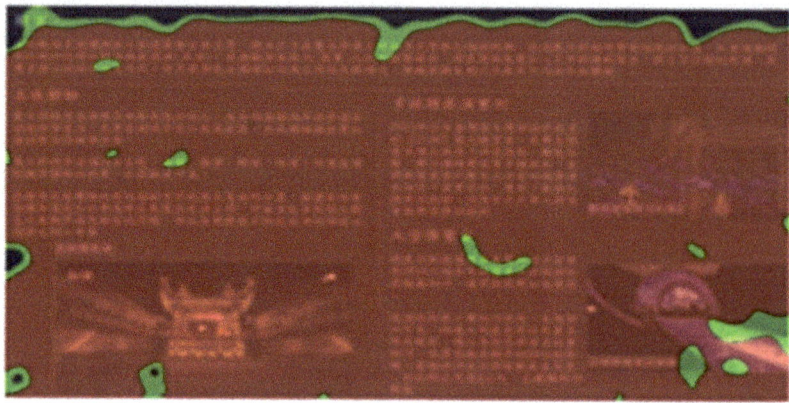

Figure 12. Experiment group (session 4).

5. Discussion and Conclusions

In this study, the affective computing was built on the intelligent tutoring system, which not only enhanced the learning interest of the users, but also provided a deeper learning experience. The real-time interaction between the users and the emotional agents provided emotional feedback and guidance that makes the users turn negative emotions into positive ones during the learning process and improve the learning interest of the users. SUS was used to understand the usability of the system, and eye movement statistics were analyzed to explore the fixation duration at the system. The analysis shows that the average score of the users for the usability of the system is 81.5, and the overall satisfaction is very high. As shown in the descriptive statistics, the users found it easy to use the system and the learning process was attractive, which increased the willingness to learn. Therefore, the statistics show that the design of the system can be adopted, and its usability is quite good. In the analysis of the eye movement statistics, the use of affective tutoring system increased the learning duration of the course. The eye movement statistics show that the fixation duration of the users from sessions one to four of the learning and the length and position of the fixation duration could represent the distribution and preference of personal attention. In this study, the fixation duration of the experiment group was longer than that of the control group, and the eye movement statistics analysis divided the experiment group into the two ROI blocks, the agent block and the course block, while there was only the course block in the ROI block of the control group. To further confirm whether the subjects are interested in the course contents, remove the fixation duration of the agent block in the experiment group and intercept the course block of both the experiment group and the control group to compare the course learning duration. The statistics show that the total learning duration of the course contents of the experiment group was better than that of the control group. The research proved that the system can increase the learning duration of users' courses. Through our experiments, the following items were found: (1) For the semantic emotion recognition module, the system was unable to recognize some fashionable terms used by young people according to the users' feedback. It was expected to collect some popular social platform, advertising works and even some emojis that can express emotions. (2) For the sentiment analysis and judgment of words and sentences, more considerations are needed because, for some popular words used by young people, the meaning is usually not the meaning of emotions, and there is some irony or implied meaning. It is easy to be confused with the original words. It is expected that, in the future, the system will be more fashionable to match social trends and be closer to the users. (3) For the technology of the agent module, it is expected to perform deep learning to train the machine to become a ChatBot, which can interact with users more smoothly and naturally. For this part, we have planned them into the work for the future.

6. Future Prospects

In recent years, the intelligent tutoring system has integrated users' emotional state into the intelligent tutoring system, which has led to the transformation of the intelligent tutoring system to the affective tutoring system. Therefore, affective computing is undoubtedly important in the education environment. In the future, multi-media contents can be applied in the design and development of the affective tutoring system. In addition, we expect to apply deep learning to the affective tutoring system and make the system feature a ChatBot message function. Message function has become an indispensable part of contemporary daily life. Under this premise, it is an inevitable trend to be equipped with a good ChatBot. Chatbots are no longer seen as mere assistants, for they interact in a way that brings them closer to the users as friendly companions [42]. Based on this, we will explore the user experience and evaluate the learning effectiveness in the subsequent study.

Author Contributions: Conceptualization, H.-C.K.L. and Y.-C.L.; methodology, H.-C.K.L. and Y.-C.L.; software, H.-C.K.L.; formal analysis, Y.-C.L. and H.-T.W.; writing—original draft preparation, Y.-C.L. and H.-T.W.; writing—review and editing, H.-C.K.L., Y.-C.L. and H.-T.W.; data collection, Y.-C.L. and H.-T.W. All authors have read and agreed to the published version of the manuscript.

Funding: This research received no external funding.

Institutional Review Board Statement: Not applicable.

Informed Consent Statement: Informed consent was obtained from all subjects involved in the study.

Data Availability Statement: Not applicable.

Conflicts of Interest: The authors declare that the research was conducted in the absence of any commercial or financial relationships that could be construed as a potential conflict of interest.

References

1. Morrish, L.; Rickard, N.; Chin, T.C.; Vella-Brodrick, D.A. Emotion regulation in adolescent well-being and positive education. *J. Happiness Stud.* **2018**, *19*, 1543–1564. [CrossRef]
2. Burić, I.; Sorić, I.; Penezić, Z. Emotion regulation in academic domain: Development and validation of the academic emotion regulation questionnaire (AERQ). *Personal. Individ. Differ.* **2016**, *96*, 138–147. [CrossRef]
3. Picard, R.W.; Picard, R. *Affective Computing*; MIT Press: Cambridge, MA, USA, 1997; Volume 252.
4. Picard, R.W.; Vyzas, E.; Healey, J. Toward machine emotional intelligence: Analysis of affective physiological state. *IEEE Trans. Pattern Anal. Mach. Intell.* **2001**, *23*, 1175–1191. [CrossRef]
5. Xu, J. Emotion regulation in mathematics homework: An empirical study. *J. Educ. Res.* **2018**, *111*, 1–11. [CrossRef]
6. Jiménez, S.; Juárez-Ramírez, R.; Castillo, V.H.; Ramírez-Noriega, A. Integrating affective learning into intelligent tutoring systems. *Univ. Access Inf. Soc.* **2018**, *17*, 679–692. [CrossRef]
7. Kort, B.; Reilly, R.; Picard, R. An Affective Model of Interplay Between Emotions and Learning: Reengineering Educational Pedagogy-Building a Learning Companion. In Proceedings of the IEEE International Conference on Advanced Learning Technologies, Madison, WI, USA, 6–8 August 2001; pp. 43–46.
8. Wang, C.-H.; Lin, H.-C.K. Constructing an Affective Tutoring System for Designing Course Learning and Evaluation. *J. Educ. Comput. Res.* **2006**, *55*, 1111–1128. [CrossRef]
9. Mastorodimos, D.; Chatzichristofis, S.A. Studying Affective Tutoring Systems for Mathematical Concepts. *J. Educ. Technol. Syst.* **2019**, *48*, 14–50. [CrossRef]
10. Cheng, C.-H. The Power of Positive Thinking. *Cult. Corp.* **2010**, *5*, 47–49.
11. Mejbri, N.; Essalmi, F.; Jemni, M.; Alyoubi, B.A. Trends in the use of affective computing in e-learning environments. *Educ. Inf. Technol.* **2022**, *27*, 3867–3889. [CrossRef]
12. Wang, T.-H.; Lin, H.-C.; Chen, H.-R.; Huang, Y.-M.; Yeh, W.-T.; Li, C.-T. Usability of an Affective Emotional Learning Tutoring System for Mobile Devices. *Sustainability* **2021**, *13*, 7890. [CrossRef]
13. Yadegaridehkordi, E.; Noor, N.F.B.M.; Bin Ayub, M.N.; Affal, H.B.; Hussin, N.B. Affective computing in education: A systematic review and future research. *Comput. Educ.* **2019**, *142*, 103649. [CrossRef]
14. Yu-Chun, M.; Koong, L.H.-C. A study of the affective tutoring system for music appreciation curriculum at the junior high school level. In Proceedings of the 2016 International Conference on Educational Innovation through Technology (EITT), Tainan, Taiwan, 22–24 September 2016; pp. 204–207.
15. Cabada, R.Z.; Estrada, M.L.B.; Hernández, F.G.; Bustillos, R.O. An affective learning environment for Java. In Proceedings of the 2015 IEEE 15th International Conference on Advanced Learning Technologies, Hualien, Taiwan, 6–9 July 2015; pp. 350–354.

16. Barrón-Estrada, M.L.; Zatarain-Cabada, R.; Oramas-Bustillos, R.; Gonzalez-Hernandez, F. Sentiment analysis in an affective intelligent tutoring system. In Proceedings of the 2017 IEEE 17th international conference on advanced learning technologies (ICALT), Timisoara, Romania, 3–7 July 2017; pp. 394–397.
17. Thompson, N.; McGill, T.J. Genetics with Jean: The design, development and evaluation of an affective tutoring system. *Educ. Technol. Res. Dev.* **2017**, *65*, 279–299. [CrossRef]
18. Mao, X.; Li, Z. Agent based affective tutoring systems: A pilot study. *Comput. Educ.* **2010**, *55*, 202–208. [CrossRef]
19. Duo, S.; Song, L.X. An E-learning System based on Affective Computing. *Phys. Procedia* **2012**, *24*, 1893–1898. [CrossRef]
20. Ammar, M.B.; Neji, M.; Alimi, A.M.; Gouardères, G. The affective tutoring system. *Expert Syst. Appl.* **2010**, *37*, 3013–3023. [CrossRef]
21. Gerald, C. *Reading Lessons: The Debate over Literacy*; Hill & Wang: New York, NY, USA, 2004.
22. Sin, J.; Munteanu, C. An empirically grounded sociotechnical perspective on designing virtual agents for older adults. *Hum. Comput. Interact.* **2020**, *35*, 481–510. [CrossRef]
23. Wooldridge, M.; Jennings, N.R. Intelligent agents: Theory and practice. *Knowl. Eng. Rev.* **1995**, *10*, 115–152. [CrossRef]
24. Castelfranchi, C. Guarantees for autonomy in cognitive agent architecture. In *International Workshop on Agent Theories, Architectures, and Languages*; Springer: Berlin/Heidelberg, Germany, 1994; pp. 56–70.
25. Genesereth, M.R. *Software Agents Michael R*; Genesereth Logic Group Computer Science Department Stanford University: Stanford, CA, USA, 1994.
26. Cunha-Perez, C.; Arevalillo-Herraez, M.; Marco-Gimenez, L.; Arnau, D. On Incorporating Affective Support to an Intelligent Tutoring System: An Empirical Study. *IEEE Rev. Iberoam. Tecnol. Aprendiz.* **2018**, *13*, 63–69. [CrossRef]
27. Russell, J.A. A circumplex model of affect. *J. Personal. Soc. Psychol.* **1980**, *39*, 1161. [CrossRef]
28. Ekman, P.; Friesen, W.V. Constants across cultures in the face and emotion. *J. Pers. Soc. Psychol.* **1971**, *17*, 124–129. [CrossRef]
29. Kuo, S.-C. *The Meaning of Positive Psychology and Its Application in Learning*; Graduate School of Education, Ming Chuang University: Taoyuan, Taiwan, 2010; pp. 56–72.
30. Chiang, W.-T. The Emotion Regulation of College Students: Processes and Developmental Characteristics. *Bull. Educ. Psychol.* **2004**, *35*, 249–268.
31. Sun, Y.-C. *Evaluation of Learning Emotion and Performance for Learners with Visualizer/Verbalizer Cognitive Style Enrolled in Various Types of Multimedia Materials*; Department of Applied Electronic Technology of National Taiwan Normal University: Taipei City, Taiwan, 2010; pp. 1–136.
32. Adhanom, I.B.; Lee, S.C.; Folmer, E.; MacNeilage, P. Gazemetrics: An open-source tool for measuring the data quality of HMD-based eye trackers. In Proceedings of the ACM Symposium on Eye Tracking Research and Applications, Stuttgart, Germany, 2–5 June 2020; pp. 1–5.
33. Hosp, B.; Eivazi, S.; Maurer, M.; Fuhl, W.; Geisler, D.; Kasneci, E. RemoteEye: An open-source high-speed remote eye tracker. *Behav. Res. Methods* **2020**, *52*, 1387–1401. [CrossRef]
34. Boraston, Z.; Blakemore, S.J. The application of eye-tracking technology in the study of autism. *J. Physiol.* **2007**, *581*, 893–898. [CrossRef]
35. Carter, B.T.; Luke, S.G. Best practices in eye tracking research. *Int. J. Psychophysiol.* **2020**, *155*, 49–62. [CrossRef]
36. Tang, D.-L.; Chang, W.-Y. Exploring Eye-Tracking Methodology in Communication Study. *Chin. J. Commun. Res.* **2007**, *12*, 165–211.
37. Rayner, K. Eye movements and attention in reading, scene perception, and visual search. *Q. J. Exp. Psychol.* **2009**, *62*, 1457–1506. [CrossRef]
38. Rayner, K. Eye movements in reading and information processing: 20 years of research. *Psychol. Bull.* **1998**, *124*, 372–422. [CrossRef]
39. Langton, S.R.; Watt, R.J.; Bruce, V. Do the eyes have it? Cues to the direction of social attention. *Trends Cogn. Sci.* **2000**, *4*, 50–59. [CrossRef]
40. Brooke, J. SUS: A 'Quick and Dirty' Usability Scale. *Usability Eval. Ind.* **1996**, *189*, 4–7.
41. Bangor, A.; Kortum, P.; Miller, J. Determining what individual SUS scores mean: Adding an adjective rating scale. *J. Usability Stud.* **2009**, *4*, 114–123.
42. Costa, P. Conversing with personal digital assistants: On gender and artificial intelligence. *J. Sci. Technol. Arts* **2018**, *10*, 59–72.

Article

Learners' Continuous Use Intention of Blended Learning: TAM-SET Model

Xiulan Chen [1], Xiaofei Xu [2], Yenchun Jim Wu [3,4,*] and Wei Fong Pok [5]

1. School of Foreign Language, Huaqiao University, Quanzhou 362021, China
2. School of Business Administration, Huaqiao University, Quanzhou 362021, China
3. MBA Program in Southeast Asia, National Taipei University of Education, Taipei 106, Taiwan
4. Department of Hospitality Management, Ming Chuan University, Taipei 111, Taiwan
5. Faculty of Accountancy and Management, Universiti Tunku Abdul Rahman, Kajang 43000, Malaysia
* Correspondence: wuyenchun@gmail.com

Abstract: Blended learning (BL) combines online and face-to-face teaching and learning and is thought to be an effective means to cultivate learners' sustainability literacy. The success of BL relies on learners who take the initiative to participate in the learning process. Therefore, this study aims to examine learners' acceptance of the BL system. The technology acceptance model (TAM) and the self-efficacy theory are combined to construct a systematic model to determine the learners' continuous intention to adopt BL. Seven constructs are identified, i.e., course quality (CQ), technical support (TS), perceived usefulness (PU), perceived ease of use (PEOU), satisfaction (SE), self-efficacy (SE), and behavioral intentions (BI). A survey was conducted using a close-ended questionnaire, and 461 valid responses were collected from Huaqiao University's undergraduate students. Covariance-based structural equation modelling was performed. The empirical findings show that except for the hypothesis regarding the connection between PU and PEOU, all the other hypotheses are verified. CQ stands out as having the greatest positive effect on PEOU, which highlights the importance of CQ for BL. The study also confirms that PU significantly impacts SA, SE, and BI, and both SA and SE significantly influence BI. Based on these results, some suggestions are provided for educators and administrators as to how to better design BL systems to strengthen sustainability education.

Keywords: blended learning; continuous use intention; technology acceptance model; self-efficacy theory

Citation: Chen, X.; Xu, X.; Wu, Y.J.; Pok, W.F. Learners' Continuous Use Intention of Blended Learning: TAM-SET Model. *Sustainability* 2022, *14*, 16428. https://doi.org/10.3390/su142416428

Academic Editor: Hao-Chiang Koong Lin

Received: 8 November 2022
Accepted: 5 December 2022
Published: 8 December 2022

Publisher's Note: MDPI stays neutral with regard to jurisdictional claims in published maps and institutional affiliations.

Copyright: © 2022 by the authors. Licensee MDPI, Basel, Switzerland. This article is an open access article distributed under the terms and conditions of the Creative Commons Attribution (CC BY) license (https://creativecommons.org/licenses/by/4.0/).

1. Introduction

Blended learning (BL) is one of the emerging trends in education. According to Oxford Dictionary, BL can be defined as a style of education in which students learn via electronic and online media, as well as traditional face-to-face teaching. However, it is challenging to accurately define BL (or hybrid learning) due to dynamic combinations of online and face-to-face components. One scholar points out that "blended learning is a thoughtful combination of face-to-face learning experience in class and online learning experience" [1]. Web-based technologies, such as free or charging online courses, MOOCs, electronic textbooks, websites, and social media apps, are often adopted in blended learning. The mix of online and face-to-face components depends on the teaching objectives, curriculum, teachers' teaching experience, students' learning styles, etc. The key to blended teaching design is to cultivate students' learning ability, with students as the main body and "learning as the center," so that students can adapt to and develop the habit of active learning under the environment of deep integration of information technology and traditional teaching. Therefore, it is crucial to determine learners' attitudes toward BL to help them build a firm belief in the adoption and continued usage of BL.

There is consensus among most universities that BL can be a source of sustainable education [2]. Currently, the world is encountering challenges in the protection of world sustainability. One of the key responsibilities of higher education is to develop sustainability literacy, i.e., the knowledge and skills that enable them to build a sustainable future for society, among students. Therefore, it is crucial for educational institutions to understand the students' perceptions, attitudes, and continuous use intention related to blended learning.

Sustainability literacy (SL) has become a popular issue in education [3–5]. Critical thinking, self-study, and cooperative learning are needed to build one's SL. BL has been advocated in higher education as an effective way to raise students' awareness of environmental challenges and help them form the courage, confidence, and qualities to deal with environmental issues [4,5]. Accelerated environmental deterioration calls for environmental professionals who have mastered skills related to problem-solving, critical thinking, creative thinking, self-control, communication, and teamwork to solve environmental issues. Higher education shoulders the responsibility to help develop students' life-long SL [6–8]. BL, which allows students to pursue their studies in a flexible, exploratory, collaborative way, is thought to be able to enhance learners' SL.

As an innovative invention in education, online learning is drawing more and more attention due to its potential for self-enrichment. However, since learning is about communication and cooperation, traditional face-to-face instruction is regarded by most learners as indispensable. In addition, some technical problems regarding online communication are difficult to solve [9]. Researchers have found that learners still want offline learning to help them to improve and consolidate the knowledge acquired online [10]. Through online learning, students become familiar with course content in advance, discuss related topics in a virtual community with peers or teachers, complete assignments, review course materials, etc. When they meet face-to-face in the classroom, they are more confident that they are able to achieve the planned learning outcomes. Yet, no two BL modes are identical in design, due to variations in the characteristics of the courses and learners, as well as the goal of the learning. In such cases, only the learners can provide meaningful input to evaluate the effectiveness of the BL mode.

BL can be an effective way to solve the problem of large class size and increase learning outside the traditional face-to-face learning environment [11–13]. If properly adopted, BL can transform higher education into a more flexible and agile state, which allows for quick adaptation to the changes in the learning environment and eventually, improves its cost-effectiveness [14]. What is certain is that well-designed BL has the potential to achieve the best learning outcomes. However, BL design is a complex subject involving many factors that determine its effectiveness, and what motivates learners' continuous use intention remains unclear. The learning experience between traditional face-to-face courses and online learning differs significantly, so a good implementation of BL is bound to encounter challenges, and these must be solved jointly by administrators, educators, and learners.

Since the late 1990s, discussions on BL have evolved from the application of technology to the concern of learners' learning motivations and strategies [15,16]. The implementation of BL involves three parties—administrators, teachers, and students. Administrators need to provide reliable and accessible technology infrastructure for a smooth learning process, whereas educators take the responsibility of designing the blended course based on course features and learner backgrounds. Learners are the actual executors of BL. Their acceptance determines, to large extent, the achievement of expected learning outcomes. Therefore, it is necessary to identify the factors affecting learners' intentions to adopt the BL mode. Currently, there are limited studies focusing on the factors influencing the acceptance of BL from the learners' perspective [17]. Most of the studies focus on the administrators' perspective or the educational management issues of BL [18,19].

As BL involves self-regulated learning, learners' self-efficacy beliefs are an indispensable attribute in the BL system. So far, the literature concerning this issue has not received enough attention, and some scholars merely focus on relative factors, such as the function of collaborative learning, social presence, and self-regulating without combining them into a holistic system [20–22]. To identify the constructs that determine the continuous intention to adopt BL, the technology acceptance model (TAM) is adopted in this study because of its simplicity, strong explanatory power, and ease of operationalization. Due to the learner-centered nature of BL, learners' self-efficacy determines the influence of their motivation, confidence, and satisfaction. To reveal learners' acceptance of BL, the level of learners' self-efficacy should be included.

2. Theoretical Model and Hypotheses Development

The technology acceptance model (TAM) was first proposed by Davis (1986) in his doctoral dissertation [23]. The underlying theory of this model is the rational behavior theory. The model also assimilates other theories, i.e., expectation theory, self-efficacy theory, input-output theory, and change adoption theory. It mainly consists of three independent constructs, namely perceived useful (PU), perceived ease of use (PEOU), and attitude to using technology (AT).

The self-efficacy theory (SET) sheds light on the development of TAM, as Davis noticed that self-efficacy determines the acceptance of technology-connected systems. SET is a subset of Bandura's (1986) social cognitive theory [24]. According to this theory, the two key determinants of behavior are self-efficacy and outcome expectancy. Obviously, SET is often adopted when the behavior intention is concerned. In the context of BL, learners' engagement plays an important role in achieving the expected outcome. Nonetheless, how the BL mode leads to the continuous behavior intention of the learner remains a question.

Various types of research have examined learner satisfaction with online learning environments [25,26]. However, few studies have focused on the blended learning context, despite the fact that more higher education institutions are adopting BL because of its flexibility and low cost, while maintaining the learner-teacher face-to-face interaction [17]. BL includes both online and offline learning, so it poses more challenges to educators and learners. There are studies investigating the factors that affect learner satisfaction in the context of BL, but these are limited to some exterior factors such as online resources, learning support services, etc. [11,18,27,28]. There is limited research exploring the attributing factors for learner satisfaction from a theoretical background. Despite the fact that the BL mode is widely implemented in many universities, the continuous use intention of learners is insufficiently studied. This paper aims to establish a TAM-SET model to examine learners' continuous use intention regarding the BL mode. The findings will be used to propose solutions to boost their intentions.

In this study, seven constructs are identified in the research model: course quality (CQ), technological support (TS), perceived usefulness (PU), perceived ease of use (PEOU), satisfaction (SA), self-efficacy (SE), and behavior intention (BI). The hypothesis model is shown in Figure 1.

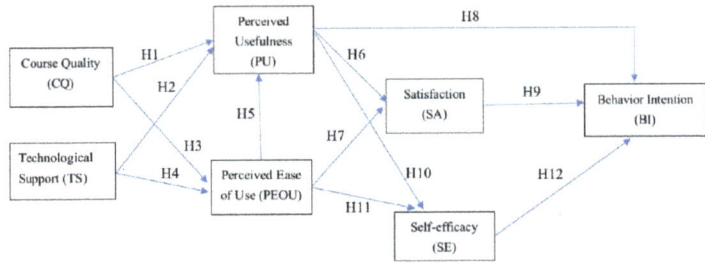

Figure 1. Research model and hypotheses.

2.1. Course Quality (CQ)

Based on Davis's TAM (1986) [23], two external constructs are identified in the context of BL: course quality (CQ) and technology support (TS). CQ can be measured from five aspects: course characteristics, teaching and learning design, interaction platform, course content, and learning resources. The external constructs directly impact the two main constructs (PU and PEOU) that determine the attitudes and indirectly affect the use intention.

2.2. Technological Support (TS)

Blended learning requires the adoption of tools, e.g., learning management systems, network conferences, digital textbooks, simulations, and games. These pose great challenges to administrators. They need to provide resources and timely technological support (TS) in accordance with the functional characteristics of the teaching and learning tasks. A smooth network connection, system stability, compatibility, convenience, and friendly navigation settings are within their routine working obligations.

2.3. Perceived Usefulness (PU)

Perceived usefulness (PU) refers to the degree to which users subjectively believe that using a system can improve their work performance [29]. In most cases, PU is considered to play the most decisive role affecting users' attitudes [30]. PU has been proven to be an essential construct to increase learners' self-regulation in e-learning environments [31]. TAM proposes that both PU and PEOU have a significant impact on SA.

2.4. Perceived Ease of Use (PEOU)

Perceived ease of use (PEOU) can be defined as the degree to which users subjectively believe that using a particular system will require little effort [29]. PU and PEOU are often regarded as the two most important constructs in TAM. The extant literature proves that individuals are more inclined to adopt new technology if they think it is easy to use [29]. Studies concerning TAM have also suggested that PEOU positively influences PU [29,32].

2.5. Satisfaction (SA)

Attitude refers to the positive or negative feelings an individual has in the process of performing a certain behavior. Satisfaction (SA) is usually conceptualized as the aggregate of a person's feelings or attitudes toward the various factors that affect a person's decision. In this study, SA predicts a person's willingness to continuously use a certain system when it involves some degree of self-motivation. Learner satisfaction is proven as one of the important factors contributing to the effectiveness of blended and purely online courses [33]. It has an important reference value for educators to improve course design and for administrators to improve service quality to ensure a satisfactory outcome.

2.6. Self-Efficacy (SE)

Self-efficacy is an individual's judgment regarding his/her ability to engage in certain behavior, and it determines to what degree an individual will persist and commit efforts after he/she has made a choice. Self-efficacy, as an important component of emotion, plays a crucial role in the learning process because of its impact on learners' motivation, self-regulation, and academic performance. The self-efficacy theory (SET) was first developed in 1977 by Albert Bandura, who proposed SET as the determining force for behavior change [34]. SET emphasizes the relative importance of personal factors, but acknowledges that behavioral and environmental factors have profound effects on outcomes as well.

2.7. Behavioral Intention (BI)

Behavioral intention describes an individual's future intention to engage in certain behavior. It can be an immediate antecedent of actual behavior [35]. In the context of BL, it encompasses the likelihood that learners will again use the BL mode when it is made available to them. They may get involved in a wide variety of learning activities, such as self-regulated study, communication with teachers and friends, interaction online and offline, sharing information and materials, etc.

3. Research Methodology

This paper aims to establish a combined TAM-SET model to predict learners' intentions to continuously use BL. After we identified the key contributing constructs and analyzed the relationships among them, we proposed how to enhance learners' enthusiasm and interest in BL. A survey was adopted in this empirical study to test the hypotheses among these constructs. The subjects of this study were undergraduates from Huaqiao University who experienced using the BL mode for at least a total of one year. The courses offered in Huaqiao University can be divided into public courses (including compulsory courses and elective courses), professional basic courses, and professional elective courses. Most of the courses are available on MOOC platforms, which offer abundant online resources for blended teaching and learning practices. Students can directly use these existing MOOCs to complete online learning, and teachers can design classroom discussions and interactive exchanges based on MOOC resources. A total of 472 students responded to the online questionnaires, and 461 valid responses were included in the analysis. The data were then analyzed using IBM SPSS Statistics (Chicago, IL, USA) 24.0 and Amos (Chicago, IL, USA) 21.0. The reliability, the convergent and discriminant validity, the goodness-of-fit, and the truth of the hypothesis were tested.

The scale compilation involved two main processes. First, the contributing constructs of the model were sorted out based on the existing literature [36–44]. Then, 22 students who participated in BL for at least one year were selected as interviewees to explore possible constructs for the scale. By combining the findings of the two processes, seven factors were identified that might affect blended learning adoption from the learners' perspective, namely course quality (CQ), technological support (TS), perceived usefulness (PU), perceived ease of use (PEOU), satisfaction (SA), self-efficacy (SE), and behavioral intentions (BI). Most of the items under each construct were adapted from well-tested scales, and some new items were designed according to the characteristics of BL used in the present study.

To further improve the validity of the questions, the draft of the questionnaire was sent to experts for their suggestions and improvement. After some amendments, the final questionnaire contained 7 constructs with 26 sub-items using a 7-point Likert scale (1 = strongly disagree; 7 = strongly agree). CQ contains 5 sub-items; TS contains 3 sub-items; PU contains 3 sub-items; PEOU contains 4 sub-items; SA contains 3 sub-items; SE contains 5 sub-items, and BI contains 3 sub-items. The complete questionnaire consisted of two parts: a survey regarding the subjects' demographic characteristics, including gender, major, grade, and scale. The data were analyzed to test their reliability and validity. Confirmatory factor analysis (CFA) was performed to examine the construct validity and composite reliability of the model.

4. Analysis and Findings

4.1. Reliability and Construct Validity Analysis

The reliability and validity of the scale were evaluated using reliability and convergent validity criteria. Reliability was established by calculating Cronbach's alpha to measure the internal consistency of the measurement. A pilot study was carried out in which 30 students who completed undergraduate courses conducted with the BL mode for at least one year were invited to complete the online questionnaire posted on a questionnaire-sharing website called "The Scale Star." As Hair et al. pointed out, Cronbach's alpha coefficient must be at least 0.7 [45]. As shown in Table 1, Cronbach's alpha values for all constructs were above 0.7. The Cronbach's alpha for CQ, PEOU, and BI are above 0.9, indicating a high degree of internal consistency of these constructs.

Table 1. Pilot test of Cronbach's alpha reliability.

Code	Pilot Test
CQ	0.912
RT	0.830
PU	0.772
PEOU	0.914
SE	0.895
AT	0.784
BI	0.918

Next, a massive survey was carried out, and 483 students participated in the online survey. A total of 461 valid questionnaire results were collected after excluding invalid answers or those that were not completed within the time limit. The first part of the survey consisted of the demographic characteristics of the respondents. The results indicated the representativeness of the subjects. As is shown in Table 2, in terms of gender, there was nearly an equal number of male and female learners. As for the major allocation, there were more science majors than arts majors, which was within the acceptable level. The majority of the respondents were juniors, which was due to the fact that many freshmen and sophomores did not meet the sampling inclusion criteria. Students in their senior year were required to perform an internship; therefore, they were not as motivated as juniors to participate in this survey.

Table 2. Demographic characteristics of the respondents.

Items	Description	N	%	Cumulative %
Gender	Male	251	54.4	54.4
	Female	210	45.6	100
Grade	Sophomore	134	29.1	29.1
	Junior	202	43.8	72.9
	Senior	125	27.1	100
Major	Arts	186	40.4	40.4
	Science	275	59.4	100

Instead of using an exploratory factor analysis (EFA), the study conducted a confirmative factor analysis (CFA) to test the convergent validity of each construct, since most of the items in each construct were adapted from mature and effective scales. To achieve a satisfactory construct validity, the values of standardized loading estimated for all the items should be higher than 0.7, while the composite reliability (CR) is recommended to be higher than 0.7, and the average variance extracted (AVE) should be higher than 0.5 [46–48]. As is shown in Table 3, the values for the standardized loading of all constructs were above 0.7, and AVE and CR were all higher than 0.5 and 0.7.

Next, the discriminant validity, which provides evidence of the external validity of the measurement instrument, was assessed. It is determined by comparing the squared correlation between two constructs and their AVE values. It is recommended that all of the squared correlations should be less than the AVE values, which indicates sufficient discriminant validity [47–49]. Table 4 presents the discriminant validity values for the constructs.

Table 3. Construct reliability and convergent validity.

Factors	Items	Standardized Loading	Cronbach's Alpha	CR	AVE
CQ	CQ1	0.753	0.861	0.863	0.558
	CQ2	0.716			
	CQ3	0.826			
	CQ4	0.701			
	CQ5	0.749			
RT	RT1	0.739	0.794	0.799	0.571
	RT2	0.793			
	RT3	0.735			
PU	PU1	0.761	0.766	0.766	0.522
	PU2	0.703			
	PU3	0.707			
PEOU	PEOU1	0.870	0.886	0.887	0.662
	PEOU2	0.772			
	PEOU3	0.772			
	PEOU4	0.841			
SE	SE1	0.758	0.894	0.901	0.651
	SE2	0.761			
	SE3	0.893			
	SE4	0.893			
	SE5	0.706			
SA	AT1	0.700	0.768	0.773	0.535
	AT2	0.782			
	AT3	0.701			
BI	BI1	0.900	0.933	0.934	0.825
	BI2	0.914			
	BI3	0.910			

Table 4. Discriminant validity.

	CQ	RT	PEOU	SE	AT	BI	PU
CQ	0.747						
RT	0.461	0.756					
PEOU	0.649	0.428	0.814				
SE	0.418	0.477	0.418	0.807			
AT	0.456	0.448	0.406	0.436	0.731		
BI	0.509	0.511	0.463	0.534	0.490	0.908	
PU	0.360	0.419	0.292	0.361	0.399	0.456	0.722

4.2. Model Fit Measurement

To assess how well the proposed structural equation model fits the data, measures of goodness-of-fit, such as chi-square testing, the goodness-of-fit index (GFI), root mean square error approximation (RMSEA), the residual root mean quarter residual (RMR), the comparative fit index (CFI), the normed fit index (NFI), and the non-normed fit index (NNFI) are examined [45,50]. Table 5 presents the rules of thumb indicating acceptable model fit and the analysis results. As is shown, all the goodness of fit indices fell within the recommended range, suggesting that the proposed research model provided a good fit to the data.

Table 5. Goodness of fit indices for the measurement model.

Type of Measure	Acceptable Level of Fit	Values
Chi-square/degree of freedom	<3	2.051
Goodness-of-fit index (GFI)	>0.9	0.913
Root mean square residual (RMSEA)	<0.10	0.054
Root-mean residual (RMR)	<0.05	0.049
Comparative fit index (CFI)	>0.9	0.948
Normed fit index (NFI)	>0.9	0.913
Non-normed fit index (NNFI)	>0.9	0.939

4.3. Hypothesis Testing

The above findings confirm that the research measurement instruments used in this study are reliable and can be used for hypothesis testing. The path analysis of the initial model was studied from the aspects of standardized path coefficient, standard error (S.E), and critical ratio (C.R.). The result is shown in Table 6.

Table 6. Results summary.

			Estimate	S.E.	C.R.	p
PEOU	<—	CQ	0.657	0.07	10.976	0.000
PEOU	<—	TS	0.153	0.064	2.914	0.004
PU	<—	CQ	0.306	0.097	3.466	0.000
PU	<—	TS	0.502	0.084	6.819	0.000
PU	<—	PEOU	−0.118	0.078	−1.42	0.156
SA	<—	PU	0.458	0.058	7.05	0.000
SA	<—	PEOU	0.358	0.047	6.369	0.000
SE	<—	PU	0.374	0.044	6.352	0.000
SE	<—	PEOU	0.346	0.037	6.539	0.000
BI	<—	PU	0.281	0.093	4.375	0.000
BI	<—	SA	0.278	0.097	4.69	0.000
BI	<—	SE	0.32	0.096	6.392	0.000

Most of the path coefficients are significant in the expected direction. The results confirmed that external variables could include CQ and TS. Hypotheses 1 to 4 are supported. However, Hypothesis 5 is not supported. The path coefficient between PU and PEOU was negative and insignificant. This is inconsistent with many studies based on TAM [23,51–57]. Hypotheses 6 and 7 were supported, confirming the hypothetical effect of PU and PEOU on SA. Hypotheses 8 and 9 were supported, verifying again the effect of PU on BI, and SA can lead to BI. Both SE and SA were found to positively affect BI. Hypothesis 10, which proposed a positive relationship between PU and SE, was supported as well, as was proved in some previous studies [57–62]. Similarly, Hypothesis 11, which projected a positive relationship between PEOU and SE, was also supported, and this is consistent with the results of previous studies [63]. Hypothesis 12 was also supported, meaning that a higher level of SE will lead to greater BI, and this opinion has been proven to be true as well [62,64]. The path standardized coefficients of the structural model are depicted in Figure 2. The results indicate that TAM and SET can well be combined to predict learners' continuous use intention of BL.

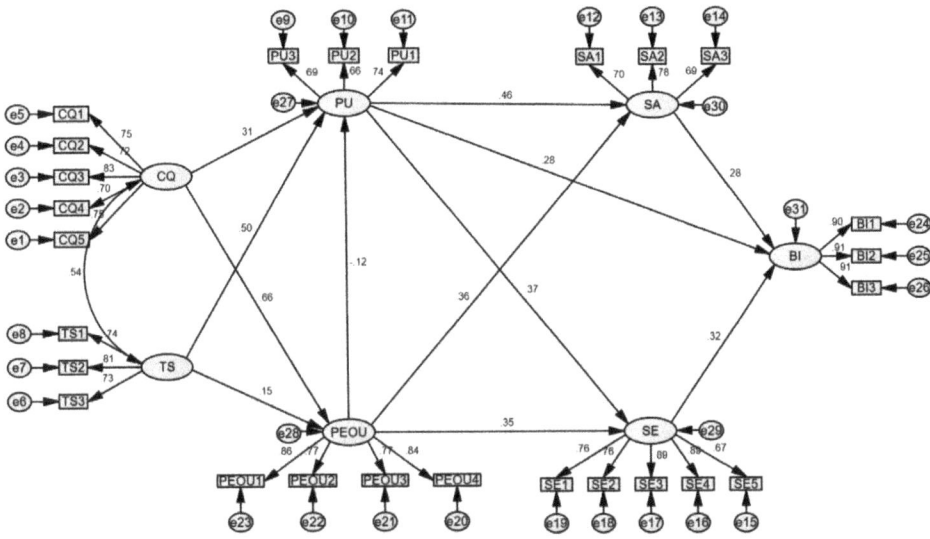

Figure 2. Structural equation model.

5. Discussion and Implications

The increasing popularity of BL indicates its vitality and sustainability. This study explores the comprehensive influencing factors regarding learners' continuous use intention of the BL mode and the relationship among these factors. As shown in Figure 2, the impact of CQ on PEOU is far greater than that of PU, implying that learners pay more attention to the content a course can offer. If a course includes abundant resources, it will trigger more motivation and enthusiasm in learners, thus lowering the perceived difficulty level of using it. The richer and friendlier the interface and the communication tools, the more eager learners are to use the course. The more self-efficacy they have, the more belief they hold regarding their ability to overcome any technological problems in learning and focus only on the learning process. This implies that the most important determinant of BL is the usefulness of the learning content. The holistic design of the course will induce more confidence and curiosity in the study. As CQ is mainly presented through course resources and teaching methods, teachers must be very careful in designing the course syllabus to meet the needs of the learners.

The influence of TS on PU (path coefficient is 0.502, $p < 0.05$) is greater than its influence on PEOU (path coefficient is 0.153), which is also out of expectations. It can be seen that in BL, TS no longer focuses on solving technological problems such as equipment and system failures or network failures because currently, the advancement of technology has caused this to be rare, and even if there are such problems, they can be solved without much effort or delay. The new form of technological support that learners need is convenient instruction regarding the use of BL. Once they become familiar with it, TS seems to have done its work. All that remains is for learners to carry out the course requirements on schedule.

In this study, PU and PEOU continue to play a huge role in affecting use intention indirectly through SA and SE. PU has a significant positive impact on SA and SE (path coefficients are 0.458 and 0.374). PEOU also has a significant positive impact on SA and SE (path coefficients are 0.358 and 0.346). This shows that SA is more likely to be affected by PU. This result echoes the above findings that information technology is no longer a big barrier for learners. This conclusion can also be supported by the only false hypothesis in this model.

In TAM, PEOU has been proven to have a direct positive influence on PU [18]. However, in this study, PEOU has a negative but insignificant influence on PU. This is consistent with some studies [65–68]. In the past, when new technology was put into use, potential users tended to feel anxious about it. To quickly eliminate this anxiety, IT technicians made every effort to make users familiar with the new technology. As the practice went on, they came to realize that basic technological skills should not be barriers to the use of technology. New technological design should be more humanized and friendly to advocate the use of new technology. At the same time, learners' technological skills are improving. In this case, IT technicians' responsibilities are greatly reduced, and they just need to list all the possible problems in a guidebook for learners to refer to whenever a problem comes up.

In this model, there is still a strong positive relationship between SA and BI (path coefficient = 0.278, $p < 0.05$), and there is also a positive relationship between SE and BI (path coefficient = 0.32, $p < 0.05$). These two impacts are close, with SE having a little higher effect on BI. It can be seen from the study that TAM alone is not enough for predicting learners' BI for BL. Their self-efficacy also plays a crucial role in the decision-making process. Although SE has been proven to have a significant impact on PU and PEOU [69,70], their relationship is actually two-way. In this study, to show the importance of the design of BL, PU and PEOU were tested to determine their impact on SE, and the result did show that there is a strong relationship between them. In the study, BI is mainly affected by learners' self-efficacy, followed by learners' satisfaction with blended learning. The affirmation of the effect of SA and SE on BI supports the necessity to build a TAM-SET model to predict learners' continuous intention to use BL.

To help achieve the goal of the study, active exploration and reform can be carried out from the following five aspects. First, improve the teaching quality of online and offline instruction. Teachers must expand their teaching knowledge scope, optimize the teaching design and help learners to gain more personalized learning experience in a timely manner. At the same time, technical support staff should strengthen the service level of online learning support to ensure learners' smooth implementation of BL. Second, enhance learners' perception of the usefulness of BL. Since PU has a significant impact on the continuous use intention of the BL mode, teachers should enhance the course quality to form a valuable curriculum knowledge system for learners and to attract them to study actively. Third, improve the usability of the learning platform. Online learning platforms are essential media for BL. This study finds that the difficulty of using the platform should not be the barrier to adopting the BL mode. Platform designers (mostly teachers and technical support staff) should provide learners with more complex platforms to encourage more active learning. Fourth, improve learners' self-efficacy. Self-efficacy plays a huge role in the learning process. Teachers should understand the needs of learners, and guide them to establish a systematic knowledge structure. At the same time, teachers can take advantage of online and offline Q&A opportunities to strengthen their supervision and guidance of the learners' learning process, help them eliminate learning obstacles, and gain more learning achievements.

6. Conclusions and Future Work

Based on TAM and SET theories, this study proposed a model to explore the relationship among constructs that contributed to learners' continuous use of the BL mode. It identified seven constructs, i.e., course quality (CQ), technological support (TS), perceived usefulness (PU), perceived ease of use (PEOU), satisfaction (SA), self-efficacy (SE), and behavioral intention (BI). Twelve research hypotheses were proposed and tested, and eleven hypotheses are statistically significant. Among them, CQ had the greatest positive impact on PEOU, meaning that the richer the course contents are, the easier and exciting the BL system seems according to the perceptions of the learners. This reveals that students expect to derive more useful knowledge from BL, and this high desire lowers their perception of the level of difficulty regarding the operating the system. If the system is too easy to handle, it will make them feel the hollowness of the resource. Whereas, if the system is abundant, with more useful content, it will arouse their curiosity and interest, making them eager to explore more, regardless of the efforts it may require.

The study confirms again that PU has a significant impact on SA, SE, and BI, and both SA and SE significantly influence BI, with SE playing a more distinct role, which lays a solid foundation for combining TAM and SET theories for predicting learners' continuous use intention.

The main contributions of the study are two-fold. One is that it determines that learners' attitudes toward PEOU are complex. On the one hand, learners hope that the course learning system is easy and flexible to operate to give full play to their autonomous learning. On the other hand, learners want the BL system to be optimized and delicately designed to enable them to acquire more knowledge. The learners would prefer sufficiency to simplicity when using the system. The other contribution of this study is that it adds the construct of SE to TAM and makes it more predictable for acceptance intention tests. Although SE is not first recognized in this field, this is the first time it has been joined with TAM for better prediction in terms of learners' behavior intention toward BI. This shows that SE plays an essential role in BL. A combined TAM-SET model seems to be more appropriate for this study. The findings have great value in helping administrators and educators to think out effective ways to boost learners' SL [71,72]. Keeping pace with the goal of sustainability education is crucial for higher education, and this study has just set an example to help hit this target.

In the future, the study can be improved from two perspectives. First, the subjects of this study come only from Huaqiao University. Although the number of questionnaires collected meets the basic demand, such samples are not representative of the whole situation. In the future, the subjects can be expanded to more colleges and universities to obtain a larger picture of how BL is perceived among learners in higher education. Second, the model in this study is built by combining the theories of TAM and SAT. To further confirm the effectiveness of this effort, future studies should include the outcome of BL to more deeply consider how the model helps build learners' confidence in BL, thus improving their SL.

BL can be an effective means for sustainability education, as it helps cultivate the necessary qualities, such as critical thinking, creative thinking, problem-solving, and cooperative spirit. The increasing popularity of BL makes traditional "teaching" and "learning" undergo profound changes. By merging the advantages of online learning and traditional face-to-face learning, BL has a great potential to arouse learners' learning enthusiasm, strengthen their learning experience, and help them better prepare themselves for constructing a sustainable society for mankind in the future.

Author Contributions: Conceptualization, X.C. and X.X.; methodology, X.C. and X.X.; validation, Y.J.W.; formal analysis, X.C.; investigation, X.C. and X.X.; writing—original draft preparation, X.C., X.X., Y.J.W. and W.F.P.; writing—review and editing, X.C., X.X., Y.J.W. and W.F.P. All authors have read and agreed to the published version of the manuscript.

Funding: This research was funded by Huaqiao University's first-class undergraduate online and offline blended curriculum construction projects and National Science and Technology Council, Taiwan (111-2410-H-003-072-MY3).

Institutional Review Board Statement: Ethical review and approval was not required for this study on human participants, in accordance with the local legislation and institutional requirements.

Informed Consent Statement: Written informed consent from the participants was not required to participate in this study, in accordance with the national legislation and the institutional requirements.

Data Availability Statement: The raw data supporting the conclusions of this article will be made available by the authors, without undue reservation, to any qualified researchers.

Conflicts of Interest: The authors declare no conflict of interest.

References

1. Garrison, D.R.; Kanuka, H. Blended learning: Uncovering its transformative potential in higher education. *Internet High. Educ.* **2004**, *7*, 95–105. [CrossRef]
2. Yao, C. An investigation of adult learners' viewpoints to a blended learning environment in promoting sustainable development in China. *J. Clean. Prod.* **2019**, *220*, 134–143. [CrossRef]
3. Chan, M.N.; Nagatomo, D. Study of STEM for sustainability in design education: Framework for student learning and outcomes with design for a disaster project. *Sustainability* **2021**, *14*, 312. [CrossRef]
4. Ling, S.; Landon, A.; Tarrant, M.; Rubin, D. The influence of instructional delivery modality on sustainability literacy. *Sustainability* **2021**, *13*, 10274. [CrossRef]
5. Micklethwaite, P. Sustainable Design Masters: Increasing the sustainability literacy of designers. *Sustainability* **2022**, *14*, 3255. [CrossRef]
6. Lozano, R. Incorporation and institutionalization of SD into universities: Breaking through barriers to change. *J. Clean. Prod.* **2006**, *14*, 787–796. [CrossRef]
7. Læssøe, J.; Schnack, K.; Breiting, S.; Rolls, S.; Feinstein, N.; Goh, K.C. Climate Change and Sustainable Development: The Response from Education. A Cross-National Report from International Alliance of Leading Education Institutes. Ph.D. Thesis, Aarhus University, Aarhus, Denmark, 2009.
8. Wals, A.E.; van der Hoeven, E.M.M.M.; Blanken, H. *The Acoustics of Social Learning: Designing Learning Processes That Contribute to a More Sustainable World*; Wageningen Academic Publishers: Wageningen, The Netherlands, 2009.
9. Herbert, C.; Velan, G.M.; Pryor, W.M.; Kumar, R.K. A model for the use of blended learning in large group teaching sessions. *BMC Med. Educ.* **2017**, *17*, 197. [CrossRef]
10. Pei, L.; Wu, H. Does online learning work better than offline learning in undergraduate medical education? A systematic review and meta-analysis. *Med. Educ. Online* **2019**, *24*, 1666538. [CrossRef]
11. Oakley, G. From Diffusion to Explosion: Accelerating Blended Learning at the University of Western Australia. In *Blended Learning for Quality Higher Education: Selected Case Studies on Implementation from Asia-Pacific*; Lim, C.P., Wang, L., Eds.; UNESCO: Paris, France, 2016; pp. 67–102.
12. Yen, J.C.; Lee, C.Y. Exploring problem solving patterns and their impact on learning achievement in a blended learning environment. *Comput. Educ.* **2011**, *56*, 138–145. [CrossRef]
13. Makhdoom, N.; Khoshhal, K.I.; Algaidi, S.; Heissam, K.; Zolaly, M.A. 'Blended learning' as an effective teaching and learning strategy in clinical medicine: A comparative cross-sectional university-based study. *J. Taibah Univ. Med. Sci.* **2013**, *8*, 12–17. [CrossRef]
14. Xiong, S. The construction of evaluation mode for blended teaching based on the Kirkpatrick's model. *J. Wuxi Inst. Technol.* **2017**, *16*, 24–27.
15. McCombs, B.L.; Vakili, D. A learner-centered framework for e-learning. *Teach. Coll. Rec.* **2005**, *107*, 1582–1600. [CrossRef]
16. Graham, C.R.; Woodfield, W.; Harrison, J.B. A framework for institutional adoption and implementation of blended learning in higher education. *Internet High. Educ.* **2013**, *18*, 4–14. [CrossRef]
17. Anthony Jnr, B. An exploratory study on academic staff perception towards blended learning in higher education. *Educ. Inf. Technol.* **2022**, *27*, 3107–3133. [CrossRef]
18. O'Connor, C.; Mortimer, D.; Bond, S. Blended learning: Issues, benefits and challenges. *Int. J. Employ. Stud.* **2011**, *19*, 63–83.
19. Khan, A.I.; Shaik, M.S.; Ali, A.M.; Bebi, C.V. Study of blended learning process in education context. *Int. J. Mod. Educ. Comput. Sci.* **2012**, *4*, 23. [CrossRef]
20. So, H.J.; Brush, T.A. Student perceptions of collaborative learning, social presence and satisfaction in a blended learning environment: Relationships and critical factors. *Comput. Educ.* **2008**, *51*, 318–336. [CrossRef]
21. Pammer, M.; Pattermann, J.; Schlgl, S. Self-regulated learning strategies and digital interruptions in Webinars. In *Communications in Computer and Information Science*; Springer: Berlin/Heidelberg, Germany, 2021.
22. Wu, J.H.; Tennyson, R.D.; Hsia, T.L. A study of student satisfaction in a blended e-learning system environment. *Comput. Educ.* **2010**, *55*, 155–164. [CrossRef]
23. Davis, F.D. A Technology Acceptance Model for Empirically Testing New End-User Information Systems: Theory and Results. Ph.D. Thesis, MIT Sloan School of Management, Cambridge, MA, USA, 1986.
24. Bandura, A. *Social Foundations of Thought and Action: A Cognitive Social Theory*; Prentice-Hall: Englewood Cliffs, NJ, USA, 1986.
25. Sahin, I.; Shelley, M. Considering students' perceptions: The distance education student satisfaction model. *J. Educ. Technol. Soc.* **2008**, *11*, 216–223.
26. Zheng, W.; Yu, F.; Wu, Y. Social media on blended learning: The effect of rapport and motivation. *Behav. Inf. Technol.* **2022**, *41*, 1941–1951. [CrossRef]
27. Porter, W.W.; Graham, C.R. Institutional drivers and barriers to faculty adoption of blended learning in higher education. *Br. J. Educ. Technol.* **2016**, *47*, 748–762. [CrossRef]
28. Anthony, B.; Kamaludin, A.; Romli, A.; Raffei, A.F.M.; Phon, D.N.A.; Abdullah, A.; Ming, G.L. Blended learning adoption and implementation in higher education: A theoretical and systematic review. *Technol. Knowl. Learn.* **2020**, *27*, 531–578. [CrossRef]
29. Davis, F.D.; Bagozzi, R.P.; Warshaw, P.R. User acceptance of computer technology: A comparison of two theoretical models. *Manag. Sci.* **1989**, *35*, 8. [CrossRef]

30. Virvou, M.; Katsionis, G. On the usability and likeability of virtual reality games for education: The case of VR-ENGAGE. *Comput. Educ.* **2008**, *50*, 154–178. [CrossRef]
31. Sharma, S.; Dick, G.; Chin, W.; Land, L. *Self-Regulation and E-Learning*; University of St. Gallen: St. Gallen, Switzerland, 2007.
32. Nov, O.; Ye, C. Users' personality and perceived ease of use of digital libraries: The case for resistance to change. *J. Am. Soc. Inf. Sci. Technol.* **2008**, *59*, 845–851. [CrossRef]
33. Wang, W.; Zhao, Y.; Wu, Y.; Goh, M. Interaction strategies in online learning: Insights from text analytics on iMOOC. *Educ. Inf. Technol.* **2022**, *205*, 1. [CrossRef]
34. Bandura, A. *Social Learning Theory*; Prentice Halls: Englewood Cliffs, NJ, USA, 1977.
35. Ajzen, I. Perceived behavior control, self-efficacy, locus of control, and the theory of planned behavior. *J. Appl. Soc. Psychol.* **2002**, *32*, 665–683. [CrossRef]
36. Abdullah, F.; Ward, R. Developing a general extended technology acceptance model for E-learning (GETAMEL) by analysing commonly used external factors. *Comput. Hum. Behav.* **2016**, *56*, 238–256. [CrossRef]
37. Zhu, Z.L.; Li, C. Research on evaluation model and index system of distance learning support service. *China Audio-Vis. Educ.* **2007**, *2*, 42–45.
38. Pan, C.C. System use of WebCT in the light of the technology acceptance model: A student perspective. Ph.D. Thesis, University of Central Florida, Orlando, FL, USA, 2003.
39. Al-Emran, M.; Arpaci, I.; Salloum, S.A. An empirical examination of continuous intention to use m-learning: An integrated model. *Educ. Inf. Technol.* **2020**, *25*, 2899–2918. [CrossRef]
40. Wu, B.; Zhang, C. Empirical study on continuance intentions towards E-Learning 2.0 systems. *Behav. Inf. Technol.* **2014**, *33*, 1027–1038. [CrossRef]
41. Kim, T.; Suh, Y.K.; Lee, G.; Choi, B.G. Modelling roles of task-technology fit and self-efficacy in hotel employees' usage behaviours of hotel information systems. *Int. J. Tour. Res.* **2010**, *12*, 709–725. [CrossRef]
42. Brahim, M.; Mohamad, M. Awareness, readiness and acceptance of the learners' in polytechnic of sultan abdul halim mu'adzam shah on m-learning. *Asian J. Sociol. Res.* **2018**, *1*, 21–33.
43. Siegel, D. *Accepting Technology and Overcoming Resistance to Change Using the Motivation and Acceptance Model*; Proquest, Umi Dissertation Publishing: Ann Arbor, MI, USA, 2008.
44. Zheng, Q.H.; Li, Q.J.; Li, C. Investigation of MOOCs teaching mode in China. *Open Educ. Res.* **2015**, *6*, 71–79.
45. Hair, J.F.; Sarstedt, M.; Ringle, C.M.; Mena, J.A. An assessment of the use of partial least squares structural equation modeling in marketing research. *J. Acad. Mark. Sci.* **2012**, *40*, 414–433. [CrossRef]
46. Šumak, B.; Šorgo, A. The acceptance and use of interactive whiteboards among teachers: Differences in UTAUT determinants between pre- and post-adopters. *Comput. Hum. Behav.* **2016**, *64*, 602–620. [CrossRef]
47. Chauhan, S.; Jaiswal, M. Determinants of acceptance of ERP software training in business schools: Empirical investigation using UTAUT model. *Int. J. Manag. Educ.* **2016**, *14*, 248–262. [CrossRef]
48. Tosuntaş, Ş.B.; Karadağ, E.; Orhan, S. The factors affecting acceptance and use of interactive whiteboard within the scope of FATIH project: A structural equation model based on the unified theory of acceptance and use of technology. *Comput. Educ.* **2015**, *81*, 169–178. [CrossRef]
49. Cheung, M.F.; To, W.M. Service co-creation in social media: An extension of the theory of planned behaviour. *Comput. Hum. Behav.* **2016**, *65*, 260–266. [CrossRef]
50. Byrne, B.M. *Structural Equation Modeling with Mplus: Basic Concepts, Applications, and Programming*; Routledge: Oxfordshire, UK, 2013.
51. Po-An Hsieh, J.J.; Wang, W. Explaining employees' extended use of complex information systems. *Eur. J. Inf. Syst.* **2007**, *16*, 216–227. [CrossRef]
52. Yang, K.C. Exploring factors affecting the adoption of mobile commerce in Singapore. *Telemat. Inform.* **2005**, *22*, 257–277. [CrossRef]
53. Kim, T.; Chiu, W. Consumer acceptance of sports wearable technology: The role of technology readiness. *Int. J. Sport. Mark. Spons.* **2018**, *20*, 109–126. [CrossRef]
54. Amin, M.; Rezaei, S.; Abolghasemi, M. User satisfaction with mobile websites: The impact of perceived usefulness (PU), perceived ease of use (PEOU) and trust. *Nankai Bus. Rev. Int.* **2014**, *5*, 258–274. [CrossRef]
55. Tang, T.T.; Nguyen, T.N.; Tran, H.T.T. Vietnamese teachers' acceptance to use E-assessment tools in teaching: An empirical study using PLS-SEM. *Contemp. Educ. Technol.* **2022**, *14*, 375. [CrossRef] [PubMed]
56. Wong, T.K.M.; Man, S.S.; Chan, A.H.S. Exploring the acceptance of PPE by construction workers: An extension of the technology acceptance model with safety management practices and safety consciousness. *Saf. Sci.* **2021**, *139*, 105239. [CrossRef]
57. Huarng, K.H.; Yu, T.H.K.; Fang Lee, C. Adoption model of healthcare wearable devices. *Technol. Forecast. Soc. Chang.* **2022**, *174*, 121286. [CrossRef]
58. Hanham, J.; Lee, C.B.; Teo, T. The influence of technology acceptance, academic self-efficacy, and gender on academic achievement through online tutoring. *Comput. Educ.* **2021**, *172*, 104252. [CrossRef]
59. Song, H.; Kim, T.; Kim, J.; Ahn, D.; Kang, Y. Effectiveness of VR crane training with head-mounted display: Double mediation of presence and perceived usefulness. *Autom. Constr.* **2021**, *122*, 103506. [CrossRef]

60. Al-Abdullatif, A.M.; Gameil, A.A. The effect of digital technology integration on students' academic performance through project-based learning in an E-learning environment. *Int. J. Emerg. Technol. Learn.* **2021**, *16*, 11. [CrossRef]
61. Malureanu, A.; Panisoara, G.; Lazar, I. The relationship between self-confidence, self-efficacy, grit, usefulness, and ease of use of elearning platforms in corporate training during the COVID-19 pandemic. *Sustainability* **2021**, *11*, 6633. [CrossRef]
62. Alalwan, A.A.; Dwivedi, Y.K.; Rana, N.P.; Simintiras, A.C. Jordanian consumers' adoption of telebanking: Influence of perceived usefulness, trust and self-efficacy. *Int. J. Bank Mark.* **2016**, *34*, 690–709. [CrossRef]
63. Venkatesh, V.; Davis, F.D. A model of the antecedents of perceived ease of use: Development and test. *Decis. Sci.* **1996**, *27*, 451–481. [CrossRef]
64. Holden, H.; Rada, R. Understanding the influence of perceived usability and technology self-efficacy on teachers' technology acceptance. *J. Res. Technol. Educ.* **2011**, *43*, 343–367. [CrossRef]
65. Hsu, C.-L.; Lu, H.-P. Why do people play on-line games? An extended TAM with social influences and flow experience. *Inf. Manag.* **2004**, *41*, 853–868. [CrossRef]
66. Flett, R.; Alpass, F.; Humphries, S.; Claire, M.; Stuart, M.; Nigel, L. The technology acceptance model and use of technology in New Zealand dairy farming. *Agric. Syst.* **2004**, *80*, 199–211. [CrossRef]
67. Chang, I.-C.; Li, Y.-C.; Hung, W.-F.; Hwang, H.-G. An empirical study on the impact of quality antecedents on tax payers' acceptance of Internet tax-filing systems. *Gov. Inf. Q.* **2005**, *22*, 389–410. [CrossRef]
68. Wu, W.W. Developing an explorative model for SaaS adoption. *Expert Syst. Appl.* **2011**, *38*, 15057–15064. [CrossRef]
69. Alalwan, A.A.; Dwivedi, Y.K.; Rana, N.P.; Williams, M.D. Consumer adoption of mobile banking in Jordan: Examining the role of usefulness, ease of use, perceived risk and self-efficacy. *J. Enterp. Inf. Manag.* **2016**, *29*, 118–139. [CrossRef]
70. Shahbaz, M.; Gao, C.; Zhai, L.; Shahzad, F.; Arshad, M.R. Moderating effects of gender and resistance to change on the adoption of big data analytics in healthcare. *Complexity* **2020**, *2020*, 2173765. [CrossRef]
71. Sayaf, A.M.; Alamri, M.M.; Alqahtani, M.A.; Al-Rahmi, W.M. Information and communications technology used in higher education: An empirical study on digital learning as sustainability. *Sustainability* **2021**, *13*, 7074. [CrossRef]
72. Alyoussef, I.Y. Massive open online course (MOOCs) acceptance: The role of task-technology fit (TTF) for higher education sustainability. *Sustainability* **2021**, *13*, 7374. [CrossRef]

Article

Students' Academic Performance and Engagement Prediction in a Virtual Learning Environment Using Random Forest with Data Balancing

Khurram Jawad [1,*], Muhammad Arif Shah [2] and Muhammad Tahir [1,*]

1 College of Computing and Informatics, Saudi Electronic University, Riyadh 11673, Saudi Arabia
2 Department of IT & Computer Science, Pak-Austria Fachhochschule Institute of Applied Sciences & Technology, Haripur 22650, Pakistan
* Correspondence: k.allo@seu.edu.sa (K.J.); m.tahir@seu.edu.sa (M.T.)

Abstract: Virtual learning environment (VLE) is vital in the current age and is being extensively used around the world for knowledge sharing. VLE is helping the distance-learning process, however, it is a challenge to keep students engaged all the time as compared to face-to-face lectures. Students do not participate actively in academic activities, which affects their learning curves. This study proposes the solution of analyzing students' engagement and predicting their academic performance using a random forest classifier in conjunction with the SMOTE data-balancing technique. The Open University Learning Analytics Dataset (OULAD) was used in the study to simulate the teaching–learning environment. Data from six different time periods was noted to create students' profiles comprised of assessments scores and engagements. This helped to identify early weak points and preempted the students performance for improvement through profiling. The proposed methodology demonstrated 5% enhanced performance with SMOTE data balancing as opposed to without using it. Similarly, the AUC under the ROC curve is 0.96, which shows the significance of the proposed model.

Keywords: student academic performance; virtual learning environment; random forest; SMOTE

1. Introduction

E-Learning systems confront a plethora of challenges but the most considerable of them is the lack of students' interest in a variety of activities. In this scenario, if students' engagements and academic performance are predicted, it will help to achieve the basic purpose of distance learning. In a virtual learning environment (VLE), a ginormous amount of data is produced by the participation of students every day. This trove of data can be utilized for student profiling as well as generating trends and hidden patterns. The focus of this study is to predict the academic performance and engagement of students in VLEs through student profiling using artificial-intelligence and machine-learning techniques. The freely available Open University Learning Analytics Dataset (OULAD) is used for this purpose. In the initial stages, students' course information is taken from VLEs, which is preprocessed and cleansed. Our built models are trained on the extracted information and tested on new data that will end up in model evaluation. The model evaluation and building is conducted iteratively until the best performance is revealed.

Information-communications-technology (ICT)-based tools have made VLEs more reliable and, therefore, more universities are now offering online education. Particularly, due to COVID-19, higher education institutions in the Kingdom of Saudi Arabia and around the world have shifted their course offerings to e-learning.

In order to guide analytics in the e-learning paradigm, it is important to have techniques that can provide true analysis of the generated data from students' interactions with the system. Students' interactions can be revealed and associated with their performance on a particular course. The primary objective of the proposed model is to predict students' academic performance and their engagement in various activities through students' profiling in VLE using random forest and data balancing.

In an e-learning environment, students usually do not take an interest in assessment and learning activities. The proposed model will be used to increase the participation level of students by letting them know about their projected performance in advance. Particularly, it will help students improve their academic performance through active participation in academic activities. Development of such models will certainly be useful in identifying social, environment and behavioral factors affecting students' overall performance in e-learning environments.

The primary contributions of this article include the following:

1. We construct students' profiles by combining their assessment scores and engagement with a VLE.
2. We utilize random forest in conjunction with a data-balancing technique to predict the students' academic performance from their profiles.
3. We investigate the performance of our proposed model by exploiting data from six different intervals, including the data for first 120 days, 150 days, 180 days, 210 days, 230 days, and 260 days.

2. Related Work

Traditional education and computer-based education are the two educational environments in practice today across academia, where the latter is well-known as e-learning [1]. Educational institutions around the world are now rapidly moving towards e-learning, with novel learning strategies that can help improve learning methodologies [2]. Innovation in information and communication technology tools have played a critical role in the growth of web-based teaching and learning processes [3], particularly in the post-COVID-19 scenario. E-learning systems have not only become an integral part of teaching over the web but also play a fundamental role in aiding face-to-face student–teacher sessions [4]. Transition from traditional learning environments to e-learning environments has created many challenges, particularly the lack of interest of the students, which affects their academic performance. Therefore, it is of the utmost importance to develop techniques which can identify reasons and forecast students' projected performance. To achieve this, a number of studies [5–10] have been conducted in the recent past to explore the e-learning domain.

Ghassen Ben Brahim [11] extracted an 86-dimensional feature space where only informative features were exploited by various machine-learning algorithms to categorize a student as an academically low performer or high performer. The author evaluated the performance of the proposed methodology under three different experimental scenarios and obtained a 97.4% accuracy using a random-forest classifier.

Nikola et al. [12] employed various machine-learning algorithms to analyze the performance of their proposed approach. The authors addressed the problem of exam prediction both as classification and regression tasks. In the case of classification, the students were identified either as "pass" or "fail" where, as in case of regression, the actual score of the student exam was predicted. Similarly, Sekeroglu et al. [13] analyzed the Student Performance Dataset and Students Academic Performance Dataset using a number of machine-learning algorithms where the former dataset was used for prediction and the latter for classification. Burgos [14] took students' online activities into account to predict their performance while using an e-learning system. The author categorized students based on their learning styles using the data obtained from their log-in history and learning management system from the Sakai platform [15]. Prior to classification, preprocessing, feature selection and parameter optimization was performed. This type of categorization will help to predict students' performance in a particular course. Another study [16] showed that machine-learning techniques can effectively use historical grades of a student to predict their final grades. A dashboard was designed to forecast students' performance in real time which may help prevent students from making premature decisions about dropping out. In another study [17], machine-learning techniques were used to predict students' engagement from their behavioral features and analyze its effect on assessment grades. Instructors can easily identify low-engagement students with the help of a dashboard that displays students' activities in the learning environment. An adaptive gamified learning system [18] was developed which utilizes educational data mining with gamification and adaptation techniques to increase the engagement of students in the learning environment and, consequently, their performance. The effectiveness of gamification against adaptive gamification was analyzed in the e-learning environment. Sana et al. [19] utilized three classifiers to develop a framework for the prediction of students' performance. The authors preprocessed the data collected from a Kalboard 360 online-learning management system by removing less important and redundant features. Next, they performed feature selection and analysis to identify the most discriminative features. Finally, classification algorithms were used to predict the students' performance. They reported the performance using accuracy, precision, recall and F-measure. Abubakar and Ahmad [20] used a random forest algorithm to predict student performance based on their interaction with an e-learning system and assessment marks. They also identified significant attributes, among others that were observed, to be more useful in performance prediction. The literature revealed that machine-learning algorithms can play a very crucial role in enhancing students' interest in e-learning environments. Forecasting the results of students will encourage them to complete their courses. This is due to the fact that students usually drop a course based on their false assumption of failing the course. In this work, we will analyze the performance of a random-forest algorithm in combination with SMOTE data balancing for its effectiveness in predicting students' projected performance.

The rest of the article is structured as follows. Section 3 describes the dataset, data-collection process, data cleansing, model-building process, and evaluation measures. Section 4 explains the experimental setup. Section 5 highlights the obtained results. Section 7 concludes the article.

3. Materials and Methods

3.1. Dataset

Open University Learning Analytics Dataset (OULAD) [21] contains data about courses, students, and the interactions of those students with the VLE. As mentioned in the original documentation of this data, there are total of 7 recorded modules denoted as AAA, BBB, CCC, DDD, EEE, FFF, and GGG. The courses were offered in February and October, respectively, denoted as B and J, where the February semesters are usually 20 days shorter than the October semesters. The data for courses CCC, EEE, and GGG are not available for the years 2013 and 2014.

The dataset was developed from data of 22 modules taught at the Open University which contains not only the demographic data of 32,593 students but also the aggregated data of their assessment results and clickstreams in the form of their interactions with the university VLE. The clickstream data is logged as daily summaries which consist of 10,655,280 entries. Figure 1 illustrates the database schema of the utilized dataset i.e., OULAD which shows student demographics, student activities, and module presentation with detailed data attributes and data types. The dataset is student-centric rather than course-centric. The "courses" relation contains data about course name (code_module), the year and semester in which it is offered (code_presentation), and the length of the module presentation in number of days (length). The "assessments" relation has information about assessments conducted in a given module presentation. In each course module, there are assessments and a final exam. Total weight of the exams and other assessments is 100 each. However, in some courses, only exams are weighted such as course GGG. Similarly, all computer-marked assessments (CMAs) are on the same date in course GGG. Another interesting fact about course GGG is that the first assessment is after 60 days, whereas in all other courses it is during the first 30 days. The "VLE" relation contains information about all the resources accessible to the students in the VLE which are usually pdf files and html pages. Studets' interactions with these online resources are recorded as resource identification number (id_site), code_module, code_presentation, activity_type, the week from which the material is scheduled to be used (week_from), and week until which the resource is scheduled to be used (week_to). The demographics of students are provided in the "studentInfo" relation. The "studentRegistration" table contains information about the registration time of a course presentation. The date of unregistration is also found here. The "studentAssessment" relation has the results of the students' submitted assessments. The value of score field in this relation ranges from 0–100, where the passing score is 40 or above.

Figure 2 highlights the gender-wise distribution of students.

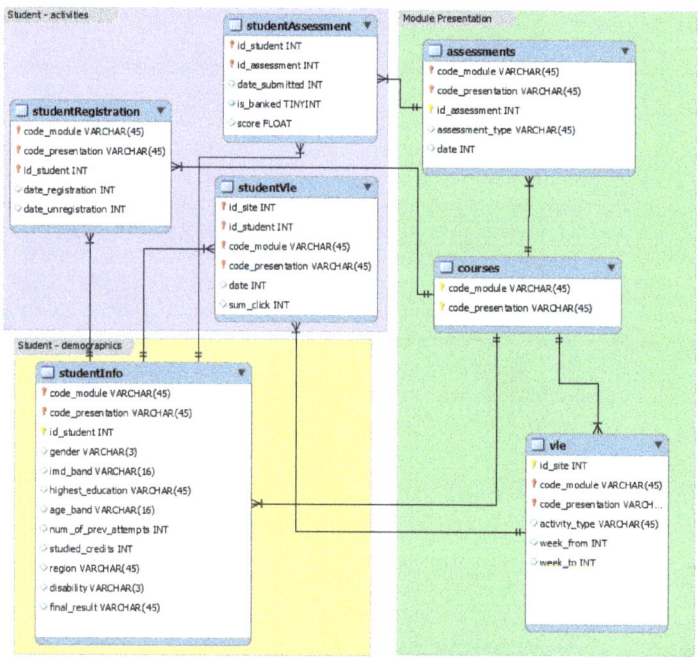

Figure 1. Open University Learning Analytics Dataset Schema [21].

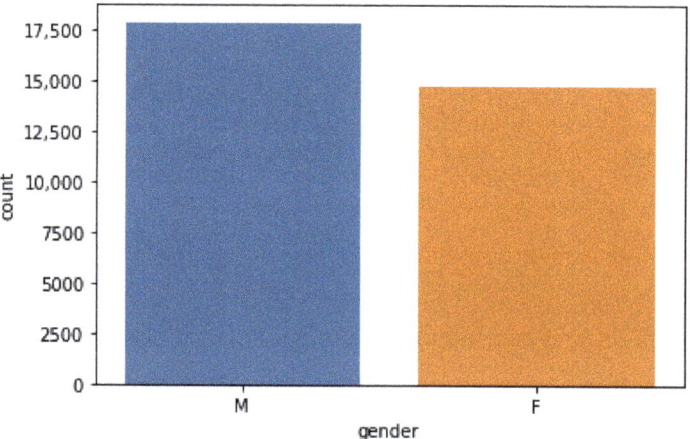

Figure 2. Gender-wise distribution of students in OULAD dataset.

3.2. Data Collection

The OULAD dataset, as mentioned in Section 3.1, was utilized in this research, and represents the data of more than 200,000 enrolled students in European Open University [17]. The dataset consists of sciences, technology, engineering, and mathematics (broadly representing STEM). Module-wise student categories can be seen in Table 1.

Table 1. Dataset Summary.

Module	AAA	BBB	CCC	DDD	EEE	FFF	GGG
Domain	Social Sciences	Social Sciences	STEM	STEM	STEM	STEM	Social Sciences
Presentations	2	4	2	4	3	4	3
Students	748	7909	4434	6272	2934	7762	2534

Its VLE is composed of the course material, course lectures and assessments. Students can interact with each other, work on assignments, watch lecture videos and use materials on VLE while the recorded videos of students interaction can be found in the log files [17]. The information of these students were tabulated as 7 modules such as student registration, subjects, students VLE, students VLE, VLE itself, and assessments [22].

The students activities are recorded in the log-file with timing based on their clicks to indicate how much time was spent on a specific activity. Students' discussion is included as forum variable which indicates a space where students can upload their queries and obtain replies [17]. The very first screen of each subject is represented by variable HomePage. The details about Open University and acronyms of higher education are kept in glossary. Relation between the dataset tables is as shown in Figure 1.

3.3. Methodology

The mechanics of our proposed research model to achieve the aim can be seen in Figure 3. The objective of the proposed methodology is to assess the students' academic performance and predict engagement with the VLE which will ultimately help in predicting the final results of the students. The students' academic performance can be computed from the scores whereas the engagement with the VLE can be measured from the number of clicks on the course-specific online resources.

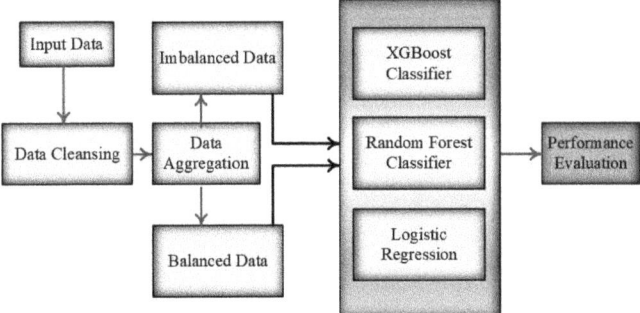

Figure 3. Our proposed research mechanics.

In order to anlyse the students' performance and engagement with the VLE, we utilized average score of a student's assessment within the first number of days from the start of the semester and average number of clicks by a student while accessing each resource category within the first number of days from the start of the semester. In order to form the final feature vector, the two features were combined with other profile information. In this process, the students who withdrew from a course within the first number of days from the start of the semester were grouped with the Fail students. During this process, the students were categorized as Fail and Pass. Note that "distinction" as a result was also replaced by Pass. The withdrawn cases were also grouped with the Fail since the students withdrew from those courses due to their poor performance.

3.3.1. Data Pre-Processing

It was necessary to perform data preprocessing before applying predictive modeling. The data preprocessing includes dealing with inconsistent data, eliminating data noise and imputing missing values through a variety of techniques and strategies. We performed these preprocessing techniques to get the data ready for model application, including creating or changing attributes and selecting the required data object [23,24].

The students' profiles were built from "assessments", "studentAssessment", "studentVle", and "vle" tables putting together student information and the relevant site. All the sites reside in the "vle" table with their ids and types (homepage, content, glossary, subpage, forum, URL, etc.).

The student's score-related information was extracted from the "assessments" and "studentAssessment" tables, which include the course name (code_module), the offered year and semester (code_presentation), the student identification number (id_student), and average score over all assessments for each student over the first number of days (mean_score_day120, i.e., 120 days in this case). Likewise, the student's engagement with VLE-related information was extracted from "studentVle" and "vle" relations, which include course name (code_module), the offered year and semester (code_presentation), student identification number (id_student), and the resources accessed (i.e., dataplus, dualpane, externalquiz, forumng, glossary, homepage, htmlactivity, oucollaborate, oucontent, ouelluminate, ouwiki, page, questionnaire, quiz, repeatactivity, resource, sharedsubpage, subpage, and url).

The students' interaction activities were calculated on different levels which depended on the number of days we considered for model development. We considered 120 days, 150 days, 180 days, 210 days, 230 days, and 260 days of activities to predict the final performance of the students while utilizing their engagement level. The engagement represents the students motivation level until the day of prediction. *Engagement* is the most impactful feature for performance prediction.

The number of students distributed in the original dataset without preprocessing is shown in Figure 4.

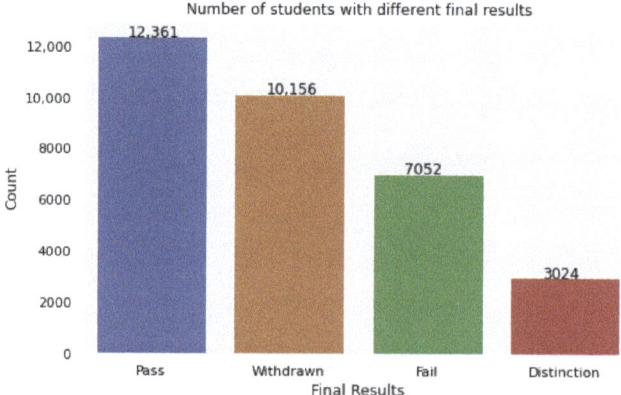

Figure 4. Distribution of the final results in 4 categories.

According to this distribution, the number of students passing the course, considering both simply pass and pass with distinction, is 15,385 whereas the number of students who are not successful is 17,208 (considering both the withdrawn and fail students), as shown in Figure 5.

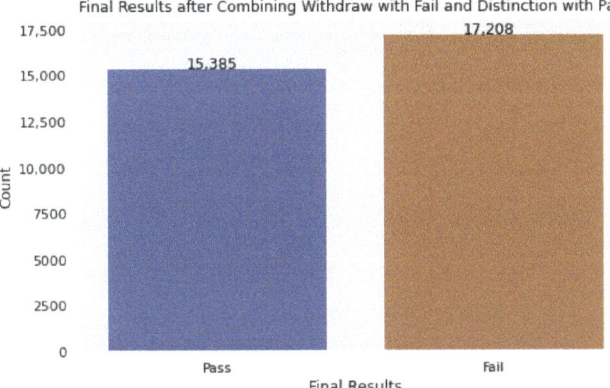

Figure 5. Distribution of the final results in 2 categories.

The input to the machine-learning algorithm was a 30-dimensional feature vector comprising of students' assessment scores and their engagement statistics with the VLE.

3.3.2. Build and Test the Predictive Model

There were a number of AI algorithms used to check their impact and capabilities in predicting the academic performance of students with respect to their profiling. We utilized random-forest classifier and, for the sake of comparison, used XGBoost classifier [25] and logistic regression as well.

A number of studies have used various AI algorithms in academic performance prediction. According to Wolpert and Macready [26], no AI classification algorithms can show better results than every other available for each problem domain. Hence, commonly adopted algorithms were taken into consideration for iteration and benchmarking to identify the best algorithm for the student-performance prediction task.

However, the computation time for training AI algorithms optimally was a bigger challenge, as there were six considered intervals.

3.4. Evaluation Measures

This section describes the performance parameters that are used in this article to evaluate the performance of our proposed models.

3.4.1. Accuracy

Accuracy is the prominent and most common quality-evaluation metric used in this study, as given in Equation (1).

$$Accuracy = (TP + TN)/(TP + FP + TN + FN) \qquad (1)$$

This basically indicates the total number of all possible correct predictions divided by the total number of samples in the dataset used, where 0 is termed as the worst accuracy and 1 as the best accuracy. Note that *TP*, *FP*, *TN*, and *FN* refer to the number of true positives, false positives, true negatives, and false negatives.

3.4.2. Receiver Operating Characteristic

Receiver operating characteristic (ROC) measures the prediction quality of a classifier especially in binary-class classification problems. ROC curve is obtained by plotting true-positive and false-positive rates along Y and X axes, respectively. In order to obtain ideal ROC curve, it is important to minimize false-positive rate while maximizing the true-positive rate. ROC curve estimates the trade off between true- and false-positive rates for a model using various probability threshold values ranging from 0.0 to 1.0.

True-positive rate, or sensitivity, describes the quality of the model at predicting the positive class and is given by Equation (2).

$$TruePositiveRate = TP/(TP+FN) \qquad (2)$$

The FP rate or false-alarm rate describes how many times the model predicted the positive class when the actual output is negative. It is given by Equation (3)

$$FalsePositiveRate = FP/(FP+TN) \qquad (3)$$

3.4.3. Precision–Recall Curve

Precision–recall curve estimates the trade off between TP rate and positive predicted value for a model on various probability thresholds. It is considered a suitable measure in the presence of imbalanced data.

Precision refers to the quality of a model at predicting positive class and is obtained using Equation (4).

$$Precision = TP/(TP+FP) \qquad (4)$$

Recall is obtained using Equation (5).

$$Recall = TP/(TP+FN) \qquad (5)$$

4. Experimental Setup

In this article, each set was generated by varying the number of days during which the students' performance and the final result were evaluated. Fewer number of days indicate that less information was available, whereas larger number of days signifies the availability of more information about students. During each set of experiments, the data was divided in training and testings sets where 67% data was reserved for training and 33% was kept for testing. The best combination of parameters was obtained using RandomizedSearchCV method with RandomForestClassifier. The data was scaled using the StandardScaler() method of sklearn library.

5. Results

5.1. Performance Analysis of Random-Forest Classifier with Random Search Optimization

Table 2 highlights the performance of the random-forest classifier in terms of training and testing accuracy values, ROC-AUC, precision–recall AUC, and F_1-score.

Table 2. Performance accuracy of the proposed technique using the random-forest classifier.

Days	Random Forest				
	Training Accuracy	Testing Accuracy	ROC-AUC	Precision–Recall AUC	F_1 Score
120	90.7	76.3	0.796	0.857	83.1
150	1.0	78.2	0.820	0.895	84.7
180	98.9	81.3	0.861	0.926	87.3
210	1.0	81.1	0.854	0.923	87.2
230	1.0	83.4	0.871	0.936	88.9
260	97.8	84.2	0.894	0.950	89.8

It is evident from the results in Table 2 that the performance of the classifier is enhanced with the increase in the engagement and score information of students to train the classifier. The highest accuracy is 84.2% when 260 days of data was used for training. Similarly, the values of area under the curves of ROC as well as precision–recall curves are higher for 260 days data as shown in Figures 6 and 7, respectively. F_1 score is also higher for the same number of days.

The obtained data for each of the number of days is highly imbalanced. Therefore, we used the SMOTE oversampling technique [27] in conjunction with the random-forest classifier using 260 days of profiling information. The training accuracy is 100% whereas the testing accuracy is 89.2%. As evident from Table 2, due to balancing the data, the testing accuracy is enhanced by 5%, which shows the significance of data balancing in predicting the students' academic performance. The ROC curve is employed to select the appropriate values of decision thresholds to establish a trade off between true- and false-positive rates across each of the six time periods. The ROC curve presented in Figure 8 achieved the AUC score of 0.96.

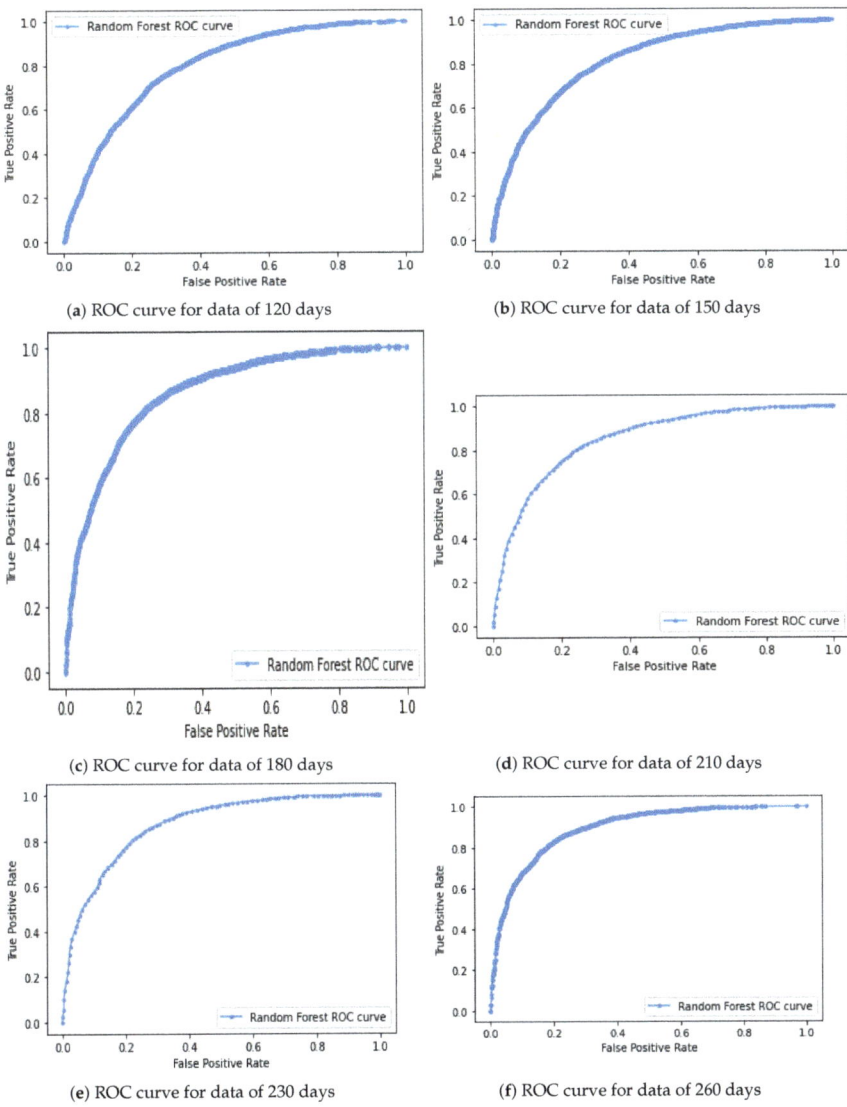

Figure 6. ROC plots of different days of data using fandom-forest classifier without SMOTE.

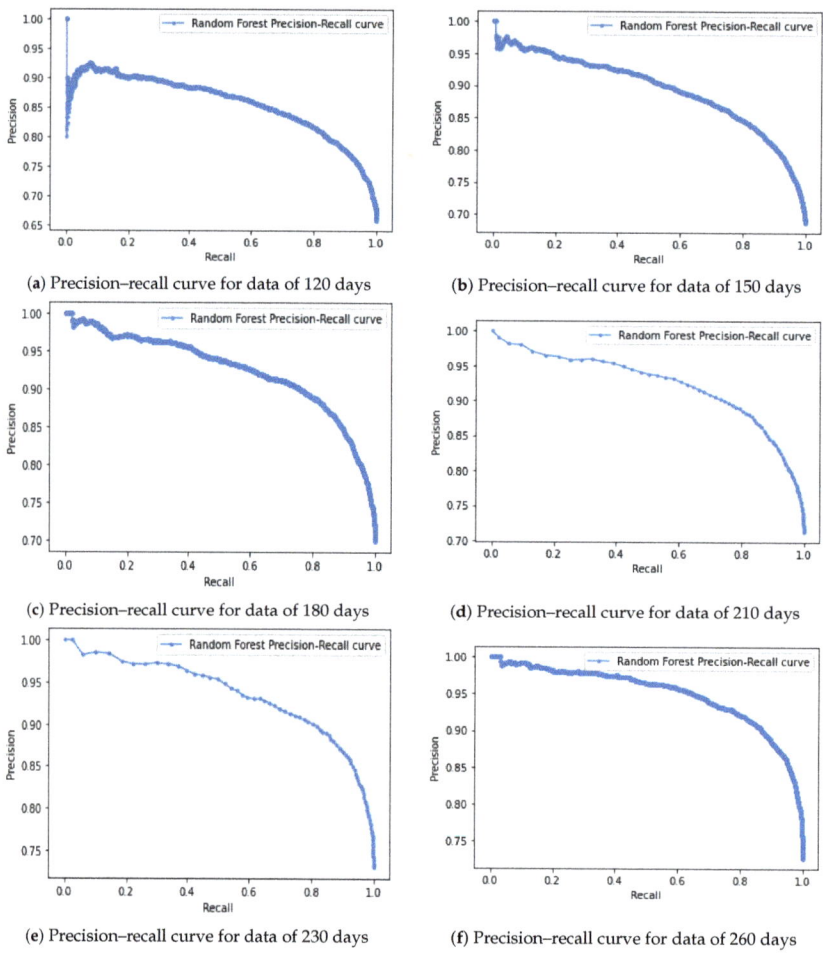

Figure 7. Precision-recall curves for data of different durations using random-forest classifier.

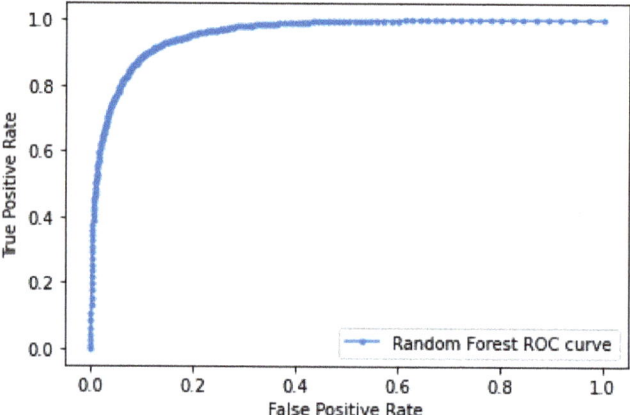

Figure 8. ROC curve for data of 260 days with random forest and SMOTE.

Precision–recall curves were also utilized to assess the performance of the proposed model. The precision–recall curve computed using balanced data is illustrated in Figure 9 where the AUC value is 0.957 and F_1-score value is 89.2.

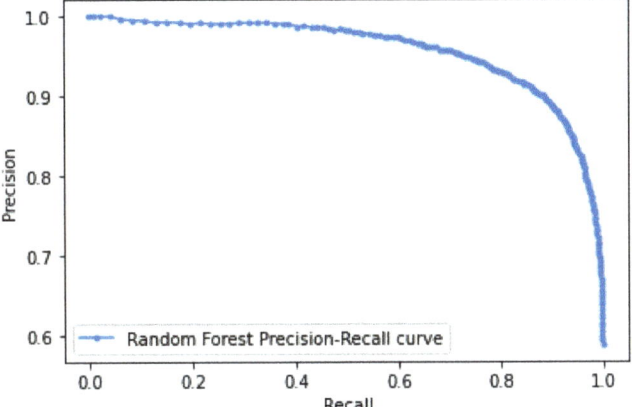

Figure 9. Precision–recall curve for data of 260 days with random forest and SMOTE.

Here, the precision–recall curve indicates the trade off between precision and recall for various threshold values. The AUC value of 0.957 indicates high precision and recall values. In the current problem, high precision shows the correct identification of failed students whereas high recall signifies the correct prediction of pass students. The proposed system produced accurate results as an indication of high precision and also achieved the majority of all pass students an an indication of high recall.

5.2. Performance Analysis of Logistic Regression and XGBoost Classifiers for 260 Days Data

In order to provide further insight, we also performed experiments using logistic regression, which achieved training and testing accuracy values of 80.4% and 80.9%, respectively. The AUC under the ROC curve is also 0.831, which is shown in Figure 10.

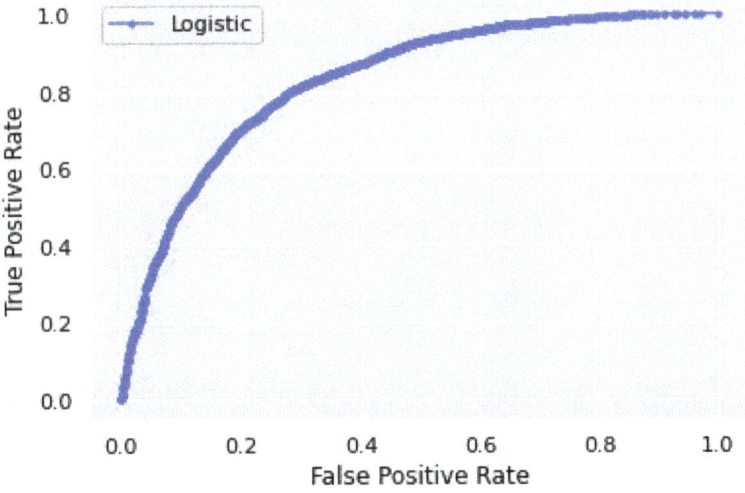

Figure 10. ROC curve for data of 260 days using logistic regression.

We also constructed the precision–recall curve as shown in Figure 11, where the AUC under the precision–recall curve is 0.912 and F_1 score is 87.5.

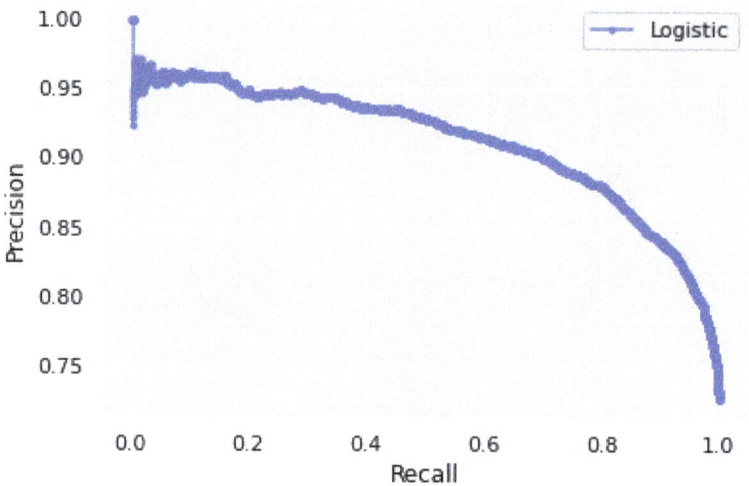

Figure 11. Precision–recall curve for data of 260 days using logistic regression.

Similarly, the XGBoost classifier was also employed to see its behaviour on the data consisting of 260 days score and engagement statistics. The obtained training and testing accuracy values are, respectively, 91.7% and 84.3%. The AUC under the ROC curve is 0.887, as shown in Figure 12.

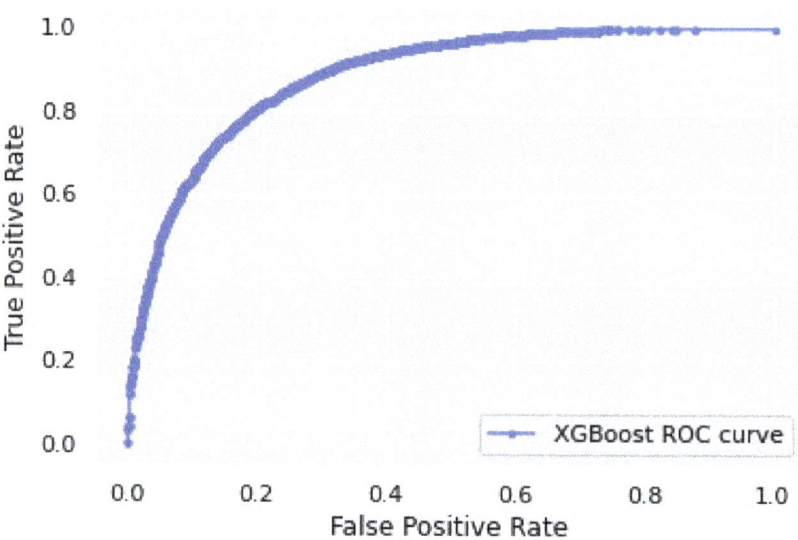

Figure 12. ROC curve for data of 260 days.

The AUC under the precision–recall curve is 0.946, which is also depicted in Figure 13, and the F_1 score is 89.7.

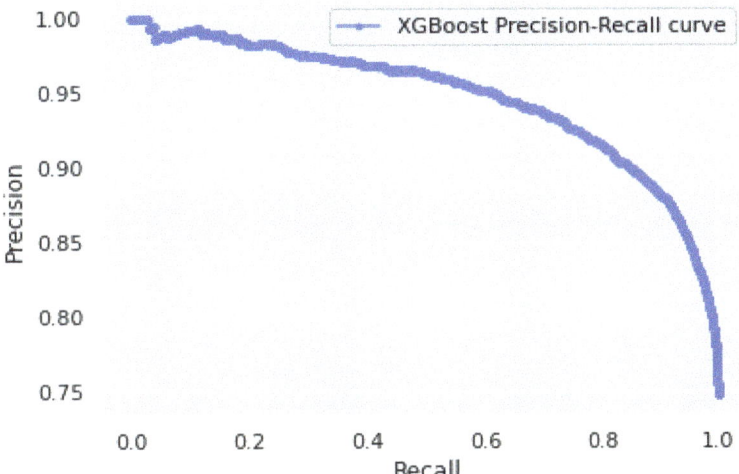

Figure 13. Precision–recall curve for data of 260 days.

6. Discussion

In this article, we investigated the effect of students' engagement with a VLE on their final results. It is observed from the obtained results that the students' engagement with the VLE plays important role in predicting their final results. It indicates that day-to-day engagement with the VLE is of higher importance compared to the students' personal information. The proposed model demonstrated that the effectiveness of engagement information is enhanced by adding data for a higher number of days. That is why the information for 260 days enabled the proposed system to demonstrate enhanced performance. The proposed random-forest-based model can inform the students about their probable failure in a course and guide them towards success. It is possible to identify an individual facing risk of failure; however, the currently proposed work can classify them as group due to the binary nature of the problem under consideration. Consequently, the privacy of individuals is maintained yet the accurate prediction of the entire class can help teachers take appropriate measures to enhance the overall performance of the students.

The trend shows better values towards the day end than from the beginning as more data is provided to the AI algorithm. It can be well-predicted from the trend that performances increase almost at the same pace as they start. Early information can help science students have the chance to improve their performances towards the end of course and before the examination. Connected to this, instructors are advised to execute the model 150 days after the commencement of the course to identify the students at risk of failure.

7. Conclusions

In this work, we analyzed students' academic performance and their engagement with a VLE using random forest in combination with SMOTE. First, the students' profile were developed from the OULAD dataset, which was then used to train a random-forest classifier.

The obtained results revealed the significant performance of the random-forest classifier in predicting the students' academic performance. Data from six different time periods were identified and it is observed that the performance of random forest with SMOTE oversampling is better for the time period of 260 days, which was almost end of the course presentation. This is due to the fact that, towards the end of the academic session, more data on the students engagement and assessments' score is available and more accurate predictions are possible.

Such analyses of students' profiles in the context of a VLE are helpful in identifying weaknesses towards the successful completion of academic session. This will certainly help academicians help students preemptively and lead them to a successful end of their studies.

Author Contributions: Conceptualization, K.J. and M.A.S.; methodology, M.T. and M.A.S.; validation, K.J., M.A.S. and M.T.; formal analysis, M.A.S.; investigation, M.T. and M.A.S.; resources, K.J. and M.A.S.; data curation, M.T. and M.A.S.; writing—original draft preparation, K.J., M.T. and M.A.S.; writing—review and editing, K.J. and M.A.S.; visualization, M.T. and M.A.S.; supervision, M.T.; project administration, K.J.; funding acquisition, K.J. All authors have read and agreed to the published version of the manuscript.

Funding: The authors extend their appreciation to the Deputyship for Research & Innovation, Ministry of Education in Saudi Arabia for funding this research work through the project number 7897.

Institutional Review Board Statement: Not applicable.

Informed Consent Statement: Not applicable.

Data Availability Statement: The data presented in this study are openly available in https://analyse.kmi.open.ac.uk/open_dataset at https://doi.org/10.1038/sdata.2017.171, accessed on 18 May 2022, reference number 170171 (2017).

Conflicts of Interest: The authors declare no conflict of interest.

References

1. Manjarres, A.V.; Sandoval, L.G.M.; Suárez, M.S. Data mining techniques applied in educational environments: Literature review. *Digit. Educ. Rev.* **2018**, *33*, 235–266. [CrossRef]
2. Zareie, B.; Navimipour, N.J. The effect of electronic learning systems on the employee's commitment. *Int. J. Manag. Educ.* **2016**, *14*, 167–175. [CrossRef]
3. Muniasamy, A.; Alasiry, A. Deep Learning: The Impact on Future eLearning. *Int. J. Emerg. Technol. Learn.* **2020**, *15*, 188–199. [CrossRef]
4. Alharthi, A.D.; Spichkova, M.; Hamilton, M. Sustainability requirements for elearning systems: A systematic literature review and analysis. *Requir. Eng.* **2019**, *24*, 523–543. [CrossRef]
5. Umer, R.; Susnjak, T.; Mathrani, A.; Suriadi, S. On predicting academic performance with process mining in learning analytics. *J. Res. Innov. Teach. Learn.* **2017**, *10*, 160–176. [CrossRef]
6. Lu, O.H.; Huang, A.Y.; Huang, J.C.; Lin, A.J.; Ogata, H.; Yang, S.J. Applying learning analytics for the early prediction of Students' academic performance in blended learning. *J. Educ. Technol. Soc.* **2018**, *21*, 220–232.
7. Widyahastuti, F.; Tjhin, V.U. Performance prediction in online discussion forum: State-of-the-art and comparative analysis. *Procedia Comput. Sci.* **2018**, *135*, 302–314. [CrossRef]
8. Zhang, W.; Huang, X.; Wang, S.; Shu, J.; Liu, H.; Chen, H. Student performance prediction via online learning behavior analytics. In Proceedings of the 2017 International Symposium on Educational Technology (ISET), Hong Kong, China, 27–29 June 2017; pp. 153–157.
9. Koutina, M.; Kermanidis, K.L. Predicting postgraduate students' performance using machine learning techniques. In *Artificial Intelligence Applications and Innovations*; Springer: Berlin/Heidelberg, Germany, 2011; pp. 159–168.
10. Alzahrani1, N.A.; Abdullah, M.A. Student Engagement Effectiveness in E-Learning System. *Biosci. Biotechnol. Res. Commun. Spec. Issue Commun. Inf. Technol.* **2019**, *12*, 208–218. [CrossRef]
11. Brahim, G.B. Predicting Student Performance from Online Engagement Activities Using Novel Statistical Features. *Arab. J. Sci. Eng.* **2022**, 10225–10243. [CrossRef]
12. Tomasevic, N.; Gvozdenovic, N.; Vranes, S. An overview and comparison of supervised data mining techniques for student exam performance prediction. *Comput. Educ.* **2020**, *143*, 103676. [CrossRef]
13. Sekeroglu, B.; Dimililer, K.; Tuncal, K. Student performance prediction and classification using machine learning algorithms. In Proceedings of the 2019 8th International Conference on Educational and Information Technology, Cambridge, UK, 2–4 March 2019; pp. 7–11.
14. Burgos, D. Background similarities as a way to predict students' Behaviour. *Sustainability* **2019**, *11*, 6883. [CrossRef]
15. Cavus, N.; Zabadi, T. A comparison of open source learning management systems. *Procedia-Soc. Behav. Sci.* **2014**, *143*, 521–526. [CrossRef]
16. Bueñano-Fernández, D.; Gil, D.; Luján-Mora, S. Application of machine learning in predicting performance for computer engineering students: A case study. *Sustainability* **2019**, *11*, 2833. [CrossRef]
17. Hussain, M.; Zhu, W.; Zhang, W.; Abidi, S.M.R. Student engagement predictions in an e-learning system and their impact on student course assessment scores. *Comput. Intell. Neurosci.* **2018**, *2018*, 6347186. [CrossRef] [PubMed]

18. Daghestani, L.F.; Ibrahim, L.F.; Al-Towirgi, R.S.; Salman, H.A. Adapting gamified learning systems using educational data mining techniques. *Comput. Appl. Eng. Educ.* **2020**, *28*, 568–589. [CrossRef]
19. Sana, B.; Siddiqui, I.F.; Arain, Q.A. Analyzing students' academic performance through educational data mining. *3C Tecnol. Glosas Innovación Apl. Pym* **2019**, *8*, 402–421.
20. Abubakar, Y.; Ahmad, N.B.H. Prediction of students' performance in e-learning environment using random forest. *Int. J. Innov. Comput.* **2017**, *7*. [CrossRef]
21. Kuzilek, J.; Hlosta, M.; Zdrahal, Z. Open university learning analytics dataset. *Sci. Data* **2017**, *4*, 170171. [CrossRef]
22. Jiang, S.; Williams, A.; Schenke, K.; Warschauer, M.; O'dowd, D. Predicting MOOC performance with week 1 behavior. In Proceedings of the Educational Data Mining, London, UK, 4–7 July 2014.
23. Baradwaj, B.K.; Pal, S. Mining educational data to analyze students' performance. *Int. J. Adv. Comput. Sci. Appl.* **2015**, *2*, 63–69.
24. Jović, A.; Brkić, K.; Bogunović, N. A review of feature selection methods with applications. In Proceedings of the 2015 38th International Convention on Information and Communication Technology, Electronics and Microelectronics (MIPRO), Opatija, Croatia, 25–29 May 2015; pp. 1200–1205.
25. Tahir, M. Brain MRI Classification Using Gradient Boosting. In *Machine Learning in Clinical Neuroimaging and Radiogenomics in Neuro-Oncology*; Springer: Berlin/Heidelberg, Germany, 2020; pp. 294–301.
26. Wolpert, D.H.; Macready, W.G. No free lunch theorems for optimization. *IEEE Trans. Evol. Comput.* **1997**, *1*, 67–82. [CrossRef]
27. Tahir, M.; Khan, A.; Majid, A.; Lumini, A. Subcellular localization using fluorescence imagery: Utilizing ensemble classification with diverse feature extraction strategies and data balancing. *Appl. Soft Comput.* **2013**, *13*, 4231–4243. [CrossRef]

Article

E-Learning Model to Identify the Learning Styles of Hearing-Impaired Students

Tidarat Luangrungruang and Urachart Kokaew *

Applied Intelligence and Data Analytics Laboratory, College of Computing, Khon Kaen University, Khon Kaen 40002, Thailand
* Correspondence: urachart@kku.ac.th

Abstract: Deaf students apparently experience hardship in conventional learning; however, despite their inability to hear, nothing can stop them from reading. Although they perform impressively in memorizing the information, their literacy and reading capability still appear to be weak since they lack the chance to revise by listening and practicing repetitively. Currently, the teaching media for deaf students are quite rare and inadequate, forcing them to face difficulties in integrating new knowledge, even though most of the contents are in a form of written, printed, downloaded, or even accessible via an e-learning platform. However, it is crucial to bear in mind that each learner is different. There is evidence showing that some learners prefer particular methods of learning, also known as learning preferences or learning styles. Thus, the present study reports the sequence of learning styles obtained by using a modified VRK + TSL model that categorized students based on their learning styles. We also propose four different ways of teaching using content-adaptive learning styles, namely visual, reading/writing, kinesthetic, and Thai sign language. Based on personal preferences and the principle of universal design under synthesized learning, an e-learning model was developed to identify deaf learners' learning styles. The objective is to provide e-learning to identify the learning styles of hearing-impaired students and to respond with up-to-date e-learning materials that can be used anywhere and at any time. These materials must support the education of deaf students. As a result, learners have increased efficiency and increased learning outcomes.

Keywords: e-learning; hearing-impaired; learning style; universal design

Citation: Luangrungruang, T.; Kokaew, U. E-Learning Model to Identify the Learning Styles of Hearing-Impaired Students. *Sustainability* **2022**, *14*, 13280. https://doi.org/10.3390/su142013280

Academic Editor: Hao-Chiang Koong Lin

Received: 19 September 2022
Accepted: 11 October 2022
Published: 15 October 2022

Publisher's Note: MDPI stays neutral with regard to jurisdictional claims in published maps and institutional affiliations.

Copyright: © 2022 by the authors. Licensee MDPI, Basel, Switzerland. This article is an open access article distributed under the terms and conditions of the Creative Commons Attribution (CC BY) license (https://creativecommons.org/licenses/by/4.0/).

1. Introduction

It is difficult for students with hearing-impaired disabilities to learn language. Their first language is sign language since they cannot hear. This can cause problems for them in learning and in communicating with others, as they must put in more effort and have more patience than normal learners. Furthermore, deaf students require more attention, assistance, and suggestions to support them in learning. Therefore, providing education for this group is composed of preparing students and facilitating them to learn and acquire knowledge.

Impaired-learning students or deaf students are considered as a special needs population when they have to access learning resources, communications, and environments [1]. Their disability cannot be physically seen, so people are not aware of the obstacles the deaf are encountering as they look similar to others. It could be concluded that, as "the deaf solely rely on their vision to access information, which differs from normal people who can use both eyes and ears, so the optimum media for the deaf is the visual ones" [2]. Therefore, the instruction created for the deaf students should be delicately constructed in terms of the curriculum, teaching method, instructional media, assessment, and educational support [3].

Education for hearing-impaired students was established on 10 December 1951. At present, there are 21 schools for deaf students under the Special Education Bureau of Thailand, namely Setsatian School for the Deaf under the royal patronage of His Royal

Highness Crown Prince Maha Vajiralongkorn, Thungmahamek School for the Deaf, Debaratana School for the Deaf, Pan Loet School for the Deaf, Anusan Sunthon School for the Deaf, Kanchanaburi School for the Deaf, Khon Kaen School for the Deaf, Chonburi School for the Deaf, Chaiyaphum School for the Deaf, Tak School for the Deaf, Nakhon Pathom School for the Deaf, Nakhon Si thammarat School for the Deaf, Nonthaburi School for the Deaf, Phang-nga School for the Deaf, Phetchabun School for the Deaf, Mukdahan School for the Deaf, Roi Et School for the Deaf, Songkhla School for the Deaf, Surin School for the Deaf, and Udon Thani School for the Deaf.

In Thailand, the Department of Empowerment of Persons with Disability has stated in the legal guide for empowering and improving the life of persons with a disability (2009) that "disabled people's right to access facility" refers to the ability to access and utilize the facility for disabled people, which is composed of the following three dimensions:

1. A universal and fair design whose principles are inclusive and idealistic;
2. The provision of assistive technology is the core of how to meet the special, personal, or group needs;
3. Reasonable accommodation between the two parties where both sides' willingness to compromise is sufficient in whatever situations occur. The matter of providing reasonable accommodation is that the government must prioritize it by assigning related sectors, such as education and vocational agencies as well as social welfare to accommodate people with disabilities. Such accommodation should include the universal and fair design, and assistive technology and equipment considering equality and personal needs.

To construct a quality education for these people requires an integration of processes to fully develop learners' potential, enabling them to be independent, autonomous learners with essential life skills. Traditional teaching methods are one of the reasons that these students can struggle. Students learn only through conventional methods, and they may find these boring and ineffective. Education and teaching styles have changed dramatically, and new forms of technology have been achieved. In addition, in today's era, where working from home and online teaching have become the new normal all over the world, technology and teaching have become inseparable [4]. Applying technology to teaching and learning will help motivate students, especially when the components of the media consist of images, videos, animations, and sign language communication. E-learning is one way to assist this group of students when they are interested in learning a certain subject. At present, several techniques are applied to make the animations more appealing. Learners then easily acquire the knowledge, are attracted and not bored, and finally accomplish satisfying academic results. These methods could help them stay focused and allow them to autonomously practice, as well as enhance their confidence [5]. Furthermore, the deaf can autonomously and independently learn anywhere and anytime they want. This could be a guideline to develop media for other subjects effectively in the future, as learners are at the center of the learning process.

E-learning is a responsive learning medium as it is a study material that can be attended and reviewed at any time. It can allow students to spend more time on the material in order to gain a greater understanding. However, the current e-learning materials did not meet the needs of the learners or did not have enough material. Even though e-learning is designed to accommodate deaf students [6–8], there is no adaptive e-learning system that can indicate the learner's learning style, although there are lessons that are built according to the learner's learning style, which adds a special feature to e-learning. Therefore, adaptive e-learning teaching materials have been created that show the lesson pages according to the learner's learning style.

This adaptive e-learning selects an appropriate learning style path based on the student's background information to select the most appropriate learning style for the hearing-impaired student through the classification of the decision tree. Learners are taught lessons according to their preferences and aptitudes, as part of an e-learning system that reduces assessment of the learner's learning style. The acquisition of technology-enabled teaching and learning has increased rapidly [9–13]. Increasing technological skills in the teaching and learning processes is called Education 4.0. This automated e-learning system is also considered as an example of Education 4.0. The teaching and learning processes that support this technology are core concepts of Education 4.0. This type of technology-based teaching and learning experience provides students with opportunities for self-learning [14].

2. Literature Review

2.1. Universal Design (UD)

Universal design (UD) is the designation of products and environments for maximum use by everyone without modifications or specific designs [15]. 'Universal' means 'everyone' or 'each person'. It is the concept of providing user-friendly products to different types of users without discrimination [16,17]. The UD view develops from the roots of the disability rights movement to an aging population, health and well-being, and social inclusion [18]. The scope of UD usage ranges from planners and designers to facility managers. In particular, it occurs in buildings, shopping malls, public facilities, the health sector, rehabilitation, and all types of disability-related groups [19–22].

In other words, universal design is dedicated to improving the quality of life through designing a better society regardless of age, gender, culture, ability, or disability [15].

Universal design facilitates everybody. No single person is targeted. Therefore, it is adopted in teaching and learning to diminish learning obstacles, make the teaching flexible, and to provide equal education for a wide range of people.

2.2. Universal Design for Learning (UDL)

The first principle underlying UDL is the belief that there are many ways to express knowledge during the learning process [23]. It involves designing teaching materials that allow diverse learners to access the content as much as possible [24]. Although UDL generally improves the learning process for all students, the impact may vary across different student groups and learning cycle [23]

In the field of special education, the universal design for learning has been adopted by applying technology to meet learners' different desires. Its principle focuses on the concept that each learner is unique, with diverse needs. That is why universal design for learning adopted in special education should be able to create optimum learning environments that meet learners' demands and encourage them to achieve their full potential in improving themselves. The universal design is an instant instructional media that teachers can promptly use with students.

The concept of universal learning was applied in the design of e-learning in this study, where different learning demands from each learner are considered and accomplished [25]. The solution to meet learners' requirements was rooted in the concept of universal learning, as it was part of the lesson plan that assists teachers in constructing effective lessons for their classes [26]. The Table 1 shows that these procedures are consistent with the three UDL principles.

The application of universal design is categorized into three levels, as follows:

- 1st Level: Presentation Level

Learning management based on universal design consists of various kinds of presentation, including the following:

- Different patterns of information, such as images, audio, or concrete information;
- Various languages and symbols;
- Opportunities to revise lessons.

- 2nd Level: Communication Level

In this level, learners are allowed to express in different ways, including the following:

- Using their body;
- Speaking;
- Using executive function.

- 3rd Level: Participation Level

    This level motivates learners using the following techniques:
    - Providing freedom to choose;
    - Encouraging an effort in performing;
    - Encouraging self-regulation.

Table 1. The development of an e-learning model to identify the learning styles of hearing-impaired students.

Universal Design Learning	Steps of Practice
Representation	- Design the content - Make it applicable and suitable - Use multimedia, such as websites, videos, images, and text - Use sign language and symbols
Actions and expressions	- Adopt heuristic evaluation and examine satisfaction using questionnaires and suggestions
Participation	- Data is applied to construct an e-learning model that identifies deaf students' learning styles through learning preferences and the principles of universal design

2.3. E-Learning

E-learning is defined as the sequence of lessons containing specific instructional content and activities in a standardized pattern embedded in electronic media. Inside it, there are objectives, lessons, learning activities, and achievement tests, as well as pre-tests and post-tests. Students can correct their information and monitor their learning outcome. Moreover, the interactions between teacher and students and vice versa can be conducted via chat boards or emails.

E-learning adopts electronic technology to create learning experiences [27,28]. E-learning can be considered as a well-designed learning guidance, putting the learning process as a center for everybody anywhere and at any time [29,30]. Currently, there are few teaching materials for deaf students. Most textbooks contain only texts and pictures that require sign language during the teaching process. If the instructors cannot convey meaning correctly and clearly, misunderstandings can occur. Developing an e-learning model can solve the problem systematically for the deaf students since the communication will become more accurate, precise, customizable, supportive of the deaf students' lifestyles, and more effective for teaching and learning. Effective learning results can be facilitated by e-learning since the model itself is available everywhere and at any time [31,32].

E-learning and its technology can be an influential factor for learning among the group of people with disabilities due to their effective functions [33]. These special needs users gradually become comfortable with using computers, the Internet, TV and radio programs, and any type of education transmission [34]. An e-learning web application can be a significant tool to assist the learning process, since it includes all of the important one-stop resources [35].

The studies about special education have made us aware of the present context. The whole concept, the insufficient components among teachers, the system, and the learning methods were depicted, and new applicable learning models were sought [36]. Currently, teaching and learning methods are mostly engaged in the mainstream structure which most schools are utilizing [37–39]. The presence of e-learning will change the conventional surroundings into the accessible system provided for everyone, everywhere, and at any time.

E-learning has been playing an important role for disabled students, especially the deaf, since it is an effective tool that smartly functions, collects, and obtains information, and makes learning simpler and faster. Several countries have now paid attention to the deafs' education equality. They help them reach the technology so that they can accomplish learning objectives and goals [40]. Consequently, e-learning has become an essential tool that facilitates everyone around the world. That is why the deaf are supposed to obtain the same rights, because they can fully benefit from the system where they can acquire knowledge and skills in a greater amount. In a conventional version, deaf students encounter some obstacles when they interact with interfaces which are not made for them. Thus, the need to construct an e-learning system specifically designed for them is apparent, since it can surely support their learning experience. The growth of e-learning usage has been obvious around the world, since it helps facilitate all related sectors in education [41]. Not only can common people take advantage of it, but deaf students will also have more options to assist in their learning [42].

2.4. Adaptive E-Learning (AEL)

Adaptive e-learning (AEL) was developed by Qazdar et al. in 2015 based on the concept that it was developed for each learner's needs, preferences, and styles. Learners will enhance their proficiency as well as performance when they adjust to new learning experiences [43]. Several studies have insisted that adaptive e-learning, with its effective e-content suitable for different learners' styles and preference, would improve their skills acquisition, experiences, and critical thinking skills [44–46]. The learning style of each learner is considered to be a crucial factor that impacts their learning performance; thus, it is normally seen as the root from which learning experiences stem [47–50].

Adaptive e-learning environments are designed by investigating student's learning styles. Different learners show different learning preferences when they interact with the content provided for them, since plenty of investigations pointed out the congruence between e-learning and learning styles, which could be prompted during the learning process. As such, learning outcomes would finally be improved [51–53].

2.5. Learning Style

Learning style is defined as the way learners collect, manage, process, and make use of the knowledge or skills that they obtain, then bring it back and utilize it in the style which shows their techniques in communicating it [54–56]. Different students possess different learning styles. They recognize and store information in their mind and perform it later until they acquire the target experiences [57].

Learning style models are various, including the VARK model, one of the most famous models identifying learning styles. In this present study, we applied the model with deaf students who use sign language in communication in the form of a VRK + TSL learning model [58].

Common learners with visual ability learn with teaching materials and submit their assignments via different means, such as maps, graphs, images, or symbols, according to [59]. Literate students can utilize written learning materials, such as glossaries, handouts, textbooks, and lecture notes. Traditional learning and teaching are useful for those without disabilities [60]. However, deaf students conduct their learning activities through Thai sign language, TSL, during conversations, lectures, and discussions.

3. Materials and Methods

3.1. Research Design

This research is a quantitative study using an e-learning model to identify the learning styles of deaf students through learning preferences and the principles of universal design.

3.2. Sample

The sample group of this study is composed of the deaf students as participants, in Matthayom 1–3 (grade 7–9), from the two schools for the deaf in the northeast region, namely Khon Kaen School for the Deaf and Udon Thani School for the Deaf. Student data were collected in the first 1/65 semester of the school year for 4 weeks.

The sample group size was calculated by using Taro Yamane's formula, as follows [61]:

$$n = \frac{N}{1 + Ne^2} \qquad (1)$$

where n is the sample size;

- N is the population size;
- e is the level of precision that always sets the value of 0.05.

3.3. Decision Tree

During the late 1970s and early 1980s, J. Loss Quinlan, a specialist in the field of machine learning, developed the algorithm of the decision tree, also known as ID3 (Iterative Dichotomiser 3), which was previously adopted in the learning system by E.B. Hunt, J. Marin, and P.T. Stone. Later, Quinlan proposed C4.5 (developed from ID3), and this has become the standard for learning algorithm comparison [62]. The decision tree can be explained as the learning process occurring when classifying the data into classes using the attributes [63]. The data obtained by classification of the decision tree let us know which attribute determines the classification process, and to what extent each attribute is significant. Therefore, data classification can assist users in terms of data analysis and more precise solution making.

A decision tree is a decision-making diagram that extracts the model rules from the machine learning process [64]. It is a well-known mathematical model used for predicting and forecasting. The learning process in the decision tree is caused by teaching and learning with labels. Its structure looks similar to a flowchart, in which the non-leaf node refers to the attribute test. Each branch shows the test result. Furthermore, each terminal node will be labeled by its group names. The node located on the top, the root node, is able to be interpreted and presented. Basically, extracting rules from the machine learning model can be conducted by using the decision tree [64].

3.4. Paired Samples t-Test

The paired samples *t*-test compares the mean of two groups, two matching cases, or the mean of a single group by checking at two different points within the specified time. If the same group is retested in the same measurement, it is repeated measures *t*-test [65]. The design of the pre-test/post-test is an experimental example of a situation in which this technique is appropriately applied [66].

3.5. Difference Score

This method is obtained from the pre- and post-study measurement scores. It is a common basic method to develop scores with the concept that improvement scores are post-scores that change from pre-scores. This concept is widely applied because it is easy to calculate and convenient, without requiring advanced statistical knowledge. The development score is the post-score minus the pre-score, as follows.

This method may not be fair for people with high pre-scores, as the scores will be lower than people with low pre-scores, because it will be limited to a full score of only 10 points. This limitation is the ceiling effect.

3.6. Relative Gain

This method is obtained from the post-score and pre-score measurement scores. Relative gain score is calculated by the difference between the post-scores and the pre-scores, with full score and pre-score difference. As a result, the ratio is multiplied by 100 to avoid decimal values [67]. The equation for calculating the relative gain score is as follows:

$$Relative\ Gain\ Score = \frac{Y_2 - Y_1}{F - Y_1} \times 100 \quad (2)$$

where
- Y_2 = Score of post-evaluation;
- Y_1 = Score of pre-evaluation;
- F = full score of the evaluation.

This measurement can solve the ceiling effect problem for people who have high pre-scores, but the additional points are less for people who have pre-scores. It can also recognize people who score the same difference, but the pre-scores are not the same. People with high pre-scores received a higher relative score than people with low pre-scores.

3.7. Instruments and Procedure

According to the findings from the study titled "*Adaptive Fleming-Type Learning Style Classifications to Deaf Students Behavior*" [58], it was found that the most effective classification was the multi-layer perceptron. However, this type of classification still contained some limitations; that is, it cannot interpret the data as humans do, and cannot identify which variable or attribute most affects the prediction. On the other hand, the decision tree provides an interpretable explanation for humans [68,69], as shown in Figure 1. Thus, it was applied to predict the learning model for deaf students. The rules synthesized by the decision tree were applied for use in e-learning lessons.

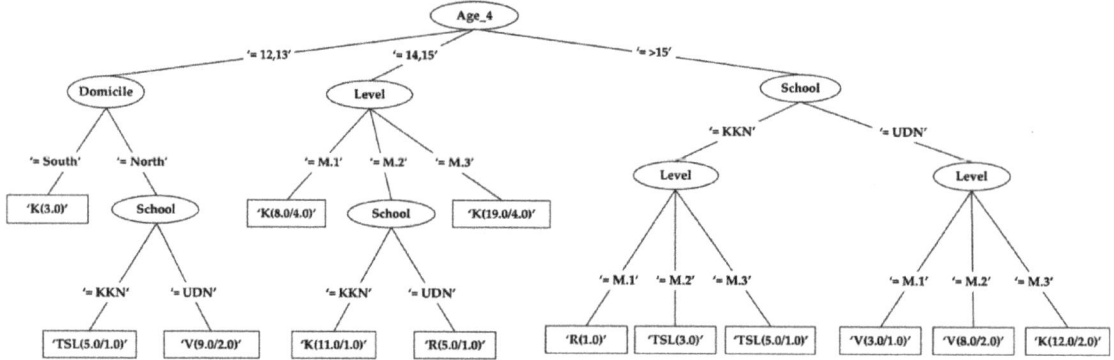

Figure 1. A decision tree obtained by classifying the VRK + TSL learning model.

According to Table 2, the rules were obtained from the analysis using the decision tree. For example, for rule 1, if the students are between 12–13 years old and live in the area of the lower northeast region, namely the south, then they would demonstrate a K (kinesthetic) learning style. Additionally, for rule 2, if the students are between 12–13 years old and live in the area of the upper northeast region, namely the north, and are studying in Khon Kaen School for the Deaf, they would demonstrate the TSL (Thai sign language) learning style.

The e-learning model to identify deaf students' learning styles through learning preferences and the principles of universal design in the computer, science, and technology department was conducted under the synthesized learning model consisting of the lessons, VRK + TSL learning activities, pre-test, achievement test, and post-test.

Table 2. An example of analysis using a decision tree technique.

No.	Decision Tree Rules	Learning Style
1	IF(Age = 12,13) and (Domicile = South)	K (Kinesthetic)
2	IF(Age = 12,13) and (Domicile = North) and (School = KKN)	TSL (Thai sign language)
3	IF(Age = 12,13) and (Domicile = North) and (School = UDN)	V (Visual)
4	IF(Age = 14,15) and (Level = M.2) and (School = UDN)	R (Reading)
5	IF(Age = 14,15) and (Level = M.2) and (School = KKN)	K (Kinesthetic)

The system checked the students' data to determine whether or not they were in line with the rules obtained from the VRK + TSL learning model. Then, it presented the lesson matching with the students' learning styles and the communication process for the deaf via the e-learning platform [70]. The content of VRK + TSL was divided into four typesm namely visual, reading/writing, kinesthetic, and Thai sign language, as shown in Figure 2. Each step and learning content were matched with each student's learning style, together with the sign language showing hand movements as well as facial expressions as a communication tool instead of verbal language [71]. The universal design was also applied.

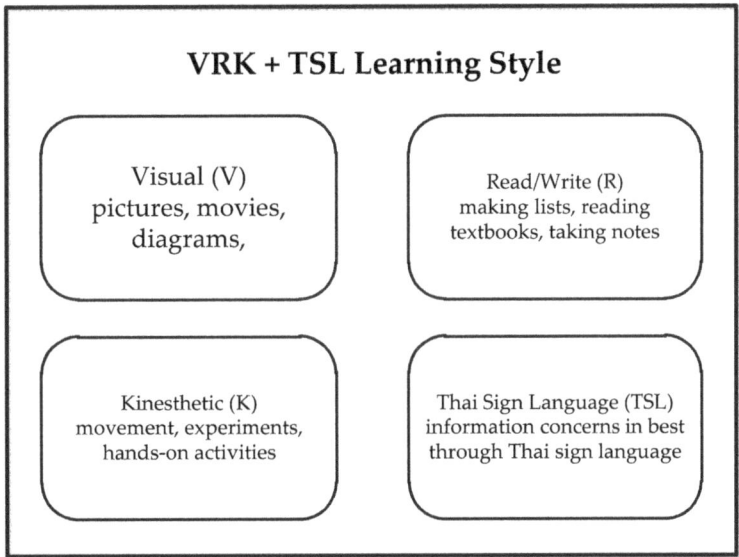

Figure 2. Dimensions and categories of VRK + TSL.

3.8. The Development of VRK + TSL Learning Model Based on ADDIE Concept

The ADDIE Model is made up of five significant activities, namely analyze, design, develop, implement, and evaluate [72,73]. This learning model is recognized as a well-known and widely accepted model and as an effective guidance in designing e-learning lessons. This model is flexible enough to adapt to different teaching environments and s isuitable for incorporating technology into teaching [74]. Its process shows inclusive steps within a closed system, and was considered from the evaluation at the final step before the data were examined, as shown in Figure 3.

The development of the VRK + TSL model based on ADDIE concept was divided into following steps:

1. Analysis (A)

The analysis and investigation of related data were illustrated below.

1.1 Data analysis: Data were collected from the teachers in the schools for the deaf in northeastern regions of Thailand, namely Khon Kaen, Udon Thani, Mukdahan, Surin,

Chaiyabhum, and Roi ET provinces. In this process, the optimum school subject was sought so that the outcome could be applied to other subjects as well as used in the competition in "Students Culture and Tradition" where they could express their different ideas and skills to reflect their academic achievement. The researcher analyzed and decided to develop a learning model for the computer subject, which is defined according to the curriculum used in Thailand and focuses on the usage of PowerPoint for teaching and learning, by following these steps:

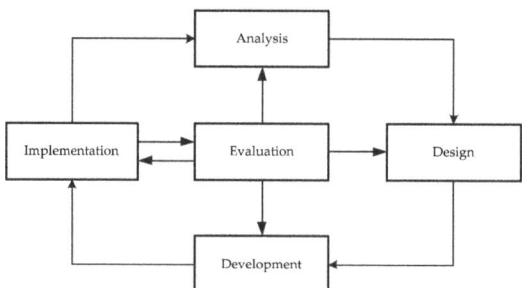

Figure 3. Learning model developed based on the ADDIE concept.

1.1.2 The examination and collection of subject-related documents, textbooks, and others;

1.1.3 The analysis of behavioral objectives to guide the learning management and to evaluate the validity of the test;

1.2 The analysis of learners who would employ the learning model, namely deaf students, Matthayom 1–3 who could understand sign language, from schools for the deaf in the Khon Kaen and Udon Thani provinces.

2. Design (D)

To develop lessons and tests in each unit, the factors that should be considered are whether the multimedia contains the components that interact with the learners or not. Such components should be presented in the form of text, pictures, animations, and videos to motivate learners so that they are interested in following the content and accessing the learning component. The process of designing the VRK + TSL learning model was conducted. The interface was simplified for students, containing the main screen, the content screen, the objective screen, the subject screen, and the test screen.

The steps that learners using the synthesized learning model should conduct are as follows. First, they must fill in their information. Then, the system checks their learning styles using the rules obtained from the analysis. It will provide the learning environment based on individual learning styles. That is, visual learners who enter the system for the first time will have to take a pre-test. Then, they study and conduct the post-test after the unit, and the system would be informed of the outcome.

3. Development (D)

To develop the synthesized learning model, the steps are as follows:

3.1 The preparation—at this phase, the learning was prepared following these steps:

3.1.1 The test was constructed based on behavioral objectives;

- The test was drafted into four-multiple choices based on the objectives;
- The test was checked whether it related to its objectives by the experts;
- The test was conducted with the students.

3.1.2 In terms of the satisfaction questionnaires, the process is as follows:

- The satisfaction questionnaire was developed as a five-point rating scale form employing Likert's method [75,76].
- The questionnaire was examined by the adviser to detect the errors and revise them.

3.2 The learning content of the e-learning model was developed under the concept of a VRK + TSL learning model analyzed by using data mining containing the following modules:

3.2.1 The first module was to classify students' learning styles of VRK + TSL. It was conducted by comparing students' data with the rules obtained from data classification to divide them into four groups, namely visual, reading/writing, kinesthetic, and Thai sign language. Thai sign language Learning style were incorporated into a Thai sign language video together with e-learning. Under the supervision of the National Electronics and Computer Technology Center (NECTEC), a QR code was embedded in the documents to connect with the sign language video.

3.2.2 The content was then developed into different topics and activities.

3.2.3 Teaching and learning process was also provided by presenting the content and activities during the lessons based on students' learning styles.

3.3 The developed system was checked to consider its suitability and revised according to the adviser's comments.

3.4 The developed system was rechecked by the experts according to the following steps:

3.4.1 The experts were selected to evaluate the developed system in terms of its technique, method, and content. The experts must be knowledgeable, with at least 5 years' experience in teaching and learning, or with an academic achievement from a university. The three-participant sample was selected using the criteria;

3.4.2 The five-point rating scale questionnaires eliciting the experts' opinion toward the techniques, method, and content were developed;

3.4.3 The questionnaires' validity was assessed to find the congruence between the objectives and the content, as well as the process, by the three experts from a secondary school and university.

The questionnaires' validity result was calculated to find the basic statistics of the content validity, the language suitability, and the question clarity by the three experts. The index of item—objective congruence, or IOC, was over 0.70, showing the congruence of the content. Some parts were revised according to the suggestions from the experts to be clearer and more comprehensible, but the original meanings still remained the same.

3.4.4 The developed system was tested by the experts and then they evaluated it using the questionnaires.

3.4.5 We revised the pilot results and had the adviser check before implementing the process.

4. Implementation (I)

The sample group, students in Grade 7–9 who could use sign language and who would employ the e-learning model for deaf students that identifies their learning styles through learning preferences and the principles of universal design, was determined at the computer laboratory of the school for the deaf in the Khon Kaen and Udon Thani provinces.

5. Evaluation (E)

The data collected from the use of the e-learning model for deaf students that identifies their learning styles through learning preferences and the principles of universal design were obtained by performing the steps illustrated below (Figure 4).

Before collecting the data, the researcher must undertake the training and obtain a certificate of Ethics for Human Research. For the data collection process, the researcher informed and asked for permission from the school before having students answer the questionnaires willingly. The details about the teaching and learning were provided for them. When they finished learning from the model, they evaluated their satisfaction, and the researcher concluded the study.

The use of e-learning lessons for students at deaf schools in the Udon Thani and Khon Kaen provinces according to the Thai sign language learning style and the scoring system summary is shown in Figure 5.

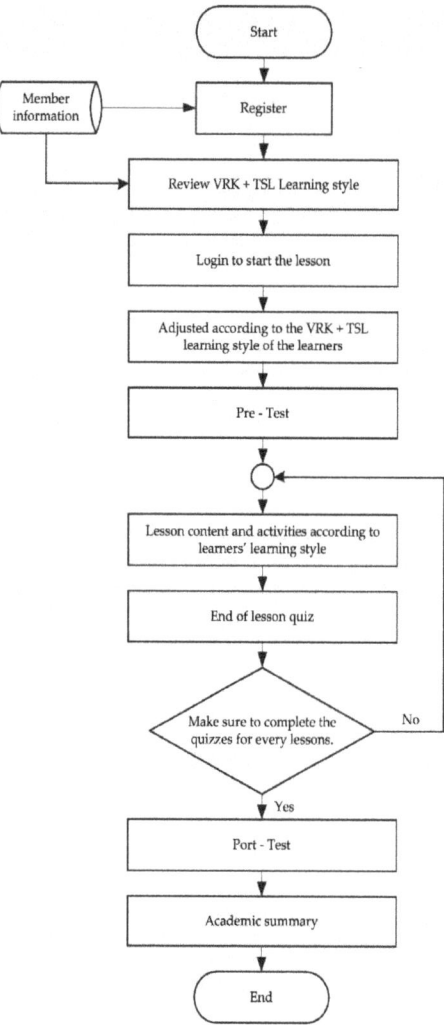

Figure 4. The process of how to use e-learning.

After students agree to voluntarily participate, they take a 10 questions pre-test that has been successfully assessed for conformance by experts. When e-learning is complete, there is a post-test with 10 original questions. After that, the system will evaluate the effectiveness and results of the pre-and post-learning of all students.

A test of e-learning materials was carried out by 50 deaf students in the Khon Kaen and Udon Thani provinces. Before starting to learn e-learning teaching materials, everyone starts by taking a pre-test. After that, when they have completed the study according to the specified content, everyone takes a post-test. From the data obtained in Table 3 from the pre- and post-study scores, the difference between the pre- and post-study scores and the relative gain Score indicates the learners' developmental scores.

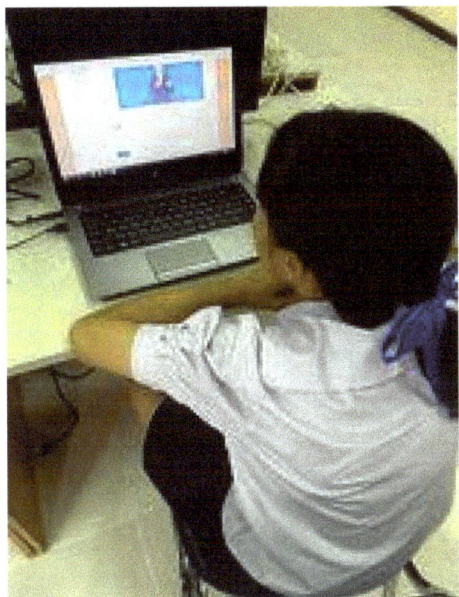

Figure 5. Test based on learning Thai sign language and the score criterion summary system.

Table 3. The results for the pre-test score, post-test score, difference score, and relative gain score.

Learning Style	Pre-Test Score	Post-Test Score	Difference Score	Relative Gain Score
V	35.00	76.67	76.67	53.87
R	22.86	72.50	72.50	54.81
K	29.03	77.10	48.06	66.92
TSL	38.00	78.00	78.00	60.71
Total	30.80	76.40	45.60	62.80

From Table 3, it was found that the students had higher average post-scores than pre-scores. The post-scores were 30.80 and the pre-scores were 76.40. It revealed that e-learning can, hypothetically, improve cognitive skills. It was revealed that the increase in different scores in the Thai sign language learning style was the highest at 78.00. Although the result of the kinesthetic learning model had an increase in the learning outcome value of the learning model that was not high, the relative gain score was at 66.92, which was the highest.

Kinesthetic learning affected students' learning for better development. Students were able to see the learning process through demonstrations, which made them understand more. Another interesting learning model is the Thai sign language learning model that audiophile students use to communicate and study vocabulary in teaching materials. In-class lessons encouraged students to review and enhance their understanding of the lesson content clearly. Students could learn more new words about computer content. As a result, students showed a better understanding and learning when using this e-learning material.

From Table 3, pre-test and post-test data are graphed, as shown in Figure 6. The X-axis represents the number of students taking the test (50). The Y-axis represents the pre-test and post-test scores, with a maximum score of 100, to compare the pre-test and post-test differences and to observe the trend of post-test scores.

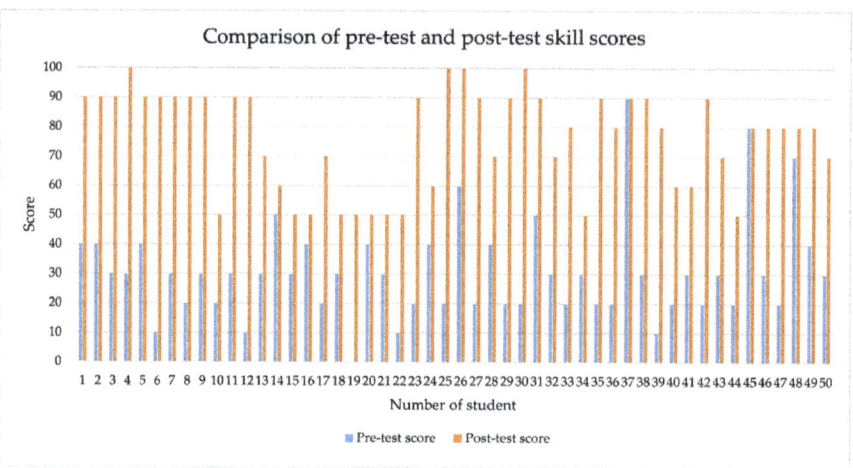

Figure 6. Comparison between pre-test scores and post-test skill scores.

From Table 3, pre-test and post-test data are graphed as shown in Figure 7. The X-axis represents the number of students taking the test (50). The Y-axis represents the difference scores and relative gain scores, with a maximum score of 100, to compare the difference scores and relative gain scores. It revealed that even the same difference scores did not show that the relative gain scores were the same. For example, this was the case with the 12th student and the 15th student. To determine student development, relative gain scores must be considered, as they are measured by the initial pre-test and post-test scores. This solves the ceiling effect problem and makes it possible to know the order of the students who really developed.

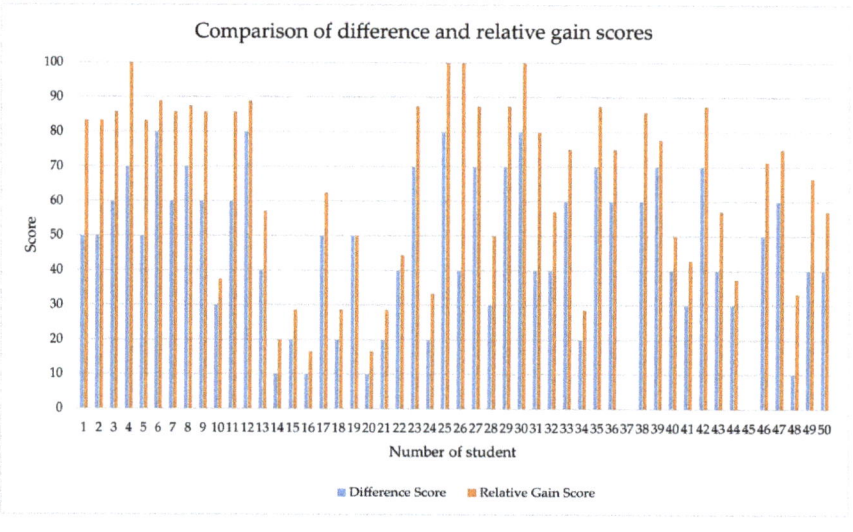

Figure 7. Comparison between difference scores and relative gain scores.

From Figures 6 and 7, the difference in scores between pre-test and post-test was the difference scores on learning gain and relative gain scores. Overall, this describes the progression of learning with increased learning outcomes.

The comparison of pre- and post-learning achievements from e-learning lessons analyzed by a dependent sample t-test are summarized in Table 4.

Table 4. Comparison between learning achievement of pre- and post-learning students using e-learning.

Testing	n	$\overline{X}$	S.D.	t
Pre-test	50	3.08	1.70	14.27
Post-test	50	7.64	1.69	

Statistical significance level or at the 0.05 level.

The researchers needed to test that the results for the pre- and post-learning sessions of e-learning users were statistically different at the 0.05 level.

Hypothesis:

$$H_0 : \mu_1 = \mu_2 \tag{3}$$

$$H_1 : \mu_1 \neq \mu_2 \tag{4}$$

The calculated t-value of 14.27 is not equal to t from the table showing the critical value of the distribution (t) of 2.01. Consequently, it was accepted that the H_1 pre- and post-test results of students using e-learning materials differed statistically at the 0.05 level. It revealed that such e-learning materials had the effect of making students study more efficiently.

Table 4 revealed that the mean of students studying e-learning lessons had a pre-scores of 3.08 and a standard deviation of 1.70, and that the post-scores had a mean of 7.64 and a standard deviation of 1.69. Test scores that differed from e-learning between pre- and post-scores showed that post-scores were statistically significantly higher than pre-scores at the 0.05 level. It was based on the assumption that e-learning lessons affected better learning achievement.

Table 5 revealed that overall satisfaction with e-learning was at the highest level. When considering each aspect, students were most satisfied with the lesson design at 4.52, followed by evaluation at 4.51, and content at 4.48.

Table 5. Summary table of student satisfaction with e-learning.

Topics	$\overline{X}$	S.D.	Level
Content	4.48	0.89	Good
Lesson design	4.52	0.84	Very Good
Evaluation aspect	4.51	0.87	Very Good
Total	4.51	0.86	Very Good

4. Discussion

The study was conducted, and the results were reported as follows. The content showed a positive correlation with adaptive students' achievement and engagement based on their different learning styles, namely kinesthetic, visual, reading/writing, and Thai sign language. It could be assumed that a few factors have affected the findings. In other words, the designed adaptive content showed the capacity in providing an idealistic learning environment for learners and supporting them with adaptive content that suits their learning preferences. Its strength helps them learn and accomplish academic targets as well as to enjoy the learning process.

The whole research method can be demonstrated as follows:

1. To develop the e-learning system that identifies students' learning styles through learning preferences and the principles of universal design, the researcher chose the computer subject for an experiment. This was to research e-learning design to accommodate deaf students. In [6–8], there is no analysis of adaptive e-learning. For this point, it is possible to indicate lessons and the learner's learning style, which adds a specific feature to

e-learning. The model was analyzed, designed, developed, implemented, and evaluated. The developed version was then brought to the experts to try out, and they evaluated it with the questionnaire. The model was completely useful for the students since it could provide optimum teaching and learning suitable with their learning styles, enhancing the whole teaching and learning process.

2. To find the relative gain of the e-learning system that identifies students' learning styles through learning preferences and the principles of universal design, data mining was conducted. The relative gain score is 66.92. The academic outcome reached the criteria, which could be explained as the learning activities met the learners' demand and their personal learning styles. Furthermore, the nature of e-learning itself allows students to review and study as much as they want.

3. To compare the academic achievement before and after using the e-learning system that identifies students' learning styles through learning preferences and the principles of universal design, the mean scores were examined. It was found that students achieved higher scores after using the model at the statistical significance of 0.05 because the developed model matched with their learning styles. Furthermore, learning activities during the course helped them to revise, and the test after each unit enhanced their potential.

4. To investigate student's satisfaction with the e-learning system that identifies students' learning styles through learning preferences and the principles of universal design, the developed model was employed with the students and their satisfaction was explored. Overall satisfaction with e-learning is at the highest level.

5. Conclusions

The present study has proposed the e-learning method and constructed an adaptive learning model with VRK + TSL based on the Fleming learning style. The target participants were the students who enrolled in a computer subject. The subject was categorized by using a decision tree classification algorithm based on their interests. Each student's learning style was different. An optimum characteristic of an e-learning system is to be able to support the learners with what they need and prefer. To reach that step, an e-learning model should be extracted and utilized based on certain factors. The model is anticipated to design and provide materials that meet learners' needs and styles. Four learning modes were embedded into the systems, i.e., visual, reading/writing, kinesthetic, and Thai sign language. Meanwhile, the model developed from various learning styles created engagement from learners. Students with unique learning styles tend to enjoy the learning process containing different teaching resources. Furthermore, the learning environment should also provide the optimum output to meet the needs of students. High-quality teaching resources and activities developed to match students' learning styles stimulate them to perform better. The results showed that most of the students had an increase in relative gain, which also increased their academic performance as a result. However, the students had low scores on the pre-study test. Students can have a relative gain with full marks. When a student who takes a post-test test gets a full score on all of them, no matter how badly the student does in the pre-test, the score is not good. However, students can still have the best learning development. Students must diligently review the material from e-learning and be able to study the content. They can review lessons anytime, anywhere, and without any limitations, allowing them to complete the post-test with full marks and the highest scores.

In terms of research limitations, the characteristics of the target group could be more varied. In this present study, the participants consisted of a group of deaf students who use Thai sign language and came from different schools and locations, with different grades and ages. We, thus, anticipate that our contribution might inspire our fellows to utilize e-learning models that support different learning styles, using adaptive e-learning techniques and universal design.

Additionally, one common problem found among the deaf students using sign language is that there are some specific words used only in one certain school. To solve this problem, some universal e-learning words were adopted from Educational Technology Substance Thai Sign Language Terminology affiliated with Ratchasuda College, Mahidol University. As such, e-learning vocabulary coordinately formulated was adopted into this study. To set up class activities based on the VRK + TSL learning model in another subject, instructors must select the activities in keeping with the subject's objective, so they can enhance learners' understanding and skills. This e-learning model can be further applied as a guideline for other courses or subjects and feasibly applied to other groups with disabilities, such as learners with speech or vision impairments or deaf students who use another sign language as their first language.

Author Contributions: Conceptualization, U.K.; methodology, U.K.; software, T.L.; validation, T.L.; formal analysis, T.L.; investigation, T.L.; resources, T.L.; data curation, T.L.; writing—original draft preparation, T.L. and U.K.; writing—review and editing, U.K.; visualization, T.L.; supervision, U.K.; project administration, U.K.; funding acquisition, U.K. All authors have read and agreed to the published version of the manuscript.

Funding: This research received no external funding.

Institutional Review Board Statement: The study was conducted in accordance with the Declaration of Helsinki and approved by the Ethics Committee of the Khon Kaen University.

Informed Consent Statement: Informed consent was obtained from all subjects involved in the study.

Data Availability Statement: The participants' datasets generated and analyzed during the current study are available on reasonable request from the corresponding author.

Acknowledgments: The authors would like to thank for all the respondents of that kindly completed the questionnaire, the teachers, and students at the School for the Deaf in the northeastern region of Thailand; namely, Khon Kaen; Udon Thani; Mukdahan; Surin; Chaiyabhum; and Roi Et for their valuable assistance. Further recognition goes to the National Electronics and Computer Technology Center (NECTEC) for the production of the document that embedded the two-dimensional barcode (QR code) within the sign language videos, as well as the entire SQR (Sign Language QR Code for the Deaf) system. Our gratitude is also extended to the College of Computing, Khon Kaen University for the research location and equipment used in this study.

Conflicts of Interest: The authors declare no conflict of interest.

References

1. Parker, A.T.; Nelson, C. Toward a comprehensive system of personnel development in deafblind education. *Am. Ann. Deaf* **2016**, *161*, 486–501. [CrossRef] [PubMed]
2. Sri-on, J. *A History of the Education of Deaf People in Thailand*; La Trobe University: Melbourne, Australia, 2001.
3. Sriorn, C. *Reading Ability and Writing Thai Language for Students with Hearing Impaired, Grade 6*; Mahidol University: Bangkok, Thailand, 2007.
4. Srivani, V.; Hariharasudan, A.; Nawaz, N.; Ratajczak, S. Impact of Education 4.0 among engineering students for learning English language. *PLoS ONE* **2022**, *17*, e0261717. [CrossRef]
5. Snajder, M.; Verlic, M.; Povalej, P.; Debevc, M. Pedagogical evaluation of e-learning courses-Adapted pedagogical index. In Proceedings of the Conference ICL2007, Villach, Austria, 26–28 September 2007.
6. Hashim, H.; Tasir, Z.; Mohamad, S.K. E-Learning Environment for Hearing Impaired Students. *Turkish Online J. Educ. Technol.* **2013**, *12*, 67–70.
7. Borgia, F.; Bianchini, C.S.; Marsico, M. De Towards Improving the e-learning Experience for Deaf Students: E-LUX. In Proceedings of the International Conference on Universal Access in Human-Computer Interaction, Heraklion, Greece, 22–27 June 2014; Springer: Berlin/Heidelberg, Germany, 2014; pp. 221–232.
8. Mohd Hashim, M.H.; Tasir, Z. An e-learning environment embedded with sign language videos: Research into its usability and the academic performance and learning patterns of deaf students. *Educ. Technol. Res. Dev.* **2020**, *68*, 2873–2911. [CrossRef]
9. Markauskaite, L. Critical review of research findings on information technology in education. *Informatics Educ.* **2003**, *2*, 65–78. [CrossRef]
10. Mashhadi, V.Z.; Kargozari, M.R. Influences of digital classrooms on education. *Procedia Comput. Sci.* **2011**, *3*, 1178–1183. [CrossRef]
11. Garavaglia, A.; Garzia, V.; Petti, L. Quality of the learning environment in digital classrooms: An Italian case study. *Procedia-Soc. Behav. Sci.* **2012**, *46*, 1735–1739. [CrossRef]

12. Chang, H.-Y.; Wang, C.-Y.; Lee, M.-H.; Wu, H.-K.; Liang, J.-C.; Lee, S.W.-Y.; Chiou, G.-L.; Lo, H.-C.; Lin, J.-W.; Hsu, C.-Y. A review of features of technology-supported learning environments based on participants' perceptions. *Comput. Human Behav.* **2015**, *53*, 223–237. [CrossRef]
13. Ragulina, Y.V.; Semenova, E.I.; Zueva, I.A.; Kletskova, E.V.; Belkina, E.N. Perspectives of solving the problems of regional development with the help of new internet technologies. *Entrep. Sustain. Issues* **2018**, *5*, 890–898. [CrossRef]
14. Hariharasudan, A.; Kot, S. A scoping review on Digital English and Education 4.0 for Industry 4.0. *Soc. Sci.* **2018**, *7*, 227. [CrossRef]
15. Baek, S.-Y.; Jeong, B.-Y. Universal Safety Design (USD) and sustainability: Comparison of guidelines between Universal Design (UD) and USD. *Appl. Sci.* **2021**, *11*, 4413. [CrossRef]
16. Jeong, B.Y.; Shin, D.S. Workplace universal design for the older worker: Current issues and future directions. *J. Ergon. Soc. Korea* **2014**, *33*, 365–376. [CrossRef]
17. Kim, J.S.; Jeong, B.Y. Universal safety and design: Transition from universal design to a new philosophy. *Work* **2020**, *67*, 157–164. [CrossRef] [PubMed]
18. Steinfeld, E.; Maisel, J. *Universal Design: Creating Inclusive Environments*; John Wiley & Sons: Hoboken, NJ, USA, 2012; ISBN 0470399139.
19. Afacan, Y.; Erbug, C. An interdisciplinary heuristic evaluation method for universal building design. *Appl. Ergon.* **2009**, *40*, 731–744. [CrossRef] [PubMed]
20. Can, G.F.; Kılıç Delice, E. A task-based fuzzy integrated MCDM approach for shopping mall selection considering universal design criteria. *Soft Comput.* **2018**, *22*, 7377–7397. [CrossRef]
21. Shea, E.C.; Pavia, S.; Dyer, M.; Craddock, G.; Murphy, N. Measuring the design of empathetic buildings: A review of universal design evaluation methods. *Disabil. Rehabil. Assist. Technol.* **2016**, *11*, 13–21. [CrossRef]
22. Preiser, W.F.E. Universal design: From policy to assessment research and practice. *Int. J. Archit. Res.* **2008**, *2*, 78–93.
23. Capp, M.J. The effectiveness of universal design for learning: A meta-analysis of literature between 2013 and 2016. *Int. J. Incl. Educ.* **2017**, *21*, 791–807. [CrossRef]
24. Courey, S.J.; Tappe, P.; Siker, J.; LePage, P. Improved lesson planning with universal design for learning (UDL). *Teach. Educ. Spec. Educ.* **2013**, *36*, 7–27. [CrossRef]
25. Rose, D.H.; Meyer, A. *A Practical Reader in Universal Design for Learning*; ERIC: Tokyo, Japan, 2006; ISBN 189179230X.
26. Spencer, S.A. Universal Design for Learning: Assistance for Teachers in Today's Inclusive Classrooms. *Interdiscip. J. Teach. Learn.* **2011**, *1*, 10–22.
27. Horton, W. *E-Learning by Design*; John Wiley & Sons: Hoboken, NJ, USA, 2011; ISBN 0470900024.
28. Kim, H.J.; Hong, A.J.; Song, H.-D. The roles of academic engagement and digital readiness in students' achievements in university e-learning environments. *Int. J. Educ. Technol. High. Educ.* **2019**, *16*, 21. [CrossRef]
29. Khan, B.H. *Managing E-Learning: Design, Delivery, Implementation, and Evaluation*; IGI Global: Hershey, PA, USA, 2005; ISBN 159140634X.
30. Guri-Rosenblit, S.; Gros, B. E-learning: Confusing terminology, research gaps and inherent challenges. *Int. J. E-Learning Distance Educ. Int. du e-learning la Form. à distance* **2011**, *25*. Available online: https://www.ijede.ca/index.php/jde/article/view/729/1206 (accessed on 9 September 2022).
31. Chen, P.-S.D.; Lambert, A.D.; Guidry, K.R. Engaging online learners: The impact of Web-based learning technology on college student engagement. *Comput. Educ.* **2010**, *54*, 1222–1232. [CrossRef]
32. Lee, J.; Song, H.-D.; Hong, A.J. Exploring factors, and indicators for measuring students' sustainable engagement in e-learning. *Sustainability* **2019**, *11*, 985. [CrossRef]
33. Debevc, M.; Stjepanovic, Z.; Holzinger, A. Development and evaluation of an e-learning course for deaf and hard of hearing based on the advanced Adapted Pedagogical Index method. *Interact. Learn. Environ.* **2014**, *22*, 35–50. [CrossRef]
34. Sandars, J.; Morrison, C. What is the Net Generation? The challenge for future medical education. *Med. Teach.* **2007**, *29*, 85–88. [CrossRef]
35. Velázquez, A.; Assar, S. Student Learning Styles Adaptation Method Based on Teaching Strategies and Electronic Media. *Educ. Technol. Soc.* **2009**, *12*, 15–29.
36. Sánchez Palomino, A.; Carrión Martínez, J.J. Una aproximación a la investigación en Educación Especial. *Rev. Educ.* **2002**, *327*, 225–247.
37. Kohli, W. Bringing Dewey into the Adult Higher Education Classroom. *New Dir. Adult Contin. Educ.* **2018**, *158*, 57–65. [CrossRef]
38. Gomez, C. Create awareness of, excitement for universal design beyond the classroom. *Disabil. Compliance High. Educ.* **2015**, *20*, 2. [CrossRef]
39. González-Zamar, M.-D.; Ortiz Jiménez, L.; Sánchez Ayala, A.; Abad-Segura, E. The impact of the university classroom on managing the socio-educational well-being: A global study. *Int. J. Environ. Res. Public Health* **2020**, *17*, 931. [CrossRef] [PubMed]
40. AlShammari, A.; Alsumait, A.; Faisal, M. Building an interactive e-learning tool for deaf children: Interaction design process framework. In Proceedings of the 2018 IEEE Conference on e-Learning, e-Management and e-Services (IC3e), Langkawi, Malaysia, 21–22 November 2018; IEEE: New York, NY, USA, 2018; pp. 85–90.
41. AlDekhail, M. E-Learning Assistance and Application for the Auditory-Impaired Population: A Review with Recommendations. *J. Basic Appl. Sci. Res.* **2015**, *5*, 36–53.

42. Li, Y. Through virtual learning community to achieve liberated learning for deaf students. In Proceedings of the 2009 2nd IEEE International Conference on Computer Science and Information Technology, Beijing, China, 8–11 August 2008; IEEE: New York, NY, USA, 2009; pp. 37–40.
43. Shi, L.; Cristea, A.; Foss, J.; Al-Qudah, D.; Qaffas, A. A social personalized adaptive e-learning environment: A case study in Topolor. *IADIS Int. J. WWW/Internet* **2013**, *11*, 13–34.
44. Abdel Aziz Ali, N.; Eassa, F.; Hamed, E. Personalized Learning Style for Adaptive E-Learning System. *Int. J. Adv. Trends Comput. Sci. Eng.* **2019**, *8*, 223–230.
45. Wu, C.-H.; Chen, Y.-S.; Chen, T. An adaptive e-learning system for enhancing learning performance: Based on dynamic scaffolding theory. *EURASIA J. Math. Sci. Technol. Educ.* **2017**, *14*, 903–913.
46. Dominic, M.; Xavier, B.A.; Francis, S. A framework to formulate adaptivity for adaptive e-learning system using user response theory. *Int. J. Mod. Educ. Comput. Sci.* **2015**, *7*, 23–30.
47. Alshammari, M.T.; Qtaish, A. Effective Adaptive E-Learning Systems According to Learning Style and Knowledge Level. *J. Inf. Technol. Educ.* **2019**, *18*, 529–547. [CrossRef]
48. El-Sabagh, H.A.; Hamed, E.H.A. The Relationship between Learning-Styles and Learning Motivation of Students at Umm Al-Qura University. *Egypt. Assoc. Educ. Comput. J.* **2020**, *8*, 1–30. [CrossRef]
49. Hussein, A.M.A.; Al-Chalabi, H.K.M. Pedagogical agents in an adaptive E-learning system. *SAR J. Sci. Res.* **2020**, *3*, 24–30. [CrossRef]
50. Normadhi, N.B.A.; Shuib, L.; Nasir, H.N.M.; Bimba, A.; Idris, N.; Balakrishnan, V. Identification of personal traits in adaptive learning environment: Systematic literature review. *Comput. Educ.* **2019**, *130*, 168–190. [CrossRef]
51. Alshammari, M. Adaptation Based on Learning Style and Knowledge Level in E-Learning Systems. Ph.D. Thesis, University of Birmingham, Birmingham, UK, 2016.
52. Alzain, A.; Clark, S.; Ireson, G.; Jwaid, A. Adaptive education based on learning styles: Are learning style instruments precise enough? *Int. J. Emerg. Technol. Learn.* **2018**, *13*, 41–52. [CrossRef]
53. Alzain, A.; Clark, S.; Ireson, G.; Jwaid, A. Learning personalization based on learning style instruments. *Adv. Sci. Technol. Eng. Syst. J.* **2018**, *3*, 108–115. [CrossRef]
54. Sajna, J.; Thomas, A.M. *Learning Styles Theories and Implications for Teaching Learning*; Horizon Research Publishing: San Jose, CA, USA, 2019.
55. Nuankaew, P.; Nuankaew, W.; Phanniphong, K.; Imwut, S.; Bussaman, S. Students Model in Different Learning Styles of Academic Achievement at the University of Phayao, Thailand. *Int. J. Emerg. Technol. Learn.* **2019**, *14*, 133–157. [CrossRef]
56. Zhang, H. Accommodating different learning styles in the teaching of economics: With emphasis on fleming and mills¡⁻s sensory-based learning style typology. *Appl. Econ. Financ.* **2017**, *4*, 72–83. [CrossRef]
57. Naqeeb, H. Learning Styles as Perceived by Learners of English as a Foreign Language in the English Language Center of The Arab American University–Jenin, Palestine. *An. Najah Univ. J. Res.* **2011**, *25*, 2232–2256.
58. Luangrungruang, T.; Kokaew, U. Adapting Fleming-Type Learning Style Classifications to Deaf Student Behavior. *Sustainability* **2022**, *14*, 4799. [CrossRef]
59. Fleming, N.; Baume, D. Learning Styles Again: VARKing up the right tree! *Educ. Dev.* **2006**, *7*, 4.
60. Willingham, D.T.; Hughes, E.M.; Dobolyi, D.G. The scientific status of learning styles theories. *Teach. Psychol.* **2015**, *42*, 266–271. [CrossRef]
61. Yamanae, T. *Statistics: An Introductory Analysis*; Harper & Row: New York, NY, USA; Evanston & London and John Weatherhill, Inc.: Tokyo, Japan, 1973.
62. Jiawei Han, M.K. *Data Mining: Concepts and Techniques*, 2nd ed.; Morgan Kaufmann Publishers: Burlington, MA, USA, 2006.
63. Amatriain, X.; Jaimes, A.; Oliver, N.; Pujol, J.M. Data mining methods for recommender systems. In *Recommender Systems Handbook*; Springer: Berlin/Heidelberg, Germany, 2011; pp. 39–71.
64. Deo, T.Y.; Patange, A.D.; Pardeshi, S.S.; Jegadeeshwaran, R.; Khairnar, A.N.; Khade, H.S. A White-Box SVM Framework and its Swarm-Based Optimization for Supervision of Toothed Milling Cutter through Characterization of Spindle Vibrations. *arXiv* **2021**, arXiv:2112.08421.
65. Ross, A.; Willson, V.L. Paired samples T-test. In *Basic and Advanced Statistical Tests*; Springer: Berlin/Heidelberg, Germany, 2017; pp. 17–19.
66. Pallant, J. SPSS Survival Manual: A Step by Step Guide to Data Analysis Using the SPSS Program. 2011. Available online: https://www.scirp.org/(S(i43dyn45teexjx455qlt3d2q))/reference/ReferencesPapers.aspx?ReferenceID=851962 (accessed on 18 April 2022).
67. Sirichai, K. *Alternative Strategies for Policy Analysis: An Assessment of School Effects on Students' Cognitive and Affective Mathematics Outcomes in Lower Secondary Schools in Thailand*; University of California: Los Angeles, CA, USA, 1989.
68. Asif, R.; Merceron, A.; Ali, S.A.; Haider, N.G. Analyzing undergraduate students' performance using educational data mining. *Comput. Educ.* **2017**, *113*, 177–194. [CrossRef]
69. Aguilar, D.L.; Perez, M.A.M.; Loyola-Gonzalez, O.; Choo, K.-K.R.; Bucheli-Susarrey, E. Towards an interpretable autoencoder: A decision tree-based autoencoder and its application in anomaly detection. *IEEE Trans. Dependable Secur. Comput.* **2022**. [CrossRef]
70. Martins, P.; Rodrigues, H.; Rocha, T.; Francisco, M.; Morgado, L. Accessible options for Deaf people in e-Learning platforms: Technology solutions for Sign Language translation. *Procedia Comput. Sci.* **2015**, *67*, 263–272. [CrossRef]

71. Zahedi, M.; Mashal, H.; Salehi, S.M. An online community for the deaf. *Procedia Comput. Sci.* **2011**, *3*, 1089–1093. [CrossRef]
72. Seels, B.; Glasgow, Z. *Making Instructional Design Decisions*; Merrill Education/Prentice Hall: Hoboken, NJ, USA, 2022.
73. Wiphasith, H.; Narumol, R.; Sumalee, C. The design of the contents of an e-learning for teaching M. 5 English language using ADDIE model. *Int. J. Inf. Educ. Technol.* **2016**, *6*, 127. [CrossRef]
74. Almelhi, A.M. Effectiveness of the ADDIE Model within an E-Learning Environment in Developing Creative Writing in EFL Students. *Engl. Lang. Teach.* **2021**, *14*, 20–36. [CrossRef]
75. Boone, H.N.; Boone, D.A. Analyzing likert data. *J. Ext.* **2012**, *50*, 1–5.
76. Allen, I.E.; Seaman, C.A. Likert scales and data analyses. *Qual. Prog.* **2007**, *40*, 64–65.

Article

Optimizing the Systematic Characteristics of Online Learning Systems to Enhance the Continuance Intention of Chinese College Students

Mengfan Li *, Ting Wang, Wei Lu and Mengke Wang

School of Economics and Management, Communication University of China, Beijing 100024, China
* Correspondence: limengfan0824@163.com

Abstract: Different from systems that directly provide online shared courses such as MOOC, online learning systems such as Tencent Classroom simulate a real classroom environment for students and teachers to realize online face-to-face teaching, utilized during the COVID-19 pandemic. Nevertheless, due to the limitation of physical distance, the intelligent design of online learning systems is necessary to provide students with a good learning experience. This study notes that an unexpected optimization effect is the impact of system characteristics on the flow experience of online learning systems, which has not been studied, but plays a vital role in the effectiveness of online learning systems. In the study, a questionnaire was created and multi-stage sampling was used to investigate 623 college students. Based on the DeLone and McLean model of IS success and flow theory, a model for optimizing system characteristics and flow experience was constructed and its effectiveness was tested. The results reveal that system characteristics have a positive impact on continuance intention and flow experience. Additionally, flow experience and learning effect have a positive impact on continuance intention. Furthermore, flow experience has a positive impact on the learning effect. This study emphasizes the flow experience of online learning systems and reveals the optimization direction of online virtual face-to-face classrooms to provide references for the Ministry of Education, schools, and enterprises providing education systems.

Keywords: online virtual classrooms; distance learning; flow experience; interactive system; education

Citation: Li, M.; Wang, T.; Lu, W.; Wang, M. Optimizing the Systematic Characteristics of Online Learning Systems to Enhance the Continuance Intention of Chinese College Students. *Sustainability* **2022**, *14*, 11774. https://doi.org/10.3390/su141811774

Academic Editor: Hao-Chiang Koong Lin

Received: 5 August 2022
Accepted: 19 September 2022
Published: 19 September 2022

Publisher's Note: MDPI stays neutral with regard to jurisdictional claims in published maps and institutional affiliations.

Copyright: © 2022 by the authors. Licensee MDPI, Basel, Switzerland. This article is an open access article distributed under the terms and conditions of the Creative Commons Attribution (CC BY) license (https://creativecommons.org/licenses/by/4.0/).

1. Introduction

Since 2020, the COVID-19 epidemic has spread rapidly around the world, posing a serious threat to human life and health. Due to the severe situation of COVID-19 and urgent prevention and control policies, universities all over the world have canceled offline courses in favor of online teaching. Before that, online courses were not widely valued in China, while they were common abroad, particularly in the United States [1,2]. Although Chinese enterprises in the field of science, technology, and education have been committed to developing new technologies to improve online learning systems and create a better online learning environment in recent years, this has not been fully utilized by schools. To prevent the spread of COVID-19, China took rigorous prevention and control measures. China's Ministry of Education has instructed schools to delay the start of school and turn to online teaching, creating an excellent opportunity for online learning systems to flourish in China.

Online learning systems are important teaching tools to support intelligent online education. Different from students with high school education or below, who mainly study recorded lessons, college students and professors use online learning systems for online face-to-face live teaching because they can freely use electronic devices and some professional courses need to be taught face-to-face [3]. The biggest difference between this new teaching mode and the traditional teaching mode is that face-to-face classrooms are moved online to enable teachers and students to interact in real-time although they are not in the same classroom space [4,5]. This teaching mode needs the support of systems, such as Tencent Classroom, Rain Classroom, and TronClass, which are the most important online learning systems providing virtual face-to-face classrooms in China. These systems pay more attention to creating a virtual online classroom for students and teachers as a functional tool to provide online communication scenarios, unlike those systems that offer online shared courses directly, such as MOOC and ZHIDAO. In contrast, it is obvious that the former has a better real-time interaction function to simulate traditional offline courses [6], and is more suitable for sustainable distance education, especially for courses with higher professionalism in universities [7]. It can be seen that it is vital to explore online learning systems providing virtual face-to-face classrooms, which are conducive to long-term online learning. These special online learning systems that provide online virtual face-to-face classrooms can be called online virtual classrooms.

Online virtual classrooms can be regarded as generalized information systems, where teachers and students transfer course information at both ends of the system [8]. Moreover, as information systems, they have the functions of processing and storing course information. For example, teachers can access statistics on students' classroom performance, and students can play back courseware. It means that the systems based on this functional design can surpass the traditional offline courses in the whole teaching experience [9,10]. It is puzzling that college students' continuance intention to use these online virtual classrooms is not high [11]. Some studies explored the influencing factors of college students' willingness to use online learning systems based on the expectation-confirmation model (ECM) and analyzed the impact of factors such as users' subjective satisfaction [12,13]. Some scholars pointed out that technical characteristics play an important role in many factors that affect the users' willingness to use the information system continuously [14–17]. However, in the field of online learning, there is limited research on college students' continuance intention to use online virtual classrooms based on system characteristics. The DeLone and McLean model of IS success (D&M model) can better examine users' continuance intention that directly shows the optimization effect of the system from system quality, information quality and service quality [18]. Therefore, it is meaningful to explore the influencing factors of college students' continuance intention to use online virtual classrooms based on the D&M model.

As a state of user experience, flow experience is closely related to the continuous use of information system users, and significantly affects the users' information system adoption and use behavior [19,20]. These online learning systems rely on the internet, so the delay and instability of the network can more or less affect classroom performance, which is also a reflection of the system quality [21]. Bao [22] pointed out that teachers generally needed to slow down when using online learning systems for teaching, which easily destroyed the immersive input of teachers and students in class, resulting in a poor overall teaching effect. In the teaching process, the use of "flow theory" can effectively stimulate students' interest in learning and improve their learning motivation, which is worth paying attention to in online learning [23]. These systems pay little attention to flow experience in current system designs, but more attention to the system infrastructure. It is of great significance to focus on the flow experience in the subsequent optimization of system characteristics, which will guide the optimization direction of system characteristics to better enhance the continuance intention of college students. In addition, Hashemi's [24] survey found that there was a strong positive correlation between students' learning effect and their satisfaction with online learning. After obviously feeling that the learning effect of using online learning systems is not good, college students will be dissatisfied with online virtual face-to-face classrooms and will not continue to use them [25]. It can be seen that flow experience and learning effect are two important factors that cannot be ignored when exploring college students' willingness to continue using online virtual classrooms. It is a pity that there is no research on them at the same time, and our research can make up for this.

This study aims to explore the general mechanism of college students' intention to use online virtual classrooms. Based on the D&M model, this study focused on the mediation effect of flow experience and the learning effect and tested the hypotheses through the survey data. The results of this study will provide important suggestions for the Ministry of Education, schools, and enterprises providing systems, and explain the optimization direction of online virtual face-to-face classrooms providing simulated offline classes in the future.

2. Literature Review

2.1. The COVID-19 Pandemic and Online Learning Systems Providing Virtual Classrooms

Due to COVID-19, China's Ministry of Education launched an initiative entitled "Ensuring learning undisrupted when classes are disrupted". In response to this directive, Chinese schools have to teach online, especially for universities with complex student sources. Online learning systems are used as functional tools to provide virtual face-to-face classrooms for college students first forced long-term online learning.

In universities, the courses of different majors vary greatly. This poses a challenge for the use of online learning platforms in universities. Husár and Dupláková [26] explored the possibility of online education as a tool to improve language education. Pather et al. [27] summarized the rapid development of online teaching after the outbreak of the pandemic in management anatomy education and found that it was helpful to realize the synchronous teaching of remote sites. Kang and Seo [28] investigated the basic practical methods of online physics teaching and revealed that online learning systems provided more development opportunities. In the study of industrial majors, further optimization can be achieved by using e-learning [29]. These studies support a view that online learning systems can provide online virtual learning for many different majors in universities. This can also reassure different kinds of universities to use online learning systems during the COVID-19 pandemic, which further demonstrates the importance and applicability of these systems.

At present, the research topics of such emerging online learning systems are relatively concentrated. Most studies analyzed the teaching mode [30], technical application [31], and teaching effect [32] of these systems from the perspective of cases. Yu [33] adopted a hybrid design to collect quantitative and qualitative data, and the comparison showed that the availability of using online learning systems for online learning as an aid to learning is significantly higher than other methods. For universities, these systems simulate the traditional offline classroom and pay attention to adding interactive functions such as raising hands, group discussions, and quizzes, to restore the classroom to the greatest extent. During the COVID-19 pandemic, the value of these systems that provide online virtual face-to-face classrooms is self-evident, but it is necessary to investigate in depth the general mechanism of students' continuance intention to use them. Therefore, this study focused on online virtual classrooms that are different from previous online learning systems.

Tencent Classroom has main functions and can be used as a representative of online virtual classrooms. An interactive interface of the class is shown in Figure 1. At the bottom of Figure 1 is the function bar including raising hands, answering questions and so on. On its right is the chat box, where you can receive and send messages. The button above the chat box can be used to invite students into the classroom. These designs ensure that students and teachers can interact promptly.

2.2. Online Virtual Classrooms and the DeLone and McLean Model of IS Success

The D&M model focuses on the three dimensions of information systems: how system quality, information quality, and service quality affect user satisfaction, use intention, and user income [34]. Some scholars used the D&M model for reference to pay attention to the impact of the three elements on users' willingness to continue using the information system [14–16]. Previous studies mostly used the ECM, technology acceptance model (TAM), and other models to investigate users' continuance intention to use online virtual classrooms. Only a few studies began to pay attention to the impact of the three elements in the D&M model in recent years and made a preliminary exploration [35].

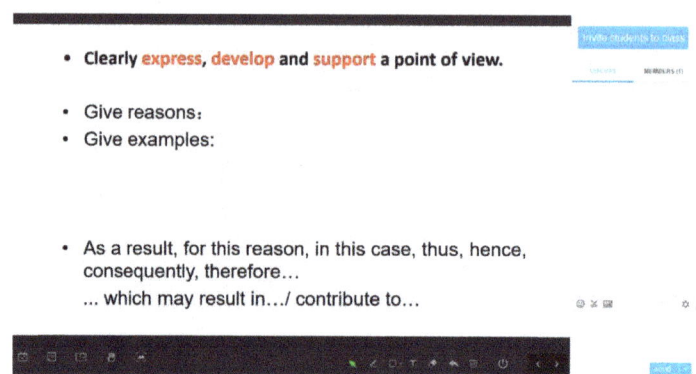

Figure 1. An Example of classroom interface in Tencent Classroom.

System availability is one of the important characteristics of system quality, which affects users' willingness to continue using these services [36]. In addition, information interaction in information systems is very important, especially for online virtual classrooms [11]. Cheng et al. [37] revealed that the timeliness of information feedback had a positive impact on users' continuance intention. When conducting online learning, teachers need to transfer course information to students through online learning systems, such as some quizzes and course tasks. These systems provide feedback for the course information input by teachers to students by displaying it on the screen or uploading it to the learning database provided by systems. This can also be called "information feedback" of online learning systems. Similar to other information systems, feedback timeliness of online learning systems may have a positive effect on the willingness of college students to continue using online learning systems. In terms of information quality, timeliness, completeness and intelligibility are important features [38]. Given the motivation of students in the use of online virtual classrooms to obtain knowledge, these characteristics are not as important as the richness and interest of teaching content. The "richness" of course content refers to the breadth, depth, and meaning of it. The "interestingness" of course content depends on ingenious and flexible teaching methods to stimulate students' interest in learning, which is conducive to their understanding of the course content. A study suggested that the richness and interestingness of course content in online virtual classrooms greatly influenced learners' willingness to attend classes [39]. Therefore, it is necessary to focus on how the content interest in information quality affects college students' continuance intention to use online virtual classrooms. Moreover, the service quality of information systems significantly affects user satisfaction [40]. The current online virtual classrooms optimize the quality of service by increasing the personalized function of the information system, with the focus on the interaction between students and teachers, such as raising hands, bullet screens, and group discussions [41]. These systems use these functions to simulate offline scenes as much as possible to bring a more real face-to-face classroom experience. Meanwhile, the BOPPPS teaching model points out that participatory interaction in students' online learning can effectively improve the classroom experience and teaching effect [42]. Students will be satisfied with a good classroom experience and are willing to continue to use online virtual classrooms [43]. Based on the above analysis, the following hypotheses were proposed:

H1. *System availability has a positive effect on college students' continuance intention to use online virtual classrooms.*

H2. *Feedback timeliness has a positive effect on college students' continuance intention to use online virtual classrooms.*

H3. *Interesting content has a positive effect on college students' continuance intention to use online virtual classrooms.*

H4. *System functionality has a positive effect on college students' continuance intention to use online virtual classrooms.*

H5. *Interactive sociality has a positive effect on college students' continuance intention to use online virtual classrooms.*

2.3. Flow Theory, Learning Effect, and Continued Intention

Flow experience is a positive psychological experience, which will give individuals such a great sense of pleasure when participating in activities that it urges individuals to repeat the same activities without getting tired [44]. With the continuous development of information technology, various types of user-oriented information systems have been launched. These information systems are designed from the perspective of user experience, and the sense of immersion is one of the important experience feelings. Therefore, the phenomenon of information users' flow experience and the impact of flow experience on information behavior was confirmed by many studies [45–47]. Online virtual classrooms also pay more attention to the application of new technologies to optimize the system interface and user experience to provide a flow experience, which can attract and retain users. The optimization direction of online learning systems is worth exploring.

Moneta and Csikszentmihalyi [48] pointed out that the relative balance between challenges and skills was an important factor in generating flow experience according to flow theory. Human–computer interaction refers to the technology that people use to realize the dialogue between people and computers in an effective way through computer input and output devices [49]. In the context of human-computer interaction, the interface usability design of information systems has an important impact on the balance of challenge skills. High system availability can reduce users' burden, and then achieve the balance between challenges and skills in the process of human-computer interaction, which is conducive to the sense of immersion [50]. At the same time, the feedback mechanism is an important condition for generating a flow experience. When the system interface of online virtual classrooms runs smoothly and quickly responds to user requests and timely feedback on the results required by users, users may be able to gain a flow experience in continuous interaction [51]. In terms of information quality characteristics, Shin confirmed that more attractive content acted on the sense of immersion [52]. In addition, online learning is prone to loneliness and distraction, so it is necessary to enhance the interaction between teachers and students to break the physical distance, to improve the sense of immersion [25]. Ma and Li [7] found that new functions of online virtual classrooms, such as bullet screens, group discussions and chat boxes, could meet the needs of communication between teachers and students, and also ensure students' immersive learning.

Individuals in flow experience can obtain pleasure and satisfaction that cannot be obtained in daily life [53]. Relevant studies found that flow experience has a significant positive impact on the continuance intention of information users [54]. A poor flow experience will make students dissatisfied with online virtual classrooms and unwilling to use online virtual classrooms [25]. Therefore, the following hypotheses were proposed:

H6. *System availability has a positive effect on the flow experience.*

H7. *Feedback timeliness has a positive effect on the flow experience.*

H8. *Interesting content has a positive effect on the flow experience.*

H9. *System functionality has a positive effect on the flow experience.*

H10. *Interactive sociality has a positive effect on the flow experience.*

H11. *Flow experience plays a mediating role in the influence mechanism of the five system characteristics on continuance intention to use online virtual classrooms.*

Due to the differences in individual psychology and behavior, students' acceptance ability in classroom learning is different [55]. This leads to differences in their level of knowledge acquired in class and their performance in completing the test. These different degrees of performance are taken as the main measures of learning effect in this study. It should be noted that online learning makes it impossible to communicate face-to-face directly. It is very easy for the technical characteristics of the system, such as an unstable network and delayed message reception, to keep up with the teaching progress and show poor learning results [56]. It can be seen that the system characteristics of online learning systems, such as system availability, feedback timeliness, have a positive effect on the learning effect. A study showed that the poor flow experience of online learning was more likely to make students feel anxious, affect their classroom performance, and achieve poor learning results [57]. However, no matter what causes the learning effect, students are extremely dissatisfied with online virtual classrooms after they perceive that using online virtual classrooms will weaken their academic performance, and then they become unwilling to continue to use online virtual classrooms [24,25]. Therefore, we hypothesized that:

H12. *System availability has a positive effect on the learning effect.*

H13. *Feedback timeliness has a positive effect on the learning effect.*

H14. *Interesting content has a positive effect on the learning effect.*

H15. *System functionality has a positive effect on the learning effect.*

H16. *Interactive sociality has a positive effect on the learning effect.*

H17. *Flow experience has a positive effect on the learning effect.*

H18. *Learning effect plays a mediating role in the influence mechanism of the five system characteristics on continuance intention to use online virtual classrooms.*

The research model in this paper is based on the D&M model and flow theory [58,59]. Based on the above hypotheses, this research model as shown in Figure 2.

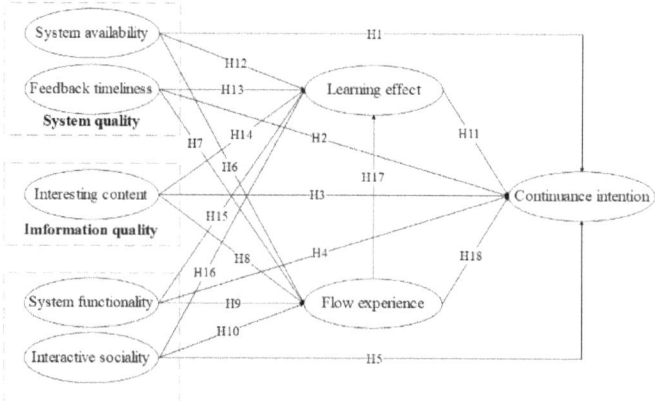

Figure 2. Proposed research model.

3. Materials and Methods

3.1. Questionnaire Items

After an extensive review of the literature on the D&M model, we developed the measurement items (as shown in Appendix A). This scale was reviewed by experts and modified by a pre-investigation test. We also repeatedly compared the Chinese and English translations of the questionnaire to ensure accuracy and consistency.

3.2. The Research Setting

Since undergraduates in Beijing used online virtual classrooms during the COVID-19 pandemic, with a high length of time and a high proportion of participation, this study limited the survey objects to undergraduates in Beijing, which is very representative in China. To obtain the most economical and effective results under the premise of fully representative samples, we adopted the multi-level sampling method to gradually sample from the types of universities, specific universities, and students. The results of each level are shown in Table 1. In addition, all participants were informed and confirmed before the questionnaire was issued.

Table 1. Sampling results of types of colleges and universities in the first stage.

Types	Number	Code Range	Random Sampling	Re-encoding
Technology	18	1–214974	2388	1
Language	8	214975–255301	253717	2
Political Law	5	255302–280862		
Comprehensive	11	280863–375911	290014	3
Normal	2	375912–397979	381557	4
Agricultural	2	397980–417178		
Medical	3	417179–432162	431765	5
Forestry	1	432163–445611		
Finance and Economics	6	445612–492027	470701	6
Physical Education	2	492028–504467		
Art	8	504468–527020		
Ethnic	1	527021–538354		

In stage 1, in order to investigate more comprehensive types of students, we first adopted PPS sampling to select school types. Before sampling, the size of the type sample box was set as 6 university types. We used random numbers to select them according to the number of undergraduates in each university. In stage 2, schools are selected by stratified sampling. One school was selected randomly from each of the six selected school types. In stage 3, simple random sampling was used to randomly select undergraduates from Beijing University of Posts and Telecommunications, Beijing Foreign Studies University, Peking University, Capital Normal University, Capital Medical University and Central University of Finance and Economics.

3.3. Description of the Sample

Due to COVID-19, we issued questionnaires online and offline to ensure the greatest accuracy of sampling and quality of questionnaires, and 716 questionnaires were collected. According to the answers to the audit questions set in the questionnaire, the length of time to fill in, the identification of reverse questions, and other judgment factors, the invalid questionnaires were eliminated item by item. Finally, 623 valid questionnaires were used for analysis with an effective rate of 87.01%. Table 2 shows the demographic characteristics of the participants.

Table 2. Demographic characteristics.

Variables	Classification	Number	Percentage
Gender	Male	270	43.34
	Female	353	56.66
Grade	Grade 1	96	15.41
	Grade 2	273	43.82
	Grade 3	190	30.50
	Grade 4	64	10.27
Major	Law	31	4.98
	Engineering	94	15.09
	Management	75	12.04
	Education	39	6.26
	Economics	92	14.77
	Military Science	6	0.96
	Science	74	11.88
	History	6	0.96
	Agronomy	11	1.77
	Literature	92	14.77
	Medical Science	74	11.88
	Art	21	3.37
	Philosophy	8	1.28

Since the issuance of questionnaires strictly followed the sampling design, the distribution of the final valid samples was also very appropriate. The results show that 270 (43.34%) are male and 353 (56.66%) are female. The respondents are mainly in grade 2 (272, 43.82%) and grade 3 (191, 30.50%). The benefit from taking into account the school type in the sampling design, respondents' professional types cover thirteen categories. Since students of different majors may need different functions and tools to match their major content when using online virtual classrooms [60–62], a full investigation of students in various majors can avoid bias caused by professional imbalance when examining students' functional requirements.

4. Results

4.1. Measurement Model

To test common method bias [63,64], the Harman single factor test was used to analyze all the measurement items of each latent variable. The explained percentage of the variance of the first common factor is 31.857%, which is lower than the critical value of 40%, indicating that the common method bias is within an acceptable range. It can be considered that there is no serious common method bias and further research can be carried out.

Next, we tested the reliability and effectiveness. Cronbach's α values and composite reliability (CR) values were used as indicators to test the effectiveness of variables. In Table 3, the Cronbach's α values of all variables are higher than 0.8, and the composite reliability (CR) values are higher than 0.7. Therefore, the scale established in this study has good internal consistency and high reliability.

Table 3. Reliability and validity test.

Constructs	Factors	Factor Loading	CR	AVE	Cronbach's α
System availability (SA)	SA1	0.910	0.891	0.733	0.885
	SA2	0.899			
	SA3	0.748			
Feedback timeliness (FT)	FT1	0.909	0.913	0.779	0.909
	FT2	0.894			
	FT3	0.855			

Table 3. Cont.

Constructs	Factors	Factor Loading	CR	AVE	Cronbach's α
Interesting content (IC)	IC1	0.943	0.908	0.769	0.899
	IC2	0.787			
	IC3	0.872			
System functionality (SF)	SF1	0.833	0.850	0.657	0.842
	SF2	0.857			
	SF3	0.716			
Interactive sociality (IS)	IS1	0.741	0.884	0.658	0.879
	IS2	0.857			
	IS3	0.733			
	IS4	0.889			
Flow experience (FE)	FE1	0.944	0.856	0.664	0.869
	FE2	0.739			
	FE3	0.744			
	FE4	0.759			
Learning effect (LE)	LE1	0.830	0.889	0.680	0.856
	LE2	0.821			
	LE3	0.795			
Continuance intention (CI)	CI1	0.909	0.884	0.719	0.879
	CI2	0.782			
	CI3	0.853			

KMO = 0.921, Bartlett spherical approximate chi-square test value is 10,709.622, $p < 0.001$.

In addition, the factor loadings and average variance extracted (AVE) values of all variable measures are higher than 0.5, indicating that the scale has good convergent validity. Meanwhile, in Table 4, the square root of AVE is significantly greater than the correlation coefficient of each variable, so the scale has good discrimination effectiveness. Finally, the results of confirmatory factor analysis show that: $\chi^2/df = 2.076 < 3.0$, GFI = 0.948 > 0.9, CFI = 0.972 > 0.9, NFI = 0.948 > 0.9, NNFI = 0.967 > 0.9, RMSEA = 0.043 < 0.1, RMR = 0.098 < 0.1, all goodness of fit indicators are within the recommended range, which shows that the model fits well.

Table 4. The square root of AVE and correlation coefficient of variables.

	SA	FT	IC	SF	IS	FE	TE	CI
SA	0.856							
FT	0.571	0.883						
IC	0.206	0.303	0.877					
SF	0.461	0.455	0.392	0.811				
IS	0.434	0.42	0.399	0.714	0.811			
FE	0.393	0.392	0.368	0.685	0.683	0.815		
TE	0.249	0.235	0.164	0.394	0.425	0.483	0.825	
CI	0.37	0.403	0.291	0.533	0.514	0.596	0.314	0.848

4.2. Structural Equation Modeling

In this study, SEM was used to test the theoretical model and hypotheses, whose strength lies in the quantitative study of the interaction between multiple variables [58,65]. The path coefficient indicates the degree of support of the data to the research model. Figure 3 shows the SEM test results of the sample. It can be seen from Figure 3 that only system availability ($\beta = 0.160$, $p < 0.001$) and interactive sociality ($\beta = 0.199$, $p < 0.001$) have significant positive effects on college students' continuance intention to use online virtual classrooms. H1 and H5 are supported, while H2–H4 are not tenable. In addition, system availability ($\beta = 0.359$, $p < 0.05$), feedback timeliness ($\beta = 0.210$, $p < 0.001$), interesting content ($\beta = 0.138$, $p < 0.001$), system functionality ($\beta = 0.188$, $p < 0.001$) and interactive sociality (β = 0.154, p < 0.001) have a positive effect on flow experience. H6–H10 are verified. At the same time, feedback timeliness (β = 0.183, p < 0.001), interesting content (β = 0.216, p < 0.001), system functionality (β = 0.224, p < 0.001) and interactive sociality (β = 0.156, p < 0.001) have a significant positive effect on the learning effect. However, system availability (β = 0.065, p = 0.077 > 0.05) has no significant effect on the learning effect, while it has a tremendous impact on flow experience. H13–H16 are proved, but H12 is not.

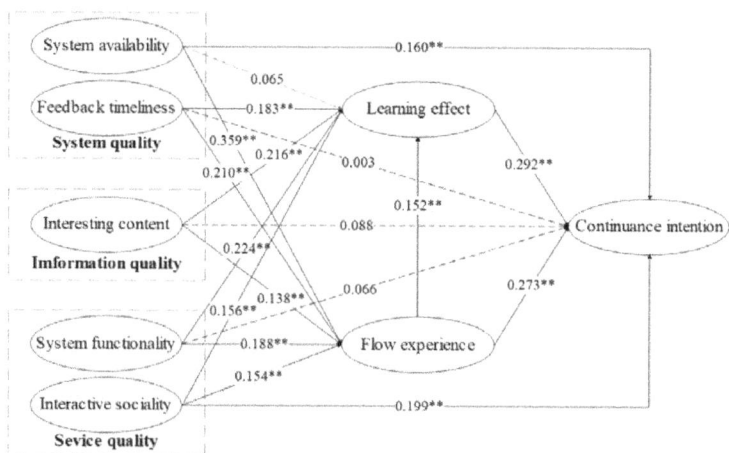

Figure 3. Path coefficient of the model. Note: All coefficients in the above figure are standardized coefficients; the solid line and the dashed line represent the significant and non-significant effects of the corresponding path, respectively; ** $p < 0.001$.

Finally, flow experience (β = 0.273, p < 0.001) and learning effect (β = 0.292, p < 0.001) have a significant positive effect on college students' continuance intention to use online virtual classrooms. Flow experience (β = 0.152, p < 0.001) has a significant positive effect on the learning effect. H11 is verified.

To sum up, the five system characteristics of the study have a positive effect on college students' continuance intention to use online virtual classrooms, of which interactive sociality has the greatest impact. Except that the system availability has no obvious effect on the learning effect, these system characteristics indirectly affect the college students' continuance intention to use online virtual classrooms by positively affecting the flow experience and learning effect. At the same time, flow experience has a positive effect on the learning effect. It is also obvious that the flow experience of students plays an important role in the entire influence mechanism.

4.3. Mediation Analysis

The theoretical model shows that there is a chained mediating relationship between system characteristics, flow experience, learning effect and continuance intention. To further verify the mediating role of flow experience and learning effect between system characteristics and college students' continuance intention to use online virtual classrooms, a bootstrap sampling test (5000 samples) was conducted using the SPSS macro program PROCESS plug-in compiled by Hayes [66]. The results are shown in Tables 5 and 6.

Table 5. Regression analysis of mediating effect.

Variables	Flow Experience	Learning Effect		Continuance Intention		
	M1	M2	M3	M4	M5	M6
Control variable						
Gender	−0.010	−0.025	−0.061	−0.058	−0.053	−0.051
Grade	−0.007	0.028	0.030	0.032	0.021	0.024
Major	−0.007	−0.012	−0.011	−0.009	−0.008	−0.006
Independent variable						
System availability	0.359 **	0.121 **	0.124 *	0.137 *	0.062	−0.156 **
Feedback timeliness	0.210 **	0.217 **	0.120 *	0.055	0.053	0.002
Interesting content	0.135 **	0.234 **	0.187 **	0.144 *	0.114 *	0.083
System functionality	0.188 **	0.254 **	0.189 **	0.13 *	0.110 *	0.066
Interactive sociality	0.155 **	0.176 **	0.292 **	0.243 **	0.237 **	0.200 **
Mediator variable						
Flow experience				0.313 **		0.270 **
Learning effect					0.312 **	0.284 **
R^2	0.853	0.780	0.483	0.497	0.504	0.515
$\triangle R^2$	0.851	0.777	0.476	0.490	0.497	0.508
F	417.587 **	254.602 **	67.062 **	63.033 **	64.809 **	60.737 **

Note: * $p < 0.05$ ** $p < 0.01$.

Table 6. Indirect effect analysis results.

Indirect Effect	Effect	Boot SE	BootLLCI	BootULCI	p
SA⇒FE⇒CI	0.091	0.029	0.040	0.154	0.002
SA⇒LE⇒CI	0.018	0.012	−0.005	0.044	0.139
SA⇒FE⇒LE⇒CI	0.014	0.007	0.004	0.033	0.049
FT⇒FE⇒CI	0.060	0.019	0.021	0.095	0.001
FT⇒LE⇒CI	0.056	0.018	0.023	0.092	0.002
FT⇒FE⇒LE⇒CI	0.010	0.004	0.002	0.019	0.025
IC⇒FE⇒CI	0.034	0.014	0.012	0.067	0.015
IC⇒LE⇒CI	0.056	0.019	0.027	0.102	0.004
IC⇒FE⇒LE⇒CI	0.005	0.003	0.001	0.013	0.088
SF⇒FE⇒CI	0.053	0.019	0.018	0.091	0.004
SF⇒LE⇒CI	0.067	0.021	0.030	0.110	0.001
SF⇒FE⇒LE⇒CI	0.008	0.004	0.002	0.017	0.026
IS⇒FE⇒CI	0.041	0.014	0.016	0.072	0.004
IS⇒LE⇒CI	0.043	0.016	0.015	0.078	0.009
IS⇒FE⇒LE⇒CI	0.007	0.003	0.001	0.015	0.060

Note: BootLLCI refers to the lower limit of the 95% interval of bootstrap sampling, and BootULCI refers to the upper limit of the 95% interval of bootstrap sampling. These grey parts are chained mediation and the rest are parallel mediation.

First, interactive sociality was studied. In Table 5, the interactive sociality (β = 0.155, $p < 0.05$) positively affects college students' continuance intention to use online virtual classrooms. Moreover, interactive sociality has significant positive effects on flow experience (β = 0.155, $p < 0.01$) and learning effect (β = 0.176, $p < 0.01$). Based on model M3, flow experience and learning effect were introduced into models M4, M5 and M6. It is found that the influence of interactive sociality, flow experience and learning effect on continuance intention is still evident, demonstrating that there is a partial mediation. In addition, Table 6 also shows a chained mediation between interactive sociality, flow experience, learning effect, and continuance intention (95% confidence interval is [0.001, 0.015]).

The results of the mediating effect analysis are provided in Table 6. Among them, the 95% interval (BootCI) values of the indirect effect do not include the number 0, indicating that it has a mediating effect. The final results show that only the learning effect has no mediating effect between system availability and continuance intention, while the mediating effect between other variables in the research model and hypothesis exists. Through the above analysis, H11 is supported and H18 is partially supported.

5. Discussions

5.1. Theoretical Implications

This study combined the D&M model and flow theory to investigate the generation mechanism of Chinese college students' continuance intention to use online virtual classrooms. The results of this study can make some theoretical contributions to future research.

First, most of the previous research on online learning systems focused on systems that provide shared online courses. They paid more attention to gameplay and course design when exploring users' continuance intention [14], and never paid attention to the flow experience. However, a study by Simamora et al., suggested that poor flow experience in learning is more likely to make students feel anxious and affect their classroom performance and willingness to attend class [56]. Although the impact of flow experience on users' willingness to use information systems has been confirmed by many studies, this aspect has not been taken into account by previous studies on online learning systems to the best of the author's knowledge. This study innovatively examines systems such as Tencent Classroom, which provide real-time online virtual classrooms for universities during the COVID-19 pandemic and expands the important role of flow experience through the D&M model. The results obtained in this study are consistent with the conclusion of Simamora et al., [56]. Second, previous research on online learning systems has commonly been conducted in conjunction with course performance [67,68]. It is undeniable that compared with course performance, the learning effect recognized through quizzes during and after class has a more intuitive impact on students' use intention and the learning effect is affected by flow experience [24]. The influence of flow experience on the learning effect is incorporated into the model, which improves the generation mechanism of the whole college students' continuance intention to use online virtual classrooms.

5.2. Practical Implications

There is an old saying in China: "a workman must first sharpen his tools if he is to do his work well." Therefore, it is more noteworthy to optimize online virtual classrooms to improve users' satisfaction and willingness to continue using them. Compared with a study investigated the way flow experience drives the online students' intention to engage in online English teaching platforms based on the flow and expectation confirmation model (ECM), which pays more attention to students' perception [69], this study applies D&M model to optimize system characteristics from the perspective of applicability and can provide more practical optimization suggestions.

This study identifies that the flow experience of college students plays an important role in the whole influence mechanism. College students with a better flow experience will show better learning effects and higher continuance intention to use online virtual classrooms. Online virtual classrooms need to pay attention to the application of new technologies to optimize the system and user experience to provide an immersive learning experience to attract and retain users. The existing online learning systems have provided basic system support and interactive functions, allowing teachers and students to communicate at both ends of the system. However, it can be seen that the flow experience it provides is not satisfactory from the feedback of teachers and students. Previous studies have shown that functions such as bullet screen, line dropping prevention, and screen cutting processing performed well in providing an immersive learning experience [70]. The survey results of this paper also indicate that system availability and feedback timeliness have a great positive impact on the flow experience. The system side can improve these. For example, these systems can optimize the system performance to adapt to more application scenarios and reduce reflection time. It can reduce errors in the system and transfer tasks assigned by the teacher to the students in a shorter time. In addition, the design of the system interface can also be more scientific, such as the clear division of modules, so that students can enter and exit the course and find information more conveniently. These will make students more accessible to use these systems to achieve a similar or even better flow experience than offline, which will optimize their learning effect and continuance intention.

This study also finds that interesting content and system functionality have a great impact on the learning effect. This reminds teachers to pay more attention to the design of courseware during online teaching, which is also a function that the system can focus on. Moreover, it is found that the functions of recording and playback courses and sharing courseware are also worth developing and optimizing to enrich the usability of the system before, during, and after class. In addition, the interaction between teachers and students is an essential part of online courses, which can effectively reduce the sense of distance and loneliness to drive students' learning mood. Online virtual classrooms can design personalized bullet screen functions and various discussion spaces to arouse students' enthusiasm for interaction.

5.3. Inadequate Research and Future Recommendations

Although the sampling design of this study is scientific and rigorous, only relatively representative college students in Beijing were investigated because of the sampling difficulties during the COVID-19 pandemic. As there may be some local policies in different regions that will affect the online learning experience of college students, the generalizability of this research conclusion needs to be strengthened and the follow-up research can further expand the scope of the investigation. Moreover, although the new structure and project were created by combining important literatures and checked repeatedly before the formal investigation, the implementation of each key point in the questionnaire could be further optimized through focus group interviews [71]. Moreover, we did not consider control variables in this study. Future research may examine the effects of control variables, such as demographic variables and personality traits; they could influence the findings [58]. More importantly, without COVID-19, online learning is often only used as an auxiliary tool rather than the main learning method [33,72]. In the future, we can compare the different effects of college students, using it both as an auxiliary tool and the main learning method.

6. Conclusions

The prevention and control of COVID-19 is a battle of resistance and difficulty. We may need to make great efforts to overcome it, but learning cannot be delayed. Online learning systems simulate the real classroom environment for college students during the COVID-19 pandemic to achieve online face-to-face teaching as much as possible. However, from a large number of blog posts on social media, college students feel widespread dissatisfaction with online courses, which reminds us that we need further analysis and optimization to enhance the experience of future online learning. Since the topic and direction of this study are relatively new and there is no directly available scale, this study developed the measurement items to investigate the generation mechanism of Chinese college students' continuance intention to use online virtual classrooms. Based on the D&M model, this study explored the relationship between flow experience, learning effect, and college students' continuance intention to use online virtual classrooms.

In this study, it is found that system characteristics are very important for online virtual classrooms to retain college students. The flow experience of college students plays an important mediating role in the whole shock mechanism. According to the investigation of this study, after considering the flow experience, these systems will be optimized in technology and function, such as increasing the personalized design of information interaction and technology to prevent screen cutting. The optimization of these system characteristics will greatly enhance the flow experience of college students, thus increasing their willingness to continue using the system. This study emphasizes the flow experience of online learning systems and reveals the optimization direction of online virtual face-to-face classrooms to provide references for the Ministry of Education, schools, and enterprises providing systems for education.

Author Contributions: Conceptualization, M.L., T.W. and W.L.; data curation, M.L. and M.W.; investigation, M.L.; methodology, M.L. and W.L.; software, M.L.; supervision, M.L. and T.W.; validation, M.L. and T.W.; visualization, M.L. and M.W.; writing—original draft, M.L. and T.W.; writing—review and editing, M.L. and W.L. All authors have read and agreed to the published version of the manuscript.

Funding: This research received no external funding.

Institutional Review Board Statement: Not applicable.

Informed Consent Statement: Informed consent was obtained from all subjects involved in the study.

Data Availability Statement: Data can be available from the corresponding author upon request.

Acknowledgments: The authors wish to thank the reviewers for their invaluable comments and suggestions that enhanced the quality of the paper.

Conflicts of Interest: The authors declare no conflict of interest.

Appendix A

Table A1. Questionnaire items.

Factors	Items	Items	Sources
System availability (SA)	SA1 SA2 SA3	Online virtual classrooms can be accessed and used normally anytime and anywhere. Online virtual classrooms have good functions and stable operations. Online virtual classrooms have a scientific interface design and clear module division.	[21,34]
Feedback timeliness (FT)	FT1 FT2 FT3	The topic pages assigned by teachers in online virtual classrooms display quickly. Online virtual classrooms can provide timely feedback for tasks assigned by teachers. The response time of online virtual classrooms is short.	[23,37]
Interesting content (IC)	IC1 IC2 IC3	When using online virtual classrooms, teachers' teaching content is abundant. When using online virtual classrooms, teachers' teaching content is interesting. When using online virtual classrooms, the teacher's mood is full during the classes.	[66]
System functionality (SF)	SF1 SF2 SF3	Online virtual classrooms provide sufficient chat functions. Online virtual classrooms provide sufficient learning tools. Online virtual classrooms provide sufficient data design.	[55]
Interactive sociality (IS)	IS1 IS2 IS3 IS4	When using online virtual classrooms, teachers ask us more questions. When using online virtual classrooms, teachers react quickly to my questions. I actively use online virtual classrooms to communicate with teachers and classmates. There is more interaction in online virtual classrooms.	[4,42]
Flow experience (FE)	FE1 FE2 FE3 FE4	When using online virtual classrooms, my attention is always focused. When using online virtual classrooms, I feel that the class time passes quickly. When using online virtual classrooms, I do not feel anxious or afraid of making mistakes. I do not cut out the interface of online virtual classrooms.	[25,34]
Learning effect (LE)	LE1 LE2 LE3	When using online virtual classrooms, I absorb and master the course knowledge. When using online virtual classrooms, I answer the teacher's questions quickly and well. When using online virtual classrooms, I finish the exercises quickly and well.	[24]
Continuance intention (CI)	CI1 CI2 CI3	I am willing to continue to use online virtual classrooms for online classes. I will not give up using online virtual classrooms in the future. If there is an alternative teaching mode, I will still use online virtual classrooms.	[54]

References

1. Allen, I.E.; Seaman, J. Growing by Degrees: Online Education in the United States. Sloan Consortium (NJ1). 2006. Available online: http://files.eric.ed.gov/fulltext/ED530063.pdf (accessed on 1 March 2006).
2. Palvia, S.; Aeron, P.; Gupta, P.; Mahapatra, D.; Parida, R.; Rosner, R.; Sindhi, S. Online education: Worldwide status, challenges, trends, and implications. *J. Glob. Inf. Technol. Manag.* **2018**, *21*, 233–241. [CrossRef]
3. Gupta, M.M. Impact of Coronavirus Disease (COVID-19) pandemic on classroom teaching: Challenges of online classes and solutions. *J. Educ. Health Promot.* **2021**, *10*, 155. [CrossRef]
4. Looi, C.K.; Chan, S.W.; Wu, L. Crisis and opportunity: Transforming teachers from curriculum deliverers to designers of learning. In *Radical Solutions for Education in a Crisis Context*; Springer: Singapore, 2021; pp. 131–145. [CrossRef]
5. Mali, D.; Lim, H. How do students perceive face-to-face/blended learning as a result of the Covid-19 pandemic? *Int. J. Manag. Educ.* **2021**, *19*, 100552. [CrossRef]
6. Xue, E.; Li, J.; Xu, L. Online education action for defeating COVID-19 in China: An analysis of the system, mechanism and mode. *Educ. Philos. Theory* **2022**, *54*, 799–811. [CrossRef]

7. Ma, S.; Li, J. Research on Construction of Online learning Platform in Colleges and Universities. In Proceedings of the 5th International Conference on Education and E-Learning, Virtual Event, 5–7 November 2021. [CrossRef]
8. Webster, J.; Hackley, P. Teaching effectiveness in technology-mediated distance learning. *Acad. Manag. J.* **1997**, *40*, 1282–1309. [CrossRef]
9. Dixson, M.D. Measuring Student Engagement in the Online Course: The Online Student Engagement Scale (OSE). Online Learn. 2015; Volume 19, p. n4. Available online: https://files.eric.ed.gov/fulltext/EJ1079585.pdf (accessed on 1 September 2015).
10. Zhu, H. Application of Rain classroom in formal classroom learning in the teaching of offshore engineering environment and loads. *Comput. Appl. Eng. Educ.* **2021**, *29*, 603–612. [CrossRef]
11. Tang, Y.M.; Chen, P.C.; Law, K.M.; Wu, C.H.; Lau, Y.Y.; Guan, J.; Ho, G.T. Comparative analysis of Student's live online learning readiness during the coronavirus (COVID-19) pandemic in the higher education sector. *Comput. Educ.* **2021**, *168*, 104211. [CrossRef]
12. Lee, M.C. Explaining and predicting users' continuance intention toward e-learning: An extension of the expectation–confirmation model. *Comput. Educ.* **2010**, *54*, 506–516. [CrossRef]
13. Chou, H.K.; Lin, I.C.; Woung, L.C.; Tsai, M.T. Engagement in e-learning opportunities: An empirical study on patient education using expectation confirmation theory. *J. Med. Syst.* **2012**, *36*, 1697–1706. [CrossRef]
14. Yang, M.; Shao, Z.; Liu, Q.; Liu, C. Understanding the quality factors that influence the continuance intention of students toward participation in MOOCs. *Educ. Technol. Res. Dev.* **2017**, *65*, 1195–1214. [CrossRef]
15. Sun, Y.; Liu, L.; Peng, X.; Dong, Y.; Barnes, S.J. Understanding Chinese users' continuance intention toward online social networks: An integrative theoretical model. *Electron. Mark.* **2014**, *24*, 57–66. [CrossRef]
16. Wu, B.; Zhang, C. Empirical study on continuance intentions towards E-Learning 2.0 systems. *Behav. Inf. Technol.* **2014**, *33*, 1027–1038. [CrossRef]
17. Wang, Y.; Asaad, Y.; Filieri, R. What makes hosts trust Airbnb? Antecedents of hosts' trust toward Airbnb and its impact on continuance intention. *J. Travel Res.* **2020**, *59*, 686–703. [CrossRef]
18. Shim, M.; Jo, H.S. What quality factors matter in enhancing the perceived benefits of online health information sites? Application of the updated DeLone and McLean Information Systems Success Model. *Int. J. Med. Inf.* **2020**, *137*, 104093. [CrossRef]
19. Lu, Y.; Zhou, T.; Wang, B. Exploring Chinese users' acceptance of instant messaging using the theory of planned behavior, the technology acceptance model, and the flow theory. *Comput. Hum. Behav.* **2009**, *25*, 29–39. [CrossRef]
20. Yang, H.; Lee, H. Exploring user acceptance of streaming media devices: An extended perspective of flow theory. *Inf. Syst. e-Bus. Manag.* **2018**, *16*, 1–27. [CrossRef]
21. Purwanto, A. University Students Online Learning System during Covid-19 Pandemic: Advantages, Constraints and Solutions. *Syst. Rev. Pharm.* **2020**, *11*, 570–576. Available online: https://ssrn.com/abstract=3986850 (accessed on 7 April 2022).
22. Bao, W. COVID-19 and Online Teaching in Higher Education: A Case Study of Peking University. *Hum. Behav. Emerging Technol.* **2020**, *2*, 113–115. Available online: https://publons.com/publon/10.1002/hbe2.191 (accessed on 7 April 2020). [CrossRef]
23. Su, L.; Li, M. The Improvement of Teaching Ideological and Political Theory Courses in Universities Based on Immersive Media Technology. *Front. Psychol.* **2022**, *13*, 877288. [CrossRef]
24. Hashemi, A. Effects of COVID-19 on the academic performance of Afghan students' and their level of satisfaction with online teaching. *Cogent Arts Humanit.* **2021**, *8*, 1933684. [CrossRef]
25. Maqableh, M.; Alia, M. Evaluation online learning of undergraduate students under lockdown amidst COVID-19 Pandemic: The online learning experience and students' satisfaction. *Child. Youth Serv. Rev.* **2021**, *128*, 106160. [CrossRef]
26. Husár, J.; Dupláková, D. Evaluation of foreign languages teaching in LMS conditions by facility and discrimination index. *TEM J.* **2016**, *5*, 44. [CrossRef]
27. Pather, N.; Blyth, P.; Chapman, J.A.; Dayal, M.R.; Flack, N.A.; Fogg, Q.A.; Green, R.A.; Hulme, A.; Johnson, I.; Meyer, A.J.; et al. Forced disruption of anatomy education in Australia and New Zealand: An acute response to the COVID-19 pandemic. *Anat. Sci. Educ.* **2020**, *13*, 284–300. [CrossRef] [PubMed]
28. Kang, N.H.; Seo, J. Emerging Online Science Teaching Practices: Insights from High School Physics Teaching Cases in South Korea during COVID-19 Pandemic. *Asia-Pac. Sci. Educ.* **2021**, *7*, 343–383. [CrossRef]
29. Mital, D.; Dupláková, D.; Duplák, J.; Mital'ová, Z.; Radchenko, S. Implementation of Industry 4.0 Using E-learning and M-learning Approaches in Technically-Oriented Education. *Assoc. Inf. Commun. Technol. Educ. Sci.* **2021**, *10*, 368–375. Available online: https://www.temjournal.com/content/101/TEMJournalFebruary2021_368_375.pdf (accessed on 1 February 2021).
30. Guo, J.; Zhu, R.; Zhao, Q.; Li, M.; Zhang, S. Adoption of the online platforms Rain Classroom and WeChat for teaching organic chemistry during COVID-19. *J. Chem. Educ.* **2020**, *97*, 3246–3250. [CrossRef]
31. Da-Hong, L.; Hong-Yan, L.; Wei, L.; Guo, J.J.; En-Zhong, L. Application of flipped classroom based on the Rain Classroom in the teaching of computer-aided landscape design. *Comput. Appl. Eng. Educ.* **2020**, *28*, 357–366. [CrossRef]
32. Yang, Y.; Zhang, H.; Chai, H.; Xu, W. Design and application of intelligent teaching space for blended teaching. *Interact. Learn. Environ.* **2022**, *2022*, 2028857. [CrossRef]
33. Yu, Z.; Yu, L. Identifying Tertiary Students' Perception of Usabilities of Rain Classroom. *Technol. Knowl. Learn.* **2021**, *26*, 1–21. [CrossRef]
34. DeLone, W.H.; McLean, E.R. The DeLone and McLean model of information systems success: A ten-year update. *J. Manag. Inf. Syst.* **2003**, *19*, 9–30. [CrossRef]

35. Aparicio, M.; Bacao, F.; Oliveira, T. Grit in the path to e-learning success. *Comput. Hum. Behav.* **2017**, *66*, 388–399. [CrossRef]
36. Lee, S.; Kim, B.G. The impact of qualities of social network service on the continuance usage intention. *Manag. Decis.* **2017**, *55*, 701–729. [CrossRef]
37. Cheng, F.F.; Wu, C.S.; Chen, Y.C. Creating customer loyalty in online brand communities. *Comput. Hum. Behav.* **2020**, *107*, 105752. [CrossRef]
38. Daradkeh, M.K. Exploring the usefulness of user-generated content for business intelligence in innovation: Empirical evidence from an online open innovation community. *Int. J. Enterp. Inf. Syst.* **2021**, *17*, 44–70. [CrossRef]
39. Gustiani, S. Students' motivation in online learning during covid-19 pandemic era: A case study. *Holistics* **2020**, *12*, 2. Available online: https://jurnal.polsri.ac.id/index.php/holistic/article/view/3029/1235 (accessed on 30 December 2020).
40. Gürkut, C.; Nat, M. Important factors affecting student information system quality and satisfaction. *Sci. Technol. Educ.* **2017**, *14*, 923–932. [CrossRef]
41. Cong, C.; Fu, D. An AI based research on optimization of university sports information service. *J. Intell. Fuzzy Syst.* **2021**, *40*, 3313–3324. [CrossRef]
42. Wang, S.; Xu, X.; Li, F.; Fan, H.; Zhao, E.; Bai, J. Effects of modified BOPPPS-based SPOC and Flipped class on 5th-year undergraduate oral histopathology learning in China during COVID-19. *BMC Med. Educ.* **2021**, *21*, 540. [CrossRef]
43. Muthuprasad, T.; Aiswarya, S.; Aditya, K.S.; Jha, G.K. Students' perception and preference for online education in India during COVID-19 pandemic. *Soc. Sci. Humanit. Open* **2021**, *3*, 100101. [CrossRef]
44. Finkelstein, S.; Nickel, A.; Lipps, Z.; Barnes, T.; Wartell, Z.; Suma, E.A. Astrojumper: Motivating exercise with an immersive virtual reality exergame. *Presence Teleoperators Virtual Environ.* **2011**, *20*, 78–92. [CrossRef]
45. Rodríguez-Ardura, I.; Meseguer-Artola, A. Imagine, feel "there", and flow! Immersive experiences on m-Facebook, and their affective and behavioural effects. *Inf. Technol. People* **2018**, *32*, 358. [CrossRef]
46. Shin, D.; Biocca, F. Exploring immersive experience in journalism. *New Media Soc.* **2018**, *20*, 2800–2823. [CrossRef]
47. Shin, D. How does immersion work in augmented reality games? A user-centric view of immersion and engagement. *Inf. Commun. Soc.* **2019**, *22*, 1212–1229. [CrossRef]
48. Moneta, G.B.; Csikszentmihalyi, M. The effect of perceived challenges and skills on the quality of subjective experience. *J. Personal.* **1996**, *64*, 275–310. [CrossRef] [PubMed]
49. Karray, F.; Alemzadeh, M.; Abou Saleh, J.; Arab, M.N. Human-computer interaction: Overview on state of the art. *Int. J. Smart Sens. Intell. Syst.* **2008**, *1*, 137–159. [CrossRef]
50. Yen, W.C.; Lin, H.H. Investigating the effect of flow experience on learning performance and entrepreneurial self-efficacy in a business simulation systems context. *Interact. Learn. Environ.* **2020**, *29*, 1–16. [CrossRef]
51. Oliver, K.; Osborne, J.; Brady, K. What are secondary students' expectations for teachers in virtual school environments? *Distance Educ.* **2009**, *30*, 23–45. [CrossRef]
52. Shin, D.H. The role of affordance in the experience of virtual reality learning: Technological and affective affordances in virtual reality. *Telemat. Inform.* **2017**, *34*, 1826–1836. [CrossRef]
53. Deng, L.; Turner, D.E.; Gehling, R.; Prince, B. User experience, satisfaction, and continual usage intention of IT. *Eur. J. Inf. Syst.* **2010**, *19*, 60–75. [CrossRef]
54. Jin, H.; Yan, J.; Zhang, Y.; Zhang, H. Research on the influence mechanism of users' quantified-self immersive experience: On the convergence of mobile intelligence and wearable computing. *Pers. Ubiquitous Comput.* **2020**, *2*, 1–12. [CrossRef]
55. Lövdén, M.; Fratiglioni, L.; Glymour, M.M.; Lindenberger, U.; Tucker-Drob, E.M. Education and cognitive functioning across the life span. *Psychol. Sci. Public Interest* **2020**, *21*, 6–41. [CrossRef] [PubMed]
56. Simamora, R.M.; De Fretes, D.; Purba, E.D.; Pasaribu, D. Practices, challenges, and prospects of online learning during COVID-19 pandemic in higher education: Lecturer perspectives. *Stud. Learn. Teach.* **2020**, *1*, 185–208. [CrossRef]
57. Doumanis, I.; Economou, D.; Sim, G.R.; Porter, S. The impact of multimodal collaborative virtual environments on learning: A gamified online debate. *Comput. Educ.* **2019**, *130*, 121–138. [CrossRef]
58. Yang, Q.; Lee, Y.-C. The Critical Factors of Student Performance in MOOCs for Sustainable Education: A Case of Chinese Universities. *Sustainability* **2021**, *13*, 8089. [CrossRef]
59. Al-Hattami, H.M. Validation of the D&M IS success model in the context of accounting information system of the banking sector in the least developed countries. *J. Manag. Control.* **2021**, *32*, 127–153. [CrossRef]
60. Varlamis, I.; Apostolakis, I. The present and future of standards for e-learning technologies. *Interdiscip. J. E-Learn. Learn. Objects* **2006**, *2*, 59–76. Available online: https://www.learntechlib.org/p/44814/article_44814.pdf (accessed on 27 August 2022). [CrossRef]
61. Tsai, C.C. Conceptions of learning versus conceptions of web-based learning: The differences revealed by college students. *Comput. Educ.* **2009**, *53*, 1092–1103. [CrossRef]
62. Simões, T.M.; Rodrigues, J.J.; de la Torre, I. Personal Learning Environment Box (PLEBOX): A new approach to E-learning platforms. *Comput. Appl. Eng. Educ.* **2013**, *21*, E100–E109. [CrossRef]
63. Podsakoff, P.M.; Organ, D.W. Self-Reports in Organizational Research: Problems and Prospects. *J. Manag.* **1986**, *12*, 531–544. [CrossRef]
64. Schwarz, A.; Rizzuto, T.; Carraher-Wolverton, C.; Roldán, J.L.; Barrera-Barrera, R. Examining the impact and detection of the "urban legend" of common method bias. *DATABASE Adv. Inf. Syst.* **2017**, *48*, 93–119. [CrossRef]

65. Qin, Z.; Fu, H.; Chen, X. A study on altered granite meso-damage mechanisms due to water invasion-water loss cycles. *Environ. Earth Sci.* **2019**, *78*, 428. [CrossRef]
66. Hayes, A.F. *Introduction to Mediation, Moderation, and Conditional Process Analysis: A Regression-Based Approach*; Guilford Publications: New York, NY, USA, 2017. [CrossRef]
67. Muilenburg, L.Y.; Berge, Z.L. Student barriers to online learning: A factor analytic study. *Distance Educ.* **2005**, *26*, 29–48. [CrossRef]
68. Wang, Y.; Dong, C.; Zhang, X. Improving MOOC learning performance in China: An analysis of factors from the TAM and TPB. *Comput. Appl. Eng. Educ.* **2020**, *28*, 1421–1433. [CrossRef]
69. Zhao, H.; Khan, A. The students' flow experience with the continuous intention of using online english platforms. *Front. Psychol.* **2021**, *12*, 807084. [CrossRef]
70. Kannadhasan, S.; Nagarajan, R.; Shanmuganantham, M.; Deepa, S. Future proofing higher education challenges in open and distance learning. *Int. J. Sci. Res. Eng. Dev.* **2020**, *3*, 1239–1245. Available online: http://www.ijsred.com/volume3/issue6/IJSRED-V3I6P110.pdf (accessed on 1 December 2020).
71. Göksün, D.O.; Gürsoy, G. Comparing success and engagement in gamified learning experiences via Kahoot and Quizizz. *Comput. Educ.* **2019**, *135*, 15–29. [CrossRef]
72. Leo, S.; Alsharari, N.M.; Abbas, J.; Alshurideh, M.T. From offline to online learning: A qualitative study of challenges and opportunities as a response to the COVID-19 pandemic in the UAE higher education context. *Eff. Coronavirus Dis. COVID-19 Bus. Intell.* **2021**, *334*, 203–217. [CrossRef]

Article

Construction of a Tangible VR-Based Interactive System for Intergenerational Learning

Chao-Ming Wang [1,*], Cheng-Hao Shao [2] and Cheng-En Han [1]

1. Department of Digital Media Design, National Yunlin University of Science and Technology, Douliu 64002, Taiwan; kevin1113k@gmail.com
2. Graduate School of Design, National Yunlin University of Science and Technology, Douliu 64002, Taiwan; shaoch108@gmail.com
* Correspondence: wangcm@yuntech.edu.tw

Abstract: The recent years have witnessed striking global demographic shifts. Retired elderly people often stay home, seldom communicate with their grandchildren, and fail to acquire new knowledge or pass on their experiences. In this study, digital technologies based on virtual reality (VR) with tangible user interfaces (TUIs) were introduced into the design of a novel interactive system for intergenerational learning, aimed at promoting the elderly people's interactions with younger generations. Initially, the literature was reviewed and experts were interviewed to derive the relevant design principles. The system was constructed accordingly using gesture detection, sound sensing, and VR techniques, and was used to play animation games that simulated traditional puppetry. The system was evaluated statistically by SPSS and AMOS according to the scales of global perceptions of intergenerational communication and the elderly's attitude via questionnaire surveys, as well as interviews with participants who had experienced the system. Based on the evaluation results and some discussions on the participants' comments, the following conclusions about the system effectiveness were drawn: (1) intergenerational learning activities based on digital technology can attract younger generations; (2) selecting game topics familiar to the elderly in the learning process encourages them to experience technology; and (3) both generations are more likely to understand each other as a result of joint learning.

Keywords: e-learning; interactive system; intergenerational learning; virtual reality; tangible user interfacing; traditional puppetry

1. Introduction

1.1. Background

According to the World Health Organization (WHO), people aged 65 or above are considered elderly. A country with the percentage of its population aged 65 and over rising to 7% is called an "aging society", and when the percentage reaches 14% and 20%, it will then be considered as an "aged society" and a "super-aged society", respectively [1]. Based on the governmental statistics of 2014, the number of people aged over 65 in Taiwan reached 1.49 million in 1993. This number accounted for more than 7% of the total population then, making Taiwan an aging society, as defined by the WHO. In addition, a 2018 report published by the government revealed that the elderly accounted for 14.1% of Taiwan's total population then, making the country an "aged society". This figure is projected to reach 20.6% by 2026, meaning that Taiwan will become a "super-aged society" at that time. Furthermore, in recent years Taiwan has been affected by a declining fertility rate, leading to even faster demographic shifts. Similar situations can be found in a great number of other countries in the world. With the advent of the aging population in these countries, it has become a constant global issue to explore methods that can help educate the elderly.

Another issue in aging societies is the serious inadequacy of intergeneration interactions. In countries such as the United States, the United Kingdom, the Netherlands, and

Sweden, the elderly and young people tend to have fewer interactions and varying opinions [2] due to their different growth backgrounds and inadequate contacts. In addition, the young people in today's societies tend to stereotype the elderly. For instance, Hall and Batey [3] revealed that most children think ill of the elderly due to the latter's declining physical function.

In response to the increasing number of senior citizens, many developed countries and international organizations have begun to formulate policies that emphasize the great importance of education for the elderly. Many countries have put forward learning methods to promote lifelong learning for the elderly, among which intergenerational learning is considered one of the best ways to bridge the generational gap. Ames and Youatt [4] believed that in the face of a larger number of older adults, the age gap has a greater impact on the older and younger generations. Hence, intergenerational programs have been found to be an effective method in providing education and service planning. Kaplan [5] also mentioned that intergenerational learning should be designed to use the advantages of one generation to meet the needs of the other to achieve meaningful and sustained resource exchange and learning between the two generations. Furthermore, Souza and Grundy [6] found that employing intergenerational interactions allowed the elderly to be more confident and positive, and so improved their self-value and happiness. Based on the perspective of the young, it was assumed that young people should be given effective channels to better exchange and cooperate with the elderly [7].

1.2. Research Motivation and Issues

In recent years, in many conventional learning activities, digital technologies have been introduced as auxiliary tools, among which virtual reality (VR) and augmented reality (AR) have been widely used. In particular, Ainge [8] suggested that students who have used VR are better at recognizing geometric shapes than those who have not, and that students in general had a positive attitude toward a VR-based learning environment. Virvou and Katsionis [9] also found that VR educational games could effectively arouse students' interest in learning and had better effects on education than other types of educational software. Meanwhile, with the developments in science and technology, VR has also been particularly adopted to help educate the elderly. For instance, MyndVR [10], a company that integrates VR with elderly health care, is assisting the elderly with diseases such as Alzheimer's and dementia by enabling them to create and experience a fulfilling and meaningful life in their later years. According to many participants, their aging diseases were relieved, and their physical health was improved. Dennis Lally, the cofounder of Rendever [11], developed a VR-based memory therapy system that brings back fond memories virtually and recreates meaningful scenes or places that older adults want to visit. Benoit et al. [12] combined VR and memory therapy by presenting scenes familiar to participants in a virtual environment with image rendering. Moreover, Manera et al. [13] argued that VR allowed patients with cognitive impairment and dementia to have more fun when performing tasks.

Ultimately, technology-based intergenerational activities can arouse more interest among the younger generations than conventional ones [14,15]. Cases related to conventional intergenerational activities indicated that due to familiarity, the elderly are more likely to have a sense of achievement in conventional activities, such as woodchopping, farming, and cooking [16]. However, only a few intergenerational activities feature combinations of technology and conventional activities, notwithstanding those based on VR and TUIs. In this study, TUIs and VR were integrated into conventional intergenerational activities to make the connections between both generations more interactive and recreational. Under the above premises, the following questions were put forward in this study. (1) Does the application of VR and TUIs to intergenerational learning facilitate emotion exchange and experience-sharing between the two generations? (2) What are the steps in setting up a VR-based system for interactive intergenerational learning for different learning tasks?

1.3. Literature Review

The literature on the elderly's physical and mental health, intergenerational learning, VR, and TUI design is reviewed in this section.

1.3.1. Physical and Mental Health of the Elderly

According to a report by the European Union, more than half of the world's population will comprise 48-year-olds or above by 2060, indicating that aging will keep accelerating in the next few decades [17]. Meanwhile, Taiwan has an aging population and a declining birth rate, giving the older and younger generations fewer opportunities to interact than they did in the past. Many studies showed that college students generally had a slightly negative view of the elderly, especially concerning the latter's physical and mental health [18–20]. However, it is worth noting that the two generations have fewer interactions. As the elderly age with time, they continue to suffer from physical and mental functional decline and become subject to increasing pain, discomfort, and inconvenience in life, giving rise to psychological changes. Furthermore, aging can be both physiological and psychological. In terms of physiology, Zajicek [21] held that the elderly could not see clearly and would easily become tired due to vision and memory degeneration. In addition, they easily forget how to operate a computer. With respect to their psychological conditions, the elderly are more likely to feel depressed in hard times, such as when they lose family members, friends, social roles, and physical functions. Thus, according to Shibata and Wada [22], some recreational activities may be adopted as an option when communicating with the elderly. Chatman [23] also found that some of the elderly in a community were so afraid of being sent to nursing institutions after retirement that they did not want to share their health conditions with others, even pretending to look healthy.

Research on the aging of seniors revealed that despite physical and mental changes of the elderly people, an aging society is blessed with a remarkable advantage—abundant older human resources. The most valuable thing that the elderly have lies in their wealth of work and life experiences, considering they lived through diverse situations. If older people can participate in more meaningful activities, their experiences can be shared with younger people to promote social progress. Moreover, their physical and mental health will be improved, reducing medical expenditures.

1.3.2. Intergenerational Learning

Intergenerational learning programs were implemented in 1963 when the P.K. Yonge Developmental Research School in the United States developed the "Adopt a Grandparent Program". Thereafter, many colleges and universities have begun studying and implementing intergenerational learning programs. In response to generational estrangement caused by population aging, intergenerational learning, which refers to the establishment of mutual learning between the older and younger generations, has emerged globally [5]. Intergenerational learning has been regarded as an informal activity passed down from one generation to another for centuries—a culture bridging tradition and modernization [24]. In modern times, influenced by an increasingly complex society, intergenerational learning is no longer limited to the family, but its influence extends to society and improves the overall social value [25].

Ames and Youatt [4] proposed a comprehensive selection model for intergenerational learning and service activities in classifying conventional intergenerational learning, which can help planners design more diverse and richer learning activities. The model can be divided into three parts: the middle generation, program categories, and selection criteria. In addition, Ohsako [26] divided intergenerational learning into four models/profiles: (1) older adults serving/mentoring/tutoring children and the youth; (2) children and the youth serving/teaching older adults; (3) children, the youth, and older adults serving the community/learning together for a shared task; and (4) children, the youth, and older adults engaged in informal leisure/unintentional learning activities.

Over the past few years, the degree of interaction has been considered a classification criterion. Kaplan [5] thought that this criterion could more effectively explain the positive or negative results of intergenerational learning, and classified intergenerational programs and activities accordingly into the following seven different levels of intergenerational engagement, ranging from initiatives (point #1 of the below) to those that promote intensive contact and ongoing opportunities for intimacy (point #7 of the below): (1) learning about other age groups; (2) seeing the other age group but at a distance; (3) meeting each other; (4) annual or periodic activities; (5) demonstration projects; (6) ongoing intergenerational programs; and (7) ongoing, natural intergenerational sharing, support, and communication. Ames and Youatt [4] put forward the most comprehensive selection model of intergenerational learning and service activities, while Ohsako [26], from a different perspective, enabled planners to design diverse and interesting activities. On the other hand, Kaplan [5] used the interaction degree as a classification criterion, and discussed how interactive methods are generated and how deep and sustainable interactions are conducted based on commonality.

Furthermore, Ames and Youatt [4] found that conventional intergenerational learning activities were mostly service-oriented. Thus, the value and significance of activities to participants must be taken into account when selecting and evaluating the topics involved in the intergenerational activities. A good intergenerational program should not only meet the expected goals, but also provide balanced and diverse activities to participants. Moreover, it is important to introduce digital technology to make intergenerational activities more interactive and recreational for the two generations.

Finally, it is worth noticing that some scholars have investigated the applications of group learning or education from wider points of view. For example, Kyrpychenko et al. [27] studied the structure of communicative competence and its formation while teaching a foreign language to higher education students. The results of the questionnaire survey of the students' responses provided grounds for the development of experimental methods for such competence formations by future studies. Kuzminykh et al. [28] investigated the development of competence in teaching professional discourse in educational establishments, and showed that the best approach was to adopt a model consisting of two stages based on self-education and group education. The research results revealed that communicative competence may be achieved through a number of activities that may be grouped under four generic categories. Singh et al. [29] proposed an intelligent tutoring system named "Seis Tutor", that can offer a learning environment for face-to-face tutoring. The performance of the system was evaluated in terms of personalization and adaptation through a comparison with some existing tutoring systems, leading to a conclusion that 73.55% of learners were strongly satisfied with artificial intelligence features. To improve early childhood education for social sustainability in the future, Oropilla and Odegaard [30] suggested the inclusion of intentional intergenerational programs in kindergartens, and presented a framework that featured conflicts and opportunities within overlapping and congruent spaces to understand conditions for various intergenerational practices and activities in different places, and to promote intergenerational dialogues, collaborations, and shared knowledge.

1.3.3. Virtual Reality

The concept of virtual reality (VR) was first proposed in 1950, but was not materialized until 1957. Heilig [31] developed Sensorama, the first VR-based system with sight, hearing, touch, and smell senses, as well as 3D images. In 1985, Lanier [32] expressed that VR must be generated on a computer with a graphics system and various connecting devices in order to provide immersive interactive experiences. Burdea [33] proposed the concept of the 3I VR pyramid, and maintained that VR should have three elements: immersion, imagination, and interaction. Currently, VR can be classified into six categories according to design technology and user interfaces: (1) desktop VR; (2) immersion VR; (3) projection VR; (4) simulator VR; (5) telepresence VR; and (6) network VR; therefore, in recent years, many experts and scholars assumed that the VR technology can improve participants' attitude toward and interest in learning, and that the interactions in learning tasks can be strengthened in an immersive environment to improve learning effects [9,34].

Many applications have been developed using VR technology in the past. A specific direction of VR applications for human welfare is the use of VR in the healthcare domain. In this research direction, Nasralla [35] studied the construction of sustainable patient-rehabilitation systems with IoT sensors for the development of virtual smart cities. The research results showed that the proposed approach could be useful in achieving sustainable rehabilitation services. In addition, Sobnath et al. [36] advocated the use of AI, big data, high-bandwidth networks, and multiple devices in a smart city to improve the life of visually impaired persons (VIPs) by providing them with more independence and safety. Specifically, the uses of strong ICT infrastructure with VR/AR and various wearable devices can provide VIPs with a better quality of life.

Table 1 summarizes the following key points in this study, based on relevant cases and the literature integrating both VR and the elderly: (1) VR is proven effective and has a positive effect on improving the body and cognition of the elderly; (2) VR-based learning activities can effectively enhance the learners' interest and help them make more progress; and (3) older people can adapt to VR, which can stimulate their memory according to their familiarity with a given scene, thereby achieving the effect of memory therapy [12]. As Davis mentioned regarding the technology-acceptance model (TAM) model [37–39], users' acceptance of science and technology is affected by "external factors", such as their living environment, learning style, and personal characteristics. Thus, it is impossible to determine whether the above method can have the same effect on the elderly in a specific society or country. In order to determine the usefulness and acceptability of VR for older Taiwanese people, Syed Abdul et al. [40] invited 30 older people over 60 years old in Taiwan to experience nine different VR games within six weeks, with each experience lasting 15 min. Then, they analyzed the users' performances with a scale based on the TAM model by Davis. The results showed that the elderly enjoyed the experience, finding VR useful and easy to use, which indicated that the elderly held a positive attitude toward the new technology.

Table 1. Relevant cases in which VR was used for the elderly.

Author, Year	Perceived Usefulness	Perceived Ease of Use
Benoit et al., 2015 [12]	Memory therapy, which used VR to present images familiar to participants, could effectively stimulate the memories of the elderly.	This case was simulator VR. Users only watched immersive projected images in a confined space similar to VR movies.
Manera et al., 2016 [13]	VR could be used to treat patients with cognitive impairment and dementia, arousing their interest in therapies.	After wearing 3D glasses, users watched a 3D projection screen and switched among pictures by clicking a mouse.
MyndVR, 2016 [10]	Immersive experiences that were diverse, meaningful, and interesting were provided to the elderly to slow down their mental aging and treat relevant diseases.	Users could see images by wearing a simple head-mounted VR display without any external operation.
George and David, 2017 [41]	After performing practical tasks in a 3D VR-based environment, the elderly held a more positive attitude toward VR.	Users wore a head-mounted display and used a controller to move around, and located their hometowns in a 3D street view.
Rendever, 2018 [11]	A memory therapy that used 3D technology to recreate meaningful scenes or places the elderly want to visit was developed, providing immersive experiences through VR.	Users could see images by wearing a simple head-mounted VR display without any external operation.

1.3.4. Tangible User Interfaces

The use of tangible user interfaces (TUIs) is a brand-new user-interfacing concept proposed by Ishii and Ullmer [42]. Unlike graphical user interfaces (GUIs), TUIs emphasize using common objects in daily life as the control interface, making the control action beyond screen manipulations. They allow users to operate the interface more intuitively by moving, grabbing, flipping, and knocking, and in other ways that people think are feasible to control the human–computer interface. Furthermore, TUIs grant a tangible form to utilize digital information or run programs [43].

More specifically, TUIs enable digital information to show in a tangible form. A digital interface consists of two important components: input and output, also known as control and representation. Control refers to how users manipulate information, while representation refers to how information is perceived. The tangible form shown in the use of TUIs may be regarded as the digital equivalent to control and representation, and the tangible artifacts operated in applying TUIs may be considered as devices for displaying representation and control. In other words, TUIs combine tangible representation (e.g., objects that can be operated by hand) with digital representation (e.g., images or sounds), as shown in Figure 1.

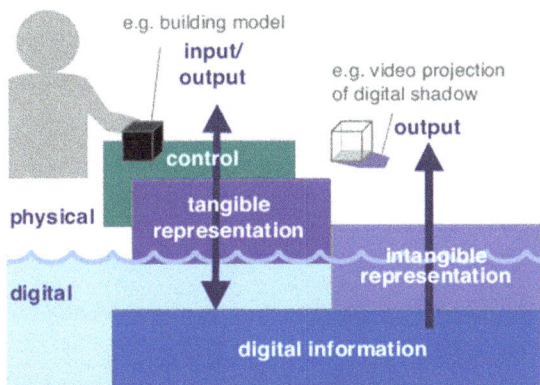

Figure 1. The conceptual framework of TUIs.

The concept of TUIs has been constantly discussed in man–machine interfacing seminars, and has been applied in various fields such as education and learning [44–46], music and entertainment [47–49], and professional solutions [50–52]. From the environmental psychology perspective, psychologists believed that TUIs had a tangible form and took advantage of the "affordance" of objects [53]. Some scholars, who employed the perceptual-motor theory as their research core, focused on user actions generated between them and TUIs, as well as on the dynamic presentation of TUIs [54–57].

Furthermore, TUIs provide a simpler and more intuitive way to help users accomplish goals. By combining physical manipulations with convenient digital technology, a TUI serves as a bridge connecting users and digital content. Moreover, TUIs have expanded the concept of interface design. Thus, scholars have conducted several discussions of the theoretical basis and scope of the conceptual framework of TUIs. In this study, it is proposed to apply TUIs in intergenerational learning activities, enabling users to intuitively operate interfaces and conduct their distinctive ways of presentation.

1.4. Brief Description of the Proposed Research and Paper Organization

Figure 2 shows the framework of this study, which was mainly derived from the literature related to the elderly's learning and technology applications. The design concept and system development were determined through interviews with experts. After constructing the system, actual intergenerational learning activities were held, and a questionnaire survey and participant interviews were conducted, with the results being analyzed and the effectiveness of the system evaluated.

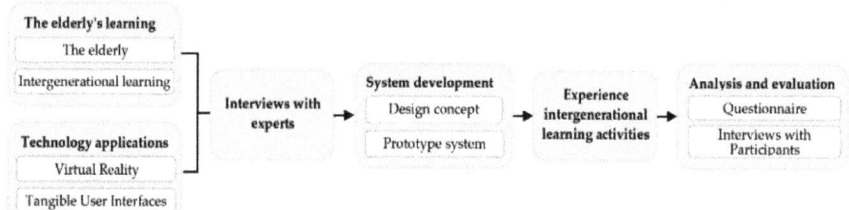

Figure 2. The framework of this study.

In this study, the research was mainly focused on intergenerational learning, and a novel tangible VR-based interactive system was proposed for such activities between the two generations of grandparents and grandchildren. Although previous studies, as mentioned in the previous literature survey, had various designs of intergenerational learning activities, the special case of adopting a traditional show performance, namely, glove puppetry, as the activity for intergenerational learning between the generations was not seen in the existing studies, which highlights the unique value of the proposed system and the resulting findings of this study.

The remainder of this manuscript is organized as follows. The proposed methods are described in Section 2. In Section 3, the results of our study are presented. The discussions of the experimental results are described in Section 4. Finally, the conclusions and discussions about the merits of the proposed system are included in Section 5.

2. Methods

A literature review, interviews with experts, the construction of a prototype system, a questionnaire survey, and interviews with participants were carried out in this study. Then, the effects of the system were analyzed. In particular, this study can be divided into four phases, as shown in Figure 3. In Phase I, the research objectives, scope, and methods were determined. Then, the relevant literature was analyzed, with key information on intergenerational learning, VR, and TUIs being collected. In Phase II, several experts in different fields were invited and interviewed to provide their comments on relevant topics that were determined according to the results of the literature review. The design principles for a VR-based intergenerational learning system using TUIs were derived based on the interview results. According to the principles, a prototype system for intergenerational learning was constructed, with relevant learning activities designed. In Phase III, users of two generations were invited to participate in the interactive intergenerational learning activities. In addition, comment data were collected through interviews with the participants and questionnaire surveys on the two aspects of intergenerational communication and the elderly's attitude. In Phase IV, the collected data were used for statistical evaluations of the effectiveness of the developed system using the SPSS and AMOS software packages, and conclusions and suggestions were put forward finally.

It is noteworthy that to use the proposed system, it requires the users' interactions through actually experiencing activities, so the users, especially the elderly, are required to have sound audio–visual ability, and be able to conduct hand movements, beat gongs and drums, and perform hand gestures.

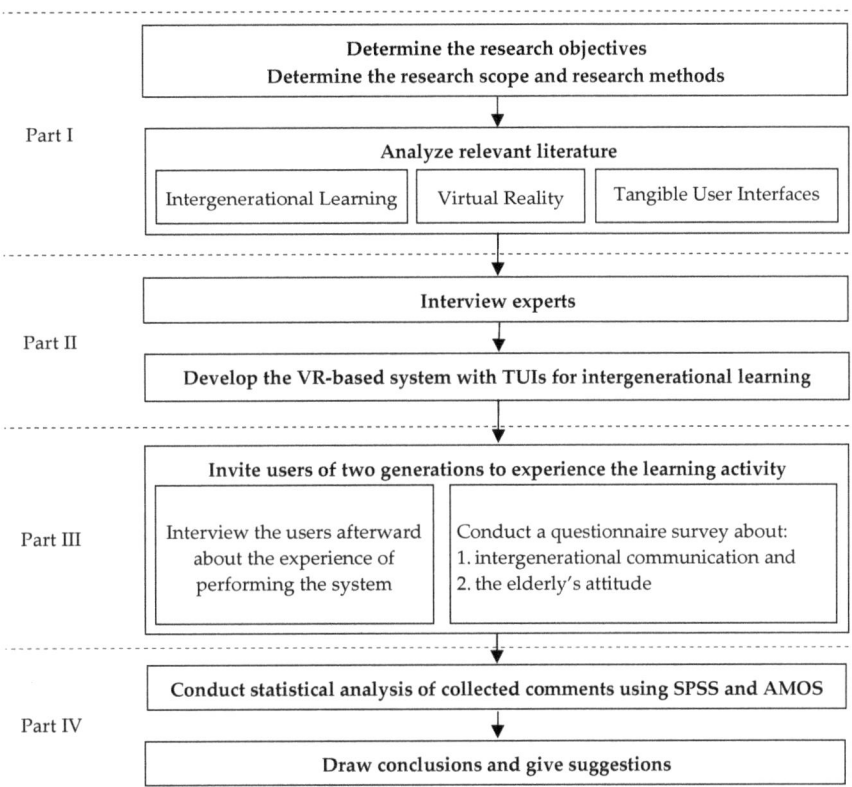

Figure 3. The flowchart of this study.

2.1. Interviews with Experts

Interviews with experts, as a form of interviews, allow interviewers to communicate with interviewees to collect research data [58]. Three experts, who were prominent in the fields of the elderly's learning, children's education, and interaction design, were invited (see Table 2 for the experts' respective backgrounds). Experts were interviewed in a semistructural form, through which they expressed their opinions on four aspects: (1) the importance of intergenerational learning; (2) the design of intergenerational learning activities; (3) the introduction of digital technology into intergenerational learning; and (4) the introduction of VR into intergenerational activities. The results of the interviews were used as a reference for designing the desired system (see Section 3 for details).

Table 2. Backgrounds of experts accepting interviews in this study.

Code	Current Company	Position	Specialty
P1	Senior Citizen Learning Center	Director	The elderly's learning and intergenerational learning
P2	Kaohsiung Municipal Jhenchang Elementary School	Homeroom teacher, PhD in adult education	Children's education and intergenerational learning
P3	RUMU Innovation	Founder of a company focused on integrated engaging technologies	Interaction design and technology art

2.2. Prototype Development

Boar's prototyping model [59] was utilized in this study to understand the users of a product in the shortest time. Through the constructed prototype, the users' responses were repeatedly evaluated, with their feedback serving as the basis for the designer to modify the product. In this way, the designer could have a clear idea of the users' needs and finally create products that met their expectations. Beaudouin Lafon and Mackay [60] believed that a prototype could allow for a concrete presentation of an abstract system, provide information during the design process, and help the designer choose the best design scheme. Thus, based on Boar's prototyping model, in this study the development of the desired intergenerational learning system based on VR and TUIs was planned in five steps, as follows: (1) planning and analyzing requirements; (2) designing the VR-based intergenerational learning system; (3) establishing a prototype of the VR-based intergenerational learning system; (4) evaluating and modifying the prototype system; and (5) completing the system development.

2.3. Questionnaire

The questionnaire for the system-effectiveness evaluation was modified several times after system development and before the experiment commenced. Fine adjustments were made later according to the evaluated effectiveness of the system to increase the stability of the system's devices. The formal experimental questionnaire adopted in this study was divided into two parts. The first part adopted the Global Perceptions of Intergenerational Communication (GPIC) scale of McCann and Giles [61], in which questions were designed to learn how the two generations thought of each other in the intergenerational learning activities. In the second part, the Elderly's Attitude Scale proposed by Lu and Kao [62] was employed to determine children's attitudes toward the elderly in the experience. The answers to questions in the questionnaire were shown on a five-point Likert scale, with 1 meaning "strongly disagree" and 5 meaning "strongly agree" (see Section 3 for the detailed analysis and description of the questionnaire).

2.4. Interviews with Participants

After conducting the questionnaire survey, five groups of 10 participants were randomly selected for interviews. This qualitative research method focused on the interviewees' self-perception and their descriptions of their life experiences. Particularly, researchers could comprehend the respondents' cognition of facts based on their responses [63]. Semistructural interviews are flexible, allowing interviewees to convey their most authentic cognition and feelings [64]. They were so adopted in this study to explore the emotional exchange between the two generations and understand their perceptions of the VR-based interactive intergenerational learning system.

In addition, based on the interaction design principles proposed by Verplank [65], the following topics were determined for use in the interview conducted in this study: (1) system operation; (2) experiences and feelings; and (3) emotions and experience transmission. As assumed by Verplank [65], the most important thing in interaction design was participants' physical and mental feelings; therefore, when designing an interaction device, designers must consider users' system operations (DO), experiences and feelings (FEEL), and emotions and experiences (KNOW). The detailed interviews with users are presented in Section 3 below.

3. Results

3.1. Interviews with Experts

The questions in the interviews with experts were based on the selection mode of intergenerational learning and service activities proposed by Ames and Youatt [4] and the technology-acceptance model by Davis [37–39] to ensure the topics and direction of this study. The questions mainly covered four dimensions. Dimension One was mainly concerned with the importance of intergenerational learning, including its significance and influence in today's society. Dimension Two involved the design of intergenerational learning activities, focusing on content presentation and other matters needing attention. Dimension Three involved the application of digital technology in intergenerational learning, focusing on the introduction method and views on the work. Dimension Four involved the introduction of VR to intergenerational activities, focusing on views of the interactive experiences, developments, and trends of VR-based intergenerational activities. Table 3 shows the outline and summary of the interviews with the experts.

Table 3. Outline and summary of the interviews with experts.

Dimension	Questions	Answers
Importance of intergenerational learning	Q1: What do you think of intergenerational learning?	1. Intergenerational learning can promote intergenerational integration between the elderly and the young, whether relatives or not. (P1) 2. It plays an increasingly important role in an aged society. Although intergenerational learning's advantages outweigh its disadvantages, intergenerational learning is not 100% healthy. (P2)
	Q2: What is the significance of intergenerational learning for the older and younger generations?	1. Intergenerational learning is about bridging the gap between the elderly and the young. (P1) 2. Intergenerational learning provides a second stage for the elderly and offers society an opportunity to redevelop the elderly as human resources. For the younger generations, the elderly set different examples for them to learn from. (P2)
	Q3: Is there any difference between the conventional and current intergenerational learning?	1. Due to the changing times, the older generations in the digital era also need to learn more about digital technology to better understand their grandchildren and become closer to them. (P1) 2. Introducing technology can attract the younger generations, but designers need to pay more attention when introducing the elderly into intergenerational programs with technological elements. (P2)
Design of intergenerational learning activities	Q4: What topics of intergenerational learning activities are more likely to arouse the interest of both grandparents and grandchildren?	1. Relaxing and easy interactive games and cooperative games such as questing and stacking allow both generations to have fun. (P1) 2. Topics must be in line with their life experience and backgrounds. The younger generations tend to be interested in cartoon characters and dolls. Thus, common points attracting both generations must be identified. (P2)
	Q5: What should be considered when designing intergenerational learning activities?	1. The elderly prefer easy and simple activities in terms of activity design, while the young emphasizes fun. Activities should not be too difficult; otherwise, one party may easily give up. (P1) 2. The difficulty of activities depends on the elderly and the young. Activities need to be interesting for both sides. Additionally, the activity time should be in line with the daily schedules of the two generations. (P2)
Introduction of digital technology to intergenerational learning	Q6: What do you think of introducing digital technology to intergenerational learning?	1. It can arouse the curiosity of the elderly, and the younger generation can learn something. The scheme's design should be carefully considered to facilitate appropriate interaction between the elderly and the young. (P1) 2. It appeals to the younger generation and provides a new learning opportunity to the two generations. (P2)
	Q7: Do you have any suggestions for the work in this study?	1. Interaction and connection between the two generations need to be enhanced. (P1) 2. Interactive methods that are more cooperative can be adopted to avoid unilateral command or control. (P2) 3. It is necessary to think about the relevance between the topics and the work. (P3)
Introduction of VR to intergenerational learning	Q8: What do you think of the current trend and development of VR?	1. It is so dependent on devices, which affect its development. The current trend mainly centers on entertainment. (P3)
	Q9: What should be taken into account when developing VR-based interactions for the elderly and children?	1. As for activity design, it is worth noting that children are more interested in brightly colored images and sound and light effects, while it is the contrary for the elderly. (P3)

In the interviews with experts, four key points were summarized. First, intergenerational learning plays an important role for the elderly and the young, bridging the gap between them and allowing them to learn from each other. Second, owing to the changes in the times and backgrounds, the progress of technology has widened the gap between the two generations. Therefore, if the elderly can actively learn about technology products and have more conversations with their grandchildren, they will find it easier to develop closer relationships with the latter. Intergenerational learning activities based on digital technology are more appealing to the young. Third, when designing intergenerational activities, the backgrounds and interests of the two generations should also be taken into account, and their common points should be identified to ensure participants' full engagement in the interaction. Meanwhile, the difficulty of activities must be appropriate so that the two generations can have fun during the interaction. Fourth, concerning the interface design of intergenerational activities, the differences between the elderly and children regarding the font size, color, and visual and sound effects chosen must be considered.

In this study, the key factors of intergenerational learning, the introduction of technology, and the application of VR to system development and design were summarized through interviews with experts. According to the recording, analysis, and sorting of the interview information, the key points were used as a reference for the subsequent system design.

3.2. System Design

In this study, a novel system for intergenerational learning activities was designed. By integrating conventional learning activities with the uses of VR and TUIs, the communication, learning, and interaction between the two generations were strengthened through multiple interaction techniques and immersive experiences.

3.2.1. The Concept of Design of Intergenerational Learning Activities

According to the literature review, it is known that the topics involved in intergenerational learning activities must be familiar to the elderly and interesting to the young in order to encourage them to have more interactions. Therefore, in this study the traditional *glove puppetry* was chosen as the topic for the intergenerational learning activities. Glove puppetry has a long history in Taiwan, reaching its peak between the 1950s and 1960s. Hence, the elderly are rather familiar with it. On the other hand, according to the interviews with experts conducted in this study, experts majoring in children's education deemed that children are easily attracted by cartoon characters and are generally interested in Muppets and dolls. Thus, they are likely to be curious about puppetry plays due to the cool sound and light effects created in such plays. Lastly, based on the selection model of intergenerational learning and service activities by Ames and Youatt [4], puppetry-based intergenerational activities suitable for this study were designed.

The theme of the designed activities was chosen to be "Recall the Play", in which the word "recall" in Chinese has the same pronunciation as the word "together", aiming at encouraging the elderly to perform glove puppetry together with the grandchildren. The elderly could recall the memories and feelings of watching puppet shows during their youth through interacting with their grandchildren. Meanwhile, sharing memories and stories of the past, as well as allusions to puppet shows, with grandchildren was a way of promoting cultural inheritance.

The activities were designed in such a way that they can be conducted through cooperation of the two generations, similar to the proscenium and backstage of a traditional open puppet-show theater, such as the example shown in Figure 4. In particular, while being assisted by instructions shown on a visible screen, a participant on the proscenium should make the corresponding gestures to manipulate the puppet in an animation. In the meantime, the other participant backstage must hit the corresponding musical instrument as instructed. If the participants follow the instructions correctly in time, the corresponding animation will be displayed correctly and smoothly.

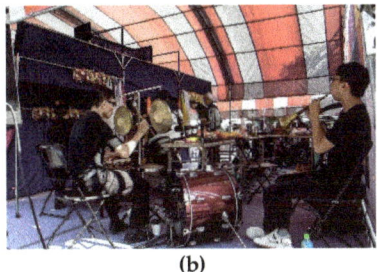

Figure 4. Real proscenium and backstage performances of a traditional glove puppet show: (**a**) proscenium; (**b**) backstage.

More specifically, regarding "Recall the Play" as a two-person cooperative experience system, its design concept is as illustrated in Figure 5, and mainly consists of two parts: *puppetry* and *sound effects*. In the puppetry part, an operator who is assumed to be on the proscenium wears an HTC VIVE headset to watch the performance of the role of a character, named *Good Man*, fighting another character, named *Evil Person*, in a puppet play from the first-person perspective, totally immersed in an on-the-spot experience. In addition, a Leap Motion sensor was mounted for gesture detection, allowing the operator to simulate the puppet gestures more intuitively. The sound effects of the second part were created to represent the soul of the puppet play in the real performance. An *interactive installation* with TUIs composed of a real drum, a gong, and a sound-sensing device was used to simulate the backstage performance in the real puppet show. The overall interactive scenario can be seen both on the headset screen and on an open system screen, which simulates what occurs during the performance in a traditional open puppet theater.

Figure 5. Schematic diagram of the proposed "Recall the Play" system.

Regarding the gesture-recognition method adopted in this research, two common gestures used in traditional glove puppet manipulation, namely, "rotation" and "flipping", were simulated, using position vector and rotation angle matching techniques (please see Algorithm 1) provided by the Leap Motion sensor to realize the gesture-recognition task. This is a feature of the gesture-recognition task implemented in this study. Since only two kinds of gestures needed to be classified, the classification process is not complicated, and in the actual operations, almost all classification outcomes were correct, yielding good user performance results.

3.2.2. System Architecture

For system development to simulate the real performance in a traditional open theater as described previously, the hardware of the proposed system was designed to include: (1) the software package Leap Motion for human gesture detection; (2) an HTC VIVE headset for immersed VR; (3) an Arduino chipset for sound-signal analysis; (4) a microphone module for sound input; (5) a drum and a gong for backstage environment simulation; (6) a PC for system control; and (7) a screen for system display, which is subsequently called the *system screen*. Note that there is another screen within the VIVE headset that is subsequently called the *headset screen*. The software used in the system include the components of Unity 3D, Blender, Adobe Illustrator, Adobe Photoshop, and Adobe after Effects. Figure 6 shows the architecture of the proposed "Recall the Play" system.

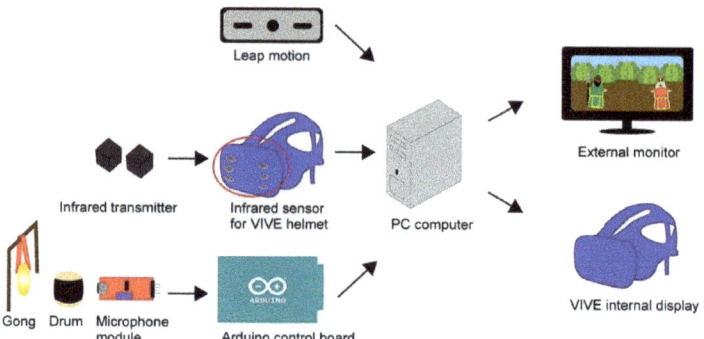

Figure 6. The framework of the proposed "Recall the Play" system.

Two types of interfacing—gesture detection and the use of the interactive installation—constitute the main input interaction part of the system. Specifically, in the gesture-detection process, the Leap Motion sensor detects the operator's hand movements, identifies the motion type, and sends the corresponding signals to the PC end. Meanwhile, the VIVE headset receives infrared signals emitted by two position-fixed infrared transmitters, and sends them to the PC end for relative spatial positioning of the operator. This scheme is needed for precise VR environment creation on the VIVE internal display.

Regarding the interface when using the interactive installation, after receiving sound signals emitted by hitting the drum or gong, the microphone module first transmits them to the Arduino chip for preliminary analysis. Then, useful signals are filtered out and sent to the PC end for further processing. It was noteworthy that all signals are of the one-way output style. Finally, the PC analyzes the received signals and generates corresponding animation effects on the VIVE headset screen and the system screen on an external monitor.

The hardware devices used in the construction of the proposed system, as described above, are all replicable, and so the system essentially can be built in a DIY manner. In addition, the interactive interface operations of gong or drum beating, as well as the hand gestures, were simple to perform. Therefore, the cost of implementation of the system is inexpensive, and if the proposed system is to be used in future studies, there should be no technical problem with replications or applications.

3.2.3. Main Technologies

The main technologies used in the proposed "Recall the Play" system include two parts: gesture detection and sound sensing. Gesture detection mainly identifies the user's hand movements. The corresponding interactive script will take effect to play the correct animations if the movements and times are in line with the given instructions. On the other hand, the sound-sensing devices check whether the user hit the correct musical instrument in the interactive installation backstage. The corresponding interactive animation will start if the instrument and beating times are consistent with the given instructions. The development environment, as well as the hardware and software used, are shown in Figure 6. Gesture detection and sound-sensing techniques using the related devices are described respectively as follows.

(1) Gesture Detection

Leap Motion, as shown in Figure 7, is a gesture sensor device developed by Ultraleap that was adopted in the proposed "Recall the Play" system. In order to capture the user's hand movements and identify the corresponding gestures in real time, two infrared cameras and three infrared LEDs in the Leap Motion sensor were used internally. The two internal infrared cameras are equipped in the device to simulate the binocular stereo vision of human eyes. By use of Leap Motion, hand movement data, especially those of the fingers, at 200 frames per second (FPS) can be acquired during the gesture-detection process and converted into the position coordinates of the hand and fingers. Specifically, in this study, when the user's hands were rotated and moved, Leap Motion is used to capture the desired data and upload them to the PC every two seconds. In turn, the PC converts the data into position coordinates, from which the corresponding gestures are defined according to the changes in the coordinate axes. Lastly, the PC compares the uploaded and the defined gesture values to scrutinize whether they match each other as the result of gesture detection and recognition.

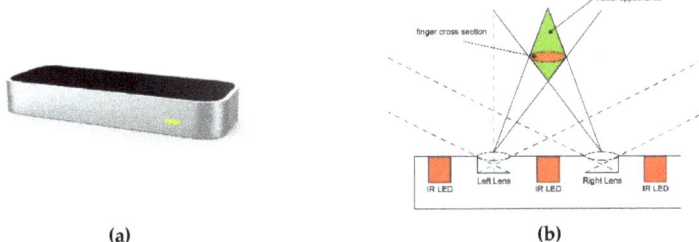

Figure 7. Device used for gesture detection: (**a**) the Leap Motion device; (**b**) the principle of binocular imaging used by the Leap Motion controller.

The proposed "Recall the Play" system mainly simulates the gestures of hand and finger manipulations of people using conventional puppets. The two major types of hand gestures selected for use in the system are *finger rotation* and *finger flipping*. These gestures are characterized by the rotations of palm joints. In order to more accurately distinguish the differences in finger rotations between the two gestures, the proposed system mainly use a rotation angle detection algorithm based on the quaternion and Euler's rotation theorems. It is noted that these are commonly used principles, given that the manner in which they are expressed is simple.

Specifically, in Euler's rotation theorem, when an object rotates in an arbitrary 3D space and at least one point is fixed, it can be interpreted that the object rotates around the fixed axis. This concept and that of quaternion rotation were used for gesture detection in this study. Quaternion represents a state of rotation in a 3D space with four numbers, namely, the three position coordinates x, y, and z, as well as the rotation angle w. Figure 8 shows the schematic diagram of the quaternion rotation matrix. A quaternion can be expressed as: $q = ((x, y, z), \theta) = (u, \theta)$, where the vector $u = (x, y, z)$ represents the coordinate values x, y, and z of the X, Y, and Z axes, respectively, and θ is a real number representing the rotation angle. In Table 4, a simple demonstration of the previously described gesture-recognition process of the proposed system is shown, which depicts how to recognize a *finger-rotation gesture* and a *finger-flipping gesture*.

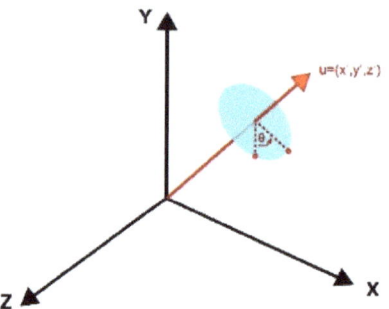

Figure 8. The Schematic Diagram of the Quaternion Rotation Matrix.

Table 4. An illustration of gesture recognition.

Gesture 1: Finger Rotation								Gesture 2: Finger Flipping							
Position coordinates and angle values of start gesture				Position coordinates and angle values of end gesture				Position coordinates and angle values of start gesture				Position coordinates and angle values of end gesture			
x	y	z	W	x'	y'	z'	w'	x	y	z	w	x'	y'	z'	w'
0.3	0.8	−0.5	0.0	0.8	0.5	0.0	0.5	0.0	−0.7	0.1	0.7	0.5	−0.5	0.6	0.5
Quaternion formula: $q = ((x, y, z), \theta) = (u, \theta)$															
$q = ((0.3, 0.8, -0.5), 0.0)$				$q' = ((0.8, 0.5, 0.0), 0.5)$				$q = ((0.0, -0.7, 0.1), 0.7)$				$q' = ((0.5, -0.5, 0.6), 0.5)$			

Algorithm 1 shows the procedure of gesture detection implemented on the proposed system. The algorithm mainly detects a hand gesture (finger rotation or finger flipping) by matching the corresponding position coordinates and rotation angle values of the fingers at three checkpoints A through C. Note that at each checkpoint, a matching of the quaternion of the input hand movement with the reference one is conducted, which is called quaternion matching.

Algorithm 1. Gesture Detection Algorithm.

Input: image frames of the finger movements of the operator on the proscenium captured by the cameras of the Leap Motion.
Output: decision about whether a finger rotation or flipping gesture G has been shown by the operator on the proscenium where the checkpoints of G are A, B and C in order.
Method:
Step 1. Detect the finger movements in each image frame F by Leap Motion and compute the corresponding position vector *u* and rotation angle θ of the quaternion of the hand in F.
Step 2. Judge whether *u* and θ reach Checkpoint A by corresponding quaternion matching: if so, go to Step 3; else, repeat this step.
Step 3. Judge whether *u* and θ reach Checkpoint B by corresponding quaternion matching: if so, go to Step 4; else, repeat this step.
Step 4. Judge whether *u* and θ reach Checkpoint C by quaternion matching: if so, go to Step 5; else, repeat this step.
Step 5. Confirm that gesture G is completed and go back to Step 1 to detect another gesture.

(2) Sound Sensing

For the purpose of sound sensing, an Arduino chipset, as shown in Figure 9a, is connected to the microphone module, as shown in Figure 9b, to determine whether the user has beat a specified instrument (the drum or the gong). At the beginning of the interaction, the microphone module attached to the instrument begins to receive sound signals. Then, the signals are sent to the Arduino for noise filtering, where the real sound of the instrument being hit is examined further. If the volume of the real sound is found to be larger than a preset value, then a decision on drum or gong hitting is made, which is finally sent to the PC for further processing to generate the corresponding animation, as described subsequently.

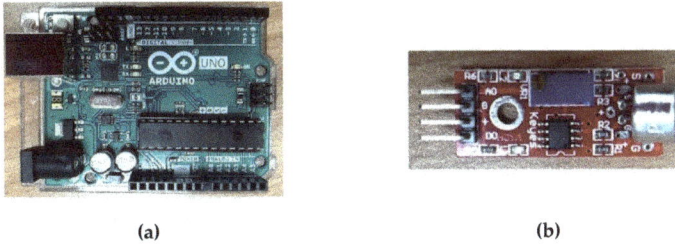

(a) (b)

Figure 9. Hardware used for sound processing: (**a**) the Arduino chipset; (**b**) the microphone module.

In more detail, the data of analog sound waves collected by the microphone were converted in this study into radio waves to demonstrate the range of the sound waves. The signal values stand around 27 dB indoors. When an instrument (the drum or the gong) of the interactive installation of the proposed "Recall the Play" system, as shown in Figure 10, was hit, the signal value significantly jumped from 27 dB to more than 60 dB, as shown in Figure 11. Since the volume of different instruments is affected by their loudness, timbre, and other factors, the preset values for sound detection can be adjusted according to the changes in the volume and the value of each instrument to avoid mutual interference of different instruments. Furthermore, to avoid ambient noise coming from the surrounding environment, it can be seen in Figure 11 that the sound signals from ambient and instrument waves are quite different, and so the ambient noise is easy to filter out. Table 5 shows the average volume values generated when the drum and the gong are played, and such values may be adopted as the threshold values for noise filtering.

(a) (b)

Figure 10. The gong and drum of the interactive installation of the proposed "Recall the Play" system and the wiring for sound-signal detection and transmission. (**a**) The front view of the installation; (**b**) the wiring.

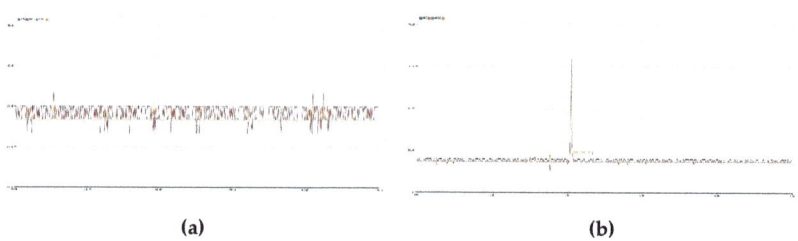

| (a) | (b) |

Figure 11. The data graphs of ambient and instrument waves: (**a**) ambient waves; (**b**) instrument waves.

Table 5. Volume values of the instruments of the interactive installation.

Instrument Name	Device	Volume Value (dB)
Drum		30–37
Gong		40–48

Algorithm 2 shows the procedure of sound-detection algorithm implemented in this study for the proposed system. The algorithm mainly examines whether the volume of the sound continuously collected by the microphone exceeds a preset value and whether the sound matches that of the instrument specified by the system to ensure whether the *correct* instrument (drum or gong) is hit.

Algorithm 2. Sound Detection and Instrument Beating Verification.

Input: (1) the instruction I of hitting an instrument (the drum or the gong) specified by the icon appearing on the screens; (2) a preset value s for determining whether the instrument is hit *with sufficient loudness*, and (3) the reference signal pattern P of the instrument specified by I.
Output: the decision *success* or *failure*, indicating whether the instrument has been hit correctly or not.
Method:
Step 1. Detect the sound S emitted around the interactive installation per second using the microphone and the Arduino chipset, and acquire its volume value v.
Step 2. Examine whether $v \geq s$: if so, go to Step 3; else, repeat this step until 20 s has passed, and at that time make the decision *failure* and exit, meaning the instruction I is not followed in time.
Step 3. If the sound S matches the reference signal pattern P, then decide that the correct instrument (the drum or the gong) has been hit loudly enough, send the decision *success* to inform the PC for further processing, and jump to Step 1 to continue the next sound detection and instrument beating verification.

---

(3) Types of gestures designed for generating animations

The proposed "Recall the Play" system designed for intergenerational learning combines VR and TUIs as the interface for interactive learning activities. It is noteworthy that the diverse interactions and immersive experiences provided by the system enhance the effects of learning and interaction between the two generations. Four types of interactive gestures, namely, *finger rotation*, *finger flipping*, *drum beating*, and *gong beating*, as shown in Table 6, were designed for use by the participants in the interactive learning activities. The total time duration of a cycle of interaction in the animation shown both on the headset screen and the system screen is 120 s. One of the icons representing the above-mentioned four types of gestures is shown *randomly* every 2 s on the screens for the two operators on the proscenium and backstage to see and follow.

Table 6. Four types of interactive gestures used in the proposed system.

Code	Gesture and Corresponding Icon	Operator and Corresponding Attack in Animation	Animation Scenario and Display on the Screens	Explanations about the Gesture
A	Gesture 1: *Finger rotation* as depicted in the icon image Icon:	Operator: The participant on the proscenium Attack 1: *Turn-causing attack*	Scenario: The "Good Man" in white gets close to the "Evil Person" in brown to attack him, causing him to turn his body around. Display:	1. During the system-experiencing process, if the icon of a *finger-rotation* gesture appears on the headset screen, the participant on the proscenium has to make Gesture 1 to create a corresponding animation shown on the screens. 2. The rotating fingers of this gesture represent exerting an invisible force toward the enemy's body to *turn* him/her around. 3. The corresponding Attack 1, *turn-causing attack*, is a basic fighting style seen in the puppet show.
B	Gesture 2: *Finger flipping* as depicted in the icon image Icon:	Operator: The participant on the proscenium Attack 2: *Flip-causing attack*	Scenario: The "Good Man" in white gets close to the "Evil Person" in brown to attack him, causing him to flip his body up. Display:	1. During the system-experiencing process, if the icon of a *finger-flipping* gesture appears on the headset screen, the participant on the proscenium has to make Gesture 2 to create a corresponding animation shown on the screens. 2. The flipping fingers of this gesture represent exerting an invisible force toward the enemy's body to *flip* him/her up. 3. The corresponding Attack 2, *flip-causing attack*, is another basic fighting style seen in the puppet show.
C	Gesture 3: *Drum beating* Icon:	Operator: The participant backstage Attack 3: *Hot-palm-wind attack with yellow light*	Scenario: The "Good Man" in white pushes a *hot palm wind with yellow light* toward the "Evil Person" in brown, to incur an internal injury in him. Display:	1. During the system-experiencing process, if the gesture icon of *drum beating* appears on the system screen, the participant backstage has to tap the drum with a stick. 2. The sound of the drum can be sensed by the system to incur an animation of a *hot-palm-wind attack with yellow light* from the "Good Man" to the "Evil Person" on the screens. 3. Pushing a hot palm wind to incur internal injury in the enemy is a third typical attack in the puppet show.
D	Gesture 4: *Gong beating* Icon:	Operator: The participant backstage Attack 4: *Cold-palm-wind attack with blue light*	Scenario: The "Good Man" in white pushes a *cold palm wind with blue light* toward the "Evil Person" in brown, to incur an internal injury in him. Display:	1. During the system experiencing process, if the gesture icon of *gong beating* appears on the system screen, the participant backstage has to hit the gong with a stick. 2. The sound of the gong can be sensed by the system to incur an animation of a *cold-palm-wind attack with blue light* from the "Good Man" to the "Evil Person" on the screens. 3. Pushing a cold palm wind to incur an internal injury in the enemy is a fourth typical attack in the puppet show.

(4) System Flow of Intergenerational Learning via Puppetry

The state diagram of the system flow for experiencing the proposed "Recall the Play" system is shown in Figure 12, and the detailed descriptions of the state transition flows are given in Algorithm 3.

Algorithm 3. State Transitions of the System Flow of the Proposed System.

Parameters: (1) the game-playing score s which shows the play skill level with the value ranging from 0 to 60; (2) the cycle time t_c of interaction; (3) the elapse time t_e in a state.
Input: the volume value v of the signal of the drum or gong of the interactive installation backstage collected continuously by the microphone module and filtered by the Arduino chipset, and a preset value S for determining whether the instrument is hit.
Output: an ending picture of the system "Recall the Play," showing a stone tablet with inscription saying that the participants are "awarded" the title of "The Worldwide Supremacy," "The Grandmaster," or "The Promising Talent," depending on the game-playing score value s obtained by the participants.

A. In the START state:
(1) Set the *cycle time* t_c = 120 s.   //Assume the time duration of a cycle of interaction to be t_c = 120 s.
(2) Set the game-playing score s = 0.   //Use s to decide the game-play skill level every 2 s, resulting in 60 decisions in a cycle
(3) In this state, show a "welcome screen" on the system screen; and
    (i) **if** no sound signal from the interactive installation is detected, **then** follow flow T to stay in the START state;
    (ii) **if** successful detection of drum beating is completed twice by Algorithm 2, **then** follow flow A to get into the GAME state.

B. In the GAME state:
(1) Start the users' experiencing of the system, and show one of the icons of the four gestures, gong beating, drum beating, finger rotation, and finger flipping (denoted as G, D, T, F, respectively) randomly every 2 s on the headset screen.
(2) Check the following cases:
    (i) **if** G is shown on the headset screen, **then** follow flow B to get into the Gong state;
    (ii) **if** D is shown on the headset screen, **then** follow flow C to get into the Drum state;
    (iii) **if** T or F is shown on the headset screen, **then** follow flow D to get into the Gesture state.

C. In the Gong state:
Detect the gong sound by Algorithm 2 using the input volume value v, and
  if the sound detection is successful, **then**
    (i) increment the game-playing score s by one, i.e., set $s = s + 1$;
    (ii) let the "Good Man" in the animation push a cold palm wind with blue light toward the "Evil Person" to injure him internally; and
    (iii) **if** the *elapse time* t_e in this state $\geq$ 2 s and the *cycle time* t_c < 120 s, **then** follow flow E1 to get into the GAME state; **else** stay in the Gong state;
  else
    if the *elapse time* t_e in this state $\geq$ 2 s and the *cycle time* t_c < 120 s, **then**
      follow flow E1 to get into the GAME state;   //Keep playing the game.
    else
      follow flow R1 to get into the RESULT state.   //Go to end the game.

D. In the Drum state:
Detect the drum sound by Algorithm 2 using the input volume value v, and
  if the sound detection is successful, **then**
    (i) increment the game-playing score s by one, i.e., set $s = s + 1$;
    (ii) let the "Good Man" in the animation push a hot palm wind with yellow light toward the "Evil Person" to injure him internally; and
    (iii) **if** the *elapse time* t_e in this state $\geq$ 2 s and the *cycle time* t_c < 120 s, **then** follow flow E2 to get into the GAME state; **else** stay in the Drum state;
  else
    if the *elapse time* t_e in this state $\geq$ 2 s and the *cycle time* t_c < 120 s, **then**
      follow flow E2 to get into the GAME state;
                                                         //Keep playing the game.
    else
      follow flow R2 to get into the Result state.   //Go to end the game.

E. In the Gesture state:
Detect the gesture of the operator on the proscenium by Algorithm 1, and
  if the *finger rotation* gesture is detected successfully, **then**
    (i) increment the game-playing score s by one, i.e., set $s = s + 1$;
    (ii) let the "Good Man" in the animation get close to the "Evil Person" to attack him, causing him to turn his body around; and
    (iii) **if** the *elapse time* t_e in this state $\geq$ 2 s and the *cycle time* t_c < 120 s, **then** follow flow E3 to get into the GAME state; **else** stay in the Gesture state;
  else
    if the *finger flip* gesture is detected successfully, **then**
      (i) increment the game-playing score s by one, i.e., set $s = s + 1$;
      (ii) let the "Good Man" in the animation get close to the "Evil Person" to attack him, causing him to flip his body up; and
      (iii) **if** the *elapse time* t_e in this state $\geq$ 2 s and the *cycle time* t_c < 120 s, **then** follow flow E3 to get into the GAME state; **else** stay in the Gesture state;
    else
      if the *elapse time* t_e in this state $\geq$ 2 s and the *cycle time* t_c < 120 s,
        then follow flow E3 to get into the GAME state;
                                                         //Keep playing the game.
      else
        follow flow R3 to get into the Result state.   //Go to end the game.

F. In the Result State:
(1) Use the game-playing score s to decide the game-play result, and show the *result picture* on the screens by checking the following cases:
    (i) **if** $s > 48$, **then** award the participants the title of "The Worldwide Supremacy";
    (ii) **if** $24 < s \leq 48$, **then** award the participants the title of "The Grandmaster";
    (iii) **if** $s \leq 24$, **then** award the participants the title of "The Promising Talent."

(2) Show a stone-tablet as the result picture with an inscription of the above-awarded title on the screen.
(3) End the game and exit.

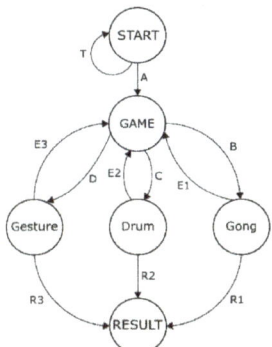

Figure 12. The state diagram of participants experiencing the proposed system.

3.2.4. Visual Design

The visual designs of the two 3D characters—the Good Man and the Evil Person—and the scene of the environment where the war between them was held in the puppet show animations are shown in Figure 13. They were designed in such a way to simulate the images of the puppets and environment in the real traditional show *Wind and Clouds of the Golden Glove-Puppet Play* so as to arouse the memory of the elderly involved in using the proposed "Recall the Play" system.

(a)

(b)

(c)

Figure 13. The 3D modeling of the characters and environment scenes of the puppet-show game played on the proposed "Recall the Play" system: (**a**) 3D model of the Evil Person; (**b**) 3D model of the Good Man; (**c**) 3D model of the environment scene.

3.2.5. An Example of Results of Running the Proposed "Recall the Play" System

The intermediate interaction results of an example of running the proposed "Recall the Play" system to perform a puppet show is shown in Table 7, which includes the intermediate animations of the major steps in the show.

Table 7. List of intermediate interaction results of an example of running the proposed system.

Stage No.	Illustration of Intermediate Result	Interaction	Involved Interaction Device	Explanation	Corresponding State in Algorithm 3
1		**B**: Complete drum beating twice (detected by sound sensing)	Drum	1. In the puppet-show game, a grandparent (called **A**) wore a VIVE headset to perform gestures, and a grandchild (called **B**) hit the drum and gong. 2. At the beginning in the START state, a "welcome screen" is shown on the screens. 3. If successful detection of drum beating is completed twice, then the system proceeds to stage 2 to engage the GAME state.	START state
2		**A**: View the icon appearing in the headset screen (one of the four ones on the left)	VIVE headset	1. If the icon of the *finger-rotation* gesture **a** is shown on the headset screen, then the system proceeds to stage 3. 2. If the icon of *finger-flip* gesture **b** is shown on the headset screen, then the system proceeds to stage 4. 3. If the icon of the *drum beating* gesture **c** is shown on the headset screen, then the system proceeds to stage 5. 4. If the icon of the *gong beating* gesture **d** is shown on the headset screen, then the system proceeds to stage 6.	GAME state
3		**A**: Complete the finger-rotation gesture (verified by gesture detection)	Leap Motion	1. Detailed explanations are given in the "Gesture state" in Algorithm 3.	Gesture state of the finger-rotation gesture
4		**A**: Complete the finger-flipping gesture (verified by gesture detection)	Leap Motion	1. Detailed explanations are given in the "Gesture state" in Algorithm 3.	Gesture state for the finger-flip gesture

Table 7. *Cont.*

Stage No.	Illustration of Intermediate Result	Interaction	Involved Interaction Device	Explanation	Corresponding State in Algorithm 3
5		**B**: Conduct drum beating repetitively. (verified by sound detection)	Drum	1. Detailed explanations given in the "Drum state" in Algorithm 3.	Drum state
6		**B**: Conduct gong beating repetitively. (verified by sound detection)	Gong	1. Detailed explanations are given in the "Gong state" in Algorithm 3.	Gong state
7		**A and B**: View the game-play result (one of the three awards)	VIVE headset and system screens	1. The game-play score s is used to decide the result of the game (i.e., three types of awards), and the result picture is shown on the screens. 2. Detail explanations are given in the "RESULT state" in Algorithm 3.	RESULT state for $s > 48$
8		Same as 7	Same as 7	Same as 7.	RESULT state for $24 < s \leq 48$
9		Same as 7	Same as 7	Same as 7.	RESULT state for $s \leq 24$

3.3. Experimental Design

In this study, both VR and TUIs technologies were applied to intergenerational learning for the two generations: the grandparent and the grandchild. Additionally, activities on the "Recall the Play" system were displayed in several exhibition halls, including the Bald Pine Forest in Nantou, the Puppets' House in Dounan, the Yunlin, and the Dali Community Care Base in Taichung, which are all located in Taiwan, as shown in Figures 14 and 15.

Figure 14. Scene setting of the proposed "Recall the Play" system.

(a)   (b)

Figure 15. Experiencing the intergenerational activity on the proposed "Recall the Play" system: (a) Case 1; (b) Case 2.

The participation of a pair including a grandparent and a grandchild was estimated to last approximately 30 min in each game play on the proposed system. When the grandparent and the grandchild entered the field, the first step taken by the staff of this study was to briefly explain the concepts and procedures of the system to them for five minutes. Then, they joined the intergenerational activity on the "Recall the Play" system for 10 min. After the experiencing process, a questionnaire survey of their opinions was conducted for five minutes. Lastly, five pairs of grandparents and grandchildren, comprising 10 participants, were randomly selected to be interviewed. The aforementioned experimental procedure is shown in Figure 16.

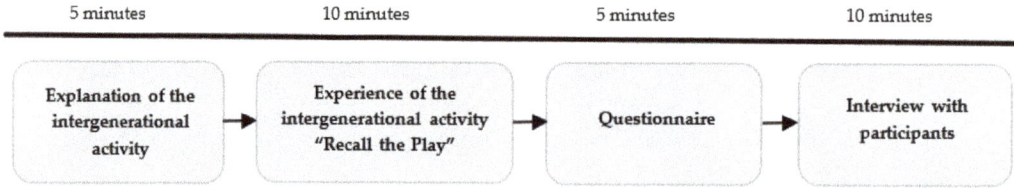

Figure 16. Design of Experimental Procedures.

The length of the total time used for the formal experimental procedure conducted in this study was the result of a deliberate decision for the test groups, which included young children and old people. In general, children cannot concentrate on an activity for very long during the system-experiencing process. On the other hand, the elderly's physical and mental conditions should be taken into consideration in the experiencing process; if the operation time is too long, they might experience slight dizziness and discomfort.

Accordingly, the activity script for the proposed mutual learning activity was designed to not be too complicated, so that the entire formal experimental procedure could be completed within 30 min; the specific time for experiencing the intergenerational activity was set to be 10 min, which was enough to complete the proposed activity.

Regarding the 10 min activity in which one user was conducting a VR experience by wearing a headset, although the user could relax his/her mind and enjoy the virtual immersive environment during this activity, if the audiovisual experience in the VR environment is too strong, it will cause contrary interference for the user. This interference is in particular more serious to the elderly users, because the visual and auditory senses of the elderly decline with age. Therefore, the VR-experiencing time must not be too long, and so was set to be 10 min, as stated above. In short, the original plan of time usage was considered appropriate. In addition, since the story script was short, a merit followed; namely, it did not require an extensive background environment for conducting the experiment.

In the future, extensions of this study can be designed to have richer story scripts and allow longer activity-experiencing times with more gorgeous background environments for use by a larger range of generations, instead of being limited to the two generations of grandparents and grandchildren.

3.4. Questionnaire Survey Results

A total of 120 copies of questionnaires were collected from 60 pairs of grandparents and grandchildren. Each questionnaire included questions about the participant's basic data, as well as the evaluations of the two indicators of the GPIC scale and the elderly's attitude scale. The basic data are shown in Table 8, in which it can be seen that 70% of the participants had never experienced VR before, while 30% of the participants had previously used a VR system.

Table 8. Basic data of the participants obtained in the questionnaire survey.

Basic Data	Categories	Samples	Percentage
Groups	Ederly	57	50%
	Children	57	50%
Sex	Male	45	39%
	Female	69	61%
Age	5–14	51	45%
	15–24	6	5%
	55–64	11	10%
	65–74	30	26%
	75–84	14	12%
	85–94	2	2%
Living together	Yes	43	38%
	No	71	62%
Having VR experience	Yes	34	30%
	No	80	70%

In addition, among the 120 collected questionnaires, 114 copies from 57 pairs were valid, and 6 from 3 pairs were invalid. Each questionnaire also included questions about and the evaluations of the two indicators of the GPIC scale and the elderly's attitude scale, with the former indicator involving both the elderly and the children, and the latter concerning only the children. The questions of the two indicators are shown in the second column of Table 9, with questions S1–S9 being related to the first indicator, and T1–T15 related to the second. Some statistics of the collected feedback data of the Likert 5-point scale of the two indicators are listed in Tables 9 and 10; these were analyzed in detail from several points of view, as described in the following.

Table 9. Questions and average statistics of the data of the two indicators of the GPIC scale and the elderly's attitude scale obtained in the questionnaire survey.

No.	Question	Min	Max	Mean	Standard Deviation
S1	During the interaction, my grandparents/grandchildren gave me support.	1	5	4.44	0.787
S2	During the interaction, my grandparents/grandchildren gave me help.	1	5	4.37	0.885
S3	During the interaction, my grandparents/grandchildren gave me useful suggestions.	1	5	4.23	0.996
S4	During the interaction, my grandparents/grandchildren outperformed me.	1	5	4.20	1.015
S5	During the interaction, my grandparents/grandchildren were more knowledgeable than I was.	1	5	4.22	1.028
S6	During the interaction, my grandparents/grandchildren were more skilled at operation than I was.	1	5	4.09	0.974
S7	I would keep silent if I disagreed with my grandparents/grandchildren during the interaction.	1	5	3.87	1.156
S8	During the interaction, I refrained from arguing with my grandparents/grandchildren.	1	5	4.11	1.092
S9	During the interaction, I would reserve my opinions.	1	5	4.07	1.028
	Average			4.17	
T1	During the interaction, I think my grandparents were kind.	1	5	4.42	0.885
T2	During the interaction, I think my grandparents were clever.	1	5	4.30	0.823
T3	During the interaction, I think my grandparents were physically healthy.	1	5	4.35	0.896
T4	During the interaction, I think my grandparents were interesting.	1	5	4.32	0.929
T5	During the interaction, I think my grandparents were calm.	1	5	4.23	0.926
T6	During the interaction, I think my grandparents were very interested in learning something new.	1	5	4.11	1.145
T7	During the interaction, I think my grandparents always seemed happy.	1	5	4.42	0.925
T8	During the interaction, I think my grandparents were trustworthy.	1	5	4.40	0.821
T9	During the interaction, I think my grandparents were experienced.	1	5	4.35	0.973
T10	During the interaction, I think my grandparents could impart me lots of knowledge.	1	5	4.33	1.041
T11	During the interaction, I think that my grandparents could empathize with me.	1	5	4.30	0.999
T12	During the interaction, I could get along well with my grandparents.	1	5	4.44	0.846
T13	During the interaction, I think that my grandparents were willing to keep learning.	1	5	4.18	1.002
T14	During the interaction, I think my grandparents were willing to do what they were interested in.	1	5	4.44	0.846
T15	During the interaction, I think my grandparents could prove their abilities.	1	5	4.33	0.932
	Average			4.33	

Table 10. Detailed statistics of the data of the two indicators of the GPIC scale and the elderly's attitude scale obtained in the questionnaire survey.

No.	Strongly Agree (5 Scores) (A)	Agree (4 Scores) (B)	No Opinion (3 Scores) (C)	Disagree (2 Scores) (D)	Strongly Disagree (1 Scores) (E)	Percentage of Agreements (F = A + B)
S1	57.0	33.3	7.9	0.0	1.8	90.3
S2	55.3	32.5	8.8	0.9	2.6	87.8
S3	49.1	35.1	8.8	3.5	3.5	84.2
S4	50.9	28.1	14.0	4.4	2.6	79.0
S5	52.6	28.1	9.6	7.9	1.8	80.7
S6	41.2	35.1	16.7	5.3	1.8	76.3
S7	35.1	36.0	15.8	7.0	6.1	71.1
S8	44.7	36.0	9.6	4.4	5.3	80.7
S9	40.4	37.7	14.9	2.6	4.4	78.1
			Average			80.9
T1	61.4	24.6	10.5	1.8	1.8	86.0
T2	47.4	38.6	12.3	0.0	1.8	86.0
T3	56.1	28.1	12.3	1.8	1.8	84.2
T4	54.4	29.8	10.5	3.5	1.8	84.2
T5	47.4	35.1	12.3	3.5	1.8	82.5
T6	50.9	22.8	17.5	3.5	5.3	73.7
T7	63.2	22.8	8.8	3.5	1.8	86.0
T8	56.1	31.6	10.5	0.0	1.8	87.7
T9	57.9	28.1	8.8	1.8	3.5	86.0
T10	63.2	15.8	15.8	1.8	3.5	79.0
T11	57.9	21.1	17.5	0.0	3.5	79.0
T12	61.4	24.6	12.3	0.0	1.8	86.0
T13	50.9	22.8	21.1	3.5	1.8	73.7
T14	61.4	24.6	12.3	0.0	1.8	86.0
T15	57.9	22.8	15.8	1.8	1.8	80.7
			Average			82.7

Table 9 includes questions about the children's feelings toward the elderly's behaviors in the system-experiencing process that were filled out by the participating children. The standard deviations of T6, T10, and T13 in the table are greater than 1, which reflect the children's divergent feelings about their grandparents' willingness to learn new things or interests in acquiring new knowledge, as well as their cognition of the elderly's passiveness in these activities.

3.4.1. Designing Processes for Testing the Properties of the Collected Data

In this study, the SPSS and AMOS software packages were used to analyze the collected questionnaire data. A series of tests were conducted to verify the properties of the collected data to ensure that the data could be analyzed to evaluate the effectiveness of the proposed system for intergenerational learning. The data properties and the methods adopted to verify them are listed in the following, with the details described later in this section.

1. Adequacy of the collected data—verified by the Kaiser–Meyer–Olkin (KMO) test and Bartlett's test of sphericity using the SPSS package.
2. Latent dimensions (scales) of the questions used in collecting the data—found by exploratory factor analysis (EFA) via the principal component analysis (PCA) method and the varimax method with Kaiser normalization using the SPSS package.
3. Reliability of the collected data—verified by using the Cronbach's α coefficient values yielded by the EFA process.
4. Suitability of the model structure of the data setup based on the found question dimensions (scales)—verified by confirmatory factor analysis (CFA) using the AMOS package.

5. Validity of the collected questionnaire data—verified by the parameter values yielded by the EFA and CFA processes.

3.4.2. Testing the Adequacy of the Collected Data

To evaluate the adequacy of the collected questionnaire data listed in Tables 9 and 10, the Kaiser–Meyer–Olkin (KMO) test and the Bartlett's test of sphericity were adopted in this study [66–71]. The KMO measure is a statistic used to indicate the proportion of variance among the variables that may possibly be caused by certain factors underlying the variables. The KMO test returns measure values in the range of 0 to 1, and Kaiser [69] assigned the returned values into six categories: (1) unacceptable—0.00 to 0.49; (2) miserable—0.50 to 0.59; (3) mediocre—0.60 to 0.69; (4) middling—0.70 to 0.79; (5) meritorious—0.80 to 0.89; and (6) marvelous—0.90 to 1.00. A KMO measure value larger than the threshold value of 0.50 is usually regarded to pass the test [66,67].

Additionally, the Bartlett's test of sphericity is employed to test the hypothesis that the correlation matrix of the data variables is an identity matrix, which indicates that the variables are unrelated. A significance value of the test result smaller than the threshold value of 0.05 is usually considered as acceptable to reject the hypothesis, or equivalently, to pass the test [67,68]. When both of the two tests are passed, the data variables are usually said to be *adequately related* for further structure analysis [70].

By using the collected questionnaire data and their statistics shown in Tables 9 and 10, the KMO measure values and the significance values of the Bartlett's test for the two indicators were computed by the SPSS, and are listed in Table 11. It can be seen in the table that for either indicator, the KMO measure value is larger than the threshold of 0.5 and the significance value of the Bartlett test is smaller than the threshold 0.05. Consequently, it was concluded that the datasets of both indicators of the GPIC Scale and the Elderly's Attitude Scale were *adequately related* for further *structure analysis*, as described next.

Table 11. The measured values of the KMO test and the significance values of Bartlett's test of the data collected for the GPIC scale and the elderly's attitude scale.

Scale	Name of Measure or Test		Value
GPIC Scale	KMO measure of sampling adequacy		0.841
	Bartlett's test of sphericity	Approx. chi-square	629.871
		Degree of freedom	36
		Significance	0
Elderly's Attitude Scale	KMO measure of sampling adequacy		0.933
	Bartlett's test of sphericity	Approx. chi-square	1005.343
		Degree of freedom	120
		Significance	0

3.4.3. Finding the Latent Dimensions (Scales) of the Questions from the Collected Data

With the adequacy of the questionnaire data being verified as described above, the SPSS package was used further to perform an exploratory factor analysis (EFA) using a principal component analysis. In addition, the varimax method with Kaiser normalization was employed to find suitable latent dimensions (scales) for the questions with the collected data as inputs. The details of the results are listed in Tables 12 and 13. It was found accordingly that the nine questions (S1–S9) of the first indicator, global perceptions of intergenerational communication (GPIC), could be divided into three groups under the question dimensions (scales) of *accommodation, nonaccommodation,* and *avoidance,* respectively. The 15 questions (T1–T15) of the second indicator, the elderly's attitude, could be divided into three groups as well under the question dimensions (scales) of *psychological cognition, social engagement,* and *life experience,* respectively. The results of such latent dimension (scale) findings, with some statistics of the data of the Likert scale included, are shown integrally in Table 14.

Table 12. Rotated component matrix of the indicator of GPIC.

No.	Question Dimension (Scale)		
	1	2	3
S2	**0.902**	0.196	0.177
S1	**0.871**	0.183	0.188
S3	**0.812**	0.337	0.142
S6	0.117	**0.837**	0.334
S4	0.300	**0.815**	0.207
S5	0.346	**0.814**	0.179
S7	−0.0021	0.322	**0.843**
S8	0.316	0.082	**0.817**
S9	0.252	0.294	**0.721**

Extraction method: principal component analysis. Rotation method: varimax with Kaiser normalization; rotation converged in 5 iterations.

Table 13. Rotated component matrix of the indicator of the elderly's attitudes.

No.	Question Dimension (Scale)		
	1	2	3
T4	**0.812**	0.251	0.234
T3	**0.792**	0.391	0.370
T2	**0.703**	0.543	0.256
T1	**0.689**	0.324	0.536
T5	**0.687**	0.298	0.498
T8	**0.643**	0.545	0.308
T13	0.435	**0.787**	0.188
T6	0.222	**0.783**	0.385
T7	0.261	**0.691**	0.501
T14	0.530	**0.674**	0.267
T15	0.367	**0.628**	0.394
T12	0.451	**0.580**	0.532
T9	0.355	0.364	**0.832**
T10	0.410	0.410	**0.772**

Table 14. Analysis of the question dimensions (scales) of GPIC and the elderly's attitude by SPSS.

No.	Question Dimension	Question	Min	Max	Mean	S.D.
S2	Accommodation (Group FS1)	During the interaction, my grandparents/grandchildren gave me help.	1	5	4.37	0.885
S1		During the interaction, my grandparents/grandchildren gave me support.	1	5	4.44	0.787
S3		During the interaction, my grandparents/grandchildren gave me useful suggestions.	1	5	4.23	0.996
S6	Nonaccommodation (Group FS2)	During the interaction, my grandparents/grandchildren were more skilled at operation than I was.	1	5	4.09	0.974
S4		During the interaction, my grandparents/grandchildren outperformed me.	1	5	4.20	1.015
S5		During the interaction, my grandparents/grandchildren were more knowledgeable than I was.	1	5	4.22	1.028
S7	Avoidance (Group FS3)	I would keep silent if I disagreed with my grandparents/grandchildren during the interaction.	1	5	3.87	1.156
S8		During the interaction, I refrained from arguing with my grandparents/grandchildren.	1	5	4.11	1.092
S9		During the interaction, I would reserve my opinions.	1	5	4.07	1.028
		Average			4.17	

Table 14. Cont.

No.	Question Dimension	Question	Min	Max	Mean	S.D.
T4	Psychological cognition (Group FT1)	During the interaction, I think my grandparents were interesting.	1	5	4.32	0.929
T3		During the interaction, I think my grandparents were physically healthy.	1	5	4.35	0.896
T2		During the interaction, I think my grandparents were clever.	1	5	4.30	0.823
T1		During the interaction, I think my grandparents were kind.	1	5	4.42	0.885
T5		During the interaction, I think my grandparents were calm.	1	5	4.23	0.926
T8		During the interaction, I think my grandparents were trust-worthy.	1	5	4.40	0.821
T13	Social engagement (Group FT2)	During the interaction, I think that my grandparents were willing to keep learning.	1	5	4.18	1.002
T6		During the interaction, I think my grandparents were very interested in learning something new.	1	5	4.11	1.145
T7		During the interaction, I think my grandparents always seemed happy.	1	5	4.42	0.925
T14		During the interaction, I think my grandparents were willing to do what they were interested in.	1	5	4.44	0.846
T15		During the interaction, I think my grandparents could prove their abilities.	1	5	4.33	0.932
T12		During the interaction, I could get along well with my grandparents.	1	5	4.44	0.846
T9	Life experience (Group FT3)	During the interaction, I think my grandparents were experienced.	1	5	4.35	0.973
T10		During the interaction, I think my grandparents could impart me lots of knowledge.	1	5	4.33	1.041
		Average			4.33	

3.4.4. Verifying the Reliability of the Collected Data Using the Cronbach's α Coefficients

Reliability is about the consistency of a measured dataset despite the repeated times [72]. In this study, the Cronbach's α coefficient [73,74] yielded by the EFA mentioned previously was adopted to analyze the reliability of the collected questionnaire data. It is known that the closer the Cronbach's α coefficient of a dataset of a scale is to the extreme value of 1.0, the greater the reliability of the dataset (regarded as variables) is. Based on Gildford [75], the following rules may be used to judge the degree of reliability of a dataset:

$$\alpha \leq 0.35 \text{ — unreliable}$$

$$0.35 \leq \alpha < 0.70 \text{ — reliable}$$

$$\alpha \geq 0.70 \text{ — highly reliable}$$

where α is the Cronbach's α coefficient value of the dataset.

The Cronbach's α coefficient values of the six question dimensions (scales) and those of the two indicators are shown integrally in Table 15. It can be seen in the table that all the Cronbach's α coefficient values are in the range of 0.35 to 0.70 or even larger, meaning that the collected questionnaire dataset of each question dimension, as well as those of each indicator are reliable.

Table 15. Collection of the data of the indicators of GPIC and the elderly's attitudes and the Cronbach's α coefficients of the six question dimensions of the two indicators.

Indicator	Question Dimension (Scale)	Cronbach's α Coefficient of the Question Dimension	Cronbach's α Coefficient of the Indicator
GPIC	Accommodation (Group FS1)	0.896	0.888
	Non-accommodation (Group FS2)	0.877	
	Avoidance (Group FS3)	0.805	
The elderly's attitude	Psychological cognition (Group FT1)	0.953	0.971
	Social engagement (Group FT2)	0.936	
	Life experience (Group FT3)	0.959	

3.4.5. Verification of the Applicability of the Structural Model Established with the Question Dimensions (scales)

Before proving the validity of the collected questionnaire data, the suitability of the structure model set up by the question dimensions (scales) need be verified [76]. For this purpose, the confirmatory factor analysis (CFA) process using the AMOS package was applied on the collected questionnaire data, yielding two three-scale structure-model graphs, as shown in Figure 17. Moreover, a list of structure-model fit indices was yielded by the CFA for each indicator, including the degrees of freedom (df), the chi-square (χ^2) statistics, the ratio of χ^2/df, the adjusted goodness-of-fit index (gfi), the comparative fit index (cfi), and the root-mean-square error of approximation (RMSEA), as shown integrally in Table 16. Accordingly, the index values of χ^2/df, gfi, cfi, and RMSEA yielded for each indicator show the fact that the structure model set up by the question dimensions (scales) of the indicator is of a reasonably good fit to the collected questionnaire data [77–81].

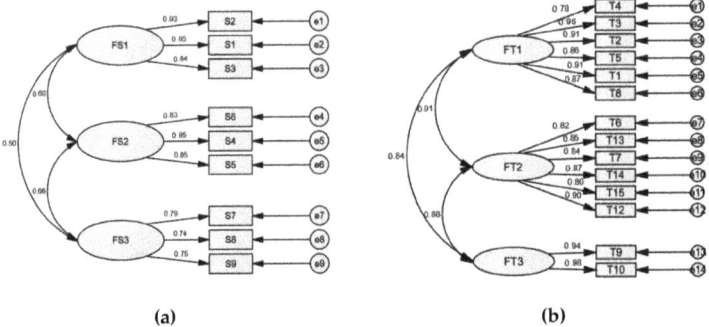

Figure 17. Results of confirmatory factor analysis (CFA) using the AMOS package. (a) Diagram of the three-scale structural model of the GPIC indicator (FS1: accommodation; FS2: nonaccommodation; FB3: avoidance) generated through CFA; (b) diagram of the three-scale structural model of the elderly's attitude indicator (FT1: psychological cognition; FT2: social interaction; FT3: life experience) generated through CFA.

Table 16. Fitness indexes of the structural models of the two indicators of GPIC and the elderly's attitudes generated through CFA.

Scale	df	χ^2/	χ^2/df	agfi	cfi	RMSEA	RMSEA (90% CI)	
							LO	HI
GPIC Scale	24	60.112	2.505	0.810	0.941	0.115	0.079	0.152
Elderly's Attitude Scale	74	102.299	1.382	0.727	0.968	0.830	0.037	0.101

Meanings of symbols—df: degree of freedom; gfi: goodness-of-fit index; agfi: average gfi; cfi: comparative fit index; RMSEA: root-mean-square error of approximation; CI: confidence interval; LO: low; HI: high.

3.4.6. Verification of the Validity of the Collected Questionnaire Data

With the model structures of the two indicators both being proved to fit reasonably to the collected questionnaire data, it was proper to analyze further the validity of the data. It can be seen from the three-scale structure model shown in Figure 17 that all the factor-loading values (also called standardized regression weights) with respect to the scales (appearing on the paths of the scales FS1–FS3 and FT1–FT3 to the questions S1–S9 and T1–T15, respectively) are all larger than the threshold of 0.5. This indicates that the construct validity of the model was verified. This fact can also be proved by the construct validity values of all the scales of the two indicators of GPIC and the elderly's attitudes yielded by the EFA process mentioned above, because such values, as listed in Table 17, can be observed to all be larger than the threshold value of 0.6 [82,83]. That is, the construct validity of the collected questionnaire data of the indicator of system usability is proven.

Table 17. Valid values of the question dimensions (scales) of the two indicators of GPIC and elderly's attitudes generated through CFA.

Indicator	Question Dimension (Scale)	Group of Related Questions	Construct Validity Value
GPIC	Accommodation (Group FS1)	FS1 = (S2, S1, S3)	0.805
	Nonaccommodation (Group FS2)	FS2 = (S6, S4, S5)	0.748
	Avoidance (Group FS3)	FS3 = (S7, S8, S9)	0.606
The elderly's attitudes	Psychological cognition (Group FT1)	FT1 = (T4, T3, T2, T1, T5, T8)	0.955
	Social engagement (Group FT2)	FT2 = (T13, T6, T7, T14, T15, T12)	0.939
	Life experience (Group FT3)	FT3 = (T9, T10)	0.960

3.4.7. Summary of Analyses Based on the Content of the Collected Questionnaire Data

It can be concluded from the above discussions that the questionnaire data collected from the participants regarding the two indicators of GPIC and the elderly's attitudes are both reliable and valid for uses in further analyses of the data contents, which lead to the following conclusions.

(A) Analysis of the Indicator of GPIC

The overall feedback on the questionnaire regarding the evaluation of GPIC was positive. As shown in the upper part of Table 10, the average percentage of agreement was 80.9%, indicating that the participants felt good about the communication between grandparents and grandchildren in the experiences of using the proposed system. Furthermore, McCann and Keaton's GPIC scale [61] consists of two perspectives for the survey data collected in this study: "perception of others' communication" and "perception of one's communication". The former perspective was divided into the dimensions of accommodation and nonaccommodation in this study. Accommodation refers to a participant's perception that the other participant is friendly and kind during the interaction. Meanwhile, nonaccommodation referred to a participant's perception that the other is more competent during the interaction and can recognize their advantages. The other perspective, "perception of one's communication," has only one dimension—avoidance. Avoidance refers to a subject making a concession for some reason or in some circumstances when interacting with others.

The average score of S1, S2, S3, S4, and S5 in the nine questions on the indicator of GPIC was higher than 4.17, indicating that more than 80% of the participants approved of the intergenerational communication during the interaction. However, the score data show in the meantime that the awareness of other people was obviously higher than self-awareness, with a sense of friendliness and intimacy. In addition, as seen in Tables 9 and 10, the question S7 yields a lower score with a standard deviation value larger than one because a small number of users gave it just one point. This fact indicates that the users had different views on compromising in the interaction process using the proposed system.

More generally, based on the data-analysis results shown in Tables 9 and 10 regarding the indicator of GPIC, the following conclusions were drawn:
1. During the interaction, the grandparents and grandchildren were friendly and kind to each other.
2. During the interaction, the grandparents and grandchildren recognized each other's strengths.
3. During the interaction, the grandparents and grandchildren would mostly restrain themselves, reserve their own opinions, and keep silent when they disagreed with each other.
4. Nevertheless, it was also found that when the two parties had different opinions, they would still acknowledge each other's advantages and friendliness during the interaction.

(B) Analysis of the Elderly's Attitudes

Most of the questions received positive feedback regarding the elderly's attitudes. As shown in the second part of Table 10, the average agreement rate was 82.7%, indicating a good overall evaluation of the interaction between the children and the elderly.

More specifically, the average scores of 9 of the 15 questions (T1, T3, T7, T8, T9, T10, T12, T14, and T15) were above 4.33. The second part of Table 10 shows that the average agreement rate was 82.7%, and according to Table 9, the children were seen to think that the elderly held positive attitudes. The highest score, T8, indicated that the children psychologically believed their grandparents were trustworthy. The two questions with lower scores are T13 and T6. Based on the data analysis of the elderly's attitudes felt by the children, the following conclusions were drawn:
1. During the interaction, the grandparents were psychologically reliable to the children.
2. During the interaction, the grandparents were kind, smart, and happy as felt by the children psychologically.
3. During the interaction, the grandparents were kind, smart, and happy as felt by the children cognitively.
4. During the interaction, the children had a positive psychological and cognitive perception of the elderly.

3.4.8. Evaluation of System Effectiveness from the Perspectives of GPIC and the Elderly's Attitudes

In the evaluation of the system effectiveness from the perspective of GPIC, the average scores of the three dimensions of "accommodation", "nonaccommodation", and "avoidance" are larger than four, and the agreement rates (including the rates of "strongly agree" plus "agree") are greater than 85%, as shown in Tables 18 and 19, which were computed using Tables 9 and 10. In addition, the average scores range from 4.02 to 4.35, all of which are greater than 4. These results indicate that grandparents and grandchildren performed well in communication during the interaction.

Table 18. Evaluation of the average scores of GPIC and the elderly's attitudes from the perspectives of the two indicators.

Question Dimension (Scale)	N	Average Mean	Standard Deviation
Accommodation	114	4.35	0.889
Nonaccommodation	114	4.17	1.006
Avoidance	114	4.02	1.092
Psychological cognition	57	4.34	0.88
Social engagement	57	4.32	0.95
Life experience	57	4.34	1.00

Table 19. Evaluation of the percentages of GPIC and the elderly's attitudes from the perspectives of the two indicators.

Question Dimension (Scale)	Strongly Agree	Agree	No Opinion	Disagree	Strongly Disagree
Accommodation	53.80	33.60	8.50	1.47	2.63
Nonaccommodation	48.23	30.43	13.43	5.87	2.07
Avoidance	40.07	36.57	13.43	4.67	5.27
Psychological cognition	53.80	31.30	11.40	1.76	1.80
Social engagement	57.61	23.40	14.60	2.05	2.83
Life experience	60.55	21.95	12.30	1.80	3.50

Meanwhile, in the evaluation of the system effectiveness from the perspective of the elderly's attitudes, the average scores of the three dimensions of "psychological cognition", "social interpersonal participation", and "life experience" are larger than four, and the agreement rates (including the rates of "strongly agree" plus "agree") are greater than 80%, as shown in Tables 18 and 19. In addition, the average scores range from 4.32 to 4.34, all of which are greater than 4. These results indicate that the elderly showed good attitudes during the interaction as felt by the children.

It is noteworthy that the average score for the elderly's attitudes is 4.33, higher than that of GPIC, which is 4.17. This fact indicates that the children had positive psychological and cognitive experiences during the interaction with the elderly, and that the psychological cognition and life experiences of the elderly were felt as positive attitudes by the children.

3.5. Analysis of Interviews with Participants

Based on Verplank's interaction design principles [65], in this study the participants' feelings about their experiences when using the proposed system were investigated via interviews with the participants. The interviews mainly focused on the aspects of system operation (labeled as DO), feeling of experiencing the system (labeled as FEEL), and communication of emotion and experience (labeled as KNOW). For DO, the questions for the participants included the aspects of system operation, interface, and design difficulty. For FEEL, the problem design was based on the participants' feelings during and after the activities, as well as other related thoughts. Lastly, the part of KNOW involved the investigation of the participants' emotional communication and inheritance of relevant memories after experiencing the system, which was also the main design purpose of this study's prototype system. After conducting the intergenerational activities and the questionnaire survey, 10 users representing five pairs of grandparents and grandchildren were randomly selected for interviews. During the interview procedure, their responses were recorded using audio recorders and in writing. The participants' responses are summarized in Table 20.

According to the results of interviews with the participants listed in Table 20, most of them gave positive feedback on the two aspects of feeling of experiencing the system (FEEL) and communication of emotion and experience (KNOW). For the aspect of system operation (DO), the participants gave many suggestions, such as making slight adjustments to the gestures, providing a greater variety of images on the screen, and making the overall operation easier to understand. In addition, the participants who had experience in manipulating puppets were faster at playing with the puppets in the VR environment. In more detail, the conclusions that are drawn based on the interview results shown in Table 20 are the following.

Table 20. Record data of interviews with participants.

Aspect	Questions	Answers
System operation (DO)	Q1: Can you operate this system?	1. The participants said they knew how to operate the system since it was easy to play the drum and gong. 2. The participants said it was easy to perform the system because they could operate puppets by moving their fingers.
	Q2: Do you have any difficulties operating this system, or what do you think needs improvement?	1. The participants said they did not know how to make gestures at first, feeling like they could not succeed. 2. The participants said that they could directly control the puppets with their hands, but it would be more interesting if they could control one puppet with each hand.
	Q3: Do you like this system's interface? Why?	1. The participants said the interface was not bad, as the scenes and characters were lifelike to a degree. 2. The participants thought that the images were a little monotonous and hoped more things could be added.
Feeling of experiencing the system (FEEL)	Q4: How do you feel when operating this system?	1. The participants said they were happy to play together with their grandchildren. 2. The participants said the system could be operated at a faster speed, making it more exciting to play.
	Q5: Would you like to continue experiencing this system?	1. The participants said "yes" because they rarely played with such things and had different feelings. 2. The participants said "no" because they felt bored quickly. 3. The participants said they would only continue to play if more activities were provided.
	Q6: How do you feel, or what do you think of this system after experiencing it?	1. The participants expressed that it was not as good as holding physical puppets in their hands. 2. The participants reported that the background music was a plus and made them more engaged.
Communication of emotion and experience (KNOW)	Q7: Do you think there is anything that reminds you of puppetry in the experience? Do you know more about puppetry?	1. The participants said characters, such as Shi Yanwen and Cangjingren, used to be very famous during their time. 2. The participants said they found puppetry a little strange, but they knew something about it because they had heard their grandparents talk about it. 3. The participants said they could recognize the puppets' names, including Shi Yanwen and Su Huan Zhen.
	Q8: How do you feel, or what do you think after interacting with your grandchildren/elders?	1. The participants said they found their grandchildren cute and were happy to play with them in this way. 2. The participants said they usually did not come back unless on holidays, so it was quite interesting to have a chance to play with grandparents like this. 3. The participants said that their grandchildren loved to play the drum and gong and enjoyed the sound effects, and that it was fun to see them play.

(1) Interview results for the aspect of system operation (DO):
  (a) After playing the drums and manipulating the puppets with VR gestures, participants found the operations of the gong and the drum more intuitive and easier to understand.
  (b) Most participants were not puppeteers, and gestures that were too professional were not easy for those inexperienced to perform.
(2) Interview results for the aspect of feeling of experiencing the system (FEEL):
  (a) The young participants preferred interactions with more sound and light effects or with more variations.
  (b) The children preferred operating the gong and the drum to performing VR actions.

(3) Interview results for the aspect of communication of emotion and experience (KNOW):
  (a) Older experienced participants learned puppetry more quickly than those without puppetry experiences, and they could impart to their grandchildren more knowledge about puppetry.
  (b) In the intergenerational learning activities, the grandparents and grandchildren would increase the exchange of mutual learning experiences.

Furthermore, usability is an important evaluation item of an interactive system. Using the content of Table 20 regarding the aspect of System Operation (DO), the following is a short summary of the usability related to our research.

(1) The participants knew how to operate the system, since it was easy to play the drum and the gong.
(2) The participants did not know how to make the gestures initially, but they succeeded later after operating the system for a while.
(3) The participants felt that it was easy to use the interface, as the scenes and characters were lifelike to a degree.

3.6. Summary of Experimental Results

The major research findings of this study drawn from the above analysis results are listed in Table 21, and are organized from the perspectives of three previously published studies: (a) McCann and Giles [61], with the perspective of global perceptions of intergenerational communication (GPIC); (b) Lu and Kao [62], with the perspective of the elderly's attitude scale; and (c) Verplank [65], with the perspective of interviews with system participants.

Table 21. Summary of the major research findings of this study.

Item	Findings
Analysis of the indicator of GPIC	During the interaction, the grandparents and grandchildren were friendly and kind to each other, and recognized each other's strengths. Furthermore, when the two parties had different opinions, they would still acknowledge each other's advantages and friendliness.
Analysis of the elderly's attitudes	During the interaction, the grandparents were psychologically reliable to the children, and were kind, smart, and happy as felt by the children psychologically. Furthermore, the children had a positive psychological and cognitive perception of their grandparents.
Analysis of interviews with participants	The participants found the operations of the gong and the drum more intuitive and easier to understand. While the children preferred operating the gong and the drum to performing VR actions, the grandparents learned puppetry more quickly than the grandchildren, and could impart more knowledge to them about puppetry.

4. Discussions

With the advent of aging societies and changes in family structures, intergenerational learning has become increasingly important in the current era. On the other hand, fast technology development has become the trend of the future in the 21st century, which makes integrating technologies into conventional intergenerational activities, as well as group learning or education, a long-term issue worthy of serious consideration. For example, Kyrpychenko et al. [27] proposed a good structure of communicative competence for teaching a foreign language to higher education students, and Kuzminykh et al. [28]

proposed self-education and group-education approaches to the development of teaching competence. These diverse research directions and results further highlight the importance of the intergenerational learning issue investigated in this study, and offer useful insights for developing the system design principles of this study.

It was the main focus of this study to educate people of the older generation who were unfamiliar with fast-developing technologies. The aim was mainly to make technology more acceptable to them to narrow the gap between the young and the old. Therefore, a novel learning system was proposed in this study, with traditional puppetry being introduced as the theme, based on the life experiences of the older generation. By introducing digital technology into intergenerational learning and applying VR and TUIs in the learning activities, the two different generations could increase their communication and interaction, thereby achieving emotional exchange and the sharing of experiences. More findings of facts in this research are elaborated in the following.

4.1. Findings of System-Development Principles

In this study, different subjects and activities based on the literature related to intergenerational activities were reviewed. In addition, existing cases on introducing intergenerational learning and VR technology to the older generation were surveyed. After deep discussions with invited experts, four design principles for the system development of VR-based intergenerational learning were created:

(1) intergenerational activity themes should be interesting to both generations;
(2) the interface should be as simple as possible;
(3) the operations of the system should be intuitive;
(4) the performance of the system should include slightly stimulating ways of interaction.

The prototype system developed in this study was based on the experts' advice and the above-mentioned design principles. After many tests and modifications, a new intergenerational learning system was constructed that was familiar to both generations and allowed them to promote emotion exchange.

4.2. Findings from Questionnaire Survey Results

The questionnaire data collected from the participants who experienced the prototype system were analyzed by SPSS and AMOS, and the results showed that the data of the two indicators, GPIC and the elderly's attitudes, were reliable and valid for further evaluation of the system's effectiveness. The average values of the data of the two indicators are both larger than 4 points on a 5-point Likert scale, indicating that the participants' attitudes toward each other in the process of experiencing the intergenerational learning activities provided by the proposed system are relatively positive. In more detail, the following conclusions were drawn from the results of the questionnaire data analyses and the interviews with the participants:

(1) The children preferred active interaction, such as playing the drum and the gong, while the older participants preferred simple and easy interactions.
(2) The interviews revealed that introducing VR into activities with traditional themes was more attractive to the children.
(3) The VR system combined with ideal themes drove more elderly people to participate in the activities.
(4) The older users expressed that they would be more pleased to join in the activities as young users influenced them.
(5) The elderly and children had positive feelings regarding each other's attitudes when experiencing the system.

4.3. Findings about Effectiveness of Technology-Based Intergenerational Learning

In this study, the new technologies of VR and TUIs were used as the interfacing techniques of the proposed system for intergenerational learning. Such new technologies were adopted with the aim of arousing the interests of the two generations in the learning activities, and the data analyses of the questionnaire survey of the participants' opinions showed that this aim was achieved by the proposed system. More findings of facts about the effectiveness of the system are elaborated in the following.

(1) Intergenerational learning activities featuring VR and TUIs can encourage the young to participate in the learning activities

Based on the interviews with participants and the observation of their experiences, most children would step toward, pick up, stare at, and study the head-mounted display, and say they want to have a try. Some children told the interviewer that they wondered what was in the VR, showing that the introduction of VR and gesture manipulations could indeed arouse the willingness of the younger generation to participate.

(2) The VR-based interaction system with the two generations' shared experiences had positive effects on the emotional communication between the two generations

According to the results of the questionnaire survey and interviews with the participants, most users gave positive comments on the proposed interactive system after experiencing it, and both generations felt happy and interested in their interactions and experiences. In addition, both generations showed positive attitudes toward each other, consistent with the findings of Souza and Grundy [6]. Through intergenerational interactions, the elderly could acquire self-confidence and positive attitudes, while the young generation could improve their self-value and obtain happiness, conducive to the accumulation of social capital of human resources and relationships.

(3) Themes familiar to the older generation can enhance their willingness to adopt high-tech products

Zajicek [21] found that one of the reasons elderly people reject high-tech products is the fear of damaging them in the process of learning. However, if the products are associated with the living environment of the older generation or are something with which they are familiar, they would be less anxious and more willing to enjoy high-tech products.

(4) By integrating VR into intergenerational learning activities, the two generations acquire more opportunities to learn and understand each other

The two generations guided each other in following instructions; for instance, in playing the drum or making the gestures. According to some interviewees, after participating in the activities, some elderly people shared the stories of the glove puppetry characters with their children. Similarly, several of the elderly reported that they had learned cartoon and game characters from some young participants, indicating that both generations have much more to talk about.

(5) Better perceptual experiences in feeling the effects of sensors, such as sound, animation, and various special effects, can improve the two generations' immersion in the system-experiencing process

It was found in the interviews that the users may have been less immersed in the activities due to certain problems occurring with the system, such as unclear screen tips, monotonous pictures, and unfamiliarity with the gestures. According to the participants' comments, it was known that if such problems could be solved, the activities would be thought to be more entertaining and interesting, and the users would immerse themselves in the activities more deeply.

5. Conclusions

5.1. Summary of Major Contributions Made by This Study

In this study, through the use of human-interfacing technologies, it was aimed to introduce innovative interactions into conventional intergenerational learning activities. An intergenerational learning system called "Recall the Play" was constructed. The architecture of the system was based on the technologies of VR and TUIs. The users' opinions obtained from the questionnaire surveys and interviews showed that emotional communication and experience inheritance between the two generations could be effectively promoted by integrating VR and TUIs into the learning process. In addition, appropriate intergenerational learning activities with the two generations each having dominant roles were designed and tested. The design was appropriate for the two generations, and was based on literature surveys related to intergenerational learning, as well as the interview comments given by experts before the activities were developed. Finally, human-interfacing hardware, including gesture detection, sound sensing, and VR, as well as software algorithms implementing an interactive game of traditional glove puppetry, were successfully integrated to construct the proposed intergenerational learning system. This integrated experience of system and game development can be used as a reference for future research in related fields.

5.2. Suggestions for Future Studies

The intergenerational learning system developed in this study is in its infancy. Based on the research results obtained using this system, for future research on intergenerational learning, more appropriate designs with better interfacing effects may be considered to make users more focused on and immersed in the learning activity. This may be achieved by improving the fluency of animation, the richness of sound effects, and the vividness of system feedback. Secondly, learning activity themes other than puppetry, such as recreation, education, public service, health care, and individual development, as mentioned by Ames and Youatt [4], may be considered for future studies. In addition, it is also worth studying constructions of systems and related learning activities for more generations with different backgrounds.

In addition, the entire formal experimental procedure was assumed to be 30 min, and the time for experiencing the intergenerational activity was set to be 10 min. It is suggested that future extensions of this study be designed to contain a richer story script, and allow for a longer activity-experiencing time with a more gorgeous background environment for use by a wider range of generations, instead of being limited to the two generations of grandparents and grandchildren. The musical instruments utilized backstage also may be expanded to include wooden hand boards, cymbals, suonas, etc., which will arouse the interests of users involved in the game activity to a greater degree. To implement this, the sound-sensing technology used in the proposed system must be upgraded to include frequency sensing in addition to volume sensing, in order to differentiate the input sounds of the musical instrument played by the user backstage.

Author Contributions: Conceptualization, C.-M.W. and C.-H.S.; Methodology, C.-M.W. and C.-H.S.; Validation, C.-M.W. and C.-H.S.; Formal Analysis, C.-M.W. and C.-H.S.; Investigation, C.-H.S. and C.-E.H.; Data Curation, C.-H.S.; Writing—Original Draft Preparation, C.-M.W., C.-H.S. and C.-E.H.; Writing—Review and Editing, C.-M.W. and C.-H.S.; Visualization, C.-H.S. and C.-E.H.; Supervision, C.-M.W.; Project Administration, C.-M.W. All authors have read and agreed to the published version of the manuscript.

Funding: This research received no external funding.

Institutional Review Board Statement: Not applicable.

Informed Consent Statement: Informed consent was obtained from all subjects involved in the study.

Data Availability Statement: The data presented in this study are available on request from the corresponding author.

Acknowledgments: The authors would like to thank Shih-Mo Tseng from the Design Institute of Yunlin University of Science and Technology for setting up the show venue during the exhibition of the system constructed in this study to the public. Thanks are also due to the director of the Chang-Tai Older People Care Center at Douliu Township of the Yunlin LOHAS Service Group, Yi-Shan Kao, for her offering of space in the center to carry out the field experiments of this study. Furthermore, we also want to express our gratitude to president of the Puppets' House in Dounan, Yi-Sha Hsu, for her offering of space to carry out the field experiments. Finally, we would like to thank Chief Chia-Wei Chang of the Bald Pine Forest in Nantou for his offering of space to carry out the field experiments.

Conflicts of Interest: The authors declared no potential conflicts of interest with respect to the research, authorship, and/or publication of this article.

References

1. Fann, G.J.; Hsu, Y.H. Socio-economic impacts of population aging in taiwan. *Taiwan Geriatr. Gerontol.* **2010**, *5*, 149–168.
2. Boström, A.K. Lifelong learning in intergenerational settings: The development of the swedish granddad program from project to national association. *J. Intergener. Relatsh.* **2011**, *9*, 293–306. [CrossRef]
3. Hall, K.W.; Batey, J.J. Children's ideas about aging before and after an intergenerational read-aloud. *Educ. Gerontol.* **2008**, *34*, 862–870. [CrossRef]
4. Ames, B.D.; Youatt, J.P. Intergenerational education and service programming: A model for selection and evaluation of activities. *Educ. Gerontol.* **1994**, *20*, 755–764. [CrossRef]
5. Kaplan, M.S. International programs in schools: Considerations of form and function. *Int. Rev. Educ.* **2002**, *48*, 305–334. [CrossRef]
6. De Souza, E.M.; Grundy, E. Intergenerational interaction, social capital and health: Results from a randomised controlled trial in Brazil. *Soc. Sci. Med.* **2007**, *65*, 1397–1409. [CrossRef]
7. Intergenerational Learning for Inclusive Societies. Available online: https://lllplatform.eu/policy-areas/intergenerational-learning-for-inclusive-societies/ (accessed on 22 March 2022).
8. Ainge, D.J. Upper primary students constructing and exploring three dimensional shapes: A comparison of virtual reality with card nets. *J. Educ. Comput. Res.* **1996**, *14*, 345–369. [CrossRef]
9. Virvou, M.; Katsionis, G. On the usability and likeability of virtual reality games for education: The case of VR-ENGAGE. *Comput. Educ.* **2008**, *50*, 154–178. [CrossRef]
10. MyndVR. Available online: https://www.myndvr.com/ (accessed on 4 April 2022).
11. Rendever VR for Seniors. Available online: https://www.rendever.com/?hsLang=en (accessed on 4 April 2022).
12. Benoit, M.; Guerchouche, R.; Petit, P.D.; Chapoulie, E.; Manera, V.; Chaurasia, G.; Drettakis, G.; Robert, P. Is it possible to use highly realistic virtual reality in the elderly? A feasibility study with image-based rendering. *Neuropsychiatr. Dis. Treat.* **2015**, *11*, 557–563.
13. Manera, V.; Chapoulie, E.; Bourgeois, J.; Guerchouche, R.; David, R.; Ondrej, J.; Drettakis, G.; Robert, P. A feasibility study with image-based rendered virtual reality in patients with mild cognitive impairment and dementia. *PLoS ONE* **2016**, *11*, e0151487. [CrossRef]
14. Benckendorff, P.; Tussyadiah, I.; Scarles, C. The Role of Digital Technologies in Facilitating Intergenerational Learning in Heritage Tourism. In *Information and Communication Technologies in Tourism*; Springer International Publishing: Berlin, Germany, 2018; pp. 463–472.
15. Meliadou, E.; Nakou, A.; Chaidi, I.; Koutsikos, L.; Giannakouloupoulos, A.; Gouscos, D.; Meimaris, M. Technology in Intergenerational Learning Research Projects in the Greek Context. In Proceedings of the 3rd International Conference on the Elderly and New Technologies, Castello, Spain, 14 April 2012.
16. Jane, B.; Robbins, J. Intergenerational learning: Grandparents teaching everyday concepts in science and technology. *Asia-Pac. Forum Sci. Learn. Teach.* **2007**, *8*, 1–18.
17. Proposal for a Council Recommendation on key Competences for Life-Long Learning. Available online: https://eur-lex.europa.eu/legal-content/EN/TXT/PDF/?uri=CELEX:52018SC0014 (accessed on 4 April 2022).
18. Kimuna, S.R.; Knox, D.; Zusman, M. College students' perceptions about older people and aging. *Educ. Gerontol.* **2005**, *31*, 563–572. [CrossRef]
19. Lee, Y.S. Measures of student attitudes on aging. *Educ. Gerontol.* **2009**, *35*, 121–134. [CrossRef]
20. Frenchs, M.; Pearl, M.; Mosher-Ashley, E. College students' attitudes toward residential care facilities. *Educ. Gerontol.* **2000**, *26*, 583–603.
21. Zajicek, M. Interface Design for Older Adults. In Proceedings of the 2001 EC/NSF Workshop on Universal Accessibility of Ubiquitous Computing: Providing for the Elderly, Alcácer do Sal, Portugal, 22 May 2001; pp. 60–65.
22. Shibata, T.; Wada, K. Robot therapy: A new approach for mental healthcare of the elderly—A mini-review. *Gerontology* **2011**, *57*, 378–386. [CrossRef]
23. Chatman, E.A. The impoverished life-world of outsiders. *J. Am. Soc. Inf. Sci.* **1996**, *47*, 193–206. [CrossRef]
24. Hoff, A. Patterns of intergenerational support in grandparent-grandchild and parent-child relationships in Germany. *Ageing Soc.* **2007**, *27*, 643–665. [CrossRef]
25. Newman, S.; Hatton Yeo, A. Intergenerational learning and the contributions of older people. *Ageing Horiz.* **2008**, *8*, 31–39.
26. The Role of Intergenerational Program in Promoting Lifelong Learning for All Ages. Available online: http://www.unesco.org/education/uie/pdf/uiestud36.pdf (accessed on 15 November 2009).
27. Kyrpychenko, O.; Pushchyna, I.; Kichuk, Y.; Shevchenko, N.; Luchaninova, O.; Koval, V. Communicative competence development in teaching professional discourse in educational establishments. *Int. J. Mod. Educ. Comput. Sci.* **2021**, *13*, 16–27. [CrossRef]
28. Kuzminykh, I.; Yevdokymenko, M.; Yeremenko, O.; Lemeshko, O. Increasing teacher competence in cybersecurity using the EU security frameworks. *Int. J. Mod. Educ. Comput. Sci.* **2021**, *13*, 60–68. [CrossRef]
29. Singh, N.; Gunjan, V.K.; Nasralla, M.M. A parametrized comparative analysis of performance between proposed adaptive and personalized tutoring system "seis tutor" with existing online tutoring system. *IEEE Access* **2022**, *10*, 39376–39386. [CrossRef]

30. Oropilla, C.T.; Odegaard, E.E. Strengthening the call for intentional intergenerational programmes towards sustainable futures for children and families. *Sustainability* **2021**, *13*, 5564. [CrossRef]
31. Morton Heilig. Available online: https://en.wikipedia.org/wiki/Morton_Heilig (accessed on 5 April 2022).
32. Lanier, J. Virtual reality: The promise of the future. *Interact. Learn. Int.* **1992**, *8*, 275–279.
33. Burdea, G.C.; Coiffet, G. *Virtual Reality Technology*; John Wiley & Sons: New York, NY, USA, 1993.
34. Merchant, Z.; Goetz, E.T.; Cifuentes, L.; Keeney-Kennicutt, W.; Davis, T.J. Effectiveness of virtual reality-based instruction on students' learning outcomes in K-12 and higher education: A meta-analysis. *Comput. Educ.* **2014**, *70*, 29–40. [CrossRef]
35. Nasralla, M.M. Sustainable virtual reality patient rehabilitation systems with IoT sensors using virtual smart cities. *Sustainability* **2021**, *13*, 4716. [CrossRef]
36. Sobnath, D.; Rehman, I.U.; Nasralla, M.M. Smart Cities to Improve Mobility and Quality of Life of the Visually Impaired. In *Technological Trends in Improved Mobility of the Visually Impaired*; Paiva, S., Ed.; Springer International Publishing: Cham, Germany, 2020; pp. 3–28.
37. Davis, F.D. A Technology Acceptance Model for Empirically Testing New End-User Information Systems: Theory and Results. Ph.D. Thesis, Sloan School of Management, Massachusetts Institute of Technology, Boston, MA, USA, 1985.
38. Davis, F.D. Perceived usefulness, perceived ease of use, and user acceptance of information technology. *MIS Q.* **1989**, *13*, 319–340. [CrossRef]
39. Davis, F.D. User acceptance of information technology: System characteristics, user perceptions and behavioral impacts. *Int. J. Man-Mach. Stud.* **1993**, *38*, 475–487. [CrossRef]
40. Syed Abdul, S.; Malwade, S.; Nursetyo, A.A.; Sood, M.; Bhatia, M.; Barsasella, D.; Liu, M.F.; Chang, C.-C.; Srinivasan, K.; Raja, M.; et al. Virtual reality among the elderly: A usefulness and acceptance study from Taiwan. *BMC Geriatr.* **2019**, *19*, 223. [CrossRef]
41. Coldham, G.; Cook, D.M. VR Usability from Elderly Cohorts: Preparatory Challenges In Overcoming Technology Rejection. In Proceedings of the National Information Technology Conference, Colombo, Sri Lanka, 14–15 September 2017; pp. 131–135.
42. Ishii, H.; Ullmer, B. Tangible Bits: Towards Seamless Interfaces between People, Bits and Atoms. In Proceedings of the ACM SIGCHI Conference on Human Factors In Computing Systems, Atlanta, GA, USA, 22–27 March 1997; pp. 234–241.
43. Ishii, H. Tangible Bits: Beyond Pixels. In Proceedings of the 2nd International Conference on Tangible and Embedded Interaction, Bonn, Germany, 18–20 February 2008; pp. 15–25.
44. Resnick, M.; Martin, F.; Berg, R.; Borovoy, R.; Colella, V.; Kramer, K.; Silverman, B. Digital Manipulatives: New Toys to Think with. In Proceedings of the SIGCHI Conference on Human Factors in Computing Systems, Los Angeles, CA, USA, 18–23 April 1998; pp. 281–287.
45. Zuckerman, O.; Arida, S.; Resnick, M. Extending Tangible Interfaces for Education: Digital Montessori-inspired Manipulatives. In Proceedings of the SIGCHI Conference on Human Factors in Computing Systems, Portland, OR, USA, 2–7 April 2005; pp. 859–868.
46. Raffle, H.; Parkes, A.; Ishii, H. Topobo: A Constructive Assembly System with Kinetic Memory. In Proceedings of the SIGCHI Conference on Human Factors in Computing, Vienna, Austria, 24–29 April 2004; pp. 647–654.
47. Jordà, S.; Geiger, G.; Alonso, M.; Kaltenbrunner, M. The reacTable: Exploring the Synergy between Live Music Performance and Tabletop Tangible Interfaces. In Proceedings of the 1st International Conference on Tangible and Embedded Interaction, Baton Rouge, LA, USA, 15–17 February 2007; pp. 139–146.
48. Dunn, H.N.; Nakano, H.; Gibson, J. Block Jam: A tangible Interface For Interactive Music. In Proceedings of the 2003 Conference on New Interfaces for Musical Expression, Montreal, QC, Canada, 22–24 May 2003; pp. 170–177.
49. Schiettecatte, B.; Vanderdonckt, J. AudioCubes: A Distributed Cube Tangible Interface Based on Interaction Range for Sound Design. In Proceedings of the Second International Conference on Tangible and Embedded Interaction, Bonn, Germany, 18–20 February 2008; pp. 3–10.
50. Couture, N.; Rivière, G.; Reuter, P. GeoTUI: A Tangible User Interface for Geoscience. In Proceedings of the Second International Conference on Tangible and Embedded Interaction, Bonn, Germany, 18–20 February 2008; pp. 89–96.
51. Kim, M.J.; Maher, M.L. The impact of tangible user interfaces on spatial cognition during collaborative design. *Des. Stud.* **2008**, *29*, 222–253. [CrossRef]
52. Piper, B.; Ratti, C.; Ishii, H. Illuminating clay: A 3-D Tangible Interface for Landscape Analysis. In Proceedings of the SIGCHI Conference on Human Factors in Computing Systems, Minneapolis, MN, USA, 20–25 April 2002; pp. 355–362.
53. Norman, D.A. The next UI breakthrough, part 2: Physicality. *Interactions* **2007**, *14*, 46–47. [CrossRef]
54. Dourish, P. *Where the Action is: The Foundations of Embodied Interaction*; MIT Press: Boston, MA, USA, 2004.
55. Kaptelinin, V.; Nardi, B.A. *Acting with Technology: Activity Theory and Interaction Design*; MIT Press: Boston, MA, USA, 2006.
56. Price, S.; Sheridan, J.G.; Pontual Falcão, T. Action and Representation in Tangible Systems: Implications for Design of Learning Interactions. In Proceedings of the 4th International Conference on Tangible, Embedded, and Embodied Interaction, Cambridge, MA, USA, 24–27 January 2010; pp. 145–152.
57. Ross, P.R.; Wensveen, S.A. Designing aesthetics of behavior in interaction: Using aesthetic experience as a mechanism for design. *Int. J. Des.* **2010**, *4*, 3–13.
58. Types and Methods of Interviews in Research. Available online: https://www.questionpro.com/blog/types-of-interviews/ (accessed on 4 April 2022).
59. Boar, B.H. *Application Prototyping: A Requirements Definition Strategy for the 80s*; John Wiley & Sons, Inc.: New York, NY, USA, 1984.

60. Beaudouin Lafon, M.; Mackay, W.E. Prototyping Tools and Techniques. In *Human-Computer Interaction*; CRC Press: Boca Raton, FL, USA, 2009; pp. 137–160.
61. McCann, R.M.; Giles, H. Age-differentiated communication in organizations: Perspectives from Thailand and the United States. *Commun. Res. Rep.* **2007**, *24*, 1–12. [CrossRef]
62. Lu, L.; Kao, S.F. Attitudes towards old people in Taiwan: Scale development and preliminary evidence of reliability and validity. *J. Educ. Psychol.* **2009**, *32*, 147–171.
63. Minichiello, V.; Aroni, R.; Hays, T. *In-Depth Interviewing: Principles, Techniques, Analysis*, 3rd ed.; Pearson Australia Group: Frenchs Forest, NSW, Australia, 2008.
64. Lin, J.D.; Yen, C.F.; Chen, M.H. Qualitative research method: Models and steps of interviewing. *J. Disabil. Res.* **2005**, *3*, 122–136.
65. Verplank, B. Interaction Design Sketchbook. Available online: https://www.academia.edu/37121727/Interaction_Design_Sketchbook_by_Bill_Verplank_Frameworks_for_designing_interactive_products_and_systems (accessed on 25 February 2020).
66. Kaiser-Meyer-Olkin (KMO) Test for Sampling Adequacy. Available online: https://www.statisticshowto.datasciencecentral.com/kaiser-meyer-olkin/ (accessed on 16 February 2020).
67. KMO and Bartlett's Test. Available online: https://www.ibm.com/support/knowledgecenter/SSLVMB_23.0.0/spss/tutorials/fac_telco_kmo_01.html (accessed on 25 February 2020).
68. A Guide to Bartlett's Test of Sphericity. Available online: https://www.statology.org/bartletts-test-of-sphericity/ (accessed on 8 April 2022).
69. Cerny, B.A.; Kaiser, H.F. A study of a measure of sampling adequacy for factor-analytic correlation matrices. *Multivar. Behav. Res.* **1977**, *12*, 43–47. [CrossRef]
70. Hair, J.F.; Black, W.C.; Babin, B.J. *Multivariate Data Analysis: A Global Perspective*; Pearson Education: London, UK, 2010.
71. Kaiser, H.F. A second generation little jiffy. *Psychometrika* **1970**, *35*, 401–415. [CrossRef]
72. Scott, W.A. Reliability of content analysis: The case of nominal scale coding. *Public Opin. Q.* **1955**, *19*, 321–325. [CrossRef]
73. Cronbach, L.J. Coefficient alpha and the internal structure of tests. *Psychometrika* **1951**, *16*, 297–334. [CrossRef]
74. Taber, K.S. The Use of Cronbach's alpha when developing and reporting research instruments in science education. *Res. Sci. Educ.* **2018**, *48*, 1273–1296. [CrossRef]
75. Guilford, J.P. *Psychometric Methods*, 2nd ed.; McGraw-Hill: New York, NY, USA, 1954.
76. Ho, Y.; Kwon, O.Y.; Park, S.Y.; Yoon, T.Y.; Kim, Y.-E. Reliability and validity test of the Korean version of Noe's evaluation. *Korean J. Med. Educ.* **2017**, *29*, 15–26. [CrossRef]
77. Bentler, P.M. *EQS Structural Equations Program Manual*; Multivariate Software Inc.: Encino, CA, USA, 1995; Volume 6.
78. Fan, X.; Thompson, B.; Wang, L. Effects of sample size, estimation methods, and model specification on structural equation modeling fit indexes. *Struct. Equ. Modeling A Multidiscip. J.* **1999**, *6*, 56–83. [CrossRef]
79. Hu, L.T.; Bentler, P.M. Cutoff criteria for fit indexes in covariance structure analysis: Conventional criteria versus new alternatives. *Struct. Equ. Modeling A Multidiscip. J.* **1999**, *6*, 1–55. [CrossRef]
80. MacCallum, R.C.; Hong, S. Power analysis in covariance structure modeling using GFI and AGFI. *Multivar. Behav. Res.* **1997**, *32*, 193–210. [CrossRef] [PubMed]
81. Hair, J.F.; Babin, B.J.; Anderson, R.E.; Black, W.C. *Multivariate Data Analysis*, 5th ed.; Pearson Prentice Hall: Upper Saddle River, NJ, USA, 1998.
82. Research Methods Knowledge Base. Available online: https://conjointly.com/kb/?_ga=2.202908566.666445287.1649411337-790067422.1649411337 (accessed on 23 February 2020).
83. Chung, M. *Encyclopedia of Measurement and Statistics*; SAGE: Southern Oaks, CA, USA, 2007; pp. 189–201. [CrossRef]

Article

Sustainable and Security Focused Multimodal Models for Distance Learning

Vacius Jusas [1], Rita Butkiene [1], Algimantas Venčkauskas [1], Šarūnas Grigaliūnas [1], Daina Gudoniene [1,*], Renata Burbaite [1] and Boriss Misnevs [2]

[1] Faculty of Informatics, Kaunas University of Technology, 44249 Kaunas, Lithuania; vacius.jusas@ktu.lt (V.J.); rita.butkiene@ktu.lt (R.B.); algimantas.venckauskas@ktu.lt (A.V.); sarunas.grigaliunas@ktu.lt (Š.G.); renata.burbaite@ktu.lt (R.B.)
[2] Department of Software Engineering, Transport and Telecommunication Institute, 1019 Riga, Latvia; misnevs.b@tsi.lv
* Correspondence: daina.gudoniene@ktu.lt

Abstract: The COVID-19 pandemic has forced much education to move into a distance learning (DL) model. The problem addressed in the paper is related to the increased necessity for the capacity of data, secure infrastructure, Wi-Fi possibilities, and equipment, learning resources which are needed when students connect to systems managed by institutional, national, and international organizations. Meanwhile, there have been cases when learners were not able to use technology in a secure manner, since they were requested to connect to external learning objects or systems. The research aims to develop a sustainable strategy based on a security concept model that consists of three main components: (1) security assurance; (2) users, including administration, teachers, and learners; and (3) DL organizational processes. The security concept model can be implemented at different levels of security. We modelled all the possible levels of security. To implement the security concept model, we introduce a framework that consists of the following activities: plan, implement, review, and improve. These activities were performed in a never-ending loop. We provided the technical measures required to implement the appropriate security level of DL infrastructure. The technical measures were provided at the level of a system administrator. We enriched the framework by joining technical measures into appropriate activities within the framework. The models were validated by 10 experts from different higher education institutions. The feasibility of the data collection instrument was determined by a Cronbach's alpha coefficient that was above 0.9.

Keywords: infrastructure; distance learning; security models; education

Citation: Jusas, V.; Butkiene, R.; Venčkauskas, A.; Grigaliūnas, Š.; Gudoniene, D.; Burbaite, R.; Misnevs, B. Sustainable and Security Focused Multimodal Models for Distance Learning. *Sustainability* **2022**, *14*, 3414. https://doi.org/10.3390/su14063414

Academic Editor: Hao-Chiang Koong Lin

Received: 17 February 2022
Accepted: 10 March 2022
Published: 14 March 2022

Publisher's Note: MDPI stays neutral with regard to jurisdictional claims in published maps and institutional affiliations.

Copyright: © 2022 by the authors. Licensee MDPI, Basel, Switzerland. This article is an open access article distributed under the terms and conditions of the Creative Commons Attribution (CC BY) license (https://creativecommons.org/licenses/by/4.0/).

1. Introduction

The disruption of learning processes disrupted by the COVID-19 pandemic has involved a radical transformation of education and training, and one of the sectors undergoing dramatic digital transformation globally is higher education [1]. The sudden forced closure of face-to-face teaching activities has led many academics and many students into "unfamiliar terrain" due to the need to adapt swiftly to total distance learning (DL) settings [2]. This sudden change has required universities to evolve toward DL in record time, implementing and adapting the technological resources available and involving professors and researchers who lack innate technological capacities for DL.

DL requires large resources of computers, information, and communication channels. Additionally, DL faces other challenges that are as follows: (1) organization of DL processes associated with practical and laboratory work, (2) skill testing and evaluation using information and communication technology, (3) forecasting of system load, (4) cybersecurity, and (5) data protection issues. The infrastructure of DL, which consists of three sections: management and governance, physical infrastructure, and logical infrastructure [3], is indispensable in the learning processes.

The emergence of disruptive innovation is a time of risk and uncertainty, but it is also a time of opportunities, bringing talent and innovation to the education system [4]. The questionnaire at King Saud University, Saudi Arabia [5] revealed that the success factors of DL named by the students and faculty members differ. The importance of technical skills, effective time management, individual differences, and support is fostered by the technology infrastructure of the DL environment [6]. When each of these pillars is equally prioritized in fully DL delivery, ultimately the best-equipped students succeed in their course from orientation through to graduation.

The use of technology helped educators to overcome the issue of DL during disaster times, but the educators argued that robust IT infrastructure is a prerequisite for DL [7]. The infrastructure needs to be strong enough that it can provide unrestricted services during a pandemic [8]. Huang et al. [9] underlined that reliability and sufficient availability of, for example, communication infrastructure, learning tools, and digital learning resources are of utmost importance in such severe situations.

Since DL is being improved and supported by technical innovations and infrastructure, many users of innovative infrastructure are not experts in using it, therefore, it is necessary to have a support staff and an established structural system for successful entrance to the DL market [10].

The problem addressed in the paper is related to the increased necessity for the capacity of the data, secure infrastructure, Wi-Fi possibilities, and equipment, which are needed learning resources when students connect to systems managed by institutional, national, and international organizations. Meanwhile, there have been cases when learners were not able to use technology in a secure manner since they were requested to connect to external learning objects or systems.

The research question is "How to assure secure and effective DL by developing security concept models consisting of three main components: (1) security assurance; (2) users, including administration, teachers, and learners; and (3) DL organizational processes".

One of our co-authors is employed as a security manager of a whole university network. All of his suggestions came from a practical point of view. So, he practically knows the viability of the proposed models and their technical merits to ensure the security of DL infrastructure.

This paper is structured as follows: The related work is reviewed in Section 2. Section 3 presents a problem formulation and a model of DL infrastructure. A security concept model and implementation framework are presented in Section 4. Results and discussion are provided in Section 5. The conclusions of the paper and the limitations of the research work are discussed in Section 6.

2. Literature Review

Literature reviews include 42 articles from Scopus, Web of Science, and databases related to the topic. Screening was performed in two phases. The first phase was used for screening titles and abstracts and the second phase is screening full texts. We used a reference management system for literature resources collecting for citing the most appropriate papers related to the topic.

Tyagi and Verma [11] focused on security in sustainable education and distance learning. The authors [11] presented sustainable education as an educational approach aimed at entrenching in students, schools, and communities the values and motivations to act for sustainability now and in the future—in one's own life, in their communities, and on a worldwide platform.

However, the authors of the paper present the Sustainable Multimodal Model for DL as the model suggesting to educational organizations systematic and consistent ways to effectively implement teaching and learning in the worldwide platforms.

Gaiveo [12] presents the security of the computer-based information systems, that links with the preservation of the information that is supported by those systems, controlling information and systems collection, treatment, use, support, and accesses.

The authors of the paper describe the Security Focused Multimodal Models for Distance Learning as the models for educational organizations to guide them on: (1) security assurance; (2) safe and effective management of users, including administration, teachers, and learners; and (3) DL organizational processes.

We provide a review of research works considering issues of DL infrastructure and security. We firstly review the research works devoted to the development of DL infrastructure. We then review the research works that analyze security threats to the DL infrastructure and suggest ways mitigate the security threats.

Ergüzen et al. [13] suggests improving the technological infrastructure of DL through a trustworthy hardware platform-independent remote education laboratory. The reason for this suggestion is that the students are not able to acquire the costly software needed for studies. A platform-independent remote laboratory suitable for computers, smartphones, and tablets has been developed for DL students in information technology. To access the virtual laboratory a security layer containing student-specific information and security measures was used. The developed laboratory had additional benefits as follows: (1) no need for installation on students' own computers; and (2) provides a way for students with weak computers to use server power for all transactions. The students using the newly developed laboratory got a 12.89% higher average mean score than the students using traditional methods in a web programming course.

Moore and Fodrey [14] present a model of a DL technology infrastructure. The model consists of four components: systems, objectives, evaluation, and personnel. Each of these components is required for any DL technology infrastructure. It is an IT division-level framework. There is not a specific order for this model on how projects may be initiated. For the component of the system, there are two aspects of interest within the system's component. The first is what delivery method is used to create instructional content, and the second is what tool will be used to deliver this content. It is critical to establish clear learning objectives and to align them with the technology tools that are selected and implemented. Learning objectives must be firstly considered, then only tools selected and evaluated. There are two parts of evaluation within this model. The initial evaluation of the selected tool and the continuous evaluation must occur after the implementation. Finally, the division will need to determine if it has personnel who can support this new tool for the faculty members and for live-event support. The main shortcoming of this model is that the model is provided at the IT division level. The authors of the model recognize that a technology infrastructure plan is needed for e-learning leaders. However, planning is not an activity of the model.

Thomas [15] clusters the infrastructure of DL into four layers from bottom to top: internet, hardware, software, and rules and regulations. Three groups of actors interact with the infrastructure of DL. These groups are as follows: institutions, individual instructors, and individual learners. Associating the layers of DL to actors enables a better understanding of the specific challenges. These challenges vary for different actors. For example, broadband internet is usual for the institution, but it can be a problem for the individual instructors and learners. The same is valid for hardware and software. However, Thomas [15] did not consider the security issues related to the infrastructure of DL.

García-Peñalvo [16] define a reference framework for introducing eLearning practices into face-to-face education. The proposed framework consists of seven layers. The basic level of the framework is an infrastructure that is divided into three sections: management and governance, physical infrastructure, and logical infrastructure. The government of technologies is an essential factor for the success of DL. The physical infrastructure to support DL must cover all the different needs concerning physical equipment. The logical infrastructure includes the software components and users with experience who are also part of DL infrastructure. Security is the fifth layer in this framework. The security is considered together with ethics and privacy issues. Privacy of individuals must be respected and based on General Data Protection Regulation (GDPR) [17]. However, García-Peñalvo [16] provided no details on how to solve the security issues.

Not only the infrastructure of DL, but also the security of DL platforms is a key success factor of DL [18,19]. DL platforms are important for billions of users and they rely on them to perform routine activities. The user-friendliness of the graphical user interface and their constant availability made them vulnerable. Therefore, it is important to secure web applications from attacks. Bhatia and Maitra [20] analyzed all the open-source e-learning platforms available in the market today to test their vulnerability against attacks. All the analyzed e-learning platforms had severe vulnerabilities. Moodle, which is the most popular e-learning platform [21], was not an exception. Bhatia and Maitra [20] propose a model for ensuring the security of e-learning platforms. The proposed security model is posed on a two-fold holistic view: a hierarchical approach and a distributed approach. The hierarchical approach consists of the following layers from top to bottom: system administrator, instructors, and learners. The distributed approach keeps separate security models of each element in the e-learning platform. The advantage of the hierarchical approach is centralization. The advantage of the distributed approach is scalability. The implementation of the security model could be done in four steps: (1) define security policy; (2) implement security policy within an e-learning system; (3) launch constant monitoring; and (4) react to an ongoing attack. The last step is invoked by the third step in case of need. A regular update is needed to the security model since threats change. The main disadvantage of the proposed security model is that the model was presented only as a collection of ideas. The security model of the e-learning system was not validated by experts.

Husain and Budiyantara [22] analyzed the effect of the control security and privacy on the attitude and behavioral intentions of e-learning users. The results of the investigation indicate that the control of security and privacy has a significant influence on the attitude and behavioral intention of e-learning users.

During the pandemic, the number of online resources drastically increased. However, the number of cyber-attacks increased, as well [23]. Khan et al. [24] identified ten deadly cybersecurity threats during the COVID-19 pandemic. They are as follows: (1) DDoS attacks; (2) malicious domains; (3) malicious websites; (4) malware; (5) ransomware; (6) spam emails; (7) malicious social media messaging; (8) business email compromise; (9) mobile threats; and (10) browsing apps. These threats are oriented to the general e-community rather than e-learners. It is important to know the most common cybersecurity threats since e-learners are part of the general e-community. Khan et al. [24] noticed also that the most widely used online conferencing tool, Zoom, faced massive criticism because the default settings of privacy and security are not adequately secure.

Ali and Zafar [25] stated that an institution providing e-learning must implement robust measures to protect sensitive participants' data against loss or unauthorized use. For this purpose, Ali and Zafar [25] presented a conceptual model of the information security and privacy factors related to e-learning. The factors are as follows: (1) data evaluation; (2) policies; (3) legislation/regulation; (4) architecture; (5) integration; (6) training; and (7) risk analysis. The authors analyzed all the factors and made propositions for every factor. The most compelling proposition is for the first factor. This proposition says that the participation of all stakeholders in the data evaluation step will enhance the security and privacy of e-learning technology. No reason was provided why this specific order of enumeration of the factors was chosen. The ordering of factors raises some doubts. Ali and Zafar [25] also provided recommendations for the implementation of the proposed conceptual model.

Ran et al. [26] asserted that identity verification of the user of the DL platform should not terminate at the login process, but it must proceed as the user is connected to the platform. Therefore, Ran et al. [26] developed an identity authentication model based on the private cloud. The model is based on multi-fold security approach and it provides an authentication methods repository. The repository includes classical methods and behavioral validation methods that are as follows: email verification, two-step verification (login + SMS), Captcha test, face recognition, fingerprint identification, speech recognition, and keystroke recognition. After the initial login, the process of constant verification starts. The main component of this process is face recognition. However, the method faces constraints of network bandwidth and computer hardware.

Nita and Mihailescu [27] proposed a secure framework for e-learning platforms using attribute-based encryption applied in cloud computing. The framework consists of the following components: methods and criteria, education and training, e-learning users, improved access mechanism, security layer, cloud, authorities, and owners. Improved access mechanism means attribute-based encryption. However, the proposed framework is not well-structured since it connects the different types of components. Moreover, neither validation nor experiments are provided using the proposed framework.

Amo et al. [28] analyzed how learning management systems (LMSs) store and process personal data. The authors established that these data are stored unencrypted, and these data are easily accessible to many users of LMSs. Therefore, the LMSs are vulnerable to the loss of sensitive information and such information storing is not in line with GDPR. To comply with GDPR, LMSs apply a simple solution: everything or nothing. If you do not agree with terms and conditions, you do not have access. The authors suggested solving the problem to use an access matrix. The suggestion to store the personal data in encrypted form was also provided. The suggested solution was implemented for the LMS Moodle.

Amo et al. [29] proceeded with the earlier investigation on GDPR implementation in the LMS and studied the possibility for the students to be anonymous in the LMS since GDPR delegates such a right. The LMS does not have such a function. The questionnaire was carried out among learners and educators. The educators did not contradict to teach the anonymous students. Therefore, the authors implemented an add-in for the LMS Moodle. The add-in is called "Protected Users", which allows hiding of the learner's identity. The add-in is freely available on GitHub.

Caviglione and Coccoli [30] noticed that online learning is an interplay among social, educational, and technological aspects. They suggested a model to identify and classify security threats and vulnerabilities of e-learning frameworks in smart cities. The model is called a holistic one, but no proof is provided. The model is divided into three spaces: infrastructure, data, and learner. A training and technological awareness of individuals is a prime countermeasure for learner space. No countermeasures are proposed to fight security threats in the infrastructure and data spaces.

Mahmood [31] presented an agent-based framework for providing the security and privacy of the cloud-based E-learning. An architecture of the cloud-based E-learning usually consists of five main layers: hardware resource layer, software resource layer, resource management layer, service layer, and business application layer. The service layer is comprised of the three services: SaaS (software as a service), PaaS (platform as a service), and IaaS (infrastructure as a service). The framework is introduced just to SaaS service.

Alexei and Alexei [32] observed that use of cloud computing (CC), learning management systems (LMS), and video conferencing applications (VCA) has become the mainstream for conducting distance learning. They presented a review of security threats to these three types of applications and provided common recommendations to secure CC, LMS, and VCA. These common recommendations include classifying information, implementing access policies at the application or resource level, updating systems, and using cryptographic protocols.

We provide a summary of the main features of the discussed related works in Table 1.

Table 1. Summary of related works.

Research Work	DL Infrastructure	Security Issues
Ergüzen et al. [13]	Hardware platform-independent remote laboratory.	VPN layer ensures security.
Moore and Fodrey [14]	Model consists of four components: systems, objectives, evaluation, and personnel.	Not considered.
Thomas [15]	Four layers of the DL infrastructure from bottom to top: internet, hardware, software, and rules and regulations.	Security measures are managed by IT departments. No details are provided.
García-Peñalvo [16]	Three sections of DL infrastructure: management and governance, physical infrastructure, and logical infrastructure.	Security is fifth layer in the framework. No details are provided. The security is considered together with ethics and privacy issues.
Bhatia and Maitra [20]	Not considered.	Hierarchical and distributed approaches. The hierarchical approach consists of the layers from top to bottom: system administrator, instructors, and learners. The distributed approach keeps separate security models of each element in the e-learning platform.
Ali and Zafar [25]	Not considered.	Conceptual model of the information security and privacy consists of factors in the specific ordering: (1) data evaluation, (2) policies, (3) legislation/regulation, (4) architecture, (5) integration, (6) training, and (7) risk analysis.
Ran et al. [26]	Not considered.	Identity authentication model using multi-fold security approach based on classical and behavioral validation methods.
Nita and Mihailescu [27]	Not considered.	Secure framework using attribute-based encryption consists of the components: methods and criteria, education and training, e-learning users, improved access mechanism, security layer, cloud, authorities, and owners.
Amo et al. [28,29]	Not considered.	GDPR compliant personal data storing in LMS Moodle.
Caviglione and Coccoli [30]	The model is divided into three spaces: infrastructure, data, and learner	A training and technological awareness of individuals is a prime countermeasure for learner space.
Mahmood [31]	Not considered.	The framework is introduced just to SaaS service.
Alexei and Alexei [32]	Not considered.	Common recommendations are provided to secure cloud computing, learning management systems, and video conferencing applications.

We can conclude, observing Table 1, that none of the authors of the reviewed papers have demonstrated a systematic view of the problem of the security of the DL infrastructure. Moreover, the reviewed authors demonstrated different understanding of DL infrastructure. In the next section, we will present our view on the DL infrastructure.

3. Problem Formulation and the Model of DL Infrastructure

Based on the literature review, we developed the requirements for the models of the DL infrastructure and security:

1. The model of DL infrastructure must include all the components required for distance learning.
2. The security concept model should cover: (1) IT infrastructure security profile; (2) levels of IT security; and (3) secure and reliable DL infrastructure framework.

3. The plan for the implementation of the DL infrastructure framework, which joins levels of IT security and IT infrastructure security profile, should be provided in the form of a matrix.
4. The security concept model must include the protection of personal data.
5. The security concept model must include the management of copyright and licenses for digital content and software in education.

The IT infrastructure of the organization is a set of hardware, software, technical, communication, information, organizational, and technological tools that ensure proper functioning and management. The IT infrastructure includes a combination of various applications, databases, servers, disk arrays, and network equipment, and provides users with access to information sources. IT infrastructure is a technological component of any service that ensures the delivery of the considered service following agreed rules and procedures. During the pandemic, the range of participants of DL has significantly increased, their IT skills vary greatly, and the available tools for remote work (RW) differ in terms of technical parameters: workplace equipment has different capacity, and the capacity of communication channels is often insufficient.

Therefore, carefully selected, developed, and configured IT infrastructure is essential to ensure reliable and secure DL and RW (Figure 1). Next, we present the components of the model of DL infrastructure.

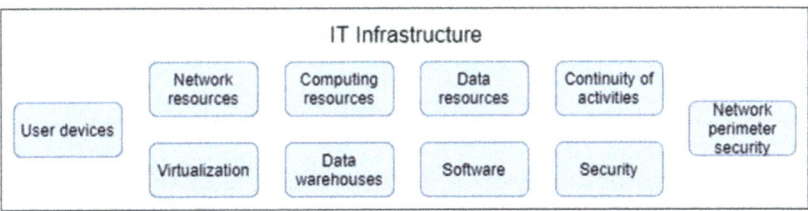

Figure 1. The model of DL infrastructure.

User devices constitute an exceptionally large spectrum of computing devices used by the participants of the DL process. This includes smartphones, tablets, and personal and desktop computers. The capabilities of these devices differ in ensuring secure and reliable DL and RW. This imposes some restrictions on the components of DL infrastructure.

Network resources include modems, routers, Wi-Fi devices, and communication lines. These resources together with user devices must ensure secure and reliable user connection with computing and information resources. To accomplish the mentioned goal the devices must use secure communication protocols (HTTPS, SSL/TLS, virtual private network, and others) and they must ensure the required bandwidth.

Virtualization is usually used in modern technologies, especially in cloud computing. Virtualization enables more effective, more flexible, and more secure use of resources. This is useful for the organization of DL and RW.

Computing resources (processors and memory blocks) are one of the most important resources, especially during the pandemic when requirements for the resources significantly increase.

Data warehouses store the digital contents of e-learning, the generated contents (individual assignments, projects, control works, and others) by e-learners, the private information of participants of DL, and others. During the pandemic, this resource is the most important since the requirements for it drastically increase.

Data resources, digital contents of e-learning, the organizational data of DL, and private data of participants of DL are critical for the process of DL. Therefore, high requirements are imposed on these resources.

The software encompasses the operational software, software of e-learning platforms, educational programs, and others. Software is one of the main components of DL infrastructure. The software is solely responsible for the ability to present e-learning material to the users of DL, for the ability of the users to communicate online and offline during the process of DL.

Continuity of activities is a set of regulations and rules that are responsible for the operation of an institution during various conditions.

Security is a set of organizational, legal, and technical regulations that are responsible for ensuring the secure operation of DL infrastructure.

Network perimeter security (firewalls, incident detection software) is a set of tools to ensure the secure operation of inner IT infrastructure.

4. Security Concept Model and Implementation Framework

4.1. Security Concept Model of DL Infrastructure

Three components take part in the DL process [16]. They are as follows: people, IT infrastructure, and organizational processes. A security model of DL infrastructure must ensure the security of the entire DL ecosystem. Figure 2 presents a security concept model that consists of security assurance, people, and organizational processes.

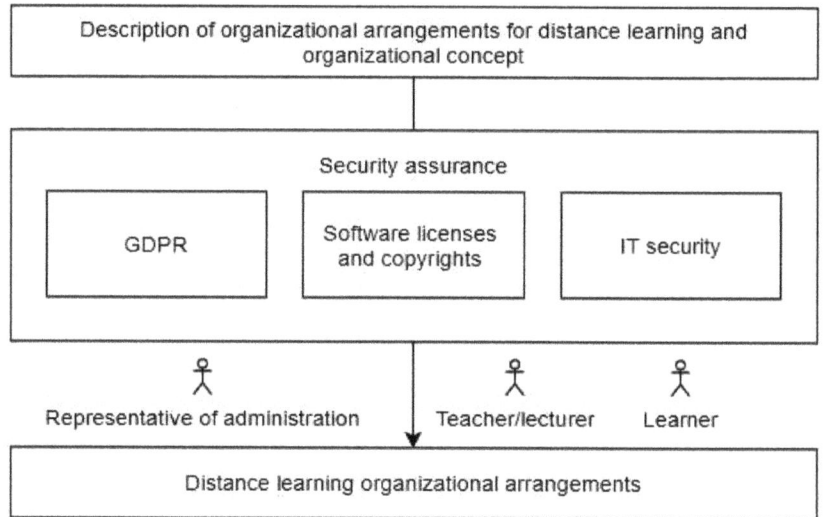

Figure 2. Security concept model of DL ecosystem.

Organizational processes of DL were considered in our previous research work [33]. They include methods of e-learning and educational technologies to support these methods.

In the security assurance, we distinguish three the most important components (Figure 2):
- Security of IT infrastructure;
- Protection of personal data (GDPR);
- Copyright and licensing of digital content and software.

Next, we will consider the implementation of these three components.

4.2. Security Profile of IT Infrastructure and Levels of IT Security

To implement security of IT infrastructure we present a security profile of IT infrastructure (Figure 3).

For the implementation of security of IT infrastructure, we used the standard ISO 27001 [34], which sets out requirements for an information security management system so that the organization can assess risks and put in place appropriate controls to protect confidentiality, integrity, and availability of information. IT infrastructure is also associated with the control of access to associated technologies. This is defined by the standard COBIT 5 [35] which is one of the most popular IT management methodologies developed and supported by the organization of ISACA (Information Systems Audit and Control Association).

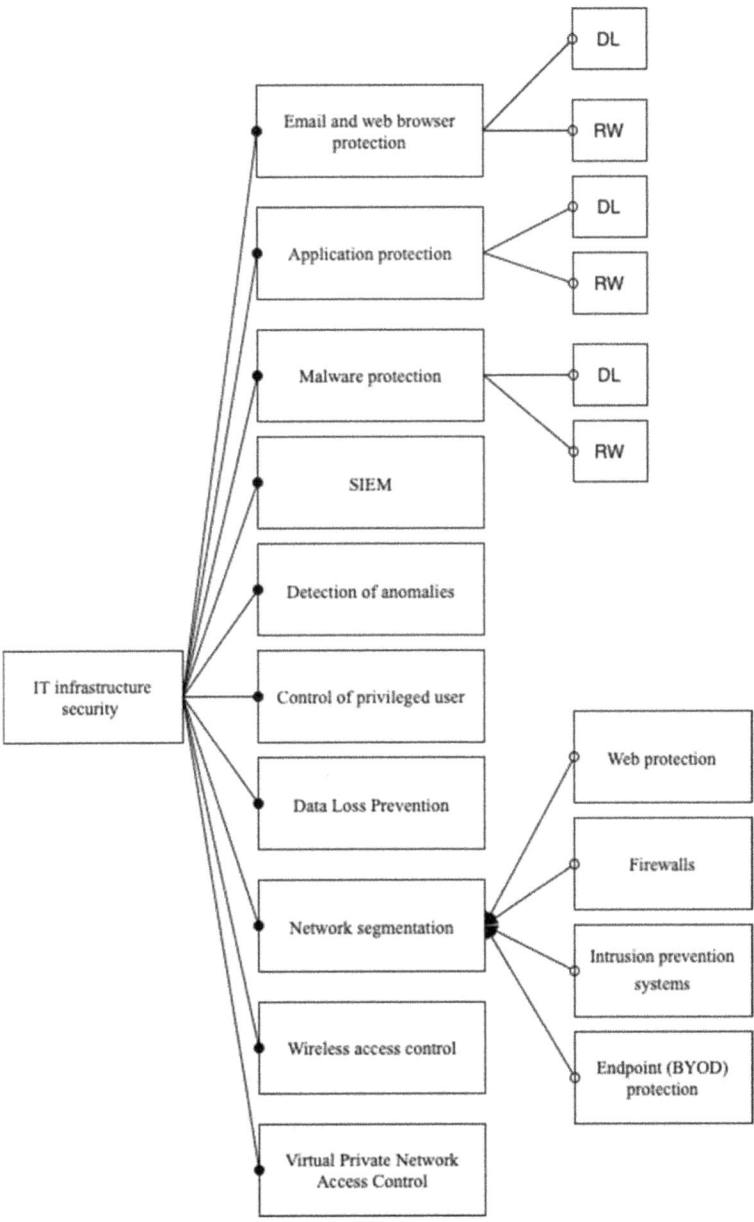

Figure 3. The security profile of IT infrastructure.

When dealing with IT infrastructure solutions, it is necessary to assess the risks and information security aspects (Figure 3):

1. Threats (external and internal): Every employee and endpoint are potential points of entry into the network. It is possible exploitation of vulnerabilities, a combination of spam, fraud, malicious URLs, and social engineering that are easier than ever to detect, automate, and deploy.
2. Risks associated with sensitive data: organizations handle many types of sensitive data, including protected learner records and data that is to be exported. The protection of sensitive data requires a good understanding of the nature of the information, knowing its location, knowing how it is generated, transmitted, shared, stored, processed, and ultimately deleted. This security profile of IT infrastructure deals with the identification, documentation, implementation, and control to protect high-value assets and sensitive information throughout its lifecycle.
3. Information security covers three main aspects:

    - Information confidentiality—protection of information against unauthorized disclosure;
    - Information integrity—protection of information against unauthorized or accidental alteration of data and/or information;
    - Access to information—ensuring that information is available when it is needed by designated users of information.

Next, we present all the components of the security profile of IT infrastructure.

Email and web browser protection is oriented to the security flaws related to the user actions. The malicious persons using different fraud strategies persuade the users of email to share sensitive information or to download the malicious programs into the network. The email protection enables the identification of spam. It can be used to identify dangerous e-letters, block attacks, and prevent sharing of sensitive data.

Application protection must enable the protection of all the application programs that can be related to the security of organization networks and security metrics. Application programs are the usual target of hackers.

Security information and event management (SIEM) tools enable a selection of data from different resources to be put into single storage for quick action in the case of need.

Anomaly detection is not a straightforward action. It can be quite difficult to find anomalies in the operations of an organization network since no one knows how the network operates in the anomaly-free mode. A careful investigation is needed to learn anomaly-free network operation mode. The available network anomaly detection tools allow analysis of the network operations. They can establish an early warning when a violation of the network operations is detected.

Data loss prevention (DLP) technologies and policy usually enable the protection of users who do not intend to use secret data improperly, and will not lose sensitive data in the network. The human factor is the weakest part of the chain of network security. Therefore, safeguards are needed to prevent either malicious or unintentional but harmful actions of the users.

Network segmentation allows assigning of the appropriate safeguard to the particular traffic in the network since traffic from different resources requires different protection. Such network partition enables application of the specific protection to each type of traffic.

Web protection is a segment of network security. Web protection is a generic term, which encompasses all the tools and measures that the organization must enable to ensure the secure usage of the internet in the inner network of the organization. Such protection does not allow the use of browsers as a means to invade the organization's network.

A firewall is a segment of network security. The goal of a firewall is to protect boundaries between an organization's network and the internet. A firewall is used to manage the network traffic and to block access to undesirable traffic.

Intrusion prevention systems (sometimes called intrusion detection systems) are a segment of network security. They constantly read and analyze the network traffic to notice as quickly as possible various attacks on the network and to react to them. These systems are founded on the basis of the known attacks [36] to recognize the known threats.

Endpoint (BYOD) protection is a segment of network security. Organizations allow users to use their owned computing devices. This is called bring your own device (BYOD). However, user-owned devices usually do not possess such strong protection as an organization's computers. Therefore, they become an easy target for hackers. Therefore, the endpoint protection adds a defensive layer between remote computing devices and organization networks, for example, a virtual private network (VPN).

Wireless access control is a separate component in the security profile of IT infrastructure since wireless networks are less secure than traditional networks. Therefore, additional measures are needed to secure wireless networks.

Virtual private network access control is used to enable authenticated communication between the endpoint device and secure organization networks. For remote VPN access authentication, either IPsec or Secure Sockets Layer protocol is used to create an encrypted communication channel that other interesting parties would not be able to access the transmitted data.

Security education is an important component of the security profile of IT infrastructure, as well. It provides four major benefits to organizations: (1) improve employee behavior; (2) increase the ability to hold employees accountable for their actions; (3) mitigate the liability of the organization for an employee's behavior; and (4) comply with regulations and contractual obligations.

The security profile of IT infrastructure can be implemented at different levels of security (Figure 4).

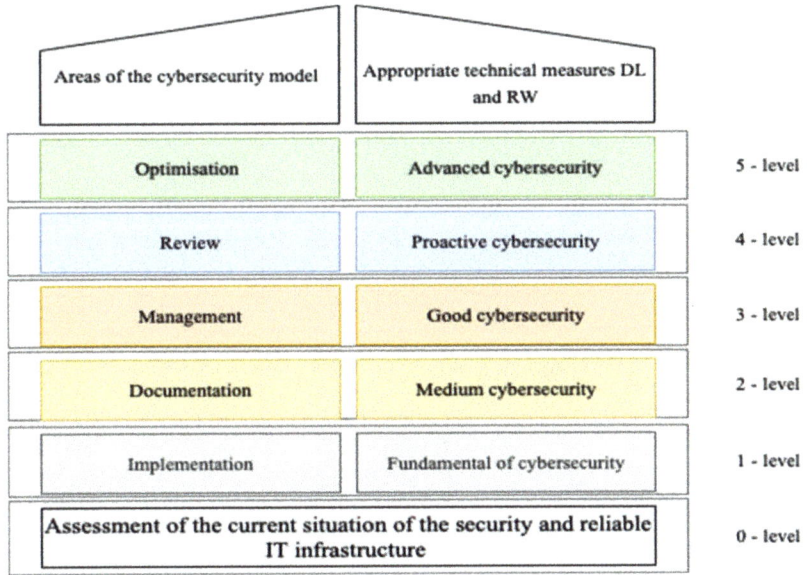

Figure 4. IT security levels.

The security levels within an organization can be ensured by appropriate technical measures that are enumerated in the security profile of IT infrastructure. To ensure that the areas of the cybersecurity model and the level of cybersecurity are sufficient, it is necessary to assess the situation of the organization's existing IT infrastructure. It is a ground level of cybersecurity.

4.3. The Framework to Ensure the Secure and Reliable DL Infrastructure

The framework to ensure a secure and reliable DL infrastructure is based on a Lean [37] methodology. It is one of the methodologies to implement agile methods. This methodology is a process improvement methodology based on reducing resources and improving the efficiency of providing them.

The first step of the Lean methodology is the most important one that is an assessment of the current security situation of DL infrastructure to eliminate wasting of resources. For this purpose, it is necessary to carry out an analysis and identify specifics of the protection level for those working and learning remotely. When all the information concerning the current situation is collected, we can start a framework that opens a never-ending loop (Figure 5). The start of the framework is usually done on the planning activity. The other title for this activity is a definition of priorities. When the priorities are defined, they have to be implemented. Threats and risks to cybersecurity change constantly. Therefore, the reviewing of threats and risks must be done permanently. The decision can be made to improve cybersecurity after reviewing the threats and risks.

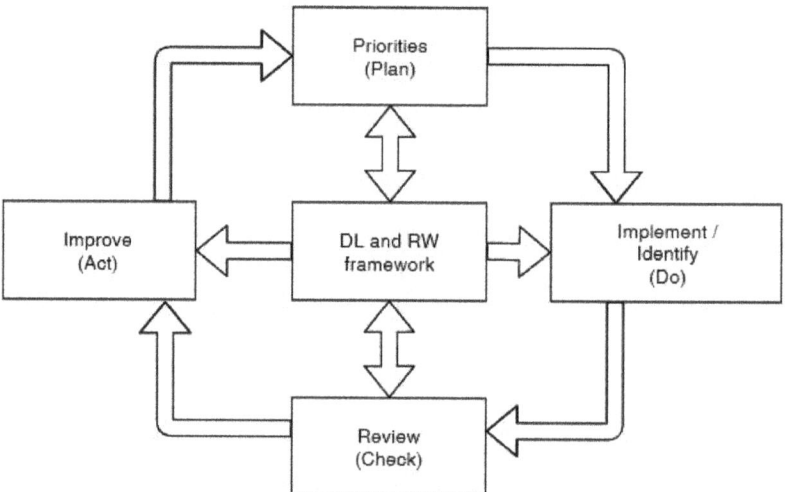

Figure 5. A framework of secure and reliable DL infrastructure.

It is also appropriate to lay down specific measures to create security appropriate to the user. As for the selection of tools, Table 2 enumerates domains of the application of cybersecurity and the technical measures applied to these domains.

Table 2. Domains of applications of a cybersecurity model.

Domains of Applications of Cybersecurity Model	Actions	Technical Measures
AC—access control	Define requirements for system access	TK—control of privileged user
	Control the access to the system from inside	UV—firewall management
	Control remote access to the system	
	Allow access to the data only to those users and processes that have a real need	
AM—asset management	Identify and document resources	TS—network segmentation
	Monitor and manage resources	UV—firewall management
AU—audit, and responsibility	Define requirements for log records	SM—SIEM
	Protect log records	DP—data loss prevention
	Monitor and manage log records	
AT—awareness and training	Inform users about threats	MV—security training
	Organize security training and education	
CM—configuration management	Define the main (minimal, baseline) configurations	TP—application protection
	Manage configuration and updates	GT—endpoint protection
IA—identification, and authentication	Allow access to authenticated resources	TK—control of privileged user
IR—incident response	Prepare an incident management plan	AN—anomaly detection
	Implement incident management	PS—intrusion prevention system
	Test incident management	UV—firewall management
MA—maintenance	Implement maintenance	SM—SIEM
MP—media protection	Define and label media	KP—Malware prevention
	Protect and control media	GT—endpoint protection
	Protect media channels	UV—firewall management

Table 2. Cont.

Domains of Applications of Cybersecurity Model	Actions	Technical Measures
PS—personal security	Protect sensitive information	DP—data loss prevention
		TK—control of privileged user
PE—physical environment	Restrict physical access	GT—endpoint protection
		TK—control of privileged user
RE—recovery	Manage backup copies	-
RM—risk management	Manage continuity of information security	SM—SIEM
	Define, assess, and manage risk	-
CA—control assessment	Prepare and manage a plan for information systems security	PS—intrusion prevention system
	Define and manage tools of control	SM—SIEM
SA—situation awareness	Implement monitoring of threats	SM—SIEM
		TP—application protection
		AN—anomaly detection
SC—system and communication	Define security requirements for systems and communication	BK—wireless access control
	Manage communication with information systems	PS—intrusion prevention system
		AN—anomaly detection
		EN—email and web browser protection
		ZS—web protection
		VT—VPN access control
SI—system integrity	Know and manage the flaws of the information system	PS—intrusion prevention system
	Identify malicious contents	KP—Malware prevention
	Monitor network and systems	SM—SIEM
	Implement enhanced protection of email	EN—email and web browser protection

We provide the information of Table 2 in concise form using a matrix to ensure secure and reliable DL infrastructure within the organization (Table 3).

Table 3. Implementation matrix of DL infrastructure framework.

Domains of Application	Appropriate Technical Measures														
	TK	KP	AN	TP	DP	EN	GT	UV	PS	TS	SM	VT	ZS	BK	MV
AC	x							x							
AM										x					
AU					x			x			x				
AT															x
CM			x				x								
IA	x														
IR		x						x	x						
MA											x				
MP		x					x	x							
PS						x	x	x							
PE															
RE	x														
RM											x				
CA										x	x				
SA			x	x							x				
SC			x			x				x		x	x	x	
SI		x			x			x			x				

The use of the secure and reliable DL infrastructure framework (Figure 5) and the description of the technical measures taken for distance learning at different IT security levels within the organization (Figure 4) in the field of cybersecurity can significantly increase the resilience to cyberattacks:

- Domains of the cybersecurity model: 17;
- Actions: 35;
- Technical measures for DL and RW: 39;
- Levels of IT security in the organization: (0–5).

The appropriate choice of technical measures and their prioritization, as shown in Figure 6, can ensure the full security of the educational institution's infrastructure during DL and RM. We can observe in Figure 6 that the specific technical measures are joint to the appropriate activities of the framework.

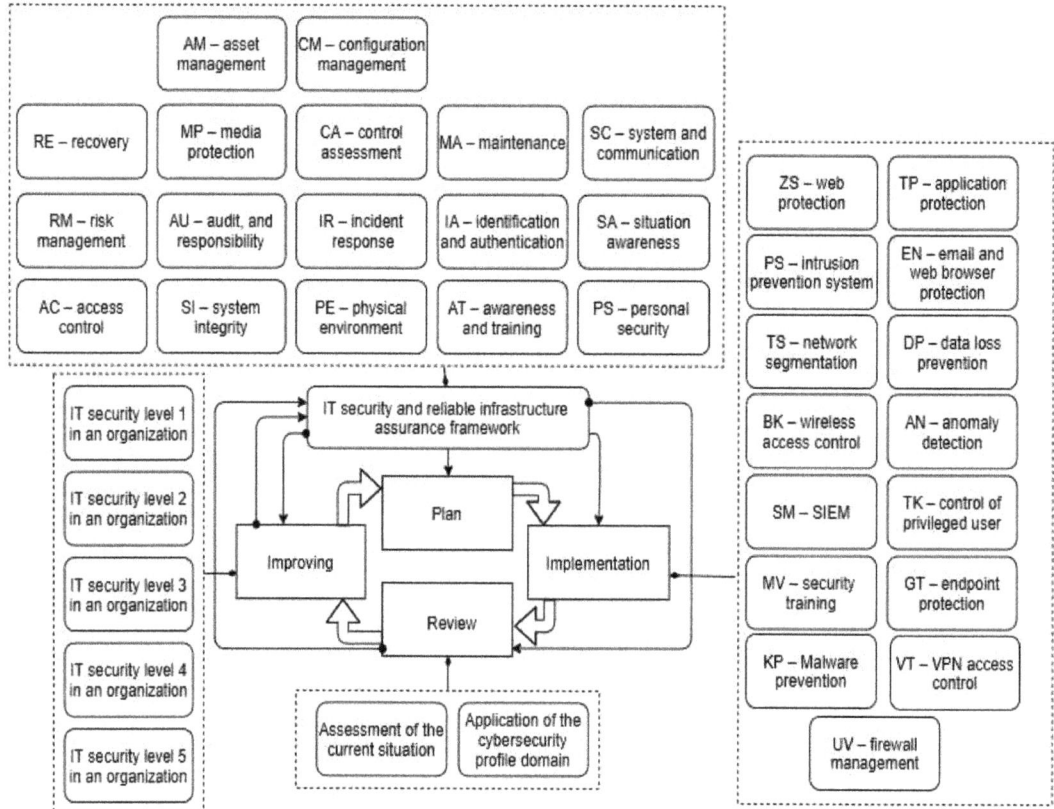

Figure 6. Secure DL infrastructure framework enriched by technical measures.

The technical measures to ensure cybersecurity may be selected for the domains that will be protected or that are of higher priority and subject to the proposed DL infrastructure framework matrix (Table 3). Capacity within the organization is also considered and is taken into account. As the level of maturity increases, the plan must be updated (Figure 5), followed by the implementation of measures and review of existing measures while ensuring the security level of DL infrastructure.

For the proper and successful application of the cybersecurity profile, we provide a matrix of ensuring secure and reliable DL infrastructure in the organization (Table 4). The matrix is used to assign the technical measures to the appropriate IT security levels.

Table 4. The level of assurance of secure and reliable IT infrastructure in the organization.

Domains of Application	Levels of IT Security					
	0	1	2	3	4	5
AC		x	x	x	x	x
AM			x	x		
AU			x	x	x	x
AT			x	x	x	
CM			x	x	x	x
IA	Assessment of the current situation	x	x	x		
IR			x	x	x	x
MA			x	x		
MP		x	x	x		
PS			x			
PE		x	x	x		
RE				x	x	x
RM			x	x	x	x
CA			x	x	x	
SA				x	x	
SC		x	x	x	x	x
SI		x	x	x	x	x

4.4. A Case Study

Each institution starts to take care of security from a level 0 to assess what measures it already has and can use. If such an institution decides to set level 1 of secure and reliable DL infrastructure, the institution uses the proposed framework (Figure 5) and reviews the domains of the application of the cybersecurity model. Level 1 of the cybersecurity model includes AC, IA, MP, PE, SC, and SI, as shown in Table 4. The technical measures for the implementation of security to the selected domains can be found in Table 3. They are as follows: TK, UV, KP, GT, AN, EN, PS, SM, VT, ZS, and BK. The joint information for the implementation of security level 1 is shown in Table 5.

Table 5. Implementation of level 1 to ensure secure and reliable IT infrastructure.

Domains of Application of the Cybersecurity Model	DL and RW Technical Measures							
AC	TK				UV			
IA	TK							
MP		KP			UV			
PE				GT	UV			
SC			AN	EN		PS	VT	ZS	BK
SI		KP		EN		PS	SM		
All measures of security level 1:	TK	KP	AN	EN	GT	UV	PS	SM	VT	ZS	BK

4.5. Protection of Personal Data

Recently, the protection of personal data has received a lot of attention. Higher education institutions possess personal data, and therefore they have a statutory and regulatory responsibility for the careful processing of personal data. Personal data protection issues are particularly relevant during the implementation of DL and RW as personal data are not processed in a relatively secure intranet environment of the organization, but the data are transmitted and processed outside the intranet. Therefore, additional security measures are needed to ensure the secure transmission of personal data over the internet as well as the processing and storage of personal data whenever a person works remotely.

As our uses and approaches to technology generate new cybersecurity challenges, regulations are growing in number and complexity. This growth in regulatory changes often overwhelms organizations as they need to become more flexible to comply quickly and simultaneously with different mandatory controls and requirements. Personal data protection is specifically mapped with Control the privileged user rights (TK) to help organizations to meet multiple General Data Protection Regulation (GDPR) [17] and ISO 27001 [34] requirements with one comprehensive solution.

The implementation of the GDPR requirements is a complex process that requires considerable resources and expertise. Depending on the nature of the institution, its activities, the volume of data managed and processed, international and national organizations offer various methodologies and models that have been developed for the implementation of the GDPR. The State Data Protection Inspectorate of Lithuania has drawn up a 12-step set of recommendations to guide the preparation process for the implementation of the GDPR [38]. These recommendations are based on the guidelines of the UK Information Commissioner's Office [39], adapting them to the case of Lithuania. These steps are as follows: (1) awareness; (2) information that you are possessing; (3) provision of privacy information; (4) rights of data subjects; (5) implementation of the subject right to acquaint with personal data; 6) legal base of personal data management; (7) consent; (8) data of children; (9) violations of management of personal data; (10) applied personal data protection; (11) officer of personal data protection; and (12) internationalization.

We can recall that the institution must periodically review the security risks of IT infrastructure and improve protection when risks change. This is prescribed according to the secure and reliable IT framework (Figure 5). The same rule must be applied to the implementation of GDPR, as well.

4.6. Licensing of Software

When purchasing (whether for payment or free) software, you are entitled to use the program, but not to become the owner of the program. The terms and conditions regarding the use of the program depend on the license in which the copyright holder defines the conditions of use of the program in a particular case. The user of the program must understand and agree to and use the terms of the license without violating the existing restrictions. If the license terms are not accepted, the software cannot be used. Generally, a license entitles you to install a program on one computer and have a backup. The license may also include other authorizations, such as free use with additional restrictions, modification of the program, and distribution under certain conditions. There are two main types of licenses: free software and proprietary. Public domain software may be distinguished as a separate group. The four types of licenses are used the most frequently. They are as follows: (1) Copyright (©); (2) Creative Commons (CC); (3) Public Domain (PD); and (4) author-defined license.

Software used in the teaching/learning process requires a careful assessment of the software distribution and use license (terms and conditions) to avoid possible legal consequences or potential security breaches. Special care should be taken when using software that is free or temporarily free and that can be unlawfully distributed, with security issues, etc.

Digital content is usually shared using the Creative Commons (CC) license. Creative Commons is an international non-profit organization that has created several standard license agreements. The authors using these types of licenses can define terms of use of their products. Creative Commons defined four types of terms of product usage [40]. Combining these four types of terms six types of Creative Commons licenses and two types of Public Domain licenses are obtained. The terms of product usage are labeled using a special graphic character and/or a short description of terms of product usage. Creative Commons licenses enable usage of products without the separate permission of authors and/or holders of property rights. Different types of licenses define different terms of product usage. Creative Commons licenses apply practice that some property rights are reserved, meanwhile, the traditional copyright applies practice that all the property rights are reserved. Creative Commons licenses restrict only some rights of product usage.

The use of software that is copied, hacked, having an uncertain origin, or without specified authorship, in some cases, may be freely distributed; however, it may lead to certain risks, as well:

- Legal or financial consequences;
- The possible distribution of malicious software;
- Possible improper, illegal processing, collection (leakage) of personal data;
- Frequently has poor or no documentation at all;
- No guarantees are given regarding the consequences of this program usage;
- Usually, such a program is not supported, updated, bugs are not fixed, and technical assistance is not provided.

Although cybersecurity has always been important, it arguably has never been more vital for organizations to protect their data and reduce the risk of being hacked with so many of us working from home these days. The larger number of employees working from home leaves an organization open to more risks, as a home set-up will often be far less restricted compared to the office-based one. By consolidating IT, systems organizations can control what software their employees utilize, identify all assets (asset management (AM)), and protect against cyberattacks. The proposed model can be provided with the data for which assets are connecting to servers. Cybersecurity can protect the services (and remote access into the organization's infrastructure) by creating policies.

5. Results and Discussion

The proposed models are validated by experts in distance learning and IT security. The experts evaluated the models anonymously. The single qualification requirement for the experts was to have at least five years' experience of employment in the studies organization process, including distance learning and/or IT security. The experts were the distance learning process coordinators in their organizations, having a possibility to compare the use of IT infrastructure before and during the pandemic, as they first identified the challenges of the pandemic and had to assure a successful and secure study process.

Experts were invited to evaluate the proposed models of DL infrastructure and security. One of our co-authors is employed as a security manager of a whole university network. So, he practically knows the viability of the proposed models and their technical merits to ensure security of distance learning infrastructure. All the suggestions came from the practical point of view.

To ensure the anonymity of expert assessments, an expert survey was conducted using the anonymous survey tool Google Forms [41].

Because the proposed models are of an applied nature, a method based on Ikoma et al. [42] and the basic validation principles described in the IEEE 1012-2012 standard [43] are applied:

1. Compliance with the requirements of the product;
2. The usability of the product.

Model evaluation criteria and scale are based on the Likert methodology presented by McLeod [44]. The Likert scale was chosen to measure the expert opinions. According to the Likert methodology, the questionnaire presents the question as a statement and several answer options. The options for an answer must show the extent to which the respondent agrees.

Five types of answers were used to assess the fulfillment of the requirements: "fulfilled", "more fulfilled than not", "neither fulfilled nor not", "more unfulfilled than fulfilled", and "unfulfilled". Their corresponding numeric values were 5, 4, 3, 2, and 1, respectively.

To assess the suitability of the model the following options were suggested: "suitable", "more suitable than not", "neither suitable nor unsuitable", "more unsuitable than suitable", and "unsuitable". Their corresponding numeric values were 5, 4, 3, 2, and 1, respectively.

The number of experts was chosen based on assumptions developed in the evaluation theory, which argues that the reliability of the aggregated solutions and the number of experts is linked to the factor determining the effectiveness of the research. Libby and Blashfield [45] have shown that the accuracy of decisions and assessments made by the group, consisting of 10 experts, is not inferior to that of a large expert group. The highest percentage of reliability is obtained with the evaluation of at least 7–10 experts, later the percentage of reliability changes very insignificantly, therefore 15 experts were invited to evaluate the validity of the distance learning models. The qualification of the experts was as follows: 14 of them had a doctoral degree, 1 had a master's degree, 10 of them were researchers in the field of technological sciences (9 of them were in the field of computer science, 1 in the field of mechanics), 5 of them were in the field of educational sciences; 6 of them were professors of universities (5 different universities), 3 of them were secondary school teachers, 5 of them were either higher or secondary school administrators, and 1 was a security expert from the business. Among the experts, eight female and seven male experts were present. Their age varied from 35 to 65 years. The mean age was 52.73 years. The standard deviation of the age was 8.99 years.

To assess the compliance of the models with the requirements, the relevant criteria for infrastructure and security models were formulated following the requirements. They are as follows:

1. The infrastructure model includes the key components of DL and RW infrastructure.
2. The security concept model covers: (1) IT infrastructure security profile, (2) levels of IT security, and (3) secure and reliable DL infrastructure framework.
3. The matrix is the appropriate form for the planning of the implementation of the DL infrastructure framework, which joins the levels of IT security and IT infrastructure security profile.
4. The security concept model includes the protection of personal data.
5. The security concept model includes the management of copyright and licenses for digital content and software in education.

In total, 15 experts were invited to verify the validity of the models and 10 experts filled out anonymous evaluation questionnaires. Table 6 presents the data provided by the experts to assess the compliance of the models with the criteria.

According to the assessment data presented in Table 6, we can observe that five experts out of ten were not critical. They thought that the presented models fully satisfied all the raised requirements and assigned the highest assessment values possible. The least assessment values among all the presented values were assigned to criterion 2, which is used to assess the security concept model. The security concept model is presented in an abstract way. Five experts out of ten thought that such a presentation did not fully reveal what is intended by it. Two experts out of ten were quite critical. They thought that there is room for the improvement of all the models.

Table 6. Compliance of the models with the requirements.

Experts	Criterion No 1	Criterion No 2	Criterion No 3	Criterion No 4	Criterion No 5	Total
1	4	4	4	4	4	20
2	4	4	4	4	4	20
3	4	4	4	5	5	22
4	4	4	5	5	5	23
5	5	4	5	5	5	24
6	5	5	5	5	5	25
7	5	5	5	5	5	25
8	5	5	5	5	5	25
9	5	5	5	5	5	25
10	5	5	5	5	5	25

The anonymous evaluation questionnaires for the usability of the models were completed by 10 experts out of 15 experts. The criteria for the evaluation were as follows:

1. The infrastructure model includes the key components of DL and RW infrastructure.
2. The security concept model covers: (1) IT infrastructure security profile, (2) levels of IT security, and (3) secure and reliable DL infrastructure framework.
3. The matrix is the appropriate form for the planning of the presentation of the implementation of the DL infrastructure framework, which joins the levels of IT security and IT infrastructure security profile.
4. The security concept model must include the protection of personal data.
5. The security concept model must include the management of copyright and licenses for digital content and software in education.

The assessment of the suitability of the models is presented in Table 7.

Table 7. Suitability of the models.

Experts	Criterion No 1	Criterion No 2	Criterion No 3	Criterion No 4	Criterion No 5	Total
1	4	3	4	4	4	19
2	4	4	4	4	4	20
3	5	4	4	5	4	22
4	5	4	5	5	5	24
5	5	4	5	5	5	24
6	5	4	5	5	5	24
7	5	5	5	5	5	25
8	5	5	5	5	5	25
9	5	5	5	5	5	25
10	5	5	5	5	5	25

According to the assessment data presented in Table 7, we can observe that four experts out of ten were not critical. They were fully satisfied with the usability of the presented models and assigned the highest assessment values possible. The least assessment values among all the presented values were assigned to criterion 2 that is used to assess the suitability of the security concept model. The security concept model is presented in a quite abstract way. Six experts out of ten thought that such a presentation did not fully reveal what is intended by it. The first expert was especially critical in assigning the value 3 that means that the model was deemed "neither suitable nor unsuitable". Two experts out of ten were quite critical. They thought that there is room for the improvement of the suitability of all the models.

We can observe in Table 1 presented at the end of the review of related work that just two research works [15,16] are devoted to the consideration of the DL infrastructure and security together. However, both research works [15,16] devoted all attention to the investigation of the DL infrastructure and security was mentioned at a very abstract level without providing any details how to ensure it. Other research works [20,25–27] summarized in Table 1 investigated only security. Different approaches were presented; however, no one approach investigated the technical measures required to implement security, and levels of IT security were not considered.

In this paper, we consider the security of DL infrastructure at the full length. We introduce a security concept model. We provide an IT infrastructure security profile, the levels of IT security, and a secure DL infrastructure framework. We enumerate the technical measures to implement the security concept model. We join the specific technical measures into appropriate activities of the framework. We show the technical measures to implement to achieve a higher security level if the institution is ready for it. We introduce an implementation of GDPR and software licensing into our security concept model. Just a few authors [28,29] discussed the problems of implementation of GDPR in the LMS and presented a possible solution. To the best of our knowledge, no author considered an implementation of GDPR as a component of the security model of the DL infrastructure. To the best of our knowledge, no author considered the problems of software licensing in any context. Consequently, we have presented the security model of the DL infrastructure, which covers all the possible domains related to the security of the DL infrastructure.

6. Conclusions

The proposed models are intended for higher education institutions whose lecturers had to adapt their teaching activities to the pandemic, integrate DL elements into their subject, and solve the new issues related to the security of the DL infrastructure. The proposed model of the DL infrastructure consists of the following components: user devices, network resources, virtualization, computing resources, data warehouses, data resources, software, continuity of activities, security, and network perimeter security.

The proposed model of the security of the DL infrastructure is presented as a hierarchical model consisting of two levels. The first level includes people, organizational processes, and security assurance. The security assurance is divided further (the second level) into the protection of personal data, copyright and licensing of digital content and software, and security of IT infrastructure. To ensure the security of IT infrastructure, an IT infrastructure security profile, the levels of IT security, and a secure DL infrastructure framework are provided. The technical measures to implement the desired security level of the institution were also presented.

The application of the proposed models will ensure security in the DL process for higher education institutions. During the assessment process, the experts decided that the proposed models fully fit the need of DL infrastructure, helping the administration to find the best solution on preparation and implementation of the DL processes. The proposed models of DL infrastructure and security fully meet the raised requirements and are suitable for use.

The first limitation of the study is that all the main contributing authors of the research to the methodology of the presentation have experience in administering university software systems. It is an advantage that the subject is well-known. On the other hand, it is a limitation since such knowledge presents an insider view. It lacks abstractions. To solve this limitation, future research should invite a co-author who would add to the study using abstractions for the representation of the subject. The second limitation of the study is that the validation by the experts was accomplished fully anonymously. It was not possible to collect information on the participating experts that would not disclose the person. For example, whether he or she is a representative of either teaching technologies or IT security, or whether he or she is a professor, administrator, or teacher. Then it would be possible to relate this information with their judgment and to decide where the possible weaknesses of the proposed models were. To solve this limitation, we suggest collecting some information, which would not disclose a person's identification to the participating experts.

The future direction of our research is the development of a model for general data protection regulation and licensing of digital content and software.

Author Contributions: Conceptualization, Š.G. and A.V.; Methodology, V.J. and D.G.; Validation, R.B. (Renata Burbaite) and A.V.; Formal analysis, R.B. (Rita Butkiene) and B.M.; Writing—Original Draft Preparation, Š.G. and D.G.; Writing—Review and Editing, V.J. and D.G.; Visualization, Š.G.; Project administration, A.V.; Funding Acquisition, A.V. and V.J. All authors have read and agreed to the published version of the manuscript.

Funding: This paper is supported in part by European Union's Horizon 2020 research and innovation program under Grant Agreement No. 830892, the project "Strategic programs for advanced research and technology in Europe" (SPARTA) and Lithuanian Research Council financed project "Model of distance working and learning organization and recommendations for extreme and transition period" (EKSTRE) (1 June 2020—31 December 2020). Grant Agreement S-COV-20-20.

Institutional Review Board Statement: Ethical review and approval were waived for this study, as this study involves no more than minimal risk to subjects.

Informed Consent Statement: Informed consent was obtained from all subjects involved in the study.

Data Availability Statement: The data presented in this study are available on request from the corresponding author. The data are not publicly available due to the data restriction policy by the grant provider.

Conflicts of Interest: The authors declare no conflict of interest.

References

1. Dwivedi, Y.K.; Hughes, D.L.; Coombs, C.; Constantiou, I.; Duan, Y.; Edwards, J.S.; Gupta, B.; Lal, B.; Misra, S.; Prashant, P.; et al. Impact of COVID-19 pandemic on information management research and practice: Transforming education, work and life. *Int. J. Inf. Manag.* **2020**, *55*, 102211. [CrossRef]
2. Carolan, C.; Davies, C.L.; Crookes, P.; McGhee, S.; Roxburgh, M. COVID 19: Disruptive impacts and transformative opportunities in undergraduate nurse education. *Nurse Educ. Pract.* **2020**, *46*, 102807. [CrossRef] [PubMed]
3. García-Holgado, A.; García-Peñalvo, F.J. A metamodel proposal for developing learning ecosystems. In *Learning and Collaboration Technologies. Novel Learning Ecosystems. Proceedings of the 4th International Conference, LCT 2017, Held as Part of HCI International 2017, Vancouver, BC, Canada, 9–14 July 2017, Proceedings, Part I*; Zaphiris, P., Ioannou, A., Eds.; Springer International Publishing: Cham, Switzerland, 2017; pp. 100–109.
4. García-Morales, V.J.; Garrido-Moreno, A.; Martín-Rojas, R. The Transformation of Higher Education after the COVID Disruption: Emerging Challenges in an Online Learning Scenario. *Front. Psychol.* **2021**, *12*, 616059. [CrossRef]
5. Alhabeeb, A.; Rowley, J. E-learning critical success factors: Comparing perspectives from academic staff and students. *Comput. Educ.* **2018**, *127*, 1–12. [CrossRef]
6. Roddy, C.; Amiet, D.; Chung, J.; Holt, C.; Shaw, L.; McKenzie, S.; Garivaldis, F.; Lodge, J.M.; Mundy, M.E. Applying Best Practice Online Learning, Teaching, and Support to Intensive Online Environments: An Integrative Review. *Front. Educ.* **2017**, *2*, 59. [CrossRef]
7. Ayebi-Arthur, K. E-learning, resilience and change in higher education: Helping a university cope after a natural disaster. *e-Learn. Digit. Media* **2017**, *14*, 259–274. [CrossRef]
8. Dhawan, S. Online Learning: A Panacea in the Time of COVID-19 Crisis. *J. Educ. Technol. Syst.* **2020**, *49*, 5–22. [CrossRef]
9. Huang, R.H.; Liu, D.J.; Tlili, A.; Yang, J.F.; Wang, H.H.; Zhang, M.; Lu, H.; Gao, B.; Cai, Z.; Liu, M.; et al. *Handbook on Facilitating Flexible Learning during Educational Disruption: The Chinese Experience in Maintaining Undisrupted Learning in COVID-19 Outbreak*; Smart Learning Institute of Beijing Normal University: Beijing, China, 2020; Available online: https://iite.unesco.org/wp-content/uploads/2020/03/Handbook-on-Facilitating-Flexible-Learning-in-COVID-19-Outbreak-SLIBNU-V1.2-20200315.pdf (accessed on 13 September 2021).
10. Carroll, N.; Conboy, K. Normalising the "new normal": Changing tech-driven work practices under pandemic time pressure. *Int. J. Inf. Manag.* **2020**, *55*, 102186. [CrossRef]
11. Tyagi, N.; Verma, S. Culturally Responsive Teaching: A Suggestive Pedagogical Framework. In *Handbook of Research on Social Justice and Equity in Education*; IGI Global: Noida, Uttar Pradesh, India, 2022; pp. 312–331.
12. Gaivéo, J.M. Security of ICTs Supporting Healthcare Activities. In *Standards and Standardization: Concepts, Methodologies, Tools, and Applications*; IGI Global: Setubal, Portugal, 2015; pp. 192–212.
13. Ergüzen, A.; Erdal, E.; Ünver, M.; Özcan, A. Improving Technological Infrastructure of Distance Education through Trustworthy Platform-Independent Virtual Software Application Pools. *Appl. Sci.* **2021**, *11*, 1214. [CrossRef]

14. Moore, R.L.; Fodrey, B.P. Distance Education and Technology Infrastructure: Strategies and Opportunities. In *Leading and Managing e-Learning*; Piña, A., Lowell, V., Harris, B., Eds.; Educational Communications and Technology: Issues and Innovations; Springer: Cham, Switzerland, 2018; pp. 87–100. [CrossRef]
15. Thomas, S.E. Digital Infrastructure. Available online: https://diiii.net/di2, (accessed on 15 February 2022).
16. García-Peñalvo, F.J. Avoiding the Dark Side of Digital Transformation in Teaching. An Institutional Reference Framework for eLearning in Higher Education. *Sustainability* **2021**, *13*, 2023. [CrossRef]
17. EUR-Lex. Available online: https://eur-lex.europa.eu/legal-content/EN/TXT/PDF/?uri=CELEX:32016R0679&from=EN (accessed on 27 April 2021).
18. Arora, M.; Goyal, L.M.; Chintalapudi, N.; Mittal, M. Factors affecting digital education during COVID-19: A statistical modeling approach. In Proceedings of the 2020 5th International Conference on Computing, Communication and Security (ICCCS), Patna, India, 14–16 October 2020; pp. 1–5.
19. Favalea, T.; Soroa, F.; Trevisana, M.; Dragob, I.; Melliaa, M. Campus traffic and e-Learning during COVID-19 pandemic. *Comput. Netw.* **2020**, *176*, 107290. [CrossRef]
20. Bhatia, M.; Maitra, J.K. E-learning Platforms Security Issues and Vulnerability Analysis. In Proceedings of the 2018 International Conference on Computational and Characterization Techniques in Engineering & Sciences (CCTES), Lucknow, India, 14–15 September 2018; pp. 276–285.
21. De Oliveira, P.C.; de Almeida Cunha, C.J.C.; Nakayama, M.K. Learning Management Systems (LMS) and e-learning management: An integrative review and research agenda. *J. Inf. Syst. Technol. Manag.* **2016**, *13*, 157–180. [CrossRef]
22. Husain, T.; Budiyantara, A. Analysis of Control Security and Privacy Based on e-Learning Users. *SAR J.* **2020**, *3*, 51–58.
23. Weil, T.; Murugesan, S. IT Risk and Resilience—Cybersecurity Response to COVID-19. *IT Prof.* **2020**, *22*, 4–10. [CrossRef]
24. Navid Ali, K.; Sarfraz Nawaz, B.; Noor, Z. *Ten Deadly Cyber Security Threats Amid COVID-19 Pandemic*; IEEE: Piscataway, NJ, USA, 2020. [CrossRef]
25. Ali, R.; Zafar, H. A Security and Privacy Framework for e-Learning. *Int. J. e-Learn. Secur.* **2017**, *7*, 556–566. [CrossRef]
26. Ran, J.; Hou, K.; Li, K.; Dai, N. A High Security Distance Education Platform Infrastructure Based on Private Cloud. *Int. J. Emerg. Technol. Learn.* **2018**, *13*, 42–54. [CrossRef]
27. Nita, S.L.; Mihailescu, M.I. Proposing a secure framework for eLearning platforms using attribute based encryption. In Proceedings of the 13th International Scientific Conference "eLearning and Software for Education", Bucharest, Romania, 27–28 April 2017; Volume 2, pp. 114–119. [CrossRef]
28. Amo, D.; Alier, M.; García-Peñalvo, F.J.; Fonseca, D.; Casany, M.J. GDPR Security and Confidentiality compliance in LMS' a problem analysis and engineering solution proposal. In Proceedings of the Seventh International Conference on Technological Ecosystems for Enhancing Multiculturality, Leon, Spain, 16–18 October 2019; pp. 253–259. [CrossRef]
29. Amo, D.; Alier, M.; García-Peñalvo, F.J.; Fonseca, D.; Casañ, M.J. Protected Users: A Moodle Plugin To Improve Confidentiality and Privacy Support through User Aliases. *Sustainability* **2020**, *12*, 2548. [CrossRef]
30. Caviglione, L.; Coccoli, M. A Holistic Model for Security of Learning Applications in Smart Cities. *J. e-Learn. Knowl. Soc.* **2020**, *16*, 1–10.
31. Mahmoud, A.M.M. An agent-based framework for providing security in a cloud-based E-learning system. *Int. J. Adv. Appl. Sci.* **2020**, *7*, 19–24. [CrossRef]
32. Alexei, A. Cyber Security Threat Analysis in Higher Education Institutions as a Result of Distance Learning. *Int. J. Sci. Technol. Res.* **2021**, *10*, 128–133.
33. Jusas, V.; Butkiene, R.; Venčkauskas, A.; Burbaite, R.; Gudoniene, D. Models for Administration to Ensure the Successful Transition to Distance Learning during the Pandemic. *Sustainability* **2021**, *13*, 4751. [CrossRef]
34. ISO/IEC 27001. Information Security Management. Available online: https://www.iso.org/isoiec-27001-information-security.html (accessed on 27 April 2021).
35. COBIT. Available online: https://www.isaca.org/resources/cobit (accessed on 27 April 2021).
36. CVE. Available online: https://cve.mitre.org (accessed on 27 April 2021).
37. Principles of Lean. Available online: https://www.lean.org/WhatsLean/Principles.cfm (accessed on 27 April 2021).
38. Pasiruošimas Taikyti Bendrąjį Duomenų Apsaugos Reglamentą (ES) 2016/679 (Preparation for the Application of the General Data Protection Regulation (EU) 2016/679). Available online: https://vdai.lrv.lt/uploads/vdai/documents/files/12zingsnius_BDAR_20170525.pdf (accessed on 15 September 2021).
39. Information Commissioner's Offise (UK). Preparing for the General Data Protection Regulation (GDPR). 12 Steps to Take Now. Available online: https://ico.org.uk/media/1624219/preparing-for-the-gdpr-12-steps.pdf (accessed on 15 September 2021).
40. About the Licenses. Available online: https://creativecommons.org/licenses/ (accessed on 27 April 2021).
41. Google Forms. Available online: https://workspace.google.com/products/forms/ (accessed on 27 April 2021).
42. Ikoma, M.; Ooshima, M.; Tanida, T.; Oba, M.; Sakai, S. Using a validation model to measure the agility of software development in a large software development organization. In Proceedings of the 2009 31st International Conference on Software Engineering -Companion Volume, Vancouver, BC, Canada, 16–24 May 2009; pp. 91–100. Available online: http://ieeexplore.ieee.org/document/5070967/ (accessed on 27 April 2021).

43. IEEE Standard for System and Software Verification and Validation. *IEEE Std 1012–2012 (Revision of IEEE Std 1012-2004)*; IEEE: Piscataway, NJ, USA, 2012; pp. 1–223. Available online: https://ieeexplore.ieee.org/document/6204026 (accessed on 27 April 2021).
44. McLeod, S.A.; Likert Scale Definition, Examples and Analysis. Simply Psychology 2019. Available online: https://www.simplypsychology.org/likert-scale.html (accessed on 27 April 2021).
45. Libby, R.; Blashfield, R.K. Performance of a composite as a function of the number of judges. *Organ. Behav. Hum. Perform.* **1978**, *21*, 121–129. [CrossRef]

Article

Effect of Adding Emotion Recognition to Film Teaching—Impact of Emotion Feedback on Learning through Puzzle Films

Shang-Chin Tsai * and Hao-Chiang Koong Lin

Department of Information and Learning Technology, National University of Tainan, Tainan City 70005, Taiwan; koong@gm2.nutn.edu.tw
* Correspondence: maneytsai@gmail.com

Abstract: In this study, the scientific puzzle film, "Story of the Comet", is taken as a case to implement scientific teaching to guide students to find correct answers, through which it can train their learning and judging abilities. The students in the experimental group received the scientific teaching guiding system of the puzzle film "Story of the Comet" with a facial emotion recognition system to recognize the emotional reaction of the subjects at the moment. According to their facial expressions of "disgust", "sadness", or "joy" appearing in the moment, the system presented differently captioned positive encouragement cards particularly designed for four different levels, for when the subjects answered the questions incorrectly at different levels and their emotions were detected at the same time. Furthermore, the positive encouragement cards encouraged the subjects to complete the puzzle film learning process. The subjects were students in the higher grades of Grade 5 and Grade 6 in elementary school. A total of 130 students participated in this experiment and were randomly divided into two groups. Both the control group (i.e., the group without emotion recognition) and the experiment group (i.e., the group with emotion recognition) received a before-watching test of learning effectiveness. After implementing the scientific teaching of the puzzle film "Story of the Comet", both the control group and the experimental group also received an after-watching test of learning effectiveness. Finally, the subjects filled out a "learning satisfaction" questionnaire, "system availability" questionnaire, and "system satisfaction" questionnaire. The analysis of the results of the two groups' tests and questionnaires: a comparative analysis of learning effectiveness indicates that there is a statistically significant difference between the choice answers of the two groups after the interactive teaching; for the experimental group, the average correct answers in the after-watching test was 5.86, which is 2.48 more than the before-watching test; that of the control group was 4.74, which is 1.47 more than the before -watching test. For comparative analysis of questionnaires for "learning satisfaction" and "system satisfaction", the statistical data analysis indicates that the experimental group was more satisfied than the control group.

Keywords: emotion recognition; puzzle film; learning satisfaction; emotion feedback; learning effectiveness

Citation: Tsai, S.-C.; Lin, H.-C.K. Effect of Adding Emotion Recognition to Film Teaching—Impact of Emotion Feedback on Learning through Puzzle Films. *Sustainability* **2021**, *13*, 11107. https://doi.org/10.3390/su131911107

Academic Editor: Carlos Salavera

Received: 20 August 2021
Accepted: 4 October 2021
Published: 8 October 2021

Publisher's Note: MDPI stays neutral with regard to jurisdictional claims in published maps and institutional affiliations.

Copyright: © 2021 by the authors. Licensee MDPI, Basel, Switzerland. This article is an open access article distributed under the terms and conditions of the Creative Commons Attribution (CC BY) license (https://creativecommons.org/licenses/by/4.0/).

1. Introduction

In this era, in public and private universities in Taiwan, despite teachers' great flow of speech on the podium, students in their seats usually mind their own business, chatting, sleeping, eating bento, playing mobile phones and video games, and watching movies; few students listen to teachers attentively [1]. The inattention of students at different levels, including elementary, junior high, and senior high schools, should not vary much. According to the concentration survey of Parenting magazine, more than 90% of teachers from elementary and middle schools believe that students do not concentrate enough, while "cannot understand contents in class", "teaching methods cannot attract students", and "teaching contents are too simple, which they have learned in continuation class and daycare centers" are the three major reasons for their inattention [2]. Therefore, learning effectiveness is very poor. How to raise students' interest in learning and guide them to study attentively is an important topic of the education circle. As positive emotion improves students' learning interest and motivation [3], by using the function of emotion detection and adding emotional feedback through encouragement cards, this study explored whether the addition of timely encouragement cards can improve the learning effectiveness of students.

Research Question

1. Explore the relationship between emotional feedback and learning effectiveness when watching films with emotion detection added for learning.
2. Explore the relationship between emotion detection and learning satisfaction when using film teaching.
3. Explore the relationship between the availability of the teaching system and emotion detection when using film teaching.
4. Explore the relationship between the satisfaction of the teaching system and emotion detection when using film teaching.

2. Literature Review

With the rapid development of science and technology and the innovation of teaching aids, the narrative teaching method in the classroom is no longer favored by students, and the visualization of an image is better than purely text description in cognition [4,5]; in the following four teaching methods—(1) digital learning by an interactive film; (2) digital learning by a non-interactive film; (3) digital learning without using film; (4) traditional teaching in class—comparing learning achievements based on the four different learning environments and learning equipment, results confirmed that students viewing interactive films in a digital learning environment achieved significantly better learning results and higher satisfaction [6]. With both sound and light effects, films are an excellent instrument to attract students' attention. The audio–visual experience of film can improve students' awareness and encourage critical thinking skills [7]. On the other hand, in addition to the function of an oral account, films allow the teacher to replay and pause, which makes them a good medium to promote learning [8–10]. Learning effectiveness is an indicator for judging students' learning outcomes. The purpose of evaluating effectiveness is to let students become aware of their own learning situation and to serve as a basis for teachers to improve teaching and students to improve learning. [11] Learning effectiveness is a measure of the performance indicators or a behavior change after a student participates in a learning activity [11,12]. Generally, we can use two data to measure the effect of learning. The first is academic achievement, such as semester grade or test score [13,14], and the second is learning satisfaction [15–17]. Correspondingly, Huang et al. [18], they also use academic achievement and learning satisfaction as the two criteria to measure the learning effect of students. Learning satisfaction can be regarded as the learner's feelings about learning activities [19,20], or the learner's attitude [19] or sense of pleasure [21]. Piccoli et al. [17] and Maki et al. [16] believe that learning satisfaction expresses learners' satisfaction with the learning process and learning results. Therefore, learning satisfaction is a very suitable criterion for evaluating learners' satisfaction with classroom learning. As a result, we can further understand the learning effect of students based on academic achievement and learning satisfaction [22].

With the rapid changes of the times, it is more important to use effective ways to enable learners to quickly absorb the information they have learned in this fast-developing environment. Because of this, digital learning has stood out from the digitization of traditional methods. So far, it has evolved from inefficient computer-aided teaching to intelligent guidance learning through intelligent classrooms and mobile devices (digital learning by mobile equipment) [23]. In addition, studies found that observation and recognition of the learners' emotional status enable teachers to adopt actions of significant impact on teaching quality and execution to a large extent and interact with students in more humanized ways. Therefore, an intelligent teaching system should consider relations among emotions, perceptions, and behaviors in the learning environment [24]. It is very important to explore students' emotions, as there are inextricably connections between emotion and perception, which facilitates effective learning. The study also found that perception plays a role in emotion generation. Positive emotions can actually improve students' learning interest and motivation [3]. Therefore, an emotion recognition system can help teachers interact fully and accurately so as to encourage students to learn actively. In this way, teachers will have the opportunity to monitor and propose appropriate expression models, especially when dealing with students' negative emotions. Therefore, "effective emotion detection" allows the design of modular and reusable activities suitable for students' learning styles, which can provide stronger and powerful educational activity planning [25]. According to the studies of Elias and Weissberg [26]; and Payton, Wardlaw, Graczyk, Bloody, Trompsett, and Weissberg [27], if children can use emotional intelligence in class, they can achieve better results in tests or other forms of academic performance. In addition, the study finds the relationship between emotional factors and students' academic performance, which believes that students with healthy emotions have the opportunity to succeed in college, and one of the basic mechanisms of learning is students' active participation. To be more exact, when a student begins to actually engage in the learning process, the student will usually be more active rather than assume passivity or total acceptance. In view of this, how to help students speed up their learning and obtain better learning results have always been the research topic of many researchers who are concerned about this issue.

Film teaching materials integrate various media materials such as images, pictures, music, sounds, and words to present information in an appropriate way and appearance. Therefore, it is normal to use films as a teaching aid in school teaching or in the daily work of industry, commerce, and society. As a cognitive theory, dual coding theory was proposed by Allan Paivio of the University of Western Ontario in 1971. Paivio believed that the "formation of imagery is beneficial to learning". According to Paivio, people can use "verbal association" and "visual imagery" to further remember what they have learned [28]. Dual coding theory proposes that both visual information and verbal information are the way to express information, which is different in their processing methods. They are processed in different blocks of the brain, and information processed by each channel creates its own unique representation. When learning information, if people use visual code and verbal code at the same time, that is, generate a relevant image in visual code and link it with a verbal code, such an ability to use the two different codes improves the chances of remembering the item [29]. In addition, some people like to receive information through visual modes such as charts and illustrations, while others like to obtain information by reading or listening to verbal information; Richardson [30] called the former a "visualizer", while the latter is a "verbalizer". Through the study, Richardson found that there are obvious differences between visualizers and verbalizers in many characteristics; visualizers tend to think specifically, while verbalizers tend to think with more abstract symbols; visualizers like to think with physical images or mental images. Their thinking mode is subjective and self-oriented, while the thinking mode of verbalizers is objective and task-oriented.

According to the Cognitive Theory of Multimedia Learning of Mayer [31–33], there are two separate channels (auditory and visual) for processing information; there is limited channel capacity; and learning is an active process of filtering, selecting, organizing, and integrating information. Mayer points out that "people learn more from words and pictures" "rather than just words" [34,35]. However, only adding words to pictures is not an effective way to achieve this goal. The purpose of multimedia learning is to make teaching media according to people's way of thinking. This is the basis of Mayer's cognitive theory of multimedia learning. When it comes to multimedia learning, the theory puts forward three main assumptions:

1. There are two separate channels (auditory and visual) for processing information (sometimes referred to as Dual-Coding theory).
2. Each channel has a limited (finite) capacity, similar to Sweller's notion of Cognitive Load. [36,37]
3. Learning is an active process of filtering, selecting, organizing, and integrating information based upon prior knowledge. Humans can only process a finite amount of information in a channel at a time, and they make sense of incoming information by actively creating mental representations.

Image, sound, action, and plots are the four characteristics of films. Combining these characteristics, it becomes a powerful force, which is far more than the media effect of pure text or ordinary text plus pictures. The advantage of film is that it has sound and light effects at the same time, giving viewers extreme sensory stimulation. Therefore, it is undeniable that film itself has a unique charm in attracting learners' attention. Furthermore, due to the development of digital audio–visual technology and the population of networks, digital audio–visual information is everywhere in our daily life. Many teachers have used film as an auxiliary tool for teaching in school classes, but the format of films is mostly in a one-way communication mode, that is, relying on the authors' intention to produce and play the content of the film, and the audience is expected to watch and accept the content. However, in the digital era, the one-way communication mode cannot meet the information audio–visual needs of the audiences. Responding to this trend, producers integrate new media materials and new technology and produce two-way films with interactive characteristics, through which users can participate and even dominate the content. In recent years, interactive films have been widely used in advertising, marketing, education, publicity, navigation, and other aspects of daily life. Interactive films have become an efficient instrument in education and communication.

3. Research Design and Method

3.1. Research Design

In this study, the interactive puzzle film "Story of the Comet" (Halley's Comet) is provided to students to watch (Figure 1); the film is modeled after puzzle-solving in a scientific teaching guidance system to study the learning process and effectiveness of students and further confirm whether this teaching mode can improve teaching effectiveness of teachers and learning effectiveness of students. In the experiment, when the emotion recognition system was added—through which doubtful students were encouraged with emotion-related feedback—to inspect the impact of emotion-related feedback on the learning process of students.

Figure 1. Student participating in this experiment watching "The Comet's Story" puzzle film.

The learning effectiveness block was divided into two groups. One group was the experimental group, and the other group was the control group. In both the experimental group and control group, the students were asked to complete the first knowledge test on Halley's Comet discovery process (Figure 2). The test had 10 true or false questions and 10 multiple-choice questions, with 5 points for each question, totaling 100 points. Then, the students in the experimental group and control group watched the interactive puzzle film "Story of the Comet" and chose their answers for four levels according to the guidance in the interactive puzzle film (Figure 3). When the students of the experimental group watched the interactive puzzle film, facial emotion detection and recognition systems were added (Figure 4). If emotions of disgust, sadness, or joy were detected when choosing answers while watching the interactive puzzle film "Story of the Comet", the corresponding encouragement card of emotion feedback was given at different levels (Figures 5–9). When watching the interactive puzzle film, students in the control group the facial emotion detection and recognition systems were not used (Figure 10); in other words, there was no encouraging emotional feedback; the content of the interactive puzzle film "Story of the Comet" was entirely about the story of discovering Halley's Comet. The 16 short films were organized into four levels, including the historical story of Halley's Comet and fabricated stories, and students were required to choose answers. After completing the interactive puzzle film, the second test on the discovery process of Halley's Comet was immediately conducted on students in the experimental group and control group. The question content and question numbers were completely the same as the first test, including 10 true or false questions and 10 multiple-choice questions, with each question valuing 5 points, totaling 100 points. After completing the interactive puzzle film and the second test, the test results were compared with those of the first test to check learning effectiveness. In addition, the students were asked to fill the questionnaire on system availability, system satisfaction, and learning satisfaction (Figure 2). Before the test, Excel was employed to generate a random number table to decide whether the students who participated in the test before and after belonged to the experimental group to join the emotional detection or to the control group without adding emotional detection.

Figure 2. Student participating in this experiment—filling out the questionnaire.

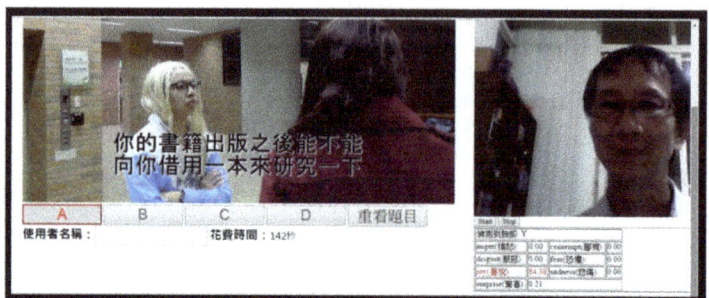

Figure 3. Puzzle film, "The Comet's Story", combined with emotion detection system.

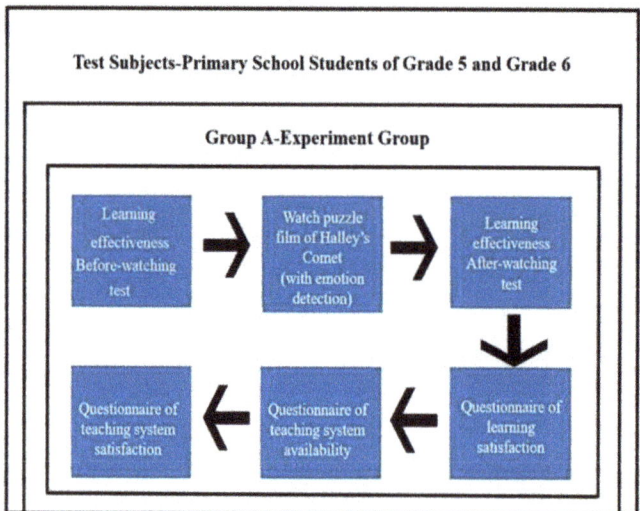

Figure 4. Research framework—experimental group.

Figure 5. Title insert 1: Go! Please work hard.

Figure 6. Title insert 2: Go, there are three levels ahead.

Figure 7. Title insert 3: Go, only two levels left.

Figure 8. Title insert 4: Go, it is almost finished.

Figure 9. Title insert 5: Now in a happy mood. Go! Let us finish it!

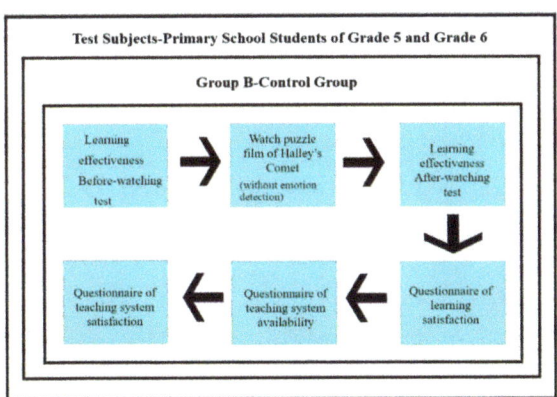

Figure 10. Research framework—control group.

The script of the film is in Appendix A.
The 5 captioned encouragement cards (Figures 5–9) are as follows:
Thus, this study proposed the following hypotheses.

3.2. Research Hypothesis

Hypothesis 1 (H1). *When using film with emotion detection for learning, emotional feedback will have a positive impact on learning effectiveness.*

Hypothesis 2 (H2). *The addition of emotion detection when using film teaching will have a positive impact on learning satisfaction.*

Hypothesis 3 (H3). *The availability of the teaching system when using film teaching will be positively impacted by the addition of emotion detection.*

Hypothesis 4 (H4). *The satisfaction of the teaching system when using film teaching will be positively impacted by the addition of emotion detection.*

3.3. Research Method

This study shot a total of four films to tell the "Story of the Comet" (Halley's Comet) and designed a teaching guidance system. By combining the films with the teaching guidance system and through emotion detection and emotion feedback, this teaching guidance system was installed in private laptops of the researcher, and the researcher took the paper questionnaires and laptops to elementary schools in different cities to conduct the experiment one school after another. The researcher made a parental consent form and then asked the fifth- and sixth-grade class teachers to distribute it to their students. The students took the forms home and obtained consent signed by their parents. The students with parental consent were the samples in this study. The elementary schools participating in this research provided a classroom with no classes as an experimental classroom. The researcher used an experimental system installed on a notebook computer to process. The class teacher assigned one student to the experimental classroom for the experiment at a time. This student filled out test paper on the discovery process of Halley's Comet for the first time and then used the notebook computer to watch puzzle film of Halley's Comet. After the puzzle film of Halley's Comet test was over, the student filled out the test paper on the discovery process of Halley's Comet for the second time. Furthermore, after filling out some other paper questionnaires at the same time, the student completed the experiment and went back to invite the next student to the experimental classroom to continue the experiment.

The four films are coded with One, Two, Three, and Four. The first film is a story about Halley and Newton, the second film is about Halley and Hooke, the third film is about Halley and Wren, and the fourth film is about Halley and Flamsteed. Except for the first film, the other three films are fabricated. Every film has four plots to form a complete film plot; therefore, the first film is about Halley and Newton, which is made up of four short plots of D, F, I, and O; the second film is about Halley and Hooke, which is made up of four short plots of C, H, J, and M; the third film is about Halley and Wren, which is made up of four short plots of B, E, K, and P; and the fourth film is about Halley and Flamsteed, which is made up of four short plots of A, G, L, and N. There are 16 short films in total, in which D, F, I, O is the right sequence, and the rest—C, H, J, M; B, E, K, P; A, G, L, N, etc.—are fabricated plots, and the 16 short films are compiled in the following mode:

First-level film: Answer (A). Flamsteed (1); Answer (B). Wren (1); Answer (C). Hooke (1); Answer (D). Newton (1).
Second-level film: Answer (E). Wren (2); Answer (F). Newton (2); Answer (G). Flamsteed (2); Answer (H). Hooke (2).
Third-level film: Answer (I). Newton (3); Answer (J). Hooke (3); Answer (K). Wren (3); Answer (L). Flamsteed (3).
Fourth-level film: Answer (M). Hooke (4); Answer (N). Flamsteed (4); Answer (O). Newton (4); Answer (P). Wren (4).

Before the first level, there was an introduction of the film's characters in words. Then, before every level, there was a part of words showing the choices of the answers, and there was a caption of plot introduction before each plot was performed by an actual person, at the beginning of which the options were shown, such as A, B, and C; then, the plot was performed by actual persons. After watching the performance of the four answers by actual persons, there was a captioned film that asked the subjects to choose the correct answer from the four options. If the subject chose the correct answer, the caption guided the subject to go on to the next level of the film; if the wrong answer was chosen, the caption told the subject to choose another film plot of the level, and the film plot was returned to the beginning page. In this way, until choosing the correct plot answers for the four levels, the subject completed the levels in sequence.

The film content sequence of the first level was as follows:

(Captioned film) Based on the story of the first level, there are four different plots A, B, C, and D. Please choose the right one.

(Captioned film) A: Halley and Flamsteed were both British astronomers and celebrities at that time. Halley paid a special visit to Flamsteed to look for the comet data he was studying.

The actors performed the above plot film.

(Captioned film) B: Halley and Wren were both British astronomers and good friends; Halley paid a special visit to Wren to look for the comet data he was studying.

The actors performed the above plot film.

(Captioned film) C: Halley, Hooke, and Wren were friends. One day, the friends met to chat. Halley asked Hooke for the calculation formula in order to look for the comet data he was studying.

The actors performed the above plot film.

(Captioned film) D: Active Halley and lonely Newton were good friends in spite of their difference in age. Halley always had doubts about the laws of planetary motion and could not find the answer.

The actors performed the above plot film.

(Captioned film) Please choose the correct answer from A, B, C, and D.

The film content order of the second level is as follows:

(Captioned film) There are E, F, G, and H, totaling four different plots in the second level. Please choose the right one.

(Captioned film) E: Three months later, Wren published a book on astronomy and astrology—*On the Revolutions of Heavenly Spheres*. One day, Halley went to Wren's house and asked for books *On the Revolutions of Heavenly Spheres*.

The actors performed the above plot film.

(Captioned film) F: In August 1684, Halley paid a special visit to Newton in Oxford to look for the comet data he was studying and borrowed the formula data of the law of planetary motion from Newton.

The actors performed the above plot film.

(Captioned film) G: Two months later, Flamsteed published a book on astronomy and astrology — *The Origins of Astrology*. One day, Halley went to Flamsteed's house and wanted to borrow the book, *The Origins of Astrology*.

The actors performed the above plot film.

(Captioned film) H: A few days later, Halley went to Hooke's house. Hooke lent the calculation formula of planetary orbit to Halley.

The actors performed the above plot film.

(Captioned film) Please choose the right answer from E, F, G, and H.

The film content order of the third level is as follows: (Captioned film) There are I, J, K, and L, totaling four different plots in the third level. Please choose the right one.

(Captioned film) I: Based on the hypothesis mentioned in *The Principia: Mathematical Principles of Natural Philosophy* of Newton, Halley analyzed all the comet observation records collected and found the movement law of a certain comet.

The actors performed the above plot film.

(Captioned film) J: After studying the data of the *Scientific Principles of Nature* written by Hooke for some time, Halley found the movement law of a certain comet.

The actors performed the above plot film.

(Captioned film) K: After studying data of *On the Revolutions of Heavenly Spheres* written by Wren for some time, Halley found the movement law of a certain comet.

The actors performed the above plot film.

(Captioned film) L: After studying data of *The Origins of Astrology* written by Flamsteed for some time, Halley found the movement law of a certain comet.

The actors performed the above plot film.

(Captioned film) Please choose the right answer from I, J, K, and L.

The film content order of the fourth level is as follows: (Captioned film) There are M, N, O, and P, totaling four different plots in the fourth level. Please choose the right one.

(Captioned film) M: Two years later, on Christmas eve, Hooke and Halley sat in a chair outside the café. Halley found that the comet he had speculated using Hooke's formula in the sky returned.

The actors performed the above plot film.

(Captioned film) N: Three years later, one night in September, Halley sat in front of his house to enjoy the cool. He found in the sky that the comet he had speculated by using the Flamsteed formula had returned.

The actors performed the above plot film.

(Captioned film) O: On December 25, 1758, this comet was observed by a German farmer and amateur astronomer, Johann Georg Palitzsch. However, Halley died in 1742 and failed to see the return of this comet.

The actors performed the above plot film.

(Captioned film) P: Seven years later, one night in March, Mary, Halley's wife, sat in front of her house to enjoy the cool. She found in the sky that the comet Halley had speculated by using the Wren formula had returned.

The actors performed the above plot film.

(Captioned film) Please choose the right answer from M, N, O, and P.

In the first level, after watching films of the four answers, when the subjects chose the wrong answer, a 10-s caption of "Sorry, you chose the wrong answer, please choose again." would appear, and the system would start to detect facial emotions. When disgust or sadness emotions were detected, the 01 captioned encouragement card would appear for 2 s, then return to the current page. For the wrong answer, when a joy expression was detected, the 05 captioned encouragement card would appear for 2 s and return to the current page. At the same level, if the wrong answers were chosen multiple times or joy expression was detected, the captioned encouragement card would appear under the same rule. The rules were the same for the second, third, and fourth levels. In the first, second, and third levels, when the subjects chose the right answer, the system would display the caption of "Congratulations! Your answer is right. Please go on to the next level." and the system would automatically be guided to the next level. In the fourth level, if the subjects chose the right answer, the system would display the caption of "Congratulations! Your answer is right, and all levels have been finished. The test is completed." The test time of interactive puzzle film "Story of the Comet" was 60 minutes; the sample was regarded as invalid if this time limit was exceeded.

Characters and Script Are Introduced as Follows

Characters in "Story of the Comet":

1. Edmond Halley (1656–1742): A British astronomer for Greenwich Observatory.
2. Isaac Newton (1643–1727): A British physicist, mathematician, astronomer, natural philosopher, and alchemist. In 1687, he released *The Principia: Mathematical Principles of Natural Philosophy*. The universal gravitation and three laws of motion were expounded, which laid the foundation of mechanics and astronomy in the next three centuries.
3. Robert Hooke (1635–1703): A British naturalist, inventor, physicist, machinist, and architect. In terms of physical research, he put forward the basic law describing material elasticity—Hooke's law. In terms of mechanical manufacturing, he designed and manufactured vacuum pumps, microscopes, and telescopes and wrote his own observations with a microscope in his book *Micrographia*. The English word "cell"

was named by him. Hooke also made important contributions to urban design and architecture, but he was barely known after his death due to a debate with Newton.
4. Christopher Wren (1632–1723): A British astronomer, architect, academician of The Royal Society, President of The Royal Society, and junior knight.
5. Mary Stuart: Wife of Halley, who married Edmond Halley in 1682 and died in 1736.
6. Johann Georg Palitzsch: A farmer and amateur astronomer in Germany in the eighteenth century.
7. John Flamsteed: The first royal astronomer in Britain in the seventeenth century. His successor was Edmond Halley. He recorded more than 3000 stars. The famous Flamsteed naming method was invented by John Flamsteed.

4. Research Results

Experimental Results: There were 130 subjects in this test and questionnaire, in which there were 125 valid samples and 5 invalid samples; the valid rate of the questionnaire was 96.15%. There were 63 valid subjects in the group with emotion recognition and 62 valid subjects in the group without emotion recognition.

1. For comparative analysis of learning satisfaction, a p-value of $0.000 < 0.05$ indicates that there is a significant difference between the learning satisfaction average of the two groups; the learning satisfaction average of the group with emotion recognition was 4.13, and that of the group without emotion recognition was 3.69. The statistical analysis shows that the group with emotion recognition was higher in learning satisfaction than the group without emotion recognition.
2. In the comparative analysis of teaching system availability, there was no significant difference between the two groups.
3. In the comparative analysis of teaching system satisfaction, with a p-value of $0.00 < 0.05$, there was a significant difference between the teaching system satisfaction of the two groups; the teaching system satisfaction average of the group with emotion recognition was 4.26, and that of the group without emotion recognition was 3.46. The statistical analysis shows that the group with emotion recognition was higher than the group without emotion recognition in terms of teaching system satisfaction.

Research Findings:

1. According to the test results before and after watching the puzzle film, results show that among the subjects, the group with emotion recognition and receiving encouragement words performed better than the group without emotion recognition and no encouraging words. The appearance of encouragement cards facilitated better learning performance.
2. According to results of the questionnaire, for comparative analysis of learning satisfaction and comparative analysis of teaching system satisfaction, the two analyses indicated that the learning satisfaction of the group with emotion recognition was higher than that of the group without emotion recognition; the increase of perception accessibility also enhanced the entertainment perception, which has a direct impact on the use intention of students and indirectly affects students' use intention.
3. Learning through multimedia aims to make teaching media according to people's thinking modes from an overall perspective. In response to this trend, we should integrate various materials and novel technologies, arrange appropriate content, determine teaching strategies based on the learning status of students, and make two-way interactive films. An interactive film can design changing story trends, increase diversified learning pathways, and provide interesting, positive, encouraging interaction when questions are answered. With adaptive learning strategies and a good learning mood, it helps to improve students' interest in watching the film.

4.1. Implementation and Collection of Test and Questionnaire

The survey subjects of this testing and questionnaire, who were tested and questioned on-site and whose answers were collected, totaled 130 cases. During the implementation of the 130 student samples in the puzzle film, all students finished the task in one hour (60 minutes). There were 125 valid test and questionnaire samples and 5 invalid test and questionnaire samples (A21, A57, B3, B8, B26), so the valid rate of the questionnaire was 96.15%.

4.2. Analysis of Basic Data

The valid questionnaires indicated that there are a total of 125 valid respondents, including 63 in the group with emotion recognition and 62 in the group without emotion recognition.

Gender and gender distribution (Table 1): there are 64 females (51.2%) and 61 males (48.8%), and there are 2.4% more females. In the group with emotion recognition, there are 11.2% more females; in the group without emotion recognition, there are 6.4% more males.

Table 1. Gender, grade, and age distribution of the two groups.

Group	Group with Emotion Recognition				Group without Emotion Recognition				Total			
Gender	Female		Male		Female		Male		Female		Male	
No.	35		28		29		33		64		61	
%	55.6		44.4		46.8		53.2		51.2		48.8	
grade	Grade 5		Grade 6		Grade 5		Grade 6		Grade 5		Grade 6	
No.	28		35		23		39		51		74	
%	44.4		55.6		37.1		62.9		40.8		59.2	
Age	10	11	12	13	10	11	12	13	10	11	12	13
No.	10	28	22	3	7	23	27	5	17	51	49	8
%	15.9	44.4	34.9	4.8	11.3	37.1	43.5	8.1	13.6	40.8	39.2	6.4
Total	63				62				125			

Grade and grade distribution (Table 1): There are 51 (40.8%) students in Grade 5. There are 74 (59.2%) students in Grade 6, which is 18.4% more than Grade 5. For the group with emotion recognition, Grade 6 is 11.2% larger than Grade 5; for the group without emotion recognition, Grade 6 is 25.8% larger than Grade 5.

Age and age distribution (Table 1): There are 17 (13.6%) students aged 10, 51 (40.8%) students aged 11, 49 (39.2%) students aged 12, and 8 (6.4%) students aged 13; students aged 11 and 12 are almost the same numbers. For the group with emotion recognition, students aged 11 account for more with a ratio of 44.4%; for the group without emotion recognition, students aged 12 account for more with a ratio of 43.5%.

Learning time (time used to finish four levels): the average learning time spent by the group with emotion recognition was 20 min 9 s, and that of the group without emotion recognition was 17 min 15 s; the group with emotion recognition spent 2 min 54 s more on average, and their emotional reaction was detected 3.3 times on average, upon which occasion they received encouragement cards. The group with emotion recognition took 16.8% more time than the group without emotion recognition.

Emotion detection data: among the 65 students in the group with emotion recognition, an emotional reaction was not detected in five respondents—A11, A27, A28, A38, and A46—during the test. Among the 65 respondents, the most detected emotional reaction was disgust, with a total number of 177 times, and for individuals, disgust was detected nine times at most; sadness was detected 11 times, and for individuals, sadness was detected three times at most; joy was detected 12 times in total, and for individuals, joy was detected three times at most. The longest time for a student to finish the four levels in the group with emotion recognition was 30 min 36 s, and the shortest time was 10 min 38 s; the longest time for a student to finish the four levels in the group without emotion recognition was 35 min 36 s, and the shortest time was 4 min 21 s.

4.3. Effectiveness Analysis of the Interactive Teaching Test

An independent sample t-test was adopted to compare whether there is a significant difference between the average of the two groups of samples. (1) There is no significant difference between the group with emotion recognition and the group without emotion recognition in the before-watching true or false questions test, with a *p*-value of 0.10 > 0.05, indicating that there is no difference between the true or false answers of the two groups before the interactive teaching; for the group with emotion recognition, the average right answers of true or false questions in the before-watching test is 5.05, and that of the group without emotion recognition is 5.42. (2) There is no significant difference between the group with emotion recognition and the group without emotion recognition in the before-watching multiple-choice questions test either. With a *p*-value of 0.69 > 0.05, it indicates that there is no difference in the multiple-choice question answers of the two groups before the interactive teaching; for the group with emotion recognition, the average right answers of multiple-choice questions in the before-watching test is 3.38, and that of the group without emotion recognition is 3.27, which indicates that there is no difference between the performances of the two groups in the before-watching test before watching the "Story of the Comet".

An independent sample t-test is used to compare whether there is a significant difference between the average of samples of the two groups. (1) There is no significant difference between the group with emotion recognition and the group without emotion recognition in the after-watching true or false questions test, with a *p*-value of 0.43 > 0.05, it indicates that there is no difference between the true or false answers of the two groups after the interactive teaching; for the group with emotion recognition, the average right answers of true or false questions in the after-watching test is 6.19, which is 1.14 more than the before-watching test; that of the group without emotion recognition is 6.39, which are 0.97 more than the before-watching test. (2) However, there is a significant difference between the group with emotion recognition and the group without emotion recognition in the after-watching multiple-choice question test; with a *p*-value of 0.00 < 0.05, it indicates that there is a difference between the choice answers of the two groups after the interactive teaching; for the group with emotion recognition, the average right answers of multiple-choice questions in the after-watching test is 5.86, which is 2.48 more than the before-watching test—that of the group without emotion recognition is 4.74, which is 1.47 more than the before-watching test, and indicates that during the interactive teaching of "Story of the Comet", the appearance of the encouragement card helps students of the group with emotion recognition to obtain better learning performance in the after-watching test of multiple-choice questions.

4.4. Construct Validity and Reliability of the Questionnaire

4.4.1. Construct Validity Analysis

After investigation and collection of all questionnaires, the valid samples collected is 125, which ensures the validity of the factor analysis. Statistics software of SPSS 18.0 for Windows is taken as the main tool for data analysis; generally, the method to measure construction validity is to use factor analysis to analyze the factor structure matrix of each item of each scale, and then retain the item only if the factor loading listed in the structure matrix is greater than 0.5, otherwise; it is deleted. To judge the validity of the framework, the greater the factor loading, the better the validity. KMO is Kaiser-Meyer-Olkin sampling adequacy. When the KMO value is greater, it means that there are more common factors among variables, which is more suitable for factor analysis. When the KMO value is less than 0.5, it is not suitable for factor analysis. When the KMO value is greater than 0.7, the effect is acceptable, and when the KMO value is greater than 0.9, the effect is the best. Factor analysis can be verified by the KMO value and Bartlett's test.

4.4.2. Reliability Analysis

To understand the validity and reliability of the questionnaire, reliability analysis should be completed. Cronbach's α coefficient is the commonly used reliability analysis method in the Likert scale. The higher the coefficient, the higher the degree of internal consistency of items. Devellis [38] and Nunnally [39] believed that the minimum reliability coefficient should be more than 0.7 to be acceptable. This study uses this method to verify the consistency of scale questionnaires in learning satisfaction, teaching system availability, teaching system satisfaction, etc.

4.4.3. Validity and Reliability Analysis of the Questionnaire

(1) Survey analysis of learning satisfaction

Factor analysis on the learning satisfaction survey is conducted. There are nine items in the scale of students' statements about learning satisfaction. KMO and Bartlett's tests are conducted to test whether it is suitable for factor analysis. With a KMO of 0.917 and Bartlett's test $p = 0.000 < 0.001$, the value reaches a significant level, indicating that the correlation matrix has common factors and is suitable for factor analysis; the α coefficient of Factor 1 is 0.899, which has reached high reliability.

(2) Survey analysis on teaching system availability

Factor analysis on teaching system availability is conducted. There are 10 items in the scale of students' statements about teaching system availability. KMO and Bartlett's tests are conducted to test whether it is suitable for factor analysis. With a factor load of 0.488, item 10 is deleted; after deleting item 10, the remaining 9 items underwent factor analysis again. With a KMO value of 0.847 and Bartlett's test $p = 0.000 < 0.001$, the value reaches a significant level, indicating that the correlation matrix has common factors and is suitable for factor analysis; the α coefficient of Factor 1 is 0.838, which has reached high reliability; that of Factor 2 is 0.776, which has also reached high reliability.

(3) Survey analysis on teaching system satisfaction

Factor analysis on teaching system satisfaction was conducted. There are six items in the scale of students' statements about teaching system satisfaction. KMO and Bartlett's tests were conducted to test whether it is suitable for factor analysis. With a KMO value of 0.890 and Bartlett's test $p = 0.000 < 0.001$, the value reaches a significant level, indicating that the correlation matrix has common factors and is suitable for factor analysis; the α coefficient of Factor 1 is 0.869, which has reached high reliability.

4.5. Comparative Analysis of the Group with Emotion Recognition and the Group without Emotion Recognition

4.5.1. Comparative Analysis of Learning Satisfaction

(1) Frequency-distribution table

Based on the questionnaire collected, there are 125 valid samples, including 63 in the group with emotion recognition and 62 in the group without emotion recognition. There are nine questions in learning satisfaction. In the group with emotion recognition, "strongly agree" accounts for most answers with a ratio of 42.2%—however, there is no "strongly disagree"; in the group without emotion recognition, "agree" accounts for most answers, with a ratio of 40.1%.

(2) Average learning satisfaction based on gender

An independent sample t-test was used to determine whether there is a significant difference between the sample average of the two groups and the average learning satisfaction of females and males; with a p-value of $0.336 > 0.05$, it indicates that there is no significant difference in the average of learning satisfaction based on gender—the average of learning satisfaction of females is 3.86, and that of males is 3.97.

(3) Average learning satisfaction based on grades

An Independent sample t-test was used to determine whether there is a significant difference between the sample average of the two groups and the average of learning satisfaction of Grade 5 and Grade 6, with a p-value of $0.000 < 0.05$. It indicates that there is a significant difference between the average learning satisfaction based on grades; the average learning satisfaction of Grade 5 is 4.18, and that of Grade 6 is 3.73, so Grade 5 is higher than Grade 6 in learning satisfaction.

(4) Learning satisfaction comparison based on groups

An independent sample t-test was used to determine whether there is a significant difference between the sample averages of the two groups and the average learning satisfaction, including the group with emotion recognition and the group without emotion recognition. With a p-value of $0.000 < 0.05$, it indicates that there is a significant difference between the average of the learning satisfaction of the two groups; learning satisfaction average of the group with emotion recognition is 4.13, and that of the group without emotion recognition is 3.69—the statistics show that the group with emotion recognition is higher in learning satisfaction than the group without emotion recognition.

(5) Learning satisfaction comparison of questions within the groups

An independent sample t-test was used to determine whether there is a significant difference between the sample averages of the two groups and the learning satisfaction averages of questions within the two groups—the group with emotion recognition and the group without emotion recognition—with a p-value < 0.05. Results indicate that the learning satisfaction of questions within groups has a significant difference. By comparing questions of learning satisfaction, * indicates a p-value < 0.05 and has a significant difference. Questions 1–9 (Table 2), except question 2, failed to reach a significant level; the learning satisfaction of the remaining 8 questions all reached a significant level, indicating that except for question 2, learning satisfaction of the remaining questions in the group with emotion recognition is better than that of the group without emotion recognition.

Table 2. Comparative analysis table of the two groups on questions of learning satisfaction.

Content of Learning Satisfaction	With Emotion Recognition	Without Emotion Recognition	p-Value
1. This learning mode can improve my learning interest.	4.22	3.87	0.022 *
2. This learning mode can improve my learning concentration.	4.06	3.76	0.054
3. Learning by this mode is relatively easy and there is no pressure.	4.21	3.60	0.000 *
4. This learning mode is completely acceptable.	4.22	3.76	0.003 *
5. Through this learning mode I can learn the scientific knowledge content of "Story of the Comet".	4.32	3.87	0.004 *
6. I am satisfied with the interesting content of "Story of the Comet".	4.03	3.56	0.004 *
7. I think the content of "Story of the Comet" is easy to understand.	3.68	3.26	0.008 *
8. I feel satisfied with the whole explanation of the content of "Story of the Comet".	4.17	3.66	0.001 *
9. I feel satisfied with the learning process of "Story of the Comet".	4.25	3.90	0.022 *

(* indicates a p-value < 0.05).

4.5.2. Comparative Analysis of Teaching System Availability

(1) Frequency distribution table

Based on the questionnaire collected, there are 125 valid samples, including 63 in the group with emotion recognition and 62 in the group without emotion recognition. There are nine questions in teaching system availability. Questions 1, 3, 5, 7, and 9 express the teaching system availability positively, in the group with emotion recognition "strongly agree" accounts for most answers with a rate of 33.3%; in the group without emotion recognition, "agree" accounts for most answers with a rate of 35.2%. Questions 2, 4, 6, and 8 express the teaching system availability negatively in the group with emotion recognition. "Ordinary" accounts for most answers with a rate of 36.9%; in the group without emotion recognition, "ordinary" accounts for most answers with a rate of 41.9%.

(2) Teaching system availability based on gender

An independent sample t-test was used to determine whether there is a significant difference between the sample average of the two groups and the average of teaching system availability based on gender. Questions 1, 3, 5, 7, and 9 express the teaching system availability positively, with a p-value of $0.613 > 0.05$. Results indicate that there is no significant difference between the positive average based on gender. For females, the positive average of teaching system availability is 3.84, and that of males is 3.90. Questions 2, 4, 6, and 8 express the teaching system availability negatively, with a p-value of $0.252 > 0.05$. Results indicate that there is no significant difference between the negative average based on gender. For females, the positive average of teaching system availability is 2.68, and that of males is 2.52. Overall, there is no significant difference between genders in ratings of teaching system availability.

(3) Teaching system availability based on grades

An independent sample t-test was used to determine whether there is a significant difference between the sample average of the two groups and the average of teaching system availability for Grade 5 and Grade 6. Questions 1, 3, 5, 7, and 9 express the teaching system availability positively, with a p-value of $0.000 < 0.05$. Results indicate that there is a significant difference between the positive average based on grades. For Grade 5, the positive average of teaching system availability is 4.19, and that of Grade 6 is 3.65. Grade 5 is higher than Grade 6. Questions 2, 4, 6, and 8 express the teaching system availability negatively, with a p-value of $0.014 < 0.05$. Results indicate that there is a significant difference between the negative average based on grades. For Grade 5, the positive average of teaching system availability is 2.39, and that of Grade 6 is 2.76, Grade 5 is lower than Grade 6. Overall, Grade 5 is higher than Grade 6 in teaching system availability.

(4) Teaching system availability comparison based on groups

An independent sample t-test was used to determine whether there is a significant difference between the sample average of the two groups and teaching system availability average of two groups, including the group with emotion recognition and the group without emotion recognition. Questions 1, 3, 5, 7, and 9 express the teaching system availability positively, with a p-value of $0.969 > 0.05$. Results indicate that there is no significant difference between the positive average based on groups. The positive average of teaching system availability of the group with emotion recognition is 3.87, and that of the group without emotion is 3.87. Questions 2, 4, 6, and 8 express the teaching system availability negatively; with a p-value of $0.378 > 0.05$, results indicate that there is no significant difference between the negative average based on groups. The negative average of teaching system availability of group with emotion recognition is 2.66, and that of the group without emotion is 2.57. Overall, for teaching system availability, there is no significant difference between the two groups.

(5) Teaching system availability comparison based on questions within the groups

An independent sample t-test was used to determine whether there is a significant difference between the sample average of the two groups and the teaching system availability average of two groups, including the group with emotion recognition and the group without emotion recognition. With a p-value < 0.05, results indicate that questions within the two groups in teaching system availability have no significant difference. All questions from 1 to 9 did not reach a significant level (Table 3), which indicates that there is no difference in the teaching system availability between the group with emotion recognition and the group without emotion recognition.

Table 3. Comparative analysis table of the two groups on questions of teaching system availability.

Applicable Content of the Teaching System	With Emotion Recognition	Without Emotion Recognition	p-Value
1. I think I would like to use this teaching system often.	3.83	3.81	0.914
2. I think this teaching system is too complicated.	2.78	2.73	0.794
3. I think this teaching system is easy to use.	3.84	3.84	0.988
4. I think I need the help of a technician to use this teaching system.	3.00	2.98	0.937
5. I think the functions of the teaching system are integrated very well.	4.11	4.16	0.750
6. I think there are too many inconsistencies in the teaching system.	2.33	2.37	0.795
7. I can imagine that most people can learn to use this teaching system very quickly.	3.94	3.94	0.995
8. I think it is very inconvenient to use this teaching system.	2.54	2.08	0.005
9. I am confident that I can use this teaching system.	3.67	3.61	0.778

4.5.3. Comparative Analysis on Teaching System Satisfaction

(1) Frequency distribution table

Based on the questionnaire collected, there are 125 valid samples, including 63 in the group with emotion recognition and 62 in the group without emotion recognition. There are six questions in teaching system satisfaction. In the group with emotion recognition, "strongly agree" accounts for most answers with a ratio of 44.7%; in the group without emotion recognition, "neutral" accounts for most answers with a ratio of 40.0%.

(2) Teaching system satisfaction based on gender

An independent sample t-test was used to determine whether there is a significant difference between the sample average of the two groups and the average of teaching system satisfaction based on the gender of males and females. With a p-value of $0.295 > 0.05$, results indicate that there is no significant difference between the average teaching system satisfaction based on gender; for females, the average teaching system satisfaction is 3.93, and that of males is 3.80.

(3) Teaching system satisfaction based on grades

An independent sample t-test was used to determine whether there is a significant difference between the sample average of the two groups and the average teaching system satisfaction for Grade 5 and Grade 6. With a p-value of $0.000 < 0.05$, results indicate that there is a significant difference between the average of teaching system satisfaction base on grades; for Grade 5, the average of teaching system satisfaction is 4.11, and that of Grade 6 is 3.70. Grade 5 is, therefore, higher than Grade 6 in teaching system satisfaction.

(4) Teaching system satisfaction comparison based on groups

An independent sample t-test was used to determine whether there is a significant difference between the sample average of the two groups and the teaching system satisfaction of the two groups, including the group with emotion recognition and the group without emotion recognition. With a p-value of $0.00 < 0.05$, results indicate that there is a significant difference between the teaching system satisfaction of the two groups; the teaching system satisfaction average of the group with emotion is 4.26, and that of the group without emotion recognition is 3.46. Statistical analysis indicates that the group with emotion recognition is higher in teaching system satisfaction as a whole than the group without emotion recognition.

(5) Teaching system satisfaction comparison in questions within the groups

An independent sample t-test was used to determine whether there is a significant difference between the sample average of the two groups and the teaching system satisfaction average of the two groups, including the group with emotion recognition and the group without emotion. With a p-value < 0.05, results indicate that there is a significant difference between teaching system satisfaction within questions of the two groups.

By comparing questions within the groups in teaching system satisfaction, * indicates p-value < 0.05, which shows a significant difference. From questions 1 to 6 (Table 4), all six questions reached the significance level in teaching system satisfaction, which indicated that the teaching system satisfaction of questions within the group with emotion recognition is better than the group without emotion recognition as a whole.

Table 4. Comparative analysis table of the two groups on questions of teaching system satisfaction.

Content of Teaching System Satisfaction	With Emotion Recognition	Without Emotion Recognition	p-Value
1. The activity design of this teaching system makes me learn the content of "Story of the Comet" more easily (easy to learn).	4.17	3.56	0.000 *
2. The activity design of this teaching system improves my learning efficiency (effectiveness).	4.27	3.44	0.000 *
3. The activity design of this teaching system makes me remember the content of "Story of the Comet" more easily (easy to remember).	4.08	3.15	0.000 *
4. The activity design of this teaching system makes me understand the content of "Story of the Comet" more correctly (correctness).	4.37	3.32	0.000 *
5. The activity design of this teaching system makes me feel useful (usefulness).	4.21	3.50	0.000 *
6. The activity design of this teaching system makes me feel satisfied (subjective satisfaction).	4.49	3.81	0.000 *

(* indicates a p-value < 0.05).

5. Conclusions

According to Elias et al., if students can use emotional intelligence in the classroom, they can achieve better results in tests or any other form of academic performance. In this study, the test results before and after watching the interactive film show that the experimental group performed better in learning (answered 2.48 more questions correctly) than the control group (answered 1.47 more questions correctly), proving that the encouragement cards enhanced the students' learning effectiveness. The results of this research fully echo the research of several scholars, such as Elias et al. In addition, Mary E. Pritchard et al.

suggested that positive emotions can increase students' learning interest and motivation. In this study, the learning satisfaction of the experimental group (average 4.13) is higher than that of the control group (average 3.69), and the system satisfaction of the experimental group (average 4.26) is also higher than that of the control group (average 3.46). Nevertheless, the teaching system availability of the two groups has no significant difference. The increase of perception accessibility also enhances the perception of entertainment, which has a direct impact on the use intention of students. The results of this research also echo the research of several scholars, such as Mary E. Pritchard. The goal of this research is to understand the impact of emotional feedback on learning when using a puzzle film in teaching. The research results also confirmed that emotions play an important role in learning. An intelligent learning system can arouse pleasant emotions and reduce learning resistance for learners who may feel frustrated or confused during learning. A positive learning mood can enhance learning effectiveness, and this teaching system improves the past teacher-oriented teaching methods. The sound and light effects of the film stimulate learning enthusiasm. The more important purpose is to increase students' continuous learning motivation and improve their learning ability. Therefore, it is recommended that teachers can make good use of film combined with emotion detection to teach, which will be of great help to improve learning results and the future development of education.

Author Contributions: Conceptualization, H.-C.K.L. and S.-C.T.; methodology, H.-C.K.L. and S.-C.T.; software, S.-C.T.; validation, H.-C.K.L. and S.-C.T.; formal analysis, H.-C.K.L. and S.-C.T.; investigation, S.-C.T.; resources, H.-C.K.L. and S.-C.T.; data curation, S.-C.T.; writing—original draft preparation, S.-C.T.; writing—review and editing, H.-C.K.L. and S.-C.T.; visualization, S.-C.T.; supervision, H.-C.K.L. and S.-C.T.; project administration, S.-C.T.; funding acquisition, H.-C.K.L. and S.-C.T. All authors have read and agreed to the published version of the manuscript.

Funding: This research received no external funding.

Institutional Review Board Statement: Not applicable.

Informed Consent Statement: Informed consent was obtained from all subjects involved in the study.

Data Availability Statement: Flipped Education, Parenting, Dialogue between Teaching and Learning, Available online: https://flipedu.parenting.com.tw/article/139, accessed on 18 August 2021.

Conflicts of Interest: The authors declare no conflict of interest.

Appendix A. Film Script

Script of the First Film

Act 1

(Caption): Although with 14 years apart, active Halley and lonely Newton were good friends. In newton's mind, Halley was the most trustworthy friend.

(Caption): In 1680.

Halley: According to Kepler's third law of planetary motion, the gravitational attraction of the sun to the planet should be inversely proportional to the square of the distance, but can this gravitational attraction comply with Kepler's first law of planetary motion that the orbit of the planet is elliptical?

(Caption): Halley could not prove it himself. He once consulted Mr. Hooke who studied the same question and other members of The Royal Society, but he couldn't get the answer. Finally, Halley decided to ask Newton.

Act 2

(Caption): In August 1684, Halley went to Oxford to visit Newton.

Halley: Mr. Newton, I'd like to ask you a question this time.

Newton: Oh, what's that?

Halley: According to Kepler's law of motion, if the planets really move around the sun along the elliptic orbit, what's the law they follow?

Newton: I calculated the inverse-square law ratio almost ten years ago, that is, the planets move around the sun along the elliptic orbit under the law of inverse-square ratio.

Halley: Really, wow! Great. Can you show me all the data of the calculation process?

Newton: OK, wait a moment. I'll get it for you.

(Caption): At that time, Kepler's law of planetary motion was only summary according to the observation records without knowing the principle. Newton could explain the reason through calculation formula. With the support of observation data, it was deduced that the motion of celestial bodies in the sky and objects on the earth could be explained by the same law, that is, the law of universal gravitation!

Act 3

(Caption): The book *The Principia: Mathematical Principles of Natural Philosophy* of Newton was published in 1686, in which a hypothesis was proposed that in addition to planets, there were also many comets had closed orbits, which meant that they would move around the sun regularly. Hoping to test this hypothesis, Halley had been collecting previous observation record since 1695. Analyzing by Newton's law of motion, he found that the orbit of a comet in 1305, 1380, 1456, 1531 and 1607 were very similar to that of the 1682, which should be the same comet.

(Caption): In 1705.

Halley: If my hypothesis is correct, the comet should come back about every 76 years, so it should reappear in 1758. I want to announce this message. If it does reappear in 1758, future generations will remember that the credit for discovering the comet belongs to a Briton.

Act 4

Johann Georg Palitzsch: Wow! It's really back. This is the comet mentioned by Mr. Halley before. Halley's prediction is correct.

(Caption): On December 25, 1758, this comet was observed by Johann Georg Palitzsch, a farmer and amateur astronomer in Germany. Halley died in 1742 and failed to live to see the return of this comet. Later, this most legendary comet, named after Halley, an Englishman, is still in use today.

Script of the Second Film

Act 1

(Caption): Halley is friends with Hooke and Wren. One day, these three people got together to chat.

Wren: The attraction between the sun and the planets should be the endless motion of the planets around the sun.

Halley: Then what orbit do the planets revolve around the sun? If it is really like Kepler said, if the planets revolve around the sun in an elliptical orbit, then what law of gravitation does this follow?

Hooke: I know the answer. If there is no error in the calculation process, the orbit of the planet should be elliptical.

Halley: So what law of gravitation does it follow?

Hooke: Of course it is based on the principle of the inverse square ratio formula.

Halley: Can you borrow me to study your calculation data?

Hooke: I'll find it and you will get it in two days.

Halley: Okay, thank you.

Act 2

(Caption): Halley went to Hooke's residence, Hooke lent the calculation data of planetary orbits to Halley.

Halley: Wow, your information is so precious, let me study it for a while.

Hooke: OK.

Halley: I suggest that you can publish these materials into books, the name of the book is called "Science Principles of Nature".

Hooke: Your suggestion is very good, but I am worried that my funds are not enough.

Halley: It's okay, I'll support you, That's it.

Act 3

(Caption): Halley happily ran to Hooke after studying the books and materials of Hooke's "Science Principles of Nature".

Halley: Mr. Hooke, Mr. Hooke, I have calculated it. This comet should come back every 38 years, so after the calculation, it should be two years later that we can see its traces again.

Hooke: Great, we will come together to welcome its visit at that time.

Act 4

(Caption): On Christmas night two years later, Hooke and Halley were sitting in chairs outside the café.

Halley: Wow, it's this one, the comet I speculated is back.

Hooke: It's true, what a beautiful comet.

(Caption): Later, in commemoration of the comet that Halley and Hooke discovered together, the world named the comet Hooke Halley's Comet.

Script of the Third Film

Act 1

(Caption): Halley and Wren are British astronomers, and they are also very good friends.

Wren: I have been observing astronomy for many years. According to my observations, the sun should be the center of the entire universe. I want to publish my observations into a book so that the general public can share my results. The title of my book will be called "Celestial movement theory".

Halley: Does the comet also orbit the sun, do you think it is?

Wren: Of course it is.

Halley: What shape do you think the orbit of the comet orbiting the sun should be?

Wren: It should be circular. There is a detailed calculation method in my book "Celestial movement theory". It operates in accordance with the formula of the law of gravitational velocity that I discovered.

Halley: Can you give me a copy after the book is published.

Wren: Of course no problem.

Act 2

(Caption): Three months later, Wren published a book "Celestial movement theory" on astronomy. On this day, Halley arrived at Wren's residence and asked him for the book on "Celestial movement theory". At this time, Wren was sitting outside the house to enjoy the cool.

Halley: Congratulations, Wren, your masterpiece has finally come out, you promised me to give me a copy.

Wren: No problem, I'll get it to you.

Wren: On page 107 of the book, there is a formula for the law of gravitational velocity when a comet orbits the sun.

Halley: Great. Recently, I am very interested in a certain comet on the celestial body. Now I have enough information to do research.

Act 3

(Caption): Halley happily ran to find Wren after studying the book materials of Wren's "Celestial movement theory" for a period of time.

Halley: Mr. Wren, Mr. Wren, I have calculated. This comet should come back every 60 years, so it should be 10 years from now.

Wren: That's great, I hope we have the honor to see it.

(Caption): Halley passed away due to overwork and illness after three years of studying comets. Halley confessed to his wife Mary Stuart before his death.

Halley: Mary, thank you very much for taking care of me for so many years. The comet I studied may come back in seven years. You must help me pay attention to this matter.

Mary: Halley, don't worry, I will help you pay attention.

Act 4

(Caption): Seven years later, one night in March, Mary sat in front of the house to enjoy the cool.

Mary: Wow, it's a comet. It's such a beautiful comet. According to the date, it is supposed to be the comet Halley was studying. It has returned again. Its cycle around the sun is really 60 years. I want to announce this message. Let the world know.

(Caption): In order to commemorate Halley's research on comets, the world named this comet Mary Halley's Comet.

Script of the Fourth Film

Act 1

(Caption): Halley and Flamsteed were both British astronomers and celebrities at that time. Halley paid a special visit to Flamsteed in order to find the comet data he was studying.

Flamsteed: I have been observing astronomy for many years. According to my observations, the sun should be the center of the entire universe. I want to publish my observations into a book so that future generations will always remember my contribution to astronomy. My book title will be called "Principle of Planetary Motion in the Universe".

Halley: May I ask Mr. Flamsteed, is the comet also orbiting the sun?

Flamsteed: Of course it is.

Halley: What shape do you think the orbit of the comet orbiting the sun should be?

Flamsteed: It should be round. There is a detailed explanation in my book "Principle of Planetary Motion in the Universe".

Halley: After your book is published, can you borrow a copy for me to study?

Flamsteed: Of course it can.

Act 2

(Caption): Two months later, Flamsteed published an astronomy book "Principle of Planetary Motion in the Universe". On this day, Halley arrived at Flamsteed's residence and wanted to borrow from him the book "Principle of Planetary Motion in the Universe". At this time, Flamsteed just taking a walk outside the house.

Halley: Congratulations, Flamsteed, your masterpiece has finally come out. You said you would lend me a copy for me to study the comet.

Flamsteed: No problem, I'll bring it to you now.

Flamsteed: On page 59 of the book, there is information about comets orbiting the sun.

Halley: Great, I can finally do my research.

Act 3

(Caption): Halley happily ran to Flamsteed after studying the book materials of "Principle of Planetary Motion in the Universe" written by Flamsteed for a period of time.

Halley: Mr. Flamsteed, Mr. Flamsteed, I have calculated that this comet should come back every three years, so we should be able to see it again in September after three years.

Flamsteed: Great, I want to include the comet you discovered in my next edition of "Principle of Planetary Motion in the Universe"

Halley: I will pay special attention to the coming of this comet in September in three years.

Flamsteed: Remember to tell me the observation data at that time.

Halley: OK

Act 4

(Caption): Three years later, one night in September, Halley sat in front of the house to enjoy the cool.

Halley: Wow, it's a comet. It's such a beautiful comet. It's the comet I studied three years ago. It is inferred from the date that it really came back again. I want to inform Flamsteed of this information as soon as possible.

(Caption): In order to commemorate Halley's research on comets, the world named this comet as Flamsteed Halley's Comet.

References

1. CTi News, Recording Taiwan. Available online: https://www.youtube.com/watch?v=M7FryY7DlRU (accessed on 13 October 2013).
2. Flipped Education, Parenting, Dialogue between Teaching and Learning. Available online: https://flipedu.parenting.com.tw/article/139 (accessed on 12 January 2015).
3. Pritchard, M.E.; Wilson, G.S. Using emotional and social factors to predict student success. *J. Coll. Stud. Dev.* **2003**, *44*, 18–28. [CrossRef]
4. McLean, G.F.; Graham, E.D.; Jernigan, M.E. A software environment for teaching image processing. In Proceedings of the ICASSP-92: 1992 IEEE International Conference on Acoustics, Speech, and Signal Processing, San Francisco, CA, USA, 23 March 1992.
5. Ageenko, E.; La Russa, G. A visualization toolkit for teaching, learning, and experimentation in image processing. In Proceedings of the 2005 IEEE Annual Conference on Frontiers in Education, F2H-21-F2H26, Indianapolis, IN, USA, 19–22 October 2005.
6. Zhang, D.; Zhou, L.; Briggs, R.O.; Nunamaker, J.F., Jr. Instructional video in e-learning: Assessing the impact of interactive video on learning effectiveness. *Inf. Manag.* **2006**, *43*, 15–27. [CrossRef]
7. Bruning, M.J. VIS: Technology for Multicultural Teacher Education. *TechTrends* **1992**, *37*, 13–14. [CrossRef]
8. Hutchinson, J.A.; Cissna, K.N.; Hall, M.E.; Backlund, P.E.; Tolhuizen, J.H. Videotape self-confrontation as a technique to enhance interpersonal communication effectiveness. *Commun. Educ.* **1978**, *27*, 245–250. [CrossRef]
9. Duhaney, D. Technology and the educational process: Transformin classroom activities. *Int. J. Instr. Media.* **2000**, *27*, 67–72.
10. Tsutsui, M. Multimedia as a Means to Enhance Feedback. *Comput. Assist. Lang. Learn.* **2004**, *17*, 377–402. [CrossRef]
11. Guay, F.; Ratelle, C.F.; Chanal, J. Optimal learning in optimal contexts: The role of self-determination in education. *Can. Psychol. Can.* **2008**, *49*, 233–240. [CrossRef]
12. Pike, G.R.; Smart, J.C.; Ethington, C.A. The Mediating Effects of Student Engagement on the Relationships Between Academic Disciplines and Learning Outcomes: An Extension of Holland's Theory. *Res. High. Educ.* **2011**, *53*, 550–575. [CrossRef]
13. Alavi, M.; Wheeler, B.C.; Valacich, J.S. Using IT to reengineer business eduaction: An exploratory investigation of collaborative telelearning. *MIS Q.* **1995**, *19*, 293–312. [CrossRef]
14. Shih, Y.C.; Huang, P.R.; Hsu, Y.C.; Chen, S.Y. A complete understanding of disorientation problems in Web-based learning. *Turk. Online J. Educ. Technol.* **2012**, *11*, 1–13.
15. Knowles, M.S. *The Modern Practice of Adult Education*; Association Press: New York, NY, USA, 1970.
16. Maki, R.H.; Maki, W.S.; Patterson, M.; Whittaker, P.D. Evaluation of a Web-based introductory psychology course: I. Learning and satisfaction in on-line versus lecture courses. *Behav. Res. Methods Instrum. Comput.* **2000**, *32*, 230–239. [CrossRef]
17. Piccoli, G.; Ahmad, R.; Ives, B. Web-Based Virtual Learning Environments: A Research Framework and a Preliminary Assessment of Effectiveness in Basic IT Skills Training. *MIS Q.* **2001**, *25*, 401–426. [CrossRef]
18. Hung, C.-Y.; Chang, T.-W.; Yu, P.-T.; Cheng, P.-J. The Problem Solving Skills and Learning Performance in Learning Multi-Touch Interactive Jigsaw Game Using Digital Scaffolds. In Proceedings of the 2012 IEEE Fourth International Conference On Digital Game And Intelligent Toy Enhanced Learning, Takamatsu, Japan, 27–30 March 2012; pp. 33–38. [CrossRef]
19. Long, H.B. Contradictory Expectations? Achievement and Satisfaction in Adult Learning. *J. Contin. High. Educ.* **1985**, *33*, 10–12. [CrossRef]
20. Allen, T. *The Adult Learning Projects*, 2nd ed.; The Ontario Institute for Studies in Education: Toronto, ON, Canada, 1982.
21. Johnson, S.D.; Aragon, S.R.; Shaik, N. Comparative analysis of learning satisfaction and learning outcomes in online and face-to-face learning environments. *J. Interact. Learn. Res.* **2000**, *11*, 29–49.
22. Kuo, F.O. Study on the Effects of Integrating Multimedia Presentation Model into Instruction. Ph.D. Dissertation, Department of Computer Science and Information Engineering, National Chung Cheng University, Minxiong, Taiwan, 2014.
23. Shen, L.; Wang, M.; Shen, R. Affective e-Learning: Using "Emotional" Data to Improve Learning in Pervasive Learning Environment. *J. Educ. Technol. Soc.* **2009**, *12*, 176–189.
24. Wegmuller, M.; von der Weid, J.P.; Oberson, P.; Gisin, N. High resolution fiber distributed measurements with coherent OFDR. *Proc. ECOC'00* **2000**, paper 11.3.4. 109.
25. Arguedas, M.; Daradoumis, T.; Xhafa, F. Analyzing the effects of emotion management on time and self-management in computer-based learning. *Comput. Hum. Behav.* **2016**, *63*, 517–529. [CrossRef]
26. Elias, M.J.; Weissberg, R.P. Primary prevention: Educational approaches to enhance social and emotional learning. *J. Sch. Heal.* **2000**, *70*, 186–190. [CrossRef]
27. Payton, J.W.; Wardlaw, D.M.; Graczyk, P.A.; Bloody, M.R.; Trompsett, C.J.; Weissberg, R.P. Social and Emotional Learning: A Framework for Promoting Mental Health and Reducing Risk Behaviour in Children and Youth. *J. Sch. Health* **2000**, *70*, 179–184. [CrossRef]
28. Paivio, A. Imagery and Verbal Processes. *Leonardo* **1972**, *5*, 359–360. [CrossRef]
29. Paivio, A. *Mental Representations: A Dual Coding Approach*; Oxford University Press: Oxford, UK, 1986.
30. Richardson, A. "Verbalizer-visualizer: A cognitive style dimension". *J. Ment. Imag.* **1977**, *1*, 109–126.
31. Mayer, R.E. *Multimedia Learning*; Cambridge University Press: New York, NY, USA, 2001.
32. Mayer, R.E. The promise of multimedia learning: Using the same instructional design methods across different media. *Learn. Instr.* **2003**, *13*, 125–139. [CrossRef]

33. Mayer, R.E. *The Cambridge Handbook of Multimedia Learning*; Cambridge University Press: Cambridge, UK, 2005.
34. Mayer, R.E. Comprehension of graphics in texts: An overview. *Learn. Instr.* **1993**, *3*, 239–245. [CrossRef]
35. Mayer, R.E.; Sims, K. For whom is a picture worth a thousand words? Extensions of a dual-coding theory of multimedia learning. *J. Educ. Psychol.* **1994**, *86*, 389–401. [CrossRef]
36. Sweller, J.; Chandler, P. Why some material is difficult to learn. *Cogn. Instr.* **1994**, *12*, 185–233. [CrossRef]
37. Sweller, J.; Van Merrienboer, J.J.; Paas, F.G. Cognitive architecture and instructional design. *Educ. Psychol. Rev.* **1998**, *10*, 251–297. [CrossRef]
38. Xie, Y.; DeVellis, R.F. Scale Development: Theory and Applications. *Contemp. Sociol. A J. Rev.* **1992**, *21*, 876. [CrossRef]
39. Nunnally, J.C. *Psychometric Theory*; McGraw-Hill: New York, NY, USA, 1978.

MDPI
St. Alban-Anlage 66
4052 Basel
Switzerland
www.mdpi.com

Sustainability Editorial Office
E-mail: sustainability@mdpi.com
www.mdpi.com/journal/sustainability

Disclaimer/Publisher's Note: The statements, opinions and data contained in all publications are solely those of the individual author(s) and contributor(s) and not of MDPI and/or the editor(s). MDPI and/or the editor(s) disclaim responsibility for any injury to people or property resulting from any ideas, methods, instructions or products referred to in the content.

www.ingramcontent.com/pod-product-compliance
Lightning Source LLC
LaVergne TN
LVHW070143100526
838202LV00015B/1882